SECOND EDITION

"So You Think I Drive a Cadillac?": Welfare Recipients' Perspectives on the System and Its Reform

Karen Seccombe

Portland State University

Boston   New York   San Francisco
Mexico City   Montreal   Toronto   London   Madrid   Munich   Paris
Hong Kong   Singapore   Tokyo   Cape Town   Sydney

Senior Series Editor: *Patricia Quinlin*
Series Editorial Assistant: *Sara Holliday*
Marketing Manager: *Laura Lee Manley*
Production Editor: *Claudine Bellanton*
Editorial Production Service: *Modern Graphics, Inc.*
Composition Buyer: *Linda Cox*
Manufacturing Buyer: *JoAnne Sweeney*
Electronic Composition: *Modern Graphics, Inc.*
Cover Administrator: *Joel Gendron*

For related titles and support materials, visit our online catalog at www.ablongman.com.

Between the time website information is gathered and then published, it is not unusual for some sites to have closed. Also, the transcription of URLs can result in typographical errors. The publisher would appreciate notification where these errors occur so that they may be corrected in subsequent editions.

Cadillac is a registered trademark of General Motors Corporation.

Library of Congress Cataloging-in-Publication Data

Seccombe, Karen,
   "So you think I drive a Cadillac?" : welfare recipients perspectives on the system and its reform / Karen Seccombe.—2nd ed.
      p. cm.
   Includes bibliographical references and index.
   ISBN 0-205-48739-4
      1. Poor women—United States. 2. Welfare recipients—United States. 3. Public welfare—United States. I. Title.

HV1445.S39 2006
362.5'80973—dc22

                                                                        2005057007

Printed in the United States of America

10   9   8   7   6   5   4   3   2   1   10   09   08   07   06

C O N T E N T S

PREFACE

I have always been self-conscious about social inequality. Growing up in a area of rich and poor neighboring communities, at a very tender age I couldn't help but notice the glaring contrast between those who have more and those who have less. It prompted me to think intellectually about inequality, and the causes and consequences of it. How is our sense of self shaped by the material goods around us? I didn't know that there was a formal discipline that pondered such questions—sociology—or a profession organized to help the casualties of inequality—social work—until much later.

This book provides insight into what it is like to be poor and live on welfare. In this era of controversial welfare reforms, we hear from lawmakers or policy "experts," but rarely from the voices of poor women themselves. We do not hear what the sting of poverty feels like, or how single mothers cope with the stigma and stresses of raising children on meager welfare benefits or low wages. Nor do we know the meanings that women attach to the label of "welfare mother." Underneath the statistics and the theories are real live human beings who are trying to make sense of their lives. While rates, correlations, and causal models are important to understanding poverty and social inequality, the old adage that "social statistics are humans with their tears washed away" also rings true. This study has been conceptualized and designed with an interpretative sociological framework that emphasizes the centrality of subjective meaning and its importance and connection to the larger social structure.

Welfare reforms, both recent and those in the past, are based on patriarchal understandings of women and their roles within the family and the paid labor market. Women's roles are now in a state of flux, and poor women are no longer excused from work in order to care for their children. Our society values their cheap market labor more than we value their labor in the home. We demand that they fill the growing number of low-tier service sector jobs that pay only minimum wages and offer no benefits such as health insurance or subsidized child care, and we ignore the fact that employment of this nature will do nothing to lift women and children from poverty. Because of the insecurity of these jobs, poor women have on-and-off-again bouts with welfare. Our society is frustrated with these repeat spells of welfare use, and therefore has imposed strict time limits and work requirements. But the real problem with welfare has little to do with lazy women, or the structure of the welfare system. Instead, the real problem with welfare is that the structure of low-wage work is so tenuous and insecure that it cannot support a family in any decent manner. The "welfare problem" is best conceptualized as a "work problem." Until we improve the structure and conditions of low-wage work, poverty will never be reduced or ameliorated, and welfare will continue to be a difficult but necessary fact of life for millions of poor families.

ACKNOWLEDGMENTS

I am fortunate to have had many family members, good friends, and helpful colleagues surrounding me throughout the many years spent on this project. Collectively, they have inspired and motivated me, and have supported my inquiry into the concerns of poor women struggling to raise their families within the confines of welfare and low-wage work in the United States.

Naturally, I want to first thank my family, since they have helped me in innumerable ways. My husband Richard read every word of this revised manuscript. His insightful comments prompted me to expand my ideas, and his keen editing skills helped me to express them. I also thank my young daughters, Natalie Rose and Olivia Lin, ages four and two, who provided the necessary diversions that both drove me crazy and kept me sane. Much of this book was written between 2 and 4 P.M.—otherwise known as naptime. After all, who can write a book when the zoo or the children's museum beckons?

This research was funded by the National Science Foundation and the Agency for Healthcare Research and Quality. Several colleagues and graduate students at the University of Florida and Portland State University assisted in the collection, transcription, and coding of these data. Christina Albo, Cheryl Amey, Sylvia Ansay, Meg Galletly, Cathy Gordon, Heather Hartley, Kim Hoffman, Richard Lockwood, Gwen Marchand, Jason Newsom, Clyde Pope, Kim Battle Walters, Goldie MacDonald, Janice Weber, and Tosha Zaback each made valuable contributions to these studies. I also acknowledge the help of friends and colleagues Beth Miller, Karen Pyke, and Becky Warner who faithfully read portions of this manuscript, lent me their ears, gave me critical advice and feedback on these chapters, and the book-writing process more generally, and taught me about the meaningful role that qualitative research can play in understanding social phenomena and informing policy debates.

Who could possibly be expected to finish a book without the playful interruptions that become all the more imperative when you are tied down to your computer? Friends in Ketchikan, Alaska, provided the scenic wonder and good cheer that made writing the first edition of this book downright enjoyable. I credit my running team, Runs in Her Stockings, particularly Michelle, Linda, and Marta, for teaching me to go from 3 to 13 miles in one year flat. And where else can you, in between pages, sneak in a kayaking trip alongside Orca whales, porpoises, and Alaskan-sized salmon, while seeing black bear along the shore, and eagles overhead? I have a special appreciation for neighbors Susan and John, who welcomed me to their community with open arms. I am grateful to the University of Florida for allowing me to have a sabbatical in one of the most spectacular places on earth.

The second edition was also written during a sabbatical, for which I am grateful—this time from the School of Community Health at Portland State University. Unfortunately, my sabbatical location was a bit more mundane this time—my home office. However, luckily for me, Portland, Oregon is also a pretty wonderful place to be, and hey, there's always the zoo and children's museum in the absence of frolicking whales. I am thankful for my friends Edith, Alice, Linda, Jeanne, and Beth who at first glance had nothing to do with this book, but actually helped me more than they probably know.

Finally, I want to express my deep and sincere gratitude to the many people in Florida and Oregon whose stories are told here. You generously opened up your lives to scrutiny, and I hope that I have conveyed your messages with the warmth, empathy, and vigor that they deserve. You are truly remarkable, and I thank you for your keen insight into the welfare system and its reform. As a token of my appreciation, a portion of the royalties from this book will be given to those programs, services, and charities that have helped you along the way. This book is dedicated to you.

Finally, thanks to the following individuals that reviewed the manuscript for the new edition: Echo E. Fields, Southern Oregon University; Jane McCandless, University of West Georgia; and Jackie Reynolds, Washington State University.

CHAPTER

1

Introduction: Putting a Face on Welfare

The house was located on a dead-end street and was difficult to find. Luckily, I left in plenty of time and found the house with five minutes to spare. It was a very modest home, but well cared for, as though the resident took tremendous pride in it. Someone living there was obviously a gardener; there were many potted flowers and plants on the porch and walkway. I thought of my mother, an avid gardener. As my thoughts drifted, I surveyed the neighborhood of junked cars, broken children's toys, dilapidated houses, and scrawny dogs roaming loose; and a chill woke the vigor within me for the task at hand. I was prepared and anxious to hear the muffled voices of women straining to be heard.

The front door was wide open, and Sheila was waiting for me to arrive. She warmly, but nervously, invited me into her home. She was a short woman, white, and looked older than her 40 years, with her graying hair pulled back. Her eyes were friendly, but reserved. We sat in her small living room, which contained a worn couch, a rocking chair with its cushion covered by a towel, a small television set, and an old-fashioned record player with many LPs and a large stack of "45s" sitting on a rack next to it. Hanging on the walls were over a dozen photos and paint-on-velvet pictures of Elvis Presley. I later learned that her primary hobby was collecting Elvis mementos, and most of the records were his early recordings. I had a wave of nostalgia.

Two preschool children were resting on the couch and slept through most of the interview. Sheila told me that they were her grandchildren, two of the "lights of her life," and the children of her 25-year-old married daughter. She was babysitting the children today. Sheila also had a daughter Melanie, aged 12, whom she spoke of with love, pride, and fierce protectiveness. For Melanie's care, she received $241 a month in Aid to Families with Dependent Children (AFDC) and $212 in food stamps from the State of Florida in 1995. In 2005, Sheila would receive the same $241 in cash, if she qualified at all, since benefits have not risen in Florida during the past ten years despite inflation. She would receive up to $274 in food stamps, an increase of $62 (Community Food, Hunger, and Nutrition Information Site, 2005).

Sheila described her daily routine: She gets up at 5:00 A.M. every morning to start her housework before she gets her daughter up for school. She spoke of going to night school two evenings a week to work toward her GED. Other than cleaning her house, taking care of Melanie, visiting her grown daughter Jamie and Jamie's husband, occasionally babysitting her grandchildren, and attending night school, Sheila is a loner. "When you got a bunch of people together, you got problems," she tells me. She has few friends, rarely socializes, and considers her daughters, son-in-law, and grandchildren her only real family, despite a husband from whom she has been separated for 14 years and a large extended family, all of whom live 200 miles away. Two hundred miles might as well be a world away. She fled abuse and an intolerable family situation. She is on her own, and her world revolves around taking care of her youngest daughter. Melanie's father has never contributed financially to Melanie's support, nor has he been involved emotionally in her life.

> He's never offered to even take care of Melanie at all. Even when we lived in the same town, he didn't have that much to do with her, except, say, when it was for his benefit. She's 12 now, and we went to court. He ain't paid a dime, he ain't trying to pay a dime, and they ain't doing nothing to him. Putting it straight, I just haven't had good luck with men. Let's put it that way. Everybody makes mistakes <laughter>, but I ain't making mine over no more. I'm tired of doing the same old thing. And I don't associate with my family. The only family I have are my daughters and my two grandbabies. That's it. When I need help, I go to her <oldest daughter>. Her and her husband. Other than that, if they can't help me, then I just do without. Because they are the only ones I'll ask anything from.

When Melanie comes home from school in the afternoon, they rarely go out again, except for Sheila's night class. Both are shy, have few friends, and do not like to socialize. Sheila told me that Melanie is self-conscious about being poor, and never invites anyone from school to come into their home. Instead, in the afternoon, Melanie tends to her homework with Sheila's supervision, completes her chores, and they watch television together. Sheila crochets or listens to her Elvis records to pass the time when she's not busy cleaning house or cooking supper. They live a quiet and very private life.

> People make comments at her school, you know. That's why she, Melanie now, that's why she's a loner too. When she comes in that door, she don't go back outside. This afternoon she's going off for the weekend with her older sister. That's about as far as she goes . . . people say, well, you can get up, you can do better for yourself, you can get a job, and this and that. They ain't never been in a situation like I've been. I mean, when you get in between a rock and a hard place, and you got a child to care of, you do what you got to do. But what goes around, comes around. So, one of these days, with all their smart comments, they might find themselves in a worser predicament than some of us have been in.

There is always a stressful undercurrent, according to Sheila. Will they have enough money to live on this month? Despite the best of planning, something "out of the ordinary" always occurs and taxes their budget. Can they afford Melanie's school field trip? She has outgrown her shoes, and can they afford a new pair? Winter is approaching, and they both need coats. Sheila feels this stress always gnawing at her, and believes it is responsible for her poor health. Some days, she doesn't "even feel like getting out of bed." The stress is affecting her physical health, and she has seen several doctors to find out what is ailing her, to no avail.

Sheila dreams of getting a good job someday. She bubbled with enthusiasm as she told me of a job at the Post Office, which she applied for, that paid over $8.00 an hour. But then again, she might have to take a test for it, and this concerned her. Sheila's reading, writing, and math skills are low, typical for someone who has not completed high school. She worries that she will not qualify for a job like this. But she is not afraid of hard work; she's spent most of her life working as a maid in hotels or cleaning private houses. Despite long hours, these jobs never pulled her out of poverty. She was born poor and has been poor all her life, living alongside the other 37 million poor Americans, or 12.7 percent of the population in 2004 (DeNavas-Walt, Proctor, & Lee, 2005). Sheila and Melanie received $241 in welfare and $212 in food stamps each month. It is a hardship, but at least the income is secure, she told me. She fears the insecurity of minimum wage jobs. The take-home pay may be more than welfare, but they don't provide health insurance. She's concerned that her food stamps will be eliminated. And there is always the dread of being laid off. If she lost her job, it would take another month or two to get back on welfare, she told me, and it would be difficult to support her daughter in the meantime.

Sheila is feeling the pressure of the changes in the welfare system:

> I'm supposed to have a job by January 1. That's what all this schooling supposed to be for. Plus I got applications out on my own. I got one at the post office, and I got one out at the mail room out on 441, Pic and Save <discount store>, Winn Dixie <grocery store>, Alachua General <hospital>. I'd like to work in a hospital, you know, like in the housekeeping department. Cleaning, that's more my line because I know what I'm doing. I don't need someone to tell me how to clean. I've been cleaning since I was 7 years old. If I ain't learned it by now, then I'll never learn. But it's hard to get a job. There aren't that many jobs out there for people who ain't finished school. Now they want a GED, or they want this, they want that. I've been going to this Career Connections thing to help me find a job, but going from nine to three, plus night school, when do I have time to do my own cooking and cleaning? Why do they want to make us old women do the things that they should be making those 15, 16-year-old girls do? Now, if I were 15 or 16 years old, I wouldn't have one complaint about this Career Connections, this and that. But I'm 40 years old. I mean, give me a break! But as far as the GED part, yes, I want to do that even if they stopped my welfare tomorrow. I'm getting my GED! I'm determined. I'll be there ten years probably before I get that GED, but I'm going to get it, and it's going to hang right there on that wall.

Sheila was the first woman I interviewed, and the first to pose these questions and concerns to me. But she was not the last. These were common concerns that ran through each and every woman's story.

Patrice, a 25-year-old African American woman, is also a "typical" welfare recipient, if there is such a thing. But unlike Sheila, she has finished high school, and was taking classes towards becoming a Licensed Practical Nurse, until her unplanned pregnancy and its complications, which required complete bed rest, forced her to quit. Nonetheless, she now works for a local hospital providing personal care in private homes, such as assisting bedridden patients with cooking, personal grooming, and housecleaning. She works part-time, and her income is low. She therefore continues to receive a partial welfare benefit for her two preschool-aged children. Patrice is proud of her education and work experience:

> I went to traveler's school, so I have experience in the traveling field, and I took business management for a short while. I was a teacher's aid for a year and a half, so, you know, I have experience here and there. I can type. I can do a variety of things. But I prefer working with people, like in nursing, over all the rest.

Patrice reveals the complexities and ironies in life. Events do not always go according to plan. Even the best of intentions, and relationships with men that were thought to be solid sometimes fall through. She shares her perceptions of women's experiences with men, their children, and the welfare system, and notes how they cope with seemingly discouraging situations.

PATRICE: Well, if you sit around moping about your condition, that's not going to better the situation. All you're going to do is become depressed, and then you become more vulnerable to different things, and people will take advantage of you. So you have to keep your head on right and think positive.

INTERVIEWER: Do you think that happens to a lot of women?

PATRICE: I really do. Well, it's like this. Being a young lady, I think a lot of women date a guy for years. And then you get pregnant. You expect him not really to marry you, but to be there for you and the child, but they jump up and leave. I believe women get depressed because of the fact that you got to just totally give up your life. Like me, I was in nursing school, and I was doing great. I came pregnant, so I got depressed because the guy left me after all those years. I had to resign in my eighth month of pregnancy. But I was working then too, because I was trying to maintain my rent and my car, you know. I think a lot of women become discouraged and depressed because what you are expecting in life—all your dreams and fantasies become nightmares. The guy leaves you, and then you know you got to turn to welfare, which everybody thinks is bad because, you know, it's taxpayer money. People be criticizing you. Then you have to stand in these long lines to get stamps. Then you have to be criticized on a daily basis. And it's just discouraging. Then you have to go for your appointments, sometimes, there for two or three hours before your worker calls you. They just blabber your business out real loud in the lobby <laughter>. You got to be embarrassed. You look around, you know? Then you have to go into the health department, and you look around, and everybody looks pitiful. You don't have the proper clothes to dress, you know, maternity wear. You be depressed. Then you be vulnerable to the situation. The first guy—well maybe not the first—but a guy promises you the world, and you are weak to the situation. You don't think your own situation is going to ever get any better, and then you end up in the same situation all over again if you don't be smart. But after two mistakes—I won't say mistakes because I love my children—but after two downfalls, you know, with men, I've learned <laughter>.

INTERVIEWER: Do you think this happens to a lot of women who are single moms?

PATRICE: Yes, I know, as a matter of fact, because a lot of my friends, we sit and talk when we aren't too depressed. We sit down and talk about it, and we've pretty much shared the same experience. You get pregnant for a guy you thought you knew; somebody you dated for years. Then he jumps up and leaves you and ends up marrying somebody they don't know for nothing but a couple of months. And you be depressed and have all the children and all the aggravation. You know, when the kids get sick, regardless of what you want to do, you got to stay up with them. And then the next morning when you're working, you've got to get up and report to work. Your employers don't want to hear that your child was sick and you kind of need to be flexible. And if you're at school, you've got to take days off when your child is sick. You got to be running from doctor's appointments, you know? Then you worry about the welfare office on your back. So, if you get depressed, you can't let your depression explode. You got to keep it under control because you got these children.

INTERVIEWER: Why do you think the guys leave at that point?

PATRICE: Well, I feel that a lot of men are scared of commitments and responsibilities. A child is a lot of responsibility. But the guys, they were older than I am by almost ten years, so I thought they would know their roles. But no. They probably felt that their life would have to stop. They couldn't do the things they wanted to do. But, as a mom, I had to give up everything, you know, stay home and take care of the children. I had to give up school, everything. But it's their responsibility too, their role. Not only are they hurting you, they are hurting the children because there are so many underprivileged kids getting into different things, drugs, and gangs and stuff because they don't have a positive male role model. They just have mom, and being a single parent I can't stay home and be with them 24 hours, seven days a week. I have to work to support me and them because they're my family. I think it's wrong because it puts me as a mom, me and other single moms, on the line because we have to give up our lives. You can't date freely because you've got children around. You don't know who is sick, you know, like a child molester.

You really got to know the guy. And then you got to make sure they are going to take to your children, and how your children like them. But I'm going to do the best I can. I'm going to provide for them, you know. I'm going to think positive and I pray and ask the Lord to assist me with, you know, raising children alone.

This is a book about welfare. It contains the intimate stories of women living in Florida and in Oregon who received cash welfare, a program now called Temporary Assistance to Needy Families (TANF). This program provides cash payments to poor families with dependent children, usually when the children are deprived of the support of one parent. For the sake of ease, I refer to TANF, and its precursor, Aid to Families with Dependent Children (AFDC) as "welfare," even though, in reality, they are only two of many programs lumped under that heading. The women interviewed graciously disclosed the experiences that led them to welfare; their appreciation for and frustration with the system, and the ways in which they cope with the frustration; their hopes, dreams, and plans for themselves and their children; the impact of welfare reform and their ideas on how the system should really be changed.

Equally important, this is a book about women. I examine the ways in which women are marginalized in our economic system, dependent in social relationships, and stigmatized for needing government aid to care for their children. These in-depth interviews reveal some of the consequences that this may have for women. Participants in this research come from all walks of life: some have been receiving welfare since childhood, others grew up in upper-middle-class families. Some bore children out of wedlock; others had children within the confines of a marriage they thought would last forever. They are a diverse group, and, at first glance, would appear to have little in common with one another. But, as their stories unfolded, many shared themes became apparent. What they have in common includes broken or intermittent relationships with men, and struggles to provide the financial security, as well as physical and emotional care, that children need. They serve as both mothers and fathers to their children, often unexpectedly.

Critical and Feminist Frameworks

I began this work because I wanted to better understand the lives of ordinary poor women on welfare and to share that information with others. I wanted to listen to their life stories: listen to the issues that engage them, the struggles that consume them, and their dreams and visions of the future that drive them. My fundamental goal is to help us better understand the lives of poor women who receive welfare by providing critical and feminist frameworks to understand their experiences. A critical perspective means that we do not blindly accept commonly touted explanations for the way things are. It requires that we examine the assumptions, values, and ideologies that are used to justify our attitudes toward women on welfare and the organization of the welfare system. Power relationships are at the heart of critical theory; it suggests that social and political arrangements often favor the dominant group, or the elite, within society. Yet these arrangements may be presented as "normal," and as reflecting the best interests of all members of society, rich and poor alike. Members of society internalize this "status quo"—the ideologies become common sense and have shared meanings. So, for example, the ideology that welfare is "a narcotic, a subtle destroyer of the human spirit," as claimed by former U.S. President Ronald Reagan in his 1986 State of the Union Address (cited in Rank, 1994, p. 19), has widespread appeal, while other evidence that contradicts this view is routinely dismissed.

A feminist framework uses gender as a central lens and as a key variable in the current controversy over welfare. Feminist research is based on the belief that women continue to be devalued and oppressed, and as a result, their experiences have been neglected or distorted by science. Reconstructing knowledge designed to empower women and challenge the status quo is at the heart of feminist research and is my ultimate purpose (Cook and Fonow, 1986; Thompson, 1992). In this book I utilize a feminist framework to present research that is both *on* and *for* women. Research on women hopes to unmask biases and expand our knowledge about women. My goal is to sensitize people to the reality of women's lives. Research for women is "consciously aimed at emancipating women and enhancing their lives," (Thompson, 1992). In particular it embeds personal experience in a broader social context. The rich personal experiences of all women are grounded in a social, historical, cultural, and political context. Women have certain experiences because society is organized by gender. Research for women illuminates far beyond simply filling in the gaps of our knowledge about women; it emphasizes the importance of context, social processes, and subjective experience.

I acknowledge that some recipients of cash assistance welfare programs are men, but I suggest that welfare is a women's issue for two reasons. First, only a small percentage of households that receive cash assistance contain two parents; by far the most prevalent household is one in which a never-married, separated, or divorced mother is the sole "head of household," (U.S. Department of Health and Human Services, Administration for Children and Families, 2004).

Second, and perhaps even more important, welfare is a women's issue because many women are simply one man away or one crisis away from welfare themselves. In reality, many middle and upper-middle-class women are more vulnerable than they reveal, and if they lost the support from their husband or partner, they too would be impoverished. Women are not a particularly wealthy group of individuals. Working full-time, women earned an average of $31,200, or 77 percent of men's earnings (DeNavas-Walt, Proctor, & Lee, 2005), this figure masks the variation in earnings. About 63 percent of women employed in wage and salary jobs were paid by the hour in 2003, with median hourly earnings of $10.08 (U.S. Department of Labor, 2004). Despite working, many women would quickly become impoverished if they lost the support of a spouse, experienced a crisis such as an injury or illness, or experienced even a short-term lay-off or reduction in work hours. These disastrous events are rarely planned, but they can happen to any and all women with only minimal notice. Certainly, men are also vulnerable. But women's wages are so much less than men's, that they walk the fine line between subsistence and impoverishment. Moreover, women's economic status is often more tentative than is the case for men. This is particularly true if a mother is not employed and is deriving her economic status through her partner, as is the case with about 40 percent of married women with children under the age of six (U.S. Census Bureau, Statistical Abstract of the U.S., 2005, Table 579). But even when employed, women face unique challenges in the gendered workplace. Lower wages for work of comparable worth, occupational segregation, and unequal returns on education are ties that bind women together, whether or not women acknowledge them. For many affluent women, this insight is particularly troubling. It breaks down the barriers that society tends to impose between "us," defined as anyone who is not on welfare, and "them," and asks that we acknowledge our common experiences as women, which transcend social class or race.

We also know, however, that there is no single meaning or given experience of being a woman. Feminist theories acknowledge difference in women's experiences. A woman is never really only a woman; many other structural and social features shape the lived experience of being female. For example, social class, as well as race and ethnicity shape experiences of women. The experience of growing up poor and black in the rural south, as vividly described by Anne Moody in *Coming of Age in Mississippi* (1968), differs from the experiences portrayed by Dorothy Allison in *Bastards Out of Carolina* (1992), a story of a white girl's experience growing up in rural southern poverty. Womanhood is not a static or unidimensional status. It is, instead, shaped by social, historical, and cultural surroundings that influence the ways in which women experience, interpret, and construct their reality.

Yet there are some shared patterns of meaning and some commonalities of experience that can be noted. We live in a patriarchal society where male dominance is maintained and supported through law, religion, culture, and societal norms. For example, women, as a collective group of people, are more likely to be economically dependent upon others; they are more likely to be poor; they are more likely to hold low-wage work; and they are more likely to be a single parent than are men. Moreover, women around the world are routinely subjected to physical and sexual violence, simply because they are women. One of the "necessities" of patriarchy, according to Dorothy Miller in *Women and Social Welfare* (1992), is the need to separate the sexes and devalue and control women. From the Chinese ritual of footbinding, to the epidemic of female genital mutilation affecting more than 100 million women today (Amnesty International, February 17, 2004; Mackie, 1996; Yount, 2004), women are routinely raped, beaten, and tortured because of patriarchal norms. In her provocative book, *Against Our Will: Men, Women and Rape* (1975), Brownmiller suggested that the threat of rape, as well as the act itself, perpetuates and enhances patriarchy by limiting women's freedoms and encourages their dependency on men for protection.

Gender is both an interactional and a political process, and is at the center of this analysis. This is one of the challenges of this book: to analyze women's experiences with welfare in a way that captures their individuality, but also recognizes the shared patterns of meaning and their commonalities of experience as women within the social structure. They are active participants in creating meaning of the welfare experience, developed through interaction with their families, friends, and with acquaintances such as the staff in the welfare office. Moreover, they create meaning through their interactions with strangers in such public places as grocery stores, where they immediately become identified and labeled as "welfare mothers" when using their food stamps.

Specific Contributions of This Study of Lived Experience

Women who receive welfare are a distorted and stigmatized group. They are seen as "different," and as something "less than" the more affluent. They are not viewed as whole human beings, with a full range of needs and experiences. Rather, we compartmentalize and focus on narrow aspects of their lives such as their checks, their alleged fraud, or whether or not there is a man in the house. As Dorothy Miller (1992) argues, women on welfare are "manless" and therefore constitute a threat to the patriarchal order. They therefore must be punished and controlled so that their numbers will not multiply. This is accomplished in our social welfare system through such mechanisms as inadequate benefit levels, and by stigmatizing recipients.

Both men and women buy into these negative images of women on welfare. Women fail to see welfare as an issue of importance to all women and do not recognize that they too could be poor and on welfare in the event of an unfortunate, yet possible change in circumstances. Women, like men, draw sharp class lines around themselves—lines that, especially for women who are dependent upon men for their class position, are relatively arbitrary and possibly tenuous. They blanket themselves in their class position, denying their commonalities with other women. A schism occurs based on class position rather than gender inclusiveness. This lack of a "gender consciousness" is divisive. I hope to increase women's collective feeling by peeling away the mostly negative opinions about the "welfare mother," and through their stories, uncover the meaning of motherhood, family, welfare, work, and dependency in their everyday lives. Negative opinion falls away easily in light of a balanced rendering of perspective and factual data.

As I explore women's experiences with welfare, I capture the shared meaning of motherhood within our society. This book illustrates that poor women share many of the same struggles and concerns about their children's lives that others who are more affluent do. They are passionately concerned about being good mothers—a job that was considered the most important job of all. They strive to promote the well-being of their children in multiple ways. They fear for the safety of their neighborhoods. They want to get out of the housing projects, which they say are crime-ridden and filled with despair. They dream of their own house with a picket fence around it. They search for jobs, particularly ones that will pay them enough money to let them provide basic necessities for their families, such as food, adequate shelter, health insurance, and clothing. Being able to offer their children some semblance of a middle-class lifestyle, such as name-brand athletic shoes, or cable television, was considered paramount for their children's self-esteem. These are shared goals. Thus, one theme of this book is *that nonpoor women have more in common with poor women than they probably realize, and may care to know.* Without making heroes of the women interviewed, I show that the distinctions between "us" and "them" are largely arbitrary and are artifacts of having or not having enough money to cushion the blows dealt by life.

Understanding these similarities and the lived experience of poverty and welfare can inform our discussions of welfare reform, and perhaps create a more rational, humane, and empowering policy. I uncover the oppressive features of welfare in the lives of the women who use it, and provide new insights into a workable alternative. A second theme of this book is that *current reforms are predicated on changing assumptions about appropriate women's roles within the marketplace and within the family, and beliefs that poor women enjoy the "free ride" they get from the welfare system at taxpayer expense.* Both of these assumptions reveal patriarchal dictums that women must be under the control and supervision of men. The policy-relevant question should not be: How can we simply and expeditiously move more women off welfare, but rather, how can we improve women's lives so that they will no longer be poor and need welfare in the first place? These are two different issues. Forcing women off welfare into low-paying, dead-end jobs without critical health insurance or other benefits may be fruitful for creating a reserve and cheap labor force desired by a capitalist economy, but it does little to improve the lives of women and their children.

This leads to my third theme, *that the real "welfare problem" has little to do with the welfare system at all, but instead lies in the insecurity of low-wage work.* Until we strengthen the bottom tier of our employment structure so that these jobs provide more security through higher wages, critical benefits such as health insurance, and dependable hours, women who have families to support will be hesitant to take them. This does not represent a failure on the part of the welfare system. It represents a failure on the part of our government to ensure the quality and security of work. The thought is abhorrent, but welfare, with all its limitations, provides more security to vulnerable families than does employment within the lowest tiers of our labor market. It is therefore not surprising that poor women who strive to be good mothers will choose welfare over work. It may be irresponsible to do otherwise.

The specific contribution of this research is unique and moves us beyond current political or social treatises. My fourth theme is straightforward, yet often overlooked: *social policies designed to ameliorate poverty and human suffering will be more successful if we take into account the specific needs that poor women articulate themselves.* We need to begin with the participants' understandings and meanings of poverty and welfare (Blumer, 1969). An interpretation derived from those with direct experience with the welfare system is a highly effective way to better understand the strengths and limitations of our current system, and to gain insight into those who rely upon it. It provides rich description and analysis, and can, at the same time, generate an analytic schema to better understand their experiences and ideas on welfare reform. Used in conjunction with the myriad of quantitative studies that examine trends in welfare use, in-depth interviews can infuse new ideas in the discussion and answer old questions in creative new ways. Consider, for example, the numerous quantitative studies which suggest the primary reason that women stay on welfare, or return to welfare quickly, is lack of childcare. Lack of childcare slots has been identified as a critical social policy problem, and was taken into consideration under former President Clinton's welfare reform plan. However, these interviews revealed the issue is more complex than this. Namely, the reason that some women do not use childcare is not simply because it is unavailable, but because they do not *trust* strangers taking care of their children. As one woman told me, "I'm not putting my daughter in daycare until she's old enough to tell me what happened there!" Paranoia? Not necessarily, given the high percentage of girls and women who have been sexually and physically abused. Simply creating more childcare slots is admirable, but it alone will not resolve the issue of trust. Thus, qualitative studies like this one can inform our understanding of welfare, from the vantage point of the recipients themselves.

Welfare and Public Policy

Welfare recipients are denigrated because welfare itself is considered to be the scourge of public policy. It is liked by neither Democrats nor Republicans, conservatives nor liberals (Hancock, 2004). It is criticized by all sides, and is considered an extravagant and costly program that is spiraling out of control, and is responsible for a sizable component of our federal deficit. In reality, however, total AFDC expenditures actually decreased from $22.2 billion in 1992 to $22.0 billion in 1995, prior to welfare reform. The law that created TANF provided for mandatory block grants to the states totaling only $16.5 billion each year for six years (Coven, 2003). This is a flat dollar amount, not adjusted for inflation. As a result, the real value of the block grant has already fallen by more than 11 percent. Consequently, only 19 states have increased their maximum grant amounts in the 7 years between 1995 and 2002 despite inflation, and three states actually reduced their benefit level (U.S. Department of Health and Social Services, 2004). Despite the concern, expenditures for cash welfare are a small component of the overall social welfare budget, constituting only 1 percent of the federal government's total spending (Congressional Digest, 1995; U.S. Ways and Means Committee, U.S. House of Representatives, 1996, Table 8-26, p. 470).

Although money is often cited as the source of these tensions, American values of financial independence and hard work are usually at the heart of welfare hostilities (Hancock, 2004; Herbert, 1996; U.S. Department of Health and Human Services, 2005). The welfare system has been accused of encouraging long-term dependency among women, family break-ups, and illegitimacy, while discouraging work incentives and motivation. A review of newspaper articles published in 1995–1996, on the eve of welfare reform, revealed that most often they alluded to the fact that women on welfare "don't work," that they were "teen mothers," that they were "overly fertile," or "drug users" (Hancock, 2004).

Public policy makers also hold these values, and these were the heart of the 1996 debate about welfare reform. Dick Armey, a former member of the U.S. House of Representatives argues that welfare stimulates poverty, rather than reduces it. He suggests that welfare makes marriage economically unsound for low-income parents; that women marry welfare instead of their children's father (Armey, 1994). A public display by John Mica, member of the House of Representatives (R-Florida), during the debate on welfare cuts took a feverish pitch as he held up a sign, which read "Don't feed the alligators." He explained, "We post these warnings because unnatural feeding and artificial care create dependency. When dependency sets in, these otherwise able alligators can no longer survive on their own." He then noted that while "people are not alligators . . . we've upset the natural order. We've created a system of dependency" (Pear, March 25, 1995).

This line of thought closely parallels that of Charles Murray in his famous book, *Losing Ground* (1984), that welfare breeds dependency, and he has successfully persuaded many people that welfare contributes more harm than good to society. To ensure that welfare isn't too easy to get, some regions impose rigorous application procedures. For example, New York City's TANF application is among the most complex, and requires applicants to attend two eligibility interviews in two different locations, undergo fingerprinting and photographing for fraud-prevention purposes, receive a home visit from an eligibility verification investigator, attend a mandatory workforce orientation, and attend daily job search classes (five days per week) for the duration of the 30-day eligibility determination period (Holcomb, Tumlin, Koralek, Capps, & Zuberi, 2003).

The real problem with welfare is that our society no longer feels comfortable paying mothers to stay home and take care of their children. In 2004, over two-thirds of married women with dependent children under age 18 were employed outside the home. Fifty-three percent of women with children under age three were employed (U.S. Department of Labor, May, 2005). This dramatic change in the behavior of married women with children has contributed to our rethinking of welfare. As mothers' employment becomes the rule rather than the exception, people question the value of paying single mothers to stay home with their children. They ask, is it necessary to subsidize poor and single mothers so that they do not have to work outside the home when most middle-class mothers are employed? Ignored in the discussions are the differing circumstances between the two groups. Poor single mothers must be both mothers and fathers to their children. They have no one else to rely upon to share the financial and emotional strains that accompany parenting. Without money to cushion the difficulties of life, their strains may be substantial. It is therefore unfair and inappropriate to assume that poor single mothers and middle-class mothers are on a level playing field.

On August 22, 1996 President Clinton signed a bill before him to eliminate AFDC and to revamp welfare "as we know it." From the Personal Responsibility and Work Opportunity Reconciliation Act (PRWORA) (P.L. 104-193), TANF was created (Coven, 2003; U.S. Department of Health and Human Services, May, 2004). This critical welfare reform legislation went into effect as federal law on July 1, 1997, and set lifetime welfare payments at a maximum of five years, with the majority of able-bodied recipients being required to work after two years. In other words, welfare was no longer an entitlement program available to parents who otherwise meet the financial criteria. Other changes under this reform included minimal childcare assistance, at least one year of transitional medical benefits, the required identification of the children's biological fathers so that child support could more easily be pursued, and the requirement that unmarried minors live at home and stay in school in order to receive benefits.

Furthermore, more power was granted to individual states, with less power residing in the federal government. Under these general parameters, the federal government provides fewer mandates, and instead allows more local and state authority in deciding how best to meet the needs of their impoverished residents. The federal government provides a block grant to states, which use these funds to operate their own programs. Some hail this as a boon to local control; others fear that poor states have little to offer their poorest residents and consequently either eliminate some families who were previously deemed eligible, or else siphon off money from other state-funded programs such as education or job training programs (Carney, 1995; Coven, 2003). The state-run programs that run under different names (e.g., CAL-WORKS in California, POWER in Wyoming, JOBS in Oregon) are designed to meet any of the four purposes set out in federal law: (1) provide assistance to needy families so that children may be cared for in their own homes or in the homes of relatives; (2) end the dependence of needy parents on government benefits by promoting job preparation, work, and marriage; (3) prevent and reduce the incidence of out-of-wedlock pregnancies; and (4) encourage the formation and maintenance of two-parent families (Coven, 2003). States can use their TANF funds in a variety of ways, including cash assistance (including wage supplements); childcare; education and job training; transportation assistance; other services to help families secure and maintain employment; and the administration of these various programs.

Two important assumptions underlie these reforms, and they shed light on the suspicion and contempt we have for women who need government assistance. First, we as a populace apparently no longer believe that the most important job of single mothers is to care for the emotional and physical needs of their own children. Instead, single mothers should now be wage-earners first, and leave the caretaking to someone else, rather than vice versa. The norms and expectations for motherhood have changed. Single mothers no longer constitute a category of "worthy poor."

Second, reforms are based on the belief that recipients do not want significant changes made in the structure of the welfare system and do not really want to work, and therefore we must force these changes upon them. Welfare reforms have been developed within a context of antagonism—that we must force recipients to get off the public dole whether they want to or not.

Since the passage of PRWORA, almost all states have limited the number of months a family may receive TANF benefits (Rowe and Russell, 2004). Many states have enacted welfare reform policies that are more stringent than those imposed by the federal government. There are two types of limits that states can impose on recipients. The first is a *lifetime time limit*, which states when benefits can be permanently eliminated. While the federal government established a limit of five years, at least nine states have opted for shorter limits. For example, the limit in Arkansas is 24 months, the limit in Florida is 48 months, and the limit in Utah is 36 months. Some exemptions may be granted in cases of hardship (the definitions of which vary by state), usually up to 20 percent of the caseload. For example, 17 states will provide an exemption to verifiable victims of domestic violence, and 7 states will provide an exemption if caring for an infant under a few months of age.

Thirteen states impose an additional type of time limit that limits benefits *temporarily* for a specific period of time. For example, in Nevada, families who receive TANF for 24 months are then ineligible to receive benefits for the next 12 months, even though ultimately they could receive 5 years of lifetime benefits.

The federal government requires that every recipient be working as soon as the state determines she is able or after 24 months of benefit receipt, whichever is earlier. Most states require recipients to begin work or finish their high school education immediately, and to work a minimum of 30 hours per week. Post-secondary education is now exempt, despite the fact that a college degree would significantly improve job prospects, pay, and job benefits like health insurance coverage. Again, some exemptions are allowed, and these vary by state. Thirty-seven states provide an exemption to care for an ill or incapacitated person, and 45 states allow exemptions to care for a young infant, usually defined as less than 12 months of age, but 11 states require work after the child is over 3 months of age.

Twenty-one states imposed family cap policies, even though this was not part of the federal mandate. These states have special treatment for families that have an additional child while receiving benefits. For example, in California, if a child is born ten months after a family begins TANF, there will be no increase in the cash benefit for that child (Rowe and Russell, 2004).

One year after signing reform legislation, President Clinton hailed welfare reform as a resounding success by citing statistics indicating a 1.4 million drop in welfare use. "I think it's fair to say that the debate is over. We know that welfare reform works," he said in a speech in St. Louis (Broder, August 17, 1997). By 2004, there were 3 million fewer families on welfare (U.S. Department of Health and Human Services, 2005). The Heritage Foundation claims that the 1996 welfare reform legislation "made remarkable headway in helping welfare dependents to move toward self-sufficiency. It dramatically reduced the caseload of dependents, reduced child poverty, and increased employment among single mothers" (Rector, 2004: 1). However, these statistics only indicate that the number of people on welfare fell. It tells us nothing about whether welfare reform "works," in the sense of fostering self-sufficiency, independence, and self-esteem. Furthermore, it tells us nothing about whether poverty itself has declined. Meaningful evaluations of policy changes take years, or even decades. "You can't tell whether welfare reform is working simply from caseload numbers," argues Wendell Primus, a welfare expert who quit the Clinton Administration in protest over Clinton's signing of the welfare legislation. "Those figures do not tell how many former recipients moved from welfare to work, or simply from dependency to despondency. You have to look at where these people went," he suggested (Broder, August 17, 1997).

Where Are the Voices of Welfare Recipients in the Discussion?

One fact is particularly glaring and troublesome. The participants of social welfare programs have had little input into the welfare reform process. Their needs, desires, and suggestions have not been uniformly sought. Why? Because numerous stereotypes persist regarding "able-bodied persons" who receive welfare. Mothers who are without husbands to support them and their children are suspect, and viewed as potentially undeserving, depending upon the reason that they have no husband. Our Social Security insurance program provides a considerably higher benefit to children whose father died than welfare provides to children whose father deserted them. Although the need is the same, the reason for that need determines the amount of cash assistance that they will receive. We have created a stratified system in which social insurance programs are given respect, while public assistance programs are deeply stigmatized. No one who receives benefits from social insurance would dare to say he receives "welfare," despite the fact that both were created and exist under the Social Security umbrella.

Welfare recipients are a stigmatized group, "reduced in our minds from a whole and usual person to a tainted, discounted one" (Goffman, 1963, 3–4). The attributes assigned to welfare recipients are less than positive and are familiar to us all. Recipients are thought of as being lazy, unmotivated, as cheating the system, and as having additional children simply to increase the amount of their benefit. Famous author and welfare critic George Gilder stated, "on the whole, white or black, these women are slovenly, incompetent, and sexually promiscuous" (1995, 25).

These perceptions do not simply reflect ignorance or randomly misguided information. Rather, they developed in relation to our longstanding values and beliefs: that the individual is primarily responsible for his or her own economic conditions; that work is good and idleness is a vice; and that social services are likely to dull initiative and hard work. Much of the underlying belief about women on welfare is that these women are looking for a free ride at the expense of the American taxpayer (Davis & Hagen, 1996). Unlike years gone by, women are no longer excused from work in order to care for their children. Staying home to nurture and tend to dependent children is only appropriate if you have the financial means to do so. If you do not have the means, then remaining at home to care for children now constitutes idleness.

Lost in the discussions of laziness, fraud, and dependency are the significant number of women who are eligible for public assistance but do not receive it; who choose not to receive all the programs they are eligible for; and the women who voluntarily leave programs before their eligibility terminates. Instead of focusing on ways to make welfare more inclusive, we are instead afraid that "handouts" will encourage dependency. Welfare programs stigmatize those who receive assistance in order to minimize the likelihood that those currently receiving aid will get too comfortable, and to make a statement to onlookers that aid comes at an emotionally expensive price.

A National Profile of Welfare Recipients

Many studies draw into question or refute the popular folklore surrounding lazy "welfare queens." Who then does receive welfare?

According to information compiled by the U.S. Department of Health and Human Services (HHS) 1,969,909 families, or 4,729,291 individuals, received TANF in June of 2004 (U.S. Department of Health and Human Services, 2005). This is a decline of about 60 percent prior to welfare reform. Of these recipients, about two-thirds are children under the age of 18. It is therefore fair to say that the "typical" welfare recipient is a child.

Despite the fact that the majority of those who receive TANF are children, the available data on welfare use are focused largely upon parents rather than their children. Table 1.1 describes selected characteristics of welfare recipients throughout the United States, and makes comparisons to 1994, prior to welfare reform, when available (U.S. Department of Health and Human Services, November, 2004; U.S. House of Representatives, Committee on Ways and Means, 1996).

TABLE 1.1   Characteristics of AFDC and TANF Recipients: 1994, 2002

	1994	2002
Race		
White	37.4	31.6
African American	36.4	38.3
Hispanic	19.9	24.9
Age of Adult Recipient		
Under 20	5.9	7.5
20–29	44.1	44.9
30–39	34.8	29.9
40 and over	15.2	17.7
Number of Children		
One	42.6	47.0
Two	30.0	28.0
Three	15.6	14.2
Four or more	9.6	9.8
Age of Children		
Under 2	15.2	14.6
2–5	30.7	25.1
6–11	31.7	34.4
12–15	15.4	18.3
16 and over	6.9	7.6
Age of Youngest Child		
Unborn	1.8	0.5
0–1	10.8	14.8
1–2	28.1	20.6
3–5	21.6	18.4
6–11	22.7	26.8
12–15	9.8	12.7

TABLE 1.1   Continued

	1994	2002
Adult's Employment Status		
Employed	8.3	25.3
Education Level		
1–9 Years	——————	14.7
10–11 Years	——————	28.1
12 Years	——————	51.4
More than 12 Years	——————	3.3
No Formal Education	——————	2.4
Marital Status		
Single	——————	66.6
Married	——————	14.3
Separated	——————	13.0
Divorced	——————	8.2
Widowed	——————	0.7
Child Support Receipt		
Percent	——————	10.3
Amount	——————	$189.41
Citizenship Status		
U.S. Citizen	——————	92.5
Qualified Alien	——————	7.1
Unknown	——————	0.4

Sources: U.S. House of Representatives, Committee on Ways and Means, 1996; U.S. Department of Health and Human Services, November, 2004.

Table 1.1 reveals that in the 1990s whites comprised the largest share of welfare recipients; however this has changed in recent years. By 2002, less than a third of welfare recipients were white. African Americans now comprise the largest component of TANF recipients, 38 percent. However, Hispanics have experienced the largest increases, comprising nearly 25 percent of TANF recipients in 2002, up from 20 percent in 1994, and 14 percent in 1986.

Few current welfare parents are teenagers, despite portrayals in the media to the contrary. The average age of welfare recipients is 31. However the percentage of welfare recipients under age 20 is rising, from 3.3 in 1986, to 6.3 in 1994, and to 7.5 in 2002.

Families on welfare are not large; 47 percent have only one child. Three-quarters of recipients have no more than two children. The majority of these children are far too young to contribute to their financial support. Nearly 40 percent of these children are under the age of 6, and three-quarters are under the age of 12. In over half of families, the youngest child is under the age of six. However, it should be noted that not all poor children are eligible and or otherwise receive TANF. HHS data show that about half of TANF-eligible families do not receive assistance and that nonreceipt among eligible families is increasing (Fremstad, January, 2004; Reichman, Teitler, Garfinkel & Garcia, 2003).

One-quarter of TANF recipients are employed, a three-fold increase since 1994. Most women who receive TANF have lower-than-average levels of education. Over 40 percent have less than a high school diploma. Slightly more than half have a high school degree, and very few have attended college. Most recipients are single and have never married (67 percent), although 12 percent are currently married. The remaining are separated, divorced, or widowed.

Despite the popular image of welfare recipients driving Cadillacs, the average monthly TANF cash grant was $354.76 in 2002. Only one in ten recipients receives child support, with an average payment of $189.41 per month.

We also know that recipients' stays on welfare are not long as is often imagined by program critics. Even prior to welfare reform, in 1994 the median number of months on welfare during the most recent stay was 22.8 months, down from 27 months in 1986. The length of time on welfare has been declining since the 1980s—welfare reform was not essential to encourage people to find jobs. Recipients are on welfare for short spells while they amass the skills, resources, and confidence to find work and support themselves.

Yet it is important to note that there is, and always has been, considerable movement on and off welfare among many women, which may have fueled arguments to alter the system. While for some, welfare is a temporary and short-term phenomenon, there are many others who return to welfare soon after leaving the system. Those who leave welfare for employment tend to remain off somewhat longer than do those who leave for other reasons. In the mid-1990s, nearly 60 percent who left welfare came back to it within two years, 69 percent returned within four years (U.S. House of Representatives, Committee on Ways and Means, 1996). Consequently, when totaling all stays on welfare, in 1994 48 percent had received benefits for more than five years. Those who were likely to use welfare longer than average during their lifetime had less than 12 years of education, had no recent work experience, were under age 24, were black or Hispanic, had never married, had a child younger than age 3, or had 3 or more children (U.S. House of Representatives, Committee on Ways and Means, 1996). Therefore, many aspects of the 1996 reform legislation, such as strict time limits, family caps, or efforts to strengthen marriage were designed to address these specific issues (Roberts & Greenberg, February 2005; Rowe & Russell, 2004).

However, the real question remains, why do women return to welfare? Several researchers have posed this question, and have looked at the factors that are associated with returning to welfare or remaining off welfare for good. Results from quantitative studies suggest that the most important factors influencing repeated use are those factors that shape a woman's ability to earn an income (Acs & Loprest, 2004; Cheng, 2002; Harris, 1996; Zedlewski, 2003). It appears that women who have lower levels of education; those who are younger; women who have many children, particularly children under the age of six; women who have little recent work experience, and women who are in poor physical health, suffer from mental health problems, or have children who suffer from health problems are more likely to return to welfare after leaving it, and are likely to remain on welfare for longer periods of time overall. Zedlewski (2003) reports that among women who cycle on and off welfare, 47 percent were in very poor mental or physical health, 44 percent had less than a high school diploma, 24 percent had not worked in at least three years, 19 percent had an infant, and 8 percent had a child who was receiving Supplemental Security Income (SSI) for an illness or disability. Moreover, 46 percent of women cycling on and off welfare had two or more of these barriers to work (Zedlewski, 2003).

Qualitative studies elaborate on these ideas; it appears that many women cannot sustain low-wage jobs without benefits attached to them, such as health insurance or childcare, for long periods of time (Hays, 2003). Whether this implies that they are lazy, unmotivated, and dependent on welfare, as critics would suggest, is obviously a matter for further study as well as interpretation. These interviews reveal that most women are sufficiently motivated to leave welfare. Their obstacles are not their own laziness or other personal shortcomings. Rather, they are on welfare largely because of an entanglement of constraints: relationships that have gone sour; a dearth in their levels of human capital (e.g., education, job skills); insufficient social support systems; and a lack of jobs that provide the security that families need.

Given the high rates of recidivism, some recipients have been accused of being "dependent" on the system. For example, the Heritage Foundation claims, "Currently approximately half of the 2 million mothers on the TANF rolls are idle. We must encourage productive activity that leads to self-sufficiency, rather than destructive activity that leads to dependency" (Rector, 2004).

Moreover, there is widespread concern over the intergenerational transmission of welfare. A 1990 review of seven studies conducted between 1986 and 1990 (Moffit, 1990) reports that their results provide consistent evidence of strong correlations between parents' use of welfare and the later behavior of their daughters. Daughters from welfare families are more likely to use welfare themselves later than are daughters whose parents did not use welfare. However, a correlation does not assume causality. The studies do not answer the question of whether growing up with welfare causes a daughter to use it later as well. Many other possible explanations for the observed correlation are possible. Children from homes that use welfare generally have fewer parental resources available to them, live in poorer and more dangerous neighborhoods, and go to inferior schools. Thus, deficiencies in social capital, human capital, or fewer jobs in the impoverished neighborhood, could be responsible for the correlation. However, it is important to recognize that 41 percent of women who are considered now to be "highly dependent" on welfare (defined as receiving at least 25 percent of average family income as cash welfare payments) received no welfare in their household when they were children, and most of the others received aid for only a short period (Table 8.51, p. 512.).

Gottschalk and Moffitt (1994) suggest that the best way to conceptualize "welfare dependence" is to examine the total time spent on welfare over a given period of time. Using data from the Panel Study of Income Dynamics (PSID) for the years 1974–1987, they found that dependence has not grown significantly in the population as a whole, with the exception of younger women. They propose that the increase in total time on welfare and total percentage of income dependence can be explained by the drop in age at first entry onto welfare, and not from an increase in welfare episode duration.

Sociologist Mark Rank suggests that we reconceptualize the poverty experience because most Americans will experience poverty and will turn to some form of public assistance at some point during their lives. Using national longitudinal data to estimate the likelihood of poverty spells over the life course, he found that by the time Americans have reached age 75, 59 percent would have spent at least a year below the poverty line during their adulthood. Moreover, approximately two-thirds will have received public assistance as adults for at least one year (Rank, 2004).

I maintain that the term "welfare dependency" is a misnomer, because few women are really "dependent" on the system as the term implies. Instead, the rich data from these in-depth interviews reveal an elaborate system in which women attempt to build a respectable and meaningful life for their children and for themselves. As you will see, they use their meager welfare benefits, as do women with greater incomes, to secure food, shelter, clothing, and to try to buy some semblance of a middle-class lifestyle. But because neither their welfare benefits nor their earnings are sufficient to pull them out of poverty, let alone allow for a middle-class lifestyle, they reconstruct intricate webs to help them live and survive. Orchestrating this is stressful. The lucky ones have family and friends to rely upon; the unlucky ones do not.

Terri Lynn is one of the luckier ones. I spoke with her, and her sister, one rainy winter day at their mother's house. Although her extended family is not large, she relies on them daily for her housing, childcare, and transportation. She is a 24-year-old African American woman and mother of a six-year-old daughter, who shares close bonds with her mother, sister, brother, and aunt. She currently lives with her sister in her rent-subsidized apartment while she saves money from her job to enable her to get her own apartment. She says that this living arrangement is preferable to her previous arrangement. Her former apartment cost $215 a month, and often was without heat or water because the landlord failed to pay the bill. During these times, Terri Lynn and her daughter would take the bus over to her mother's house and shower, cook, and perhaps even sleep there.

Terri Lynn is employed, working as a night cashier at a bowling alley across town. She continues to receive a partial welfare payment because the hours are sporadic, and, at minimum wage, her income does not lift her above the eligibility limits for aid. "But I wish I wasn't getting none of it," she told me. She has tried to get off welfare by taking computer classes at a for-profit business school in town. But after graduation, without experience, and without their help in finding employment, she could not find anyone to hire her. Instead, she found a job at a bowling alley, and slowly works to pay off her tuition debts.

Luckily for Terri Lynn, her mother or sister babysit her daughter for free, a savings of several hundred dollars per month. On her income and her small welfare grant,

Terri Lynn would not be able to pay them, or anyone else to take care of her child. She does not own a car, nor do her mother or sister, so Terri Lynn relies upon the bus to get her to work. Transportation logistics are a nightmare. The bus ride takes over an hour and a half each way. Thus, between working and commuting, her daughter often spends 11 hours a day with her childcare provider, in this case Terri Lynn's mother or sister. She is thankful she does not have to leave her with a stranger, and in an unfamiliar place, for such long periods of time. When she works late into the night and the bus has stopped running, she usually takes a taxi cab back to her mom's house, where her daughter is sleeping. The cab costs her $6.00, and cuts into a sizable portion of her minimum-wage earnings. She cannot afford to take the cab all the way back to her own house on the other side of town.

> I leave here at 3:45, and get downtown at 4:15. Then I wait until 4:30 to catch the #7 bus. And then by the time I get there it's 5:05. And then I have to walk on down there, and I get there at 5:30 on the dot. But after work at 1:00 in the morning, I have to catch a cab because the bus has stopped running. So I catch a cab to my mom's house where <daughter> is sleeping. I sleep there too, and then I get up real early so that we can catch the early bus back to my house so I can get her <daughter> ready for school. See, and by then I have to take her to school because she'd done missed the school bus. After that I go back home and try to get some rest, and then, after school, I go back and pick her up. We take the bus back to my mom's house so she can watch her, and then I go to work again. So, I be running back and forth all day long.

Sometimes her brother is able to pick her up from work late at night, and take her and her daughter directly home, which makes their morning routine considerably easier. She told me, in no uncertain terms, that this assistance from her family was invaluable to her. Without it, she would not be able to work. Her daughter's father, in contrast, provides no emotional or financial support.

> **TERRI LYNN:** Her dad never gave me nothing. I had to beg him to buy one bag of Pampers for her when she ran out once and I didn't have no money. He's called her maybe three times since he was out of jail. Now she asks, "When is my daddy coming?" What can I tell her? I don't know. I told him that he needs to straighten himself out and spend more time with her because she wanted to see him. Now that he's been out of jail he was supposed to come see her, but he hasn't gotten her yet. I guess he thinks I'm supposed to bring her to him, but I'm not going to bring her to him. I don't have a car.
>
> **INTERVIEWER:** Does he pay any child support?
>
> **TERRI LYNN:** No. But right now they are getting on the people who aren't paying. They are cracking down real hard on them. They want to know when was the last time you seen him, the name and address. And I have his social security number.

SISTER: My son's father isn't paying because I don't know his address. And he's using a different name instead of his name. He don't take care of him either. He's got four kids, two in Tampa, and two here, and they are five months apart. My son, and another girl's son. I have to call him to come see him. And that ticks me off. I have to do it by myself. When I see him, I have to cuss him out. To come and see him, and to give me money. When I come around that corner, he has to run because he's going to get cussed up. He came the other night when I was watching TV, and he gave me some money, but he wanted something too, if you know what I mean. He wanted me to kiss him and stuff.

Terri Lynn has received welfare since her daughter was born six years ago. Is she "dependent" on the system? By traditional definitions of welfare dependency, yes. However, a cogent argument can be made that Terri Lynn's family provides at least as much assistance to her, if not more, than does the state. A closer look reveals a portrait of a hard-working young woman who is doing her best to improve the life conditions for herself and her daughter. Yet, despite working hard, what are Terri Lynn's chances of beating poverty? Unless her income nearly doubles from her current minimum wage, her chances of pulling herself and her daughter out of poverty are slim at best. This is not due to her own laziness, personal inadequacy, or lack of family support, but because of structural features of the social system that snowball against poor women. Given the largely grim statistics of women's underemployment in general, what are the odds that a 24-year-old woman with only a high school diploma, who is without reliable transportation, who needs childcare, and whose only work experience is in the service sector, will soon land the $10 to $12 an hour job needed to really lift her out of poverty? Moreover, why does her daughter's father not contribute to her support? Can we really expect Terri Lynn, alone, to provide for all her daughter's emotional and financial needs without any help from the government?

Who Are the Participants in This Study?

Sheila, Patrice, and Terri Lynn are among 47 women in Florida who were willing to be interviewed for this book in 1995 and 552 women who were interviewed in Oregon in 2002 and again in 2003. The Floridians live in several small and medium-sized communities in the north-central region of the state. They were first introduced to this project at the county welfare office, as were most of the others, as they came to pick up their food stamps. Others were friends of those who were initially interviewed. Sheila, Patrice, Terri Lynn, and 44 others generously volunteered their time and energy to this project without pay or other compensation. They invited us into their homes where they embraced the opportunity to reveal the ways in which they live on, negotiate, and survive welfare. The interviews were often lengthy, up to several hours in some cases, as women disclosed the joys and frustrations with their children, with their extended families, with employment, and with the welfare system. They told us about their experiences that led them to welfare, and about the individual and structural constraints on their lives and on their opportunities for upward mobility. They told us of their coping and survival strategies; the stigma they face; their future goals; their attitudes toward other recipients; and their concerns with governmental aid, the welfare system, and welfare reform.

This book also reports the findings from a longitudinal study in Oregon combining both qualitative and quantitative strategies. In 2002, my research team conducted telephone interviews with 637 Oregonians from around the state who had left welfare for work 6 months prior. One year later, in 2003, 552 of these respondents were located and re-interviewed. At this point they had been off TANF for about 18 months, and were no longer eligible for the transitional medical benefits that they were provided when leaving welfare for work. These 552 respondents form the basis for the quantitative portion of the study. From these standardized telephone surveys, we have gained tremendous insight about life after leaving TANF. Respondents generously agreed to share their experiences about living and coping after welfare, particularly with respect to their own health and the health of their children, their health insurance options and access to health care, and their health-related worries and concerns.

We also completed in-person interviews in 2002 and 2003 with a subsample of respondents who were selected from four key regions in Oregon: (1) an urban metropolitan area with relatively low unemployment, higher wages, and low rates of poverty; (2) a rural coastal region that faces high unemployment and poverty as the fishing and timber industries have declined in recent decades; (3) a newly urbanized region in the central part of the state that is rapidly growing and known for tourism year-around—jobs are relatively plentiful, but seasonal and low-paying; and (4) a rural area in the eastern part of Oregon characterized by an agriculture-based economy with seasonal employment, high unemployment and poverty, and a relatively large Spanish-speaking Hispanic population. Ninety persons were interviewed in 2002; one year later, 82 of the original families were found and agreed to meet again and share their stories of hardship, pain, hope, and survival. These qualitative and quantitative interviews will be used throughout this book to complement the original interviews conducted in 1995.

My intention was to obtain stories about welfare from a diverse group of women. Since the goal of this project was to discover meaning, rather than simply to measure the distribution of attributes across the population, it was important to obtain a sample that elucidates particular population types. Therefore, respondents represented a variety of traits or conditions found among welfare recipients, such as variation in race or ethnic background, age, number of children, and housing type. This diversity was important in order to approximate natural variations in the welfare experience.

The demographic characteristics of the 47 women interviewed in Florida and 522 in Oregon are reported in Table 1.2, and are reasonably representative of welfare recipients in the area from which they came. With respect to the sample from Florida, 38 percent of respondents were white, and 62 percent were African American. Although this over-represents the proportion of African Americans on welfare in the United States overall, it does reflect the race and ethnic background of welfare recipients from the interview region. In the Oregon sample, nearly three-quarters of

TABLE 1.2   Characteristics of Florida and Oregon Samples

	Florida 1995 (n = 47)		Oregon 2002/2003 (n = 552)	
	N	*%*	*N*	*%*
Race				
White	18	38%	398	72%
African American	29	62%	30	5%
Hispanic	0	0	91	16%
Other	0	0	28	5%
Missing	0	0	5	1%
Age of Adult Respondent				
Under 21	2	4%	50	9%
21–29	24	51%	232	42%
30–39	10	21%	179	32%
40 and over	7	15%	91	17%
Missing	4	9%	0	0
Number of Children				
One	12	26%	233	42%
Two	16	34%	179	32%
Three	12	26%	88	16%
Four or more	7	15%	41	8%
Missing	0	0	11	2%
Marital Status				
Single	28	60%	215	40%
Married/Separated	4	9%	135	25%
Divorced	13	28%	194	35%
Widowed	0	0	7	1%
Missing	2	4	0	0
Employment Status				
Employed	10	21%	433	78%
Not Employed	37	79%	119	22%
Missing	0	0	0	0
Education				
Not a High School Graduate	9	19%	114	21%
High School Graduate/GED	18	38%	227	41%
Some College/Vocational	19	40%	210	38%
Missing	0	0	1	0

recipients are white, only 5 percent are African American, and 15 percent are Hispanic, reflecting the characteristics of TANF-leavers in that state.

Most respondents were young, with over half under the age of 30. Family sizes are small—60 percent of the Florida sample and 74 percent of the Oregon sample had only one or two children. Sixty percent of respondents in Florida had never been married, compared to 40 percent in Oregon. The others were divorced, separated, widowed, or currently married. Because the Oregon sample is made up of persons who have been off TANF for 18 months, it is not surprising that a higher percentage of them are married or separated.

Expectedly, four out of five respondents in Florida were not employed outside the home for pay because they were receiving welfare at the time of the interview. Twenty-one percent were "officially" employed, most commonly in the fast-food industry. These jobs are low-paying and without fringe benefits; therefore their incomes were not sufficient to pull them above the poverty line, and they continued to collect a partial welfare benefit. Several others who claimed to be "not employed" supplemented their checks by babysitting or styling hair, but these jobs were sporadic, were not a dependable source of income, and not reported to their caseworkers. Over three-quarters of the Oregon respondents—TANF recipients who left welfare for work 18 months prior—were still employed.

The majority of respondents lived in subsidized housing. Some of these women in Florida lived in large, often multi-storied projects. These tended to have inexpensive rent, only paying $10 to $20 per month. Most of these apartments were in a substantial state of disrepair, with paint peeling both inside and out, screens ripped or missing from windows, a carpet that was dirty and well worn, and drapes that were torn and tattered. Other women we interviewed lived in private apartments or single-family houses with reduced rent. These were far more desirable, although more expensive, and were usually located in "mixed" neighborhoods with others who were not on welfare. The waiting list for this type of subsidy was considerably longer than for the wait to move to the large housing projects. Other women paid full price for their housing, sometimes doubling up with family members or friends to make ends meet.

Conclusion and Organization

Using critical and feminist lenses with which to examine the narratives of welfare recipients, this is both a book about welfare and a book about women's lives more generally. Poor women on welfare are stigmatized; this book calls into question the negative connotations associated with women who use welfare. What unfolded from the narratives were stories about hardship, faith, and hope that were not systematically different from other women who are more financially well-off. It reveals that, in many ways, poor mothers are strikingly similar to mothers who are more affluent. They share many of the same goals, hopes, and dreams for themselves and for their children. But trying to attain these with a limited income is a constant struggle. I learned about the mechanisms that poor women need to improve their lives and lift themselves from poverty. This book explores the intricate web of informal and formal support that women need for living and surviving on welfare, and I analyze the coping strategies used by women and their children. These insights can inform and guide the ways we amend the welfare system and restructure work in the lowest tiers of our economy. These I suggest are more fruitful than simply asking, "How do we reduce the number of women on welfare?" Lifting women from poverty, and eliminating them from welfare, are two separate issues. Unfortunately, it is the latter concern that is most often addressed in welfare reforms.

Chapter 2 begins with the questions, "Why are people poor?" and "Why are they on welfare?" My goal is to put these questions into the larger framework of understanding how we have historically, and how we today, explain and legitimize social inequality. These sets of beliefs are important because they filter social perceptions and provide the cognitive structure in which to interpret the causes of poverty and welfare use. However, these explanations are not gender neutral; instead, they marginalize or ignore women's experiences within such domains as family and intimate relations, and within the domain of work.

Chapter 3 examines recipients' experience with stigma and discrimination. Themes of laziness, often racially charged, emerged frequently. How do they cope with, or manage this stigma of being a welfare mom? As social worker Frederick B. Mills reminds us, the stigma paradigm hinges on the concepts of dependence, promiscuity, illegitimacy, and addiction (1996). These stereotypes are widespread, including among welfare recipients themselves. They have important implications and serve as political tools that trivialize the plight of poor women, and consequently keep meaningful work and welfare reforms from occurring.

Chapter 4 focuses on what Scott and Lyman (1968) have labeled as "accounts"—the justifications or excuses people use to account for their own poverty and welfare use. In this chapter, I examine the economic and relationship factors that caused them to enter the welfare system for the very first time. Through their narratives, I illuminate the ways in which their histories and experiences, such as their education, work experience, and relationship with their children's fathers, in conjunction with the social structure, have influenced their economic circumstances. We can see that, for many women, their use of welfare is a result of an age-old reliance upon men that has gone awry, and a result of a social system that refuses to pay a living wage. We explore the incongruence between their accounts of their own welfare use and their perceptions of other recipients.

Chapter 5 explores the ways in which women on welfare manage their lives on a daily basis. What is it like to live and provide financially for one's family from a welfare grant? What decisions need to be made on a regular basis? After accounting for inflation, the average monthly welfare benefit has declined nearly 50 percent since 1970; thus, budgeting to make ends meet requires creativity and flexibility. Families on welfare suffer from a cultural dissonance: They are aware of consumptive patterns in the United States, but they are unable to participate. Recipients describe daily living, and the process of surviving the welfare system, while keeping their children safe and out of danger, as extremely challenging and stressful.

Several important studies identify that women on welfare do not subsist on their meager welfare grant alone. Instead, they must rely upon formal or informal sources of assistance to augment their checks. Chapter 6 explores the ways in which recipients rely upon informal supports, such as family, friends, and children's fathers, to make ends meet and to manage the stress. Most women revealed that this help was extensive and valuable, and admitted that they could not care for their families adequately without it. The chapter also examines the formal supports that women rely upon to make ends meet, such as charities or food banks, and the "hidden" income and gifts they receive and rely upon. How important are these to women? How do they assemble a "survival package" to live and cope with welfare? Their stories offer a striking portrayal of the ways in which impoverished families construct relationships so that the effects of poverty can best be eased.

Recipients are often portrayed by the media as people who like the welfare system and take delight in receiving monthly benefits from it. Yet the women interviewed here portray a markedly different point of view. Chapter 7 focuses on recipients' perceptions of the strengths and weaknesses of the welfare system. Criticisms of welfare were vast and widespread. Women spoke with a heightened sense of concern and passion as they relayed their firsthand experiences with a system they deemed as frustrating, demoralizing, and in need of considerable change and repair. Because welfare policy varies significantly by state, I examined welfare reform in one particular state— Florida, which is where the women who were interviewed reside. Respondents shared their ideas on what the role of the federal government should be in helping poor people. They commented on three critical reforms: (a) time limits for receiving aid; (2) work requirements; and (3) family caps, which limit or deny additional aid for children born to women already receiving welfare. Furthermore, they share their perspectives of what meaningful reforms would entail.

Chapter 8 examines the challenges faced by women as they leave the welfare system. While human capital enhancement programs would be helpful to some women, the difficulties they are likely to face, as they transition off of welfare due to TANF time limits, extend far beyond increasing their education or job skills. The structure of the labor market, including a lack of unskilled jobs, low pay, the increasing number of temporary positions, and the lack of health insurance among low-wage jobs, has a profound effect on their likelihood of success in finding and maintaining work.

As families leave TANF for work they are given one year of medical benefits to help them with the transition in their lives. Chapter 9 discusses the importance of medical benefits for the security of families leaving welfare. The chapter also examines what happens to families after their automatic one-year benefits expire. Do families remain insured through government programs or employers, or do they lose their medical benefits? Are they able to access the health care that they need? Access to health care is at the core of sound welfare reform because it is a critical source of security and well-being, particularly for poor and low-income families who cannot afford to purchase health insurance privately and may not qualify for government programs. Without access to health care, families risk not only their health, but their entire economic viability.

Chapter 10 revisits the themes introduced in this chapter. It concludes that welfare is not simply about providing money for women who are too lazy to work. Welfare provides security for single mothers and their children, and other vulnerable groups in society. The way to resolve the "welfare problem" is to intervene in the structure of low-tier work in the United States, not to force families off of assistance. Until the structure of work in the bottom tier is deliberately made more secure by human and rational government intervention, many single mothers will not risk their children's health and well-being by accepting low-wage, exploitive, and unreliable employment.

CRITICAL THINKING QUESTIONS

1. Is it easier for an older woman like Sheila or a younger woman to find a good job? Defend your answer.

2. Why is cash welfare stigmatized, but programs such as Social Security or Medicare are not?

3. Is it more likely that poverty causes depression, or that depression causes poverty?

4. Do you think that most Americans associate welfare with African Americans? Do they associate it with Hispanics, Asians, and Native Americans as well? Why or why not?

5. Is the term "welfare dependency" a misnomer, as the author suggests? Why or why not?

6. The author presents four themes in Chapter 1 that she will discuss throughout the book. At this point in your reading, critique these themes.

7. What can we really learn from in-depth interviews with fewer than 50 people? Would you trust a telephone survey with 552 people more? Why or why not? What are the strengths and weaknesses of each approach?

2

Historical and Persisting Dilemmas: How Do We Explain Poverty, What Should We Do About It?

Why are people poor? Why are they on welfare? These seemingly straightforward questions have a multitude of contradictory and conflicting answers. Opinions about welfare and welfare recipients reflect general beliefs that people hold regarding not only poverty, but also wealth in our nation.

This chapter provides a summary of the frameworks Americans use to explain and to legitimate poverty and social inequality. It offers a glimpse into the historical and persistent dilemmas that plague our nation. Most of the opinions in fashion today are derived from age-old questions and answers about poverty, and the distribution of wealth more generally. They reflect longstanding questions about if, how, and under what circumstances we should care for others who cannot or do not seem able to care for themselves. They reflect our views about human nature, about the importance of hard work and our dislike of idleness, and our expectations of appropriate roles for men and women in society.

Our history of rugged individualism, a spirit of Calvinism, and the idea that hard work will reap results, set the backdrop for the development of the social welfare system in this country. Poverty was considered part of the natural social order and was not necessarily taken as a defect of the social structure. Fueled by Social Darwinism, the competitive struggle to secure one's economic status allowed the "fittest" to win out over others. Government should not hamper this competitive struggle, we reasoned. Borrowing from the Poor Laws of England, we distinguished early on between the "worthy poor" (e.g., the disabled, the aged), and the "non-worthy poor" (e.g., the able-bodied). Our social welfare system developed within this framework of duality and continues to operate in this fashion today. Our system has been described as "reluctant," indicating our generosity towards the worthy poor, while demonstrating callous disregard for others (Jansson, 1988). Thus, current decisions about who constitutes the worthy poor, and at what level they should be taken care of, reflect our longstanding debates.

The "welfare problem" has been, and is today, defined primarily in terms of the moral values of work (Handler & Hasenfeld, 1991, Hancock, 2004). The most consistent part of our evolving welfare policy is to reinforce the work ethic. Traditionally, American social policy attempts to encourage people to work, not to choose welfare. Only those people who cannot work are deemed worthy of assistance. Thus, our approach to welfare has been to make the conditions of assistance less desirable than the lowest-wage work. But some welfare critics suggest that this is no longer the case; instead, welfare has become a more desirable alternative than low-wage work (Gilder, 1981; Heritage Foundation, 2004; Mead, 1986; Murray, 1984, 1988). Our attitudes toward single mothers reflect these concerns. The Heritage Foundation writes,

> Rather than being materially poor, American's "poor" suffer from the effects of behavioral poverty, meaning a breakdown in the values and conduct that leads to the formation of healthy families, stable personalities, and self-sufficiency. This includes eroded work ethic and dependency, lack of educational aspirations and achievement, inability or unwillingness to control one's children, increased single parenthood and illegitimacy, criminal activity, and drug and alcohol abuse (The Heritage Foundation, 2004, p. 2).

Historically, our policies ponder whether single mothers, as a group, are worthy of assistance. Should we pay them to stay home to take care of their children, or should we require them to work? Does government assistance undermine their incentive to work, encourage loose morals, and undermine their willingness to enter marriage—and thus perpetuate their poverty?

History of Cash Assistance

Welfare programs, at least in theory, were created and designed to help protect women and their children who were seen as more vulnerable than men to conditions of poverty, and thus potentially deserving of assistance. The concept of "Mother's Pensions," the forerunner of the AFDC program, arose during the Progressive Era (1896–1914) and was to provide greater government responsibility for the well-being of poor women and children—particularly those who were white and who were widows. Some reformers were particularly concerned over (1) that the 5.3 million women who were working for wages outside the home were taking jobs away from men; (2) the large numbers of children residing in orphanages because their mothers could not support them or care for them while they were employed; and (3) the increasing rate of delinquency among children left at home unsupervised (Abramovitz, 1996a,b; Gordon, 1994; Mink, 1995). The future of our nation depended on the proper upbringing of children by their mothers, reformers clamored. Mothers' Pensions were designed as payment for the services of motherhood, thus giving it legitimacy, and attempting to remove the stigma associated with public aid.

In reality, however, Mother's Pensions continued the traditional charity models of assistance. Benefits were low, and the emphasis was placed on moral reform. They strongly enforced patriarchal norms about women's moral character. In exchange for aid, poor mothers were forced to conform to rules and policies designed to weed out the suspected fraud, and to ensure that women followed strict gender role norms. For example, agency caseworkers monitored the women for signs of drinking, poor housekeeping, improper childrearing techniques, and relationships with men. Foreign-born women were urged to assimilate and to adopt white, middle-class values; reformers generally held the view that immigrants were inferior to the native-born (Abramovitz, 1996b).

Modern-day welfare emerged from these values of moral reform. "Welfare," as we have come to call it, was created in 1935 as Title IV of the Social Security Act, a critical piece of legislation produced during the New Deal when millions of families were suffering financial hardship. Approximately one-quarter of the workforce lost their jobs during the Great Depression. Homelessness, hunger, malnutrition, and begging were widespread. Private charities and churches stepped up their efforts to help the needy, but the problem had become so rampant that their efforts could not keep pace with the need. A wide variety of safety net programs were created to assist vulnerable populations under President Franklin D. Roosevelt. The Social Security Act established several key social security and unemployment programs, and responsibility for social welfare was transferred from individual states to the federal government.

Originally called Aid to Dependent Children (ADC), its focus was to keep single mothers from being dependent on their children for labor and income, and to keep both mothers and children out of the work force. It was "designed to release from the wage-earning role the person whose natural function is to give her children the physical and affectionate guardianship necessary not alone to keep them from falling into social misfortune, but more affirmatively to make them citizens capable of contributing to society" (Committee on Economic Security, 1985, pp. 5–6). Welfare was to be synonymous with well-being, prosperity, good health, and good spirits, and therefore faced relatively little opposition in Congress. It was considered a pro-family program: it kept mothers in the home so that they could care for, nurture, and protect their children. Mothers were not expected to work and raise their children at the same time (Abramovitz, 1996a).

ADC was a fundamental departure from the inequitably distributed "Mother's Pensions," which served almost exclusively white widows. ADC recipients included mothers who were abandoned, divorced, never married, or mothers whose husbands were unable to work. ADC was, theoretically at least, supposed to provide help to African American as well as to white women. Fourteen percent of all children who received ADC in the 1937–1938 fiscal year were African American, a figure far below true need, but it at least represented an improvement over Mother's Pensions (Sterner, 1943). However, as Quadagno (1994) points out, ADC and other components of Social Security were marked with racism. To keep African Americans from receiving benefits many states, particularly in the south, tightened their eligibility requirements so as to exclude them.

Although ADC's goals were admirable, it fell short of significantly reducing poverty in many respects. For example, although it was a means-tested "federal" program, ADC gave individual states great authority over eligibility and benefit levels. Southern congressmen fought to limit federal control and would only support ADC if the states were allowed to establish their own eligibility requirements and benefit levels (Quadagno, 1988, 1994). This resulted in dramatic statewide differences in the level of benefits. For example, in 1939 ADC benefits ranged from an average of $2.46 per child per month in Arkansas to $24.53 in New York (U.S. Social Security Board, 1940). Southern states rationalized their lower-than-average benefit levels by declaring that black families needed less than did white families (Abramovitz, 1996b). Benefits continue to vary dramatically by state; benefits ranged in 2002 from a high of $923 per month in Alaska for a family with one adult and two children, to a low of $170 per month in Mississippi (Department of Health and Human Services, November, 2004). Cost of living differentials do exist in the United States; however, they are not large enough to warrant differences in benefits of this magnitude.

Moreover, upon its creation, ADC benefits were considerably less than those provided for adults receiving Old Age Assistance (OAA) and Aid to the Blind (AB), even though recipients of these latter two programs were less likely to have children in the home. Initially, ADC did not include money for the child's caretaker—generally the mother. Furthermore, the program continued the practices, commonly employed with Mother's Pensions, of using aid to enforce behavioral standards and cultural norms. Home visits and periodic eligibility checks were routine measures to scrutinize women's parenting, domestic, and sexual behaviors. Most state programs distinguished between deserving and undeserving mothers, closely perpetuating the old model associated with Mother's Pensions.

Congress amended ADC in 1939 and separated out the assistance given to widows, moving it to Social Security's Old Age Insurance (OAI) program. The movement of widows out of ADC resulted in its further stigmatization. Marital status became a defining characteristic of ADC recipients; it was increasingly viewed as a program for children born to "unworthy" women who had never married, or were separated or divorced. At the same time, many African American widows, and widows from other racial or ethnic minority groups, were unable to receive benefits under the newly restructured OAI program because their husbands did not qualify for Social Security benefits. Thus, these widows had no choice but to turn to ADC. These policy changes have contributed to the enduring hostility surrounding "welfare" as a program for unworthy women: unmarried mothers and minority groups, especially African Americans.

ADC continued to be amended, and a relative was allowed to be included with a dependent child as a recipient. The number of persons receiving AFDC continued to grow as the program was expanded, and by 1950, there were approximately 1.6 million recipients. Still, not all single mothers received these benefits. Only 25 percent of single mothers and children received ADC, while the remaining 75 percent did not.

The 1950s have been characterized as a decade of economic optimism. A post–World War II recession was averted, in part because of the generous monetary and educational provision of the GI Bill, and because of the enormous backlog of demand for major consumer goods unavailable during the war. There was a new faith in the vigor of the economic system during the 1950s after the war. Affluence was seen as within the grasp of all hardworking people, and an attack on AFDC began to take shape. People failed to acknowledge that other more popular programs were also forms of "welfare": the G.I. Bill and VA housing loans are just two of the programs that benefited many middle-class citizens. Despite providing for the security and welfare of its citizens, these programs, along with those under the Social Security Act that targeted the elderly or widows were able to avoid the stigma of being categorized or labeled "welfare."

During the 1950s, the composition of various social welfare programs began to change radically. With a focus on mothers and children, ADC began to overshadow other programs, such as those serving the elderly. Poor mothers with children quickly and dramatically increased from one-half to nearly three-quarters of the entire public assistance population between 1950 and 1960. These changes reflect normal population growth, changing family structures, labor market dislocations, the success of Social Security in reducing poverty among the elderly, and gender and racial discrimination. The costs of ADC alone increased over 90 percent, to over $1 billion (Axin & Levine, 1975, p. 235). As a reaction to this growth, the public focused on rising costs of the program and the moral fitness of welfare mothers. Punitive state policies were enacted to remove people from ADC. State residency requirements were enforced, names of welfare recipients were publicized, and entire caseloads were closed with recipients required to reapply with new application investigations (Axin and Levine, pp. 235–236). Politicians and the media blamed the expansion of ADC on the immoral behavior of poor women and the availability of assistance. They were frequently touted as being lazy, unmotivated, immoral, and fraudulent, spending money on lavish cars, jewelry, and clothing. Racist attitudes, prevalent in the United States, continued to plague ADC. African Americans were overrepresented among ADC recipients given their size in the population, as were never-married mothers, and the public was outraged that their tax dollars were being spent on undeserving groups. Sympathy was replaced with increasing criticism. Mothers who applied for aid were threatened with child removal. Caseworkers informed them that a negative assessment might force the welfare office to remove their children and place them in institutions or foster homes (Abramovitz, 1996a).

Feminist welfare state theorists suggest that the heightened hostility towards AFDC and its recipients was motivated by several forces (Abramovitz, 1996a,b; Gordon, 1994; Miller, 1992). First is the competing demand for women's unpaid labor in the home and cheap labor in the labor market. After World War II, the occupations that relied heavily on women's labor and low wages were expanding, while at the same time, the number of women employed outside the home was shrinking. As Betty Friedan notes in her book *The Feminine Mystique* (1963), during the 1950s women dreamed of husbands, children, station wagons, and houses in the suburbs. Most did not dream about full-time employment. Women's average age at first marriage dropped to 20 years, the lowest in over 100 years (Saluter, 1989) and the number of married women in the labor market plummeted. In the early 1950s, The Women's Bureau was reporting severe shortages of typists, stenographers, nurses, social workers, teachers, and medical aides (Kessler-Harris, 1982). Consequently, welfare benefits became all the more stigmatized and restricted in order to encourage more women into the labor pool. This was particularly seen in the south, where, for example, Louisiana refused ADC to "employable" mothers with young children, especially during the harvest season, as did Georgia when extra pickers were needed in the tobacco and cotton fields (Abramovitz, 1996b). Forcing women on welfare to work, or discouraging them from getting aid to which they were entitled, helped fill jobs at the bottom rungs of the employment sector—jobs that men did not want and that could go unfilled.

Second, feminist welfare theorists suggest that welfare critics also targeted poor women's marriage, sexuality, and childbearing patterns. The divorce rate skyrocketed to levels unprecedented after World War II. Hasty shot-gun marriages were short-lived, and the divorce rate climbed to 16 divorces per 1,000 married women aged 15 and older, double the rate before the war (Singh, Mathews, Clarke, Yannicos, & Smith, 1995). Nonmarital births also increased, almost tripling for white women, and increasing, although somewhat less, for African Americans. These changes in family structure have been blamed for the breakdown in "family values"—an emotionally charged term heavy with moral overtones about a woman's proper role. Women who had children outside of the confines of marriage were looked down upon with disdain. Only women who lived under the safe confines of a husband-as-breadwinner escaped widespread scrutiny. Working mothers were criticized for neglecting their children's needs, contributing to juvenile delinquency, truancy, and child abuse. Yet women receiving ADC were also harshly criticized and blamed for a wide variety of social ills. Because widows, considered among the worthy poor, were separated out into a less stigmatized program, ADC recipients were subject to tremendous moral criticism. Policies designed to enforce behavioral, sexual, and gender norms once again flourished and were incorporated with gusto. Recipients were subject to midnight raids and other intrusions into their lives so that authorities could try to catch men staying over at recipients' homes. Some states would penalize a woman for having a relationship with a man who was not the father of her children. Arkansas, for example, denied aid to mothers in a "non-stable, non-legal union." Alabama eliminated 25 percent of their welfare clients by cutting off women who were "going with a man." Michigan cut aid to families with "male boarders" (Abramovitz, 1996b).

The 1960s contained both some gains and setbacks for the ADC program. On one level, several events occurred during the 1960s that are credited with an increased concern, compassion and a "rediscovering" of poverty. First, a series of recessions and periods of high unemployment occurred in the late 1950s and early 1960s. The economy bounced back after each of these periods, but with less energy after each time. Second, the extent of poverty was exposed during the 1960s, due in part to books or essays such as Michael Harrington's *The Other America* (1963). In this popular book, Harrington vividly reported the poverty experienced by millions of America's forgotten people in geographically isolated pockets of our country. Third, the Social Security Administration had developed an official poverty index, and thus, the number of poor people and groups in the United States could be systematically counted and compared from year to year. Fourth, the civil rights movement brought increasing attention to the racism and poverty experienced by African Americans and other minority groups. And finally, the shift in the composition of public assistance rolls that began in the 1950s continued and showed no signs of abatement in the 1960s.

"Welfare" was increasingly becoming synonymous with impoverished never-married women and their illegitimate children.

When elected in 1960, President Kennedy stressed the issues of poverty, unemployment, and rehabilitation of the poor, and so began a major effort to reduce their numbers. He believed that people were poor because they lacked adequate human capital, such as education, job skills, and experience in the labor market, and that they needed social services to help them succeed. He therefore argued for greater resources, such as education and job training programs so that the poor could eventually pull themselves out of poverty. Moreover, as a believer in the Culture of Poverty perspective, he was concerned with the anti-work subcultural values and norms that he believed develop among the poor. President Kennedy sought to create programs that would focus on instilling positive attitudes among poor children to allow them to become more economically mobile and join the ranks of the middle class. Given the expanded family focus, the name of the program changed to Aid to *Families* with Dependent Children (AFDC). The 1962 amendments to the Social Security Act, referred to as the Social Service Amendments, increased federal funding for social services, "services in addition to support, rehabilitation instead of relief, and training for useful work instead of prolonged dependency . . . to maintain family life where it is adequate and to restore it where it is deficient," claimed President Kennedy (cited in Bandler, 1975, p. 380).

Kennedy's assassination did not stop his ideals from materializing. President Johnson shared Kennedy's vision of reducing poverty, fueled in part by the annual government reports that were now effective in counting the numbers of poor persons and identifying sociodemographic groups that were particularly vulnerable: children, the elderly, large families, single-mother families, rural families, and minority group members. Like Kennedy before him, he believed the government had a critical role in reducing the incidence of poverty and the suffering experienced by millions. In his State of the Union Address in 1964, Johnson announced that "this administration today, here and now, declares unconditional war on poverty in America. . . . " In this War on Poverty, President Johnson called for a wide array of legislation for children and adults designed to provide them with the tools, resources, and human capital to lift themselves from poverty. The underlying assumption of the War on Poverty in the 1960s was that poverty is largely the result of inadequate education, job training, and marketable skills. This approach, known as "human capital enhancement" posited that the numbers of poor could be significantly reduced with adequate training programs to increase the level of "human capital" that could be exchanged for wages in the job market. If we could train everyone for a job, and then find them one, poverty will be ameliorated or significantly reduced, human capitalists argued. This logic was beginning to be extended to single mothers—should they too be required to work?

During President Johnson's administration, programs were created that focused on job training, education, improving health and providing jobs, such as the Economic Opportunity Act, Head Start, Medicare, and Medicaid. Volunteers in Service to America (VISTA) was designed to help rehabilitate slums and other impoverished areas. Not all programs were created at the federal level; Johnson's War on Poverty also shared a concern that programs should be structured and carried out on the local level. Federal dollars were often targeted to these local efforts. These programs received extensive media attention, leading the public to believe that these efforts would eventually move women off welfare and out of the ranks of the impoverished.

During this national War on Poverty, the United States was also involved in another war—Vietnam. As the Vietnam War escalated, attention and dollars were diverted from needs at home. The war in Vietnam, demographic changes, the growth in the civil rights movement and its white backlash, and the expansion of welfare benefits contributed to what became known as a "welfare crisis." By the late 1960s and early 1970s, many Americans had grown tired and weary of the clamor for social change and had grown resentful of the concerns afforded the poor, ethnic minorities, and other disadvantaged groups. Because of changing eligibility rules, such as allowing women on AFDC to work, allowing some two-parent families to be eligible for aid, and extending benefits to children between the ages of 18 and 21 who were still in school, the number of families receiving welfare continued to rise. The number of welfare recipients soared from 3.5 million in 1961 to almost 5 million in 1967. Costs jumped to $2.2 billion (Abramovitz, 1996a). Welfare programs, AFDC in particular, came under swift attack again. Politicians and the media referred to these as bloated programs, claiming that they had become too large and needed to be reformed.

At the same time, many social changes of the 1960s and 1970s became increasingly accepted. In particular, with an increasing number of women with children in the paid labor force a large number of people questioned whether poor mothers really constitute a category of the "worthy poor" any longer. By 1975, 52 percent of married women with children between the ages of six and 17 and 37 percent of married women with children under age six were employed outside the home (U.S. Department of Labor, 1994). Employment among mothers was becoming increasingly commonplace among all income groups. Consequently, some politicians raised serious doubts about the appropriateness of paying single mothers to stay home and take care of their children. They suggested that welfare benefits had become too attractive to women; that benefits had increased faster than wages, and thus more women were opting to receive AFDC rather than to work in the paid labor market. "For the hard-core welfare recipient, the value of the full range of benefits substantially exceeds the amount the recipient could earn in an entry-level job. As a result, recipients are likely to choose welfare over work, thus increasing long-term dependence," proclaimed the self-appointed experts, as they discussed the motivation of recipients (Tanner, Moore, & Hartman, 1995).

President Nixon mirrored these views. He expressed concern about the rising welfare caseloads, increased costs, welfare fraud, federal involvement in services to individuals and communities, and elitist government bureaucrats. He initiated the "Family Assistance Plan," or F.A.P., which guaranteed that every unemployed family of four would receive at least $1,600 a year from the federal government. The working poor would be allowed to keep benefits until their earnings reached approximately $4,000. Only then would their benefits be discontinued. The F.A.P. contained several other critical features or clauses; including that women with children over the age of three would be required to work or would be placed in a job training program.

Nixon's F.A.P. immediately sparked controversy. Some regarded it as a fair and workable plan that would get control over the burgeoning AFDC program. Critics denounced the program, noting that the minimum benefit of $1,600 was still $2,000 below the federal government's own poverty line for a family of four. Attitudes were mixed towards whether single mothers of preschool age children should be required to work outside the home. Others raised concerns over whether the labor market could actually absorb all of these additional workers.

Quadagno (1994) suggests that the F.A.P. contained an internal contradiction about women's roles because it encouraged single mothers to work, while it encouraged married mothers to stay home. Further, the F.A.P. contained few programs to really help poor women improve their job skills, or to assist them in finding jobs. Nor did it provide much support for child care. Rather, the employment component was primarily geared to men. Commenting upon the training programs, the Director of the Office of Economic Opportunity (OEO) said:

> In general, we would support giving higher priority to the training and employment of men than women. Given the greater employment opportunities for men generally available, they are more likely to achieve self-sufficiency. Moreover, training and employment will often be much more expensive for women, if child care must be provided (cited in Quadagno, 1994, p. 126).

In 1970 the F.A.P. passed the House by a vote of 243 to 155. But because of the controversy surrounding the F.A.P., it remained bogged down in a Senate committee until it expired. It was never enacted. Instead of F.A.P., a multitude of relatively poorly funded work programs were created during the 1960s, 1970s and 1980s: The Work Incentive Program (WIN), which was later replaced by WIN II; the Job Training Partnership Act (JTPA); and the more recent 1988 Family Support Act, and Job Opportunities and Basic Skills Training Program (JOBS). Each program received tremendous popular press and blaring headlines such as "The Most Sweeping Revision of the Nation's Principal Welfare Program" (Szanton, 1991). Yet most programs helped only a small fraction of the millions of poor families. At the high point of the WIN program, less than 20 percent of AFDC recipients were actively involved in the program; while funding under the more recent JOBS program covered only 13 percent of recipients (Welfare to Work, 1993). As Berrick notes (1995), these figures rarely make headlines:

> So, instead, low-income women have continued to apply for and to use welfare and do not appear to be responding to public officials' generous offer of education and training. In turn, the public has grown increasingly frustrated with welfare women's intransigence, blaming them for not trying hard enough (p. 11).

One of the most dramatic responses to these frustrations with welfare and its recipients occurred during the administration of President Ronald Reagan during the 1980s when several hundred thousand families were eliminated from AFDC eligibility. President Reagan's position on government involvement was very clear. He denounced big government; he believed that a strong business climate would provide prosperity for Americans; he felt that Americans were paying too much of their income in taxes; and he distrusted social welfare programs. He was heavily influenced by his social conservative mentors such as Martin Anderson (1978), George Gilder (1981), Charles Murray (1984), and Lawrence Mead (1986), who authored books proposing significant retrenchment of social welfare programs. They suggested that welfare policies themselves exacerbate poverty and welfare use by creating a disincentive to work and thereby promoting laziness. Charles Murray, for example, in his book *Losing Ground*, argues that more generous welfare benefits make work and marriage unattractive to women. He believed that women were rewarded for choosing idleness, single-parenting, and out-of-wedlock childbearing when "midnight raids" and "man in the house" rules were deemed illegal, and when welfare benefits are increased to approximate the pay of low-wage work. Consequently, the primary way to end these problems is to eliminate, or significantly scale back welfare programs. Likewise, Mead (1986) refers to welfare recipients, and other poor people, in an unflattering light, "in general, low income and serious behavior problems go together" (Mead, 1986: 22). President Reagan agreed that social welfare programs encourage laziness and long-term dependency on the system. A popular anecdote was his story of a Chicago welfare queen with "80 names, 30 addresses, 12 Social Security Cards, and a tax-free income of over $150,000" (cited in Lipset, 1990, p. 136).

Spending for all social welfare programs actually decreased from 57.4 percent to 47.9 percent of total government spending between 1980 and 1986. Decreases occurred at the federal, state, and local levels (cited in The Ronald Reagan Home Page: Social Spending, 1997). AFDC was not the only program that was reduced; so were Food Stamps, Medicaid, school lunch and other nutritional programs, family planning programs, subsidized housing, legal aid, and drug abuse counseling. Welfare expenditures were cut dramatically, down almost 30 percent per person, on average (Ellwood, 1988, p. 41).

With the election of George H. W. Bush as President, the philosophy toward the welfare system remained relatively consistent to that of Ronald Reagan. He argued that the best way to overcome poverty is through individual hard work and initiative rather than through government-sponsored programs. He stressed volunteer charity, school vouchers, and enterprise zones, and complained that the federal government should back away from welfare and leave programs to states and local communities.

Individual states attempted to reduce the number of people on welfare, with only scant attention paid to whether or not these reforms would actually reduce the level of poverty. For example, in 1992 lawmakers in New Jersey and Wisconsin passed welfare reform packages commonly referred to as "Bridefare." These reforms were designed to reduce welfare use among women by encouraging them to marry. Arguably fueled by conservative ideologies that are concerned with the presumed breakdown of family values, "Bridefare" extends AFDC eligibility to married women, while restricting benefits among those who are single. Only women who agree to live within the confines of legal marriage could be eligible for full welfare benefits. The intent is to reverse what politicians have defined as a transfer of power and authority away from men in traditional family settings to the welfare state (Thomas, 1995).

New Jersey in 1993 and Arkansas in 1995 enacted another attempt at state-level welfare reform, referred to as "Family Caps." These two states deny higher cash payments to women who have additional children while on welfare. Proponents suggest that a cap would remove financial incentives for AFDC recipients to have more children outside of marriage. Opponents, in contrast, argue that it is a misperception that women who receive AFDC have additional children in order to get more money. They point out that additional births do not dramatically increase the size of the welfare check; checks increase $24 to $147 per child depending on the state.

By 1996, under President Clinton's administration, approximately 14 million persons or nearly 5 million families with children received AFDC (U.S. House of Representatives, Committee on Ways and Means, 1996, Table 8-27, p. 471). This was once again a critical time for social welfare programs in the United States, as they emerged as a prominent target for reform. Welfare programs, AFDC and its recipients in particular, continued to be targeted as a primary cause of a variety of social ills (Haskins, 2001b). Some historians suggest that policymakers "rediscover" welfare when they cannot explain or reverse troubling social, economic, or political trends:

> Poor women and welfare come under attack either because it interferes with the dynamics of the free enterprise system or because it undermines the traditional family structure. During such periods of "panic," welfare and women receiving it are bashed in order to divert attention from the true causes of the nation's ills. It is these concerns, rather than making life better for poor women and children, which have been the driving force behind welfare reform for the past 150 years (Abramovitz, 1996b, p. 15).

Policymakers have abandoned the idea of really helping the welfare recipients improve their economic situation significantly, and have instead focused on reducing welfare "dependency" (Bernstein, 1993). Ameliorating poverty through human capital enhancement, or any other method, is no longer the primary issue, as it was during the War on Poverty Era. Instead, the paramount concern has become how to reduce the number of people who receive welfare assistance—that is the bottom line. Given the dominant views that welfare costs are unacceptably high and that welfare breaches cherished American values, the goal of government reform efforts were simply to reduce the welfare caseloads, or "welfare dependency." Reforms were not particularly designed to reduce the number of people impoverished, or reduce the effect that poverty has on individuals and families.

Recent Attempts at Welfare Reform

Finally, the most critical and far-reaching of recent reform efforts is President Clinton's sweeping welfare reform legislation. Clinton had long advocated reforming the welfare system, especially during his terms as governor of Arkansas. He maintained that the federal government should institute a comprehensive series of reforms in order to prevent long-term dependence on the system. He stressed that the focus of welfare should be in getting people back to work, because employment "gives hope and structure and meaning to our lives" (Clinton, 1997a). Towards this end, he argued that an assortment of services, including health insurance, should be made available to support lower-wage workers. Without these services, welfare recipients have little inducement to forgo welfare for work, he argued. As he stated in a 1994 speech about welfare reform:

> There are things that keep people on welfare. One is the tax burden of low wage work; another is the cost of child care; another is the cost of medical care . . . today you have this bizarre situation where people on welfare, if they take a job in a place which doesn't offer health insurance, are asked to give up their children's health care, and go to work. . . . That doesn't make any sense (Clinton, 1997a).

The welfare reform legislation introduced by a Republican-led Congress, and eventually signed by Bill Clinton in 1996, was a long way from his original rhetoric of strengthening poor families. It was an election year, and early on it looked as though it could be a close race between President Clinton and a Republican challenger. Clinton's Republican opponent could make the most of the fact that Clinton had twice vetoed Republican-initiated welfare reforms that came to his desk. He failed to sign them because he believed that they were too punitive and failed to provide adequate support to families.

But this time when the revised legislation came to his desk, the election-year pressure was insurmountable. Conservative Republicans were developing their own version of welfare reform, and many sat on key subcommittees in Congress (Haskins, 2001a). The most radical policy considered by Republicans was to end all or most welfare support for illegitimate births. Although a draconian policy such as this would likely not have passed even the Republican-led Congress, other versions attracted considerable support among conservative Republicans, including a version that would have denied cash benefits to unwed teen mothers (Haskins, 2001a).

Clinton signed welfare reform legislation into law, promising to make the needed changes to the legislation later. He claimed that the legislation met his general criteria for moving people from welfare to work, offered benefits such as child care and health care (albeit, only temporarily), and would further enforce child support payments on the part of absent parents. While he felt that this third attempt would produce legislation more towards his liking, he also acknowledged, "some parts of the bill still go too far, and I am determined to see that those areas are corrected" (Clinton, 1997b). In particular, he voiced concern over the deep cuts in nutritional assistance for working families with children and the exclusion of benefits for legal immigrants.

The Personal Responsibility and Work Opportunity Reconciliation Act of 1996 (PRWORA) (P.L. 104-193) abolished the AFDC program, and replaced it with a new program called Temporary Assistance to Needy Families (TANF). Under the old AFDC, all families that met federal eligibility criteria were entitled to receive cash assistance. Under TANF, eligibility is primarily determined by state rules, and families are no longer automatically entitled to assistance even if they meet financial criteria. States now decide who can receive assistance and for how long, yet these decisions are complex because of federal mandates, fiscal constraints at the state level, conflicting goals of TANF, and the myriad of exemptions to work requirements or time limits that may be granted because of extenuating circumstances (e.g., family violence).

For example, the new law retains a federal requirement that those receiving assistance must assign their child support rights over to the state. As in the past, in order to receive assistance, recipients must cooperate with the state in establishing paternity (if this is in question), obtaining a support order, and enforcing that order. A mother was required to appear at all relevant court/administrative agency hearings, and turn over to the state any child support payments received directly from the father. However, with "good cause" (i.e., the child was conceived as the result of a forcible rape or incest; pursuing support could result in physical or emotional harm; adoption was under consideration or was pending), she could be exempt from these requirements. PRWORA established stricter child support enforcement policies (Department of Health and Human Services, July 2002; November, 2004). Respondents must assign rights to child support and cooperate with paternity establishment efforts. States have the option to either deny cash assistance or reduce assistance by at least 25 percent to those individuals who fail to cooperate. While this requirement helps many families, it also has potential to harm others, depending on the situation surrounding paternity (Roberts, 1997).

Some of the most critical features of the TANF program, and the most controversial, are those related to work requirements and time limits. Federal law mandates that lifetime welfare payments can total no more than five years. Able-bodied recipients must work after two years, with few exceptions granted. In most cases, there is a two-year limit for TANF out of any 60 consecutive months.

Two-parent welfare families were targeted as the first to be cut off of welfare assistance. By October 1, 1997, a little over one year after welfare reform became law, 75 percent of two-parent welfare families were mandated by the federal government to either have jobs or be in job training programs. In the first real test of welfare reform, approximately half the states fell short of these employment goals—goals that, in retrospect, many people are suggesting were unrealistic (Deparle, 1997). This first failure to meet employment goals is being held up for its symbolism. Work requirements among two-parent families, on first glance at least, should be relatively easy to fulfill. It requires a total of 35 hours per week between two adults, and while one is working, the other should seemingly be able to provide childcare. If the difficulties of employing two-parent households has been so seriously underestimated, then what does that suggest about the other, more challenging cases involving single parents? Despite the severity of federal guidelines, states are free to impose stricter time limits and work requirements, which many have elected to do.

The Balanced Budget Act (BBA) of 1997 made a number of changes to the TANF program, by partially restoring funding for several of the most extreme cuts enacted in the 1996 welfare law (Haskins, 2001b). As a result, changes include such provisions as (a) an increase of $3 billion over a two-year period was enacted to help states pay for a variety of employment-related activities aimed toward persons with significant work barriers; (b) victims of family violence may be exempt from TANF work and time-limit provisions, and further study of domestic violence will be undertaken by the Government Accounting Office; (c) it restores SSI benefits to many disabled elderly legal immigrants; (d) several of the restrictions on food stamp eligibility will be waived for adults aged 18–50 who are not caring for minor children; and (e) a $20 billion child health block grant is designated to provide health insurance over the next five years to many of the 10 million uninsured children in the United States (Center for Law and Social Policy, 1997).

Because it was recognized that many TANF-leavers would likely lose their health insurance benefits when they left welfare for work, the welfare reform bill allows for 12 months of transitional Medicaid assistance for families who would otherwise lose eligibility because of their earnings (U.S. Department of Health and Human Services, 2004). After this one-year period, families can apply for continued Medicaid benefits, although most would not qualify because their incomes would push them above the stringent eligibility requirements.

It was also recognized that requiring mothers to work full- or part-time meant that someone needed to care for their children. Child care assistance is an essential part of any strategy to help families avoid or leave welfare (Fremstad, 2004). A study of TANF recipients in Michigan found that recipients who had subsidized childcare increased their months employed by 50 percent, and increased their earnings by 100 percent (Danziger, Ananat, & Browning, 2004). The final bill included an additional $4.5 billion in child care to states to be used over the next six years to offset the costs for families who leave welfare for work.

Despite these provisions, many analysts fear that welfare reform will erode the social safety net for vulnerable individuals and families. They wonder what will happen to the many poor people who won't be able to find work for one reason or another when they reach the government's time limit. They question whether jobs are available for all the people now on assistance, without a massive job creation effort. They lament that even the lucky people who do find employment will most likely be paid wages that fail to bring their incomes above the poverty line, and will probably not receive health insurance from their employers. They are concerned that job training will be superficial in nature, and will not really be effective in increasing recipients' employment prospects. They want to know why welfare recipients are no longer allowed to go to college to further their education. They ask who will care for the children of parents when child care reimbursements are inadequate to pay for quality child care? And they wonder how the health care needs of the influx of low income workers and their children will be met, after their transitional Medicaid expires.

These are critical matters because, despite a multitude of welfare reforms over this century, they have never been adequately addressed. Past reforms have been primarily symbolic efforts to appease the public over what to do with the large and growing number of women and children who are poor and need assistance. Policy makers wring their hands in anguish as their poorly funded efforts do little to reduce the large numbers of women needing aid. Democrats and Republicans alike find welfare to be the scourge of government policy—it's that nasty little problem that won't go away.

Welfare recipients, as beneficiaries of this much-maligned program, become the focus of intense hostility. Most people think that government spending on welfare should decrease rather than increase (Dowd, 1994), less than a third believe that welfare recipients truly need the assistance, and over two-thirds believe that recipients are cheating the system (USA Today, 1996). In the early 1990s, California Governor Pete Wilson proposed a 25 percent cut in AFDC benefits for recipients within the state. He trivialized the effect of such a drastic cut, suggesting that its impact might mean that welfare recipients "would have less for a six-pack of beer" (Bristro-Brown, 1991). Implicit in his comments are the assumptions that welfare benefits are too high, that women waste welfare benefits and are fraudulent.

The 1996 TANF law expired on September 30, 2002, and is operating under a temporary extension. President George W. Bush proposes to reauthorize welfare reform, and his appointees are stern believers in the merits of PRWORA. U.S. Department of Health and Human Services Secretary Mike Leavitt announced with pride that TANF rolls continued to decline in 2004, "Throughout the first four years of the Bush Administration we have seen caseloads decline continuously. Now it is important to work with Congress to reauthorize welfare reform so more families can be strengthened by work instead of weakened by welfare dependency" (U.S. Department of Health and Human Services, February 9, 2005, p. 1). Likewise, Dr. Wade F. Horn, HHS assistant secretary for children and families reports, "More Americans are leaving welfare and entering the economic mainstream. The Bush Administration is dedicated to welfare reform because it replaces dependency with self-sufficiency" (U.S. Department of Health and Human Services, February 9, 2005, p. 1).

Recent sentiments are grounded in the historical and persistent questions and dilemmas: Why are people poor; why are they on welfare; and under what conditions are people worthy of assistance from the government? We pose these questions in the generic, but it is crucial to remember that the vast majority of those affected are women. Welfare programs reflect our ambivalent attitudes towards "manless women" (Miller, 1992)—women who have children and live outside the traditional family structure.

Explanations of Poverty and Welfare Use

Several frameworks have been offered as a way to catalog explanations about poverty, welfare use, women's roles, and beliefs about government responsibility. If we think of these perspectives as residing upon a continuum, we find *Individualism* and *Social Structuralism* at each end. The Individual perspective focuses on the achievement of the individual, arguing that we are ultimately responsible for our own economic position, while social structuralism would stress that the inequality found in social institutions such as the labor market, families, and government affect our economic positions. Other perspectives, such as the *Culture of Poverty* or *Fatalism* combine features of these two perspectives to explain the ways in which our social structure shapes individual action.

These perspectives are on first glance gender-neutral. They refer to attributes of the individual or of the social structure that supposedly transcend gender. However, I suggest that they are not gender-neutral, but rather represent the male experience. Claims of "gender neutrality" marginalize or ignore women's contributions or experiences. For example, what gets defined as "achievement," so important to those espousing Individualism, is gendered. The result of women's hard work and the fruits of her labor may look considerably different from her male counterpart's. During much of our history, and for many women today, having a successful marriage, and raising and nurturing children are the pinnacles of "achievement." Women have not been socialized to define success through an occupation or income, as is the case for men. Consequently, women who fail to seek employment, who are not driven by occupational roles, or who prefer to stay home to care for their dependent children should not be interpreted as failing to meet some generic criteria for "achievement." It would be unfair to render them as lazy or unmotivated. Therefore, it is critical here that we provide a fresh perspective by acknowledging the ways in which gender interacts with our explanations of social inequality, poverty, and welfare use.

Individualism

Soon after welfare reform passed, a newspaper ran an article describing the consequences of welfare reform in the lives of recipients (Chandler, January 8, 1997). One woman in particular was profiled: Kathy Sanding received AFDC for two years, after bearing a child conceived during a rape. When interviewed, the 26-year-old mother was only one semester away from receiving an associate of arts (AA) degree from a community college, and had hoped to transfer to a nearby university for a four-year degree and study to become a teacher. Despite her 3.4 grade point average and making the Dean's List, the state of Florida's welfare department informed her that, within two months, federal and state welfare guidelines under TANF would require her to be either employed, actively searching for a job, or to be involved in vocational training. If she did not comply, she would risk losing her cash assistance, food stamps, and Medicaid coverage. She was told that going to a community college, with the goal of transferring to a four-year university, is not classified as either "work" or "learning a trade" according to the work-oriented policies enacted by the Florida legislature. Although this young woman is determined to get her AA degree, she now doubts that she can pursue a bachelor's degree from a university. Her dreams of becoming a teacher have been dashed by Florida's welfare reform policy. She knows that, like many other former welfare recipients, she will now likely end up working in a low-paying job in the expanding Florida service sector, most likely the fast-food industry, earning near minimum wage. In her own words, she says,

> I think they should let people who are going to school continue until they've finished. I feel like I've busted my butt trying to have integrity; to do what the welfare system is intends for me to do. Now the government has taken away my dreams and aspirations for having a successful life and changed them into having a mediocre or just poverty-level life (Chandler, January 8, 1997).

The story in the local newspaper was designed to provide an inside look at the way that welfare reform has eclipsed the dreams of at least one hard working, achievement-oriented woman. Yet, for some people the article did not evoke sympathy. The tension and hostility felt towards welfare recipients runs deep, as was evidenced by a letter to the newspaper's editor soon after the original article was printed (The Gainesville Sun, January 22, 1997):

> First, I commend reporter Chandler on her superb ability to write an article that is able to put the welfare situation in such a sympathetic light for the recipients. I, however, tend to sympathize with the taxpaying public that has been burdened by this system for too many years now. . . . I do not feel it my responsibility to put her through school when I cannot afford to put members of my own family through school.
>
> . . . I worked a full-time and a part-time job to put myself through night school. I am also one of the millions of people in this country who have "a mediocre or just poverty-level life," whose hard-earned tax dollars Miss Sanding seems to feel are there to make her endeavor easy.
>
> I do not blame Miss Sanding for her attitude. The government has created and nurtured this attitude in the American people for too long, and the blame lies primarily there. I do, however believe that articles of the nature of this one . . . are irresponsible and insulting to the millions of people in this country who have had the fortitude and perseverance to take the hard road to accomplish their dreams of attaining higher education.
>
> . . . The time has come for those people that have had a free ride for so many years to get down in the trenches with the rest of us and take responsibility for their own lives and livelihoods.

This letter to the editor of the newspaper expresses the sentiment of Individualism. It suggests that individuals are largely responsible for their own economic position in society; that opportunities are available to all who are willing to work hard, and to all who are sufficiently motivated. Because virtually everyone has an equal opportunity to acquire the skills, traits, and training needed for upward mobility, those that fail to make it have largely themselves to blame. The Individualistic perspective is reflected in our country's response to the poor throughout most of our history. Tales of Horatio Alger types abound—the "rags to riches stories"—the moral being that everyone can pull themselves up by their bootstraps with hard work, sweat, and motivation. Welfare recipients are a particularly blatant example of those who have failed to make it and therefore reside at the bottom of the economic hierarchy. They are at worst lazy and unmotivated, and at best simply uneducated and untrained. Either way, they are held largely responsible for their own economic plight.

Notice that the focus is on the individual—the argument is that we need to change the individual, to increase her or his motivation and to increase her or his level of human capital in order to be competitive for jobs. Little attention is given to features of our social structure such as the growing number of service-sector jobs which generally pay sub–poverty-level minimum wage. Yet, what proponents of this perspective fail to ask themselves is, if the bulk of new jobs are being created in the low paying service sector, can we really train people out of poverty? Won't someone else then occupy these roles? Poverty may be transferred to someone else, but it will not be eliminated.

Studies conducted over the past several decades show the persistent popularity of the Individual perspective in this country. Although there are important gender, race, and income variations, generally individualism is a highly popular explanation of inequality among women and men, African Americans and whites, and the affluent and poor (Feagin, 1975; Hancock, 2004; Hunt, 1996; Seccombe, James, Battle Walters, 1998; Smith & Stone, 1989; Zimmerman, 2001). One large study conducted in 1969 by sociologist Joe Feagin, with 1,017 randomly selected adults from all regions of the United States, illustrated how deeply rooted this perspective is (1975). Over half of the sample evaluated lack of thrift, laziness and lack of effort, and lack of ability and talent as very important reasons for poverty. Nearly 90 percent said that these were at least somewhat important explanations of poverty. Only 18 percent suggested that poverty was due to being taken advantage of by rich people (Feagin, 1975, p. 97). Those persons most likely to espouse Individualistic explanations were white Protestants and Catholics, residents of the South and North Central regions of the United States, persons over age 50, middle-income groups, and those with moderate levels of education (p. 98).

Additionally, Feagin found little tolerance for welfare recipients, with most respondents indicating a high degree of suspicion and distrust of them. Eighty-four percent of respondents agreed with the statement that "there are too many people receiving welfare who should be working," 71 percent agreed that "many people getting welfare are not honest about their need" and 61 percent felt that "many women getting welfare money are having illegitimate babies to increase the money they get" (p. 103).

A poll by the Joint Center for Political and Economic Studies noted that in response to a national survey evaluating the welfare system and its biggest problems, there was little difference among blacks, whites, or Hispanics. Seventy-two percent of Blacks reported that fraud and abuse by welfare recipients is a problem, as did 70 percent of Whites, and 79 percent of Hispanics. Likewise, 70 percent of blacks felt that welfare encouraged poor women to have babies out of wedlock by giving cash assistance for children, as did 74 percent of whites and 70 percent of Hispanics (Hancock, 2004).

Opinions about welfare recipients reflect the deeply held beliefs that the poor are largely responsible for their own economic circumstances because of laziness, lack of thrift, or lack of talent. Most Americans are relatively unconcerned about poverty and do not see the increasing inequality as a problem for the country. In fact, one out of five Americans thought that there were too *few* rich people (Zimmerman, 2001).

Welfare recipients are perhaps the most stigmatized subset of the poor. We assume that they should be able to improve their economic circumstances on a whim. Yet we are ignoring a critical social fact: the vast majority of welfare recipients are unmarried women with dependent children. Given their daily parental responsibilities, tasks, and time constraints, they do not have the same opportunities to pull themselves up by their bootstraps as do other adults who are without children, e.g., poor men. To ignore the emotional and time commitment involved in taking care of dependent children, and to fail to recognize the ways in which caretaking can inhibit women's ability for social mobility, ignores the reality of many women's existence. Is it correct to assume that unmarried women who stay home to take care of their dependent children are lazy, lacking in thrift, or have little or no talent?

Social Structuralism

A social structural perspective, in contrast, assumes that poverty is a result of economic or social imbalances within our social structure that serve to restrict opportunities for some people. Social structure is defined as the social institutions, organizations, groups, statuses and roles, values, and norms that exist in our culture. Three distinct themes exist under this broad perspective: (a) a concern with capitalism; (b) a focus on a changing economy; and (c) a concern that the welfare system itself exacerbates poverty. Social conservatives seeking to dismantle the welfare system have often invoked this last theme.

Concerning the first theme, some in our society contend that poverty is an inherent feature of capitalism (Marx & Engels, 1968). The subsequent control over other social structures, such as education and the polity is designed to serve the interests and maintain the dominance of the wealthy class. Karl Marx's early writings draw attention to the exploitative relationships found within capitalistic societies. They feature a greater division of labor, where workers do not work for themselves but sell their labor for wages to capitalists. Marx argued that workers are not paid wages that reflect their true worth (e.g., their output). Instead, capitalists prefer to keep wages low, pocketing the remainder as profit. Producing more goods, with fewer workers, especially when they are not paid wages equivalent to their output, ensures higher profits. Capitalism thrives on a reserve labor force; people who are available to work in times of booming economic expansion or union busting. This reserve labor force is expendable, and many are discarded when the boom subsides. Consequently, their poverty is an inevitable feature of capitalism.

Marx paid little attention to the ways in which capitalism affects women directly. More recent socialist feminists have pointed out that doing away with capitalism may not necessarily improve the lives of women appreciably. Until women are liberated from their privatized domestic roles, they are likely always to be exploited. They suggest that a more collectivist approach to carrying out housework and childcare, alongside the development of a more socialist economy, is needed to really eliminate poverty and improve women's lives.

The second theme points to the features of a changing economy, such as the growth in low-paying service-sector jobs, the erosion of the minimum wage, or the relocation of jobs from the inner city (Wilson, 1987; 1996). For example, dual labor market theory posits that the economy can be divided into at least two sectors, primary and secondary. Workers' location in one or the other sector systematically affects their earnings, bargaining power, and likelihood of fringe benefits such as health insurance—even when workers have similar levels of education, training, tenure on the job, other skills, or human capital. Furthermore, there is little mobility, and workers tend to become trapped in one sector or the other. The characteristics of the job vary dramatically in these two sectors. Jobs in the primary sector tend to offer positions possessing higher wages, better working conditions, more opportunities for advancement, greater employment stability, and generous fringe benefits. The secondary sector, in comparison, offers lower wages, fewer possibilities for promotion, higher turnover rates or seasonal employment, and fewer critical fringe benefits.

Women tend to be concentrated in relatively few occupations, and most of these fall into the secondary sector. The majority of women work in clerical, sales, and service jobs. Additionally, gender inequality exists within these sectors. Women do not receive the same returns that men do when they are employed in jobs with similar occupational characteristics, occupational prestige, or within identical job classifications (U. S. Department of Labor, May, 2005). For example, the average weekly pay of a registered nurse, an occupation comprised of primarily women, is $895 for women, and $1,031 for men (U. S. Department of Labor, May, 2005).

The third structural theme suggests that social programs and welfare policies themselves contribute to poverty and exacerbate welfare use by trapping people into poverty and welfare dependency instead of helping them escape. This theory is popular with social conservatives and welfare critics (Anderson, 1978; Murray, 1984; 1988) and is used as an argument favoring a dismantling of welfare programs. They claim, as did Tocqueville over a hundred years ago, that people are inherently lazy, and will lose motivation and incentive if they know that governmental programs are there to take care of them (2004). People will snub work at low-paying jobs, and will instead rely upon the free money of welfare if given the opportunity. These proponents argue that eliminating or drastically reducing welfare is a critical first step to curbing poverty. However, these discussions are problematic because they assume that welfare is a gender-neutral program. It is not. Recipients are predominantly women, and the needs and concerns embedded in women's real life experiences as caretakers of dependent children are not contextualized within their recommendations to reduce or eliminate welfare.

Culture of Poverty

The culture of poverty perspective blends features of the above two perspectives. It suggests that a subcultural set of values, traits, and expectations has developed as a direct result of the structural constraints associated with living in isolated pockets of poverty. People in poverty are said to live in a subculture with a weak family structure and present-time orientation, and they display a helplessness and resignation toward work (Burton, 1992). The subculture is at odds with the dominant middle-class culture because it downplays the importance of hard work, self-discipline, and deferring gratification. Although there is a wide range of opinion regarding the specific antecedents, features, and consequences of the subculture (Gilder, 1981; Lewis, 1966; Mead, 1992; Moynihan, 1965; Valentine, 1968; Wilson, 1987; 1993), concern is voiced about the transmission of these values from parents to children. The question of whether poverty and welfare use are intergenerational—

that is, are passed on from parents to their children—is an enduring theme in the poverty literature.

Oscar Lewis first introduced this perspective as he studied poor barrios in Latin American communities. The idea of a poverty subcultural phenomenon caught the media by storm. He wrote:

> The culture of poverty is both an adaptation and a reaction of the poor to their marginal position in a class-stratified, highly individuated, capitalistic society. It represents an effort to cope with feelings of hopelessness and despair which develop from the realization of the improbability of achieving success in terms of the values and goals of the larger society. Indeed, many of the traits of the culture of poverty can be viewed as attempts at local solutions for problems not met by existing institutions and agencies because the people are not eligible for them, cannot afford them, or are ignorant or suspicious of them. The culture of poverty, however, is not only an adaptation to a set of objective conditions about the larger society. Once it becomes into existence it tends to perpetuate itself from generation to generation because of its effect on the children. By the time slum children are age six or seven they have usually absorbed the basic values and attitudes of their subculture and are not psychologically geared to take full advantage of changing conditions or increased opportunities which may occur in their lifetime (Lewis, 1966, pp. xliii–xlv).

Unfortunately Lewis' work has sometimes been misinterpreted as a victim-blaming approach in which deviant values are seen as the causes of poverty itself. This is not a correct interpretation of his work. Harvey and Reed (1996) suggest that Lewis' ideas are firmly grounded in a Marxist critique of capitalism. A subculture was constructed to ease the pain associated with being a part of the reserve and discarded labor force that is an inherent byproduct of capitalism. They suggest that the culture of poverty is "a positive social construction—the result of a process by which the poor pragmatically winnow what works from what does not, and pass it on to their children" (1996, p. 482).

More recently, Wilson attributed poverty among the African American "underclass" in inner cities (1987; 1996) to their social, economic, and geographic isolation. He argued that class, not race, is the primary factor in explaining their poverty. Wilson suggests that the loss of well-paying manufacturing jobs from urban areas has had disastrous effects upon those persons living in the area. Male unemployment and subsequent poverty increased dramatically, and consequently reduced the pool of men eligible for marriage and increased the number of children born out of wedlock and raised in single-parent families. Moreover, the middle class migrated out of urban areas, leading to development of ghettos. Their migration out to the suburbs means that those persons who remain in the urban core have few role models of mainstream success.

Wilson's work is notable on several fronts. First, he contends that, although class is more important than race as a cause of intergenerational inequality, his model applies primarily to minorities because few poor whites reside in highly poor neighborhoods. Second, his model focuses on the interaction of structure and culture. He blames labor markets and demographic changes for isolating the inner city minority poor, and it is these structural constraints that thereby affect the organization of family and community life. His concept of social isolation does not imply a self-perpetuating or permanent phenomenon. When job opportunities and appropriate social services for inner city residents are provided, the subcultural adaptation will eventually disappear.

To make the culture of poverty perspective more relevant to understanding the lives of poor women, it should examine additional aspects of the social structure that inhibit mobility, specifically those features that affect women's lives. For example, it should critique the features of marriage and family life that affect women's ability to transcend economic marginality and may therefore encourage adaptation. These may include such things as fathers' lack of involvement in direct child care, the limited availability of daycare facilities, or insufficient enforcement of child support policies by the government. In the absence of these features, women may develop their own adaptations, such as relying on extended families to care for their children or to pool their financial resources.

Fatalism

Finally, Fatalism attributes the causes of wealth and poverty to quirks of birth, chance, luck, human nature, illness, or other forces over which people have no control. Poverty is not viewed as anyone's fault, *per se*, but rather is a potential consequence of unplanned, random, or natural human events. It assumes that poverty is caused by forces outside our control, thereby denying that the behaviors of the rest of the population contribute to poverty and social inequality. Herrnstein and Murray, for example suggest that low intelligence is a primary cause of poverty and welfare dependency (1994). Arguing that intelligence is largely genetic, they argue that poor people with low IQs give birth to another cohort with low IQs and thus the children remain in poverty.

Feagin, in his 1969 survey found that people shied away from attributing poverty to simply bad luck (1975). In his survey of 1,017 adults, only eight percent of respondents emphasized that "bad luck" was a very important reason for poverty. More recently, Smith and Stone, in their study of 200 randomly selected respondents in southeast Texas, also found that fatalistic perspectives were unpopular compared to individualistic explanations. For example, only 10 percent of respondents agreed that bad luck or being born inferior is a very important explanation. Moreover, only 14 percent attributed low intelligence as a very important explanation for poverty.

It is critical to note that the above studies do not distinguish the gender of the impoverished person. These studies are not unusual; we commonly talk about poverty, and discuss the poor as though they are nameless, faceless, genderless, and generic beings. They are not. The poor, especially those who receive welfare, are primarily women and children. But when we fail to identify them as such, when we do not specifically refer to the poor as "women," or as "she," most often a male mental image emerges. I suggest that our degree of tolerance for attributing poverty to "bad luck" or "fate" is indeed gendered; that is, it varies among men and women. Men are expected to be independent; they are assumed to be able to actively construct their own lives. In our society, men are not allowed to simply have bad luck and fall into poverty and need assistance. Instead, men must have extenuating and serious circumstances in order for us to excuse their poverty. Women, in contrast, have traditionally been socialized to be more dependent upon others for their economic and social position. Therefore, they are more vulnerable to fluctuations in these statuses through no fault of their own. AFDC was originally created to protect women who are single mothers from these vulnerabilities that are beyond their control, such as violence, abuse, or desertion. Today, however, we are in a state of flux. We are less understanding and less confident of the type of protection women need, and therefore we are less enthusiastic about providing it.

These four perspectives offer competing explanations for poverty, welfare use, and social inequality more generally. They are not new; they reflect historical and persisting dilemmas about human nature, the importance of hard work and the vice of idleness, and they reflect our notions of appropriate roles for men and women. AFDC and now TANF were created from these dilemmas. Yet, these perspectives fail to acknowledge the ways that gender also influences our explanations and understandings of poverty. Little attention has been given to the ways in which individual achievement, social structure, culture, or fate may operate or be perceived differently for women and men. The goal here has been to expand these explanations so that they are more inclusive of women's lived experience. The following in-depth interviews show us the usefulness of these perspectives, and allow us to revise and reanalyze them to better fit the real-world experiences of families on welfare and those who have recently left the system for work.

CRITICAL THINKING QUESTIONS

1. In the past we assumed it was better for single mothers to stay home and take care of their children than it was for them to work. Why did we think this? Do we still think this way? If not, what changed, and why?

2. Explain how poor women's sexuality, lifestyle, or mothering has been scrutinized throughout history. Is this the case for all women, or just poor women? How is the scrutiny the same across class, or how does it differ?

3. Why did former President Clinton, a Democrat, pass such a radical program of welfare reform?

4. What do we mean when we say that welfare is no longer an "entitlement" program?

5. What are the four explanations for poverty and welfare use? At this point in your reading, which makes the most sense to you, and why?

6. The author claims that "Individualism" is a popular explanation in the United States for poverty and welfare use. Can you provide any personal examples of this from your own experiences?

7. Why is "Individualism" such a popular explanation in the United States? How does the popularity of this perspective compare with views in Europe? Defend your answer.

3 Stigma and Discrimination

Conjure up in your mind an image of a "welfare mother." What does she look like? How does she sound? Why is she on welfare? How does she feel about being on the system?

For many people, a woman like Dawn would come to mind. She embodies many of the stereotypical traits of a woman on welfare, yet, as shown in Chapter 1, Dawn is atypical in many ways of women who receive welfare. Nonetheless, she fits the largely negative images that we have of "welfare mothers"—images created by the mass media.

Dawn is a large, gregarious woman. She is African American, 31 years old, and has never been married. Her grandmother raised her, although her mother is alive and they have always been close. "Momma didn't live there, but we would always see her. She was always close by," said Dawn. "That's a trend in my family." Dawn's grandmother received welfare for her care. "Granny," as she affectionately called her grandmother, and to whom she referred several times throughout the interview, recently passed away.

Dawn has four children, fathered by four different men. Her first child was born to her when she was only 13. "Me and my oldest daughter—we were both children growing up," she told me. Dawn had her second child when she was 18 years old, her third one at age 20, and her fourth child at age 21. Her mother volunteered to raise her second child for her, a son, and her mother therefore receives welfare for him. Dawn sees her mother and her son regularly. She does not find the living arrangement odd; after all, it mirrors her own childhood. She's appreciative that her mother offered this help.

> I guess my life was going kind of fast, having children. By the time I was 21 I had four kids. And my mom, one day she came to me because by the time my son was one year old I had another baby and was pregnant. So my mom, she felt sorry for me. And so she asked me if she could take one of the kids. At first it was going to be a temporary thing. But she asked me if I wanted her to help out, to at least take one kid. She offered to take him

or the other. And he was the one I chose. And that helped me out a lot. So, she raised him since he was about a year, or something like that. But I see him all the time freely. Me and my mom, you know, we're close family. He doesn't live in the household, but he knows. I wonder if I'll raise my grand-child? I don't want to. But I don't know what will happen.

The children's fathers, in contrast, provide very little help. Only one pays child support to the county welfare office, and he pays only sporadically. When he does pay, Dawn is given an extra $50 in her welfare benefits for that month. "But, he hasn't paid lately," she tells me. "I guess he's in jail or something. But when we don't get those checks, it's a long time until my kids get shoes." Without this added assistance, Dawn receives a $365 cash grant and $345 a month in food stamps for herself and her three children who live with her (in 1995). The rent on her modest, but neatly kept single-family home is subsidized and she therefore pays only $21 a month, plus approxi-mately $150 a month for utilities. Like virtually all AFDC recipients, she and her children also receive Medicaid. By 2005, Dawn's cash grant would be virtually the same, although her food stamps would have increased to $499 for her family of four (U.S. Department of Agriculture, December, 2004).

Unlike Dawn's early relationships with men, she told me that she really no longer has an interest in men or romantic relationships. She feels that a father figure for her children, at this point, is relatively unimportant. She didn't have a father, and as she sees it, that did not harm her. Dawn was not the first woman who, after bear-ing several children, flatly told me that she was not interested in any further relation-ships. Several women expressed discomfort around men. Some alluded to be being sexually abused. Dawn, however, was more vague.

> I didn't grow up around anyone but my grandmother. I had an uncle who lived in the house for awhile, my grandmother's house, and I just didn't like that man. When he wasn't there, it was good and I loved it. But when he was there, I just didn't like him. I didn't like him at all. So I guess that's a pattern that I had. When there was a man in the house, I don't know. That's why I don't have a husband. I can't. For some reason I have real big problems in that department. So when they aren't there, I just feel kind of content. More comfortable. So I guess I don't want a husband. I wouldn't want him here all the time. Although sometimes I want a boyfriend to help out financially. And then, again, sometimes I say it's not worth it, just for-get it and go back to the way it was.

Dawn has been on and off welfare for most of her life. She also has worked at a number of jobs as well, as a cashier, a nurse's aide, and she has washed cars. She works for a few months at a time, then gets "bored" and switches jobs or quits. None of the jobs have been particularly high-paying. Several times when she was employed, she withheld her employment and income information from her case-worker and continued to receive a welfare check in addition to her earnings. She did this, only temporarily, she told me, so that she would be able to pay off her bills at the first of the month. Once when she did it, she was caught, found guilty of committing welfare fraud, and given probation for 18 months. She now has a criminal record.

On first glance, Dawn is an easy target to use in the quest for welfare reform. She corroborates the negative stereotypes we have of women on welfare: she appears to be lazy, unmotivated, and dependent on the system. We assume that she lives in a culture of poverty where her "deviant" family values and her criminal record for welfare fraud are normative and perhaps even encouraged. No more information about her life is needed for judgment. Onlookers do not probe deeper. Instead, many people suggest that *she* is the precise reason why we need to reform welfare: we need to prevent Dawn, and the suspected millions of women like her, from abusing the welfare system.

Dawn is, however, an atypical welfare recipient in most respects. Compared with an average welfare mother, Dawn has more children, and she has been on welfare for a longer time. She is an anomaly. Yet, somehow, she fits the image that Americans have of women who receive welfare—an image that is inaccurate. Perhaps the principal way in which Dawn is typical of others who received welfare is that her life is considerably more complex than it appears at first blush.

Stereotypes of women who receive welfare are fed to us regularly by multiple forms of media. It is not only the middle and upper classes who are bombarded with these negative images of welfare mothers. Poor women are bombarded as well. Are women on welfare, then, also aware of these stereotypes? If so, how do they justify being on the system, with welfare mothers so widely denigrated? How do they manage or cope with this stigma? The poor make judgments, not only from the same media and cultural influences as do the more affluent, but also from their very own personal experiences with limited employment opportunities, lack of available child care, and other constraints. This chapter addresses these questions. It examines whether recipients attribute welfare use to forces beyond their control, or whether they, instead, share the same stigmatizing view found within the general population— that welfare recipients are largely responsible for their own economic plight.

Awareness of Societal Attitudes Toward Welfare Recipients

First, let us examine the issue of recipients' firsthand experience with stigma and discrimination. We know that distrust and hostility towards welfare recipients is widespread within the more affluent population. Do women who receive welfare know the extent of the negative sentiment felt towards welfare and welfare recipients? Do they have firsthand experience with stigma and discrimination?

Other studies indicate that many welfare recipients do indeed feel stigmatized for receiving welfare (Deparle, 2004; Hays, 2003). Goodban (1985), for example, using a sample of 100 African American women on welfare, reported that nearly two-thirds claimed they experienced some sense of shame at various times for being on welfare. In his study of welfare recipients in Wisconsin, Rank (1994) found that the lack of privacy and the stigma associated with welfare, at least in part, fueled recipients' desire to exit from welfare. Another study focusing solely on African American mothers found that women felt stigmatized as nonworkers, single parents, and inner city dwellers (Jarrett, 1996). Her analysis was based on food stamp use, which is a public acknowledgment of welfare receipt, and suggests that stigma was not experienced in the same way, in all contexts, by all recipients. Likewise, in my study of 552 families who left welfare in Oregon, 41 percent of recipients who left welfare 18 months prior revealed that they felt stigmatized for using Medicaid services, another public acknowledgement of welfare (Seccombe, Hartley, Newsom, Hoffman, & Pope, 2005).

Interviews revealed that welfare recipients tend to be well aware of their stigmatized status. When asked if they ever hear negative comments about people on welfare, answers were overwhelmingly "yes," and most claimed that criticism has been directed at them personally. Dawn told me of her experiences:

> Yeah, I have had people look down at me. And it makes me feel bad. I don't want to—oh, I don't know. I'd probably be the same way, I guess. I don't know. I think they should understand though, that if I didn't need them, I would not be embarrassing myself like that. You know what I'm saying? Maybe they don't understand because they've never had to have them. I wish I could feel that way. But, you know. I kind of know how they feel, but then again, if I didn't have this, me and my children wouldn't be able to eat. Then how would you look at it?

Most welfare recipients that were interviewed, African American and white, and both young and old, reported that they hear considerable personal blame and criticism. For example, when asked what kinds of things they had heard said about welfare recipients, Rhonda, a 28-year-old white woman who has one son, told me:

> I've heard one girl was going to quit working because all the taxes come to us. Plus, you know, they downgrade us in every kind of way there is. They say we look like slobs, we keep our houses this way and that way. And our children, depending on the way they're dressed, we're like bad parents and all sorts of things like that.

The theme of laziness, an image embodied in the Individualist perspective, emerged frequently. Welfare recipients are well aware that mothers on welfare are criticized for being lazy, unmotivated, and for taking advantage of the welfare system. Leah, a 24-year-old African American woman with four children commented:

> I've had people who didn't know I was receiving assistance and everything was just fine. But when people find out you're receiving assistance, it's like, "Why? Why did you get lazy all of a sudden?" People automatically just put you in this category of people that don't do anything except sit on their butts and do nothing. It's just all out there in the community.

Mandy, another African American woman, who is 20 years old, with two young children, told me:

> They say you lazy. They say you lazy and don't want to work. You want people to take care of you. You want to sit home and watch stories all day, which I don't. And they say it's a handout.

Goffman's book *Stigma* (1963) provides an insightful analysis of this phenomenon. He is interested in the gap between the image the individual wishes his or her public identity to be, "*virtual social identity*," and what the individual's identity actually is, "*actual social identity*." A person is stigmatized when there is a discrepancy in these identities. It can be a powerfully negative social label that radically changes a person's self-concept and social identity. Goffman divided stigmatized individuals into two groups: those whose stigma is known or easily perceivable (such as a paraplegic or someone who is disfigured) and those whose stigma is hidden or not easily identified. When it is identified, the stigmatized person can become deeply discredited, labeled as deviant, and deemed to be morally flawed (Gans, 1995). The label associated with stigmatization focuses on only one aspect of the individual's character. This one aspect is elevated to the level of a "master" status—it becomes the primary mechanism through which that person is identified. One suddenly becomes, "the cripple," "the lesbian," "the person with AIDS," "the man in a wheelchair," or "the welfare mother." Other statuses, such as Sunday School teacher, school volunteer, swimmer, friend, and daughter are largely overlooked.

The stigma surrounding welfare is deep and widespread, and research has documented that it may even keep some eligible families from applying for aid (Yaniv, 1997). Because women are well aware of the ways in which welfare is denigrated, they are often embarrassed about being poor and receiving welfare. So are their children. Many women told me of this embarrassment, including Sarah. Sarah is a white, 30-year-old divorced mother who works part-time at a fast-food franchise. She also attends college, and is working toward her AA degree. Both she and her daughter are embarrassed at wearing hand-me-down clothing. She described an incident in which her daughter's only coat did not fit her because it was originally purchased for someone else.

> She inherited my mom's winter coat because we couldn't afford one. Her arm was up here, and the sleeve was down here, but hey, she wore it. She stayed warm. You do what you have to do. You try to make it so it's not as embarrassing. But it really is. I mean, the parents made more fun than the kids did.

Dawn, our "stereotypical" welfare recipient also discussed her embarrassment about receiving welfare:

> First of all, I'm embarrassed about being on welfare. I'm not going to tell you no lie. Maybe I've been on it all my life, but maybe that's why I'm em-

barrassed about it. But the kids used to go, "Momma, the check is here." And that was so embarrassing. Downstairs, upstairs could hear. I had to stop them from doing that. I had to tell them, "This is not good. Don't be happy because we're getting a welfare check. This is not nothing good."

Most women, like Sarah and Dawn, could not hide their stigma, and were publicly embarrassed by it. In Sarah's case, her family's poverty was on display every day when the coat or other hand-me-down clothing was worn. In Dawn's case, despite living in a public housing project in which all of her neighbors were on welfare, she was embarrassed when her children loudly announced the arrival of the welfare check. By her children doing this, she lost all pretenses that she was not really receiving welfare.

Racism and Welfare

One of the many reasons that welfare use is stigmatized is that it is associated with use primarily by African Americans. Welfare is put in racial terms because many whites incorrectly assume that the majority of the poor and the majority of welfare recipients are African American. They see welfare as a program primarily serving African American mothers who have never married. As shown in Table 1.1, in 1994, prior to welfare reform, whites and African Americans constituted 37 percent and 36 percent of welfare recipients, respectively. However, whites have apparently had an easier time leaving welfare for work. By 2002, whites comprised only 32 percent of welfare recipients. Meanwhile, African American representation increased slightly in 2002, and Hispanics increased by over 20 percent (U.S. Department of Health and Human Services, November, 2004).

Racial overtones were evident in the comments made to women on welfare. One woman heard welfare recipients referred to as "white and black niggers sucking off the system." The racist view that welfare is a program primarily for the African American community was epitomized in the comments made by Beth, a 27-year-old white woman with one child:

Oh they say silly stuff, prejudiced stuff, "the black people are getting it, so we might as well—you might as well go ahead and get it too while you can. They're driving Cadillacs," and this and that. It just shows how ignorant they are—to me.

Several African American women commented that the public unfairly labels welfare as a problem primarily within the African American community, "they want to say that there are more black people on the system than white people." Dee is an African American woman aged 24 with three children aged four and under, and she told us that the most negative comments she has heard come from white males:

That's mainly who I hear it from. I mean, I hear a couple of things from black guys, but a lot of black guys I know grew up on the system. You know, they are trying to get off that system. So you don't really hear it much from them. They have firsthand experience with it. Those who don't have first-hand experience have friends who have. So, the majority of them have come into contact with it sometime in their lifetime. As for the white males, a lot of them grew up in the upper middle class, you know, above the poverty line, so they never run across it, unless they had friends who were on the system. But there are as many white people on it as black people.

Many whites see African Americans' experience as having improved significantly in recent years, and tend to deny that our social structure limits their opportunities. Whites are often resentful and feel that they themselves are victimized by policies of "reverse discrimination," while African Americans and other minorities reap employment and social welfare benefits (Lamont, 2003). In the late 1990s California had a ballet measure known as Proposition 209, nicknamed the "California Civil Rights Initiative," that called for an end to discrimination or preferential treatment based on race, gender or religion in state jobs and contracts, and in admissions to state educational institutions. It was touted as possibly eliminating quota-based affirmative action programs in California. Seventy-five percent of white voters approved the ballet measure, compared to only 42 percent of minorities. (Rasinski, 1998). Likewise, the General Social Survey, which assessed public opinion from a nationally representative sample of adults in 1998, found that twice as many people believed that things have improved for blacks over the last few years compared to those who believed that things have stayed the same or gotten worse. Moreover, six times as many people opposed Affirmative Action as supported it (National Opinion Research Center, Accessed March 5, 2005). African Americans and other minorities are not seen as needing special treatment or privilege, and many whites are resentful that minorities are receiving these privileges nonetheless.

Our nation tends to deny racial inequalities, and instead embraces the idea that "we are all created equal." Consequently, we oppose affirmative action programs which demand that we acknowledge the differences among us—the inequalities in earlier life circumstances that effect ones' opportunities today. But can we really deny that adults and children are treated differently, and have different experiences and opportunities based on their skin color and position in our class structure? Even public education—supposedly the great equalizer by providing all children with the same quality education and chance for the good life perpetuates "savage inequalities," according to author Jonathan Kozol (1991). In comparing two high schools, one poor and with a 99.9 percent black student population, and one consisting of mostly white upper-middle-class students, he found dramatic differences in school funding, in their facilities, and in personnel. For example, high school students in poor East Orange can afford few athletic facilities. The track team has no field, and they must do their running in the hallway of the school. Meanwhile, in nearby upper-middle-class Montclair, money is available to buy two recreation fields, four gyms, a dance room, a wrestling room, a weight room with a universal gym, tennis courts, a track, and indoor areas for fencing. Money also is available in Montclair High to hire 13 full-time physical education teachers for their 1,900 students. East Orange High School, by comparison, has four physical education teachers for 2,000 students. Drastic differences such as these not only provide different current experiences and future opportunities, but they also send a clear message about the value of education. It should come as no surprise that graduation rates from high school are correlated with race and class. Students with lower family incomes, and members of most minority groups in the United States are significantly more likely to drop out of high school than are more affluent whites.

Individual and institutional racism is prevalent in the United States. It is manifested in many ways, including hatred and distrust towards those African Americans most in need (Gilens, 2001; Hancock, 2004). William Julius Wilson suggests that young African American women are actually *more* likely to be blamed for their economic circumstances than are their white counterparts, and they are considered less worthy of government assistance (Wilson, 1996). Many Americans associate the Culture of Poverty perspective with African Americans and criticize the supposed subcultural adaptations in the African American community as aberrant and antithetical to mainstream American values associated with hard work and family. Women's poverty, African American women's in particular, is blamed on a breakdown in women's moral virtue, which has resulted in declining marriage rates and rising illegitimacy.

These concerns stem, at least in part, from two important demographic factors, both of which can be seen in Dawn's experiences. First, African Americans are indeed less like to marry than are whites; and second, they are more likely to have a child outside of marriage. National data show that race, ethnicity, and social class affect marriage patterns in many critical ways. In 2003, 43 percent of African American males age 15 and over were married, compared with 59 percent of white males. Likewise, 36 percent of black females age 15 and over were married, compared to 57 percent of white females (Popenoe & Whitehead, 2004). Critics are quick to implicate this as a subcultural adaptation at odds with American values. But there are two primary reasons for this. Both reasons are rational and pragmatic, and have little to do with a culture of poverty, *per se*. First, high rates of unemployment and underemployment discourage young adults from marrying. Unemployment among young African American males is over twice that for whites their age. And among those males who are employed, their earnings are significantly less than those of whites. Therefore, given high rates of unemployment and underemployment, young men are less eager to take on the responsibility of a family, and young women are less apt to see these men as desirable marriage prospects.

The second reason for the lower rate of marriage among African Americans is sheer demographics. The number of eligible African American women for marriage far exceeds the number of available men. The statistics are alarming: one out of every 80 African American males is the victim of a violent death, and a disturbingly high percentage of men are incarcerated. Thus, for African American females, the search for a lifetime marriage partner can be a daunting task. There is a critical shortage of marriageable men. Like many other African American women, Dawn has not found a man to marry. Given her less-than-likely chance of finding a man to support herself and her four children, her reluctance to look for one is therefore not surprising.

Higher rates of nonmarital births among African Americans also influence the belief that a separate subculture exists that is antithetical to mainstream American values. In 2002, the nonmarital fertility rate for African Americans was about three times that of white women (68 versus 23 births per 1,000 women, respectively), and the nonmarital fertility rate among Hispanic women is about twice that of whites, at 44 births per 1,000 women (Sutton & Mathews, 2004). Part of these differences can be traced back to income or education levels, but significant racial differences persist even after the effects of socioeconomic status, and other individual and family characteristics are controlled for. These nonmarital births are not simply the result of accidental pregnancies.

Corresponding with these demographic trends, birth *intentions* also differ among racial and ethnic groups. Using a national sample of 12,686 males and females between the ages of 14 and 21 from the U.S. National Longitudinal Surveys of Labor Market Experience of Youth (NSLY), researchers compared birth intentions of African Americans, Hispanics, and whites. They report that African Americans were twice as likely to expect an adolescent birth as were whites (10.6 versus 5.5, respectively), and were nearly four times as likely to expect a nonmarital birth (15.2 versus 4.2, respectively). Hispanics fared somewhere between these two groups (Trent & Crowder, 1997). Dawn's pregnancies were not planned, but at the same time, they were not particularly surprising to her either. Yet today, the rate of teen pregnancies alarms her. Her values, and those of many other women interviewed, were not at odds with conventional expectations. She did not hold separate subcultural values that encourage or tolerate teen pregnancy. Rather, Dawn is concerned about the high rates of teenage pregnancy that plague young women, and severely limit the work and educational opportunities available to them. Consequently, she is actively trying to prevent her own daughters from becoming pregnant. Dawn, and other women, told me that they were trying to ward off teenage sexual activity, among both their daughters and their sons, through repeated warnings, keeping a watchful eye on them after school, and through a series of rewards and punishments. Referring to her oldest daughter, who is now 17 years old, Dawn said:

> I'm real proud of her, because she did not do like I did. She did not have a baby at 13, or 14, or 17. She's doing good. I told her not to. Oh, so many times. All the time, right up until this day. I don't remember how long ago I used to start talking with her. But now I have a ten-year-old daughter, and I see that she's maturing, so I know she must have been about nine or ten when I started preaching my little preach. Ten is not too early at all.

These two demographic trends—lower rates of marriage and higher rates of nonmarital births—have become the rallying cry for Individualists and Culture of Poverty enthusiasts. African American women, in particular, are assumed to be the cause of their own poverty. They are poor because of their own immoral and indiscriminant sexual behavior, and their failure to find suitable lifetime mates, or so the story line goes. "It is the moral fabric of individuals, not the social and economic structure of society, that is taken to be the root of the problem" (Wilson, 1996, p. 164). Poverty and welfare use are racialized by many white Americans, because they are increasingly weary of social programs, they believe that racism has declined, and they see African Americans as failing to expend the effort needed to improve their financial standing.

Contexts Where Stigma and Discrimination Occur

Recipients commented that they heard criticism most often in public places such as grocery stores. In this context one cannot hide being on welfare; food stamps are used in full view of anyone who cares to notice. Food stamps are what Goffman has termed, "stigma symbols." Using them forces a welfare recipient to publicly acknowledge her devalued status; her use of welfare becomes a highly visible attribute. She becomes, in the eyes of the public, a "welfare mother" with all the negative connotations that title evokes. One African American woman named Lonnie, who has been on and off of welfare several times, and mostly recently has received welfare for two years, revealed the hostilities she encountered in the grocery store when using food stamps:

> And I've went in the grocery store, and when you get ready to buy your groceries, people have made nasty little remarks about the groceries you're buying. They'll go, "we're paying for that." Once there was some university students and I guess they felt like that. They had a small amount in their buggy, and I had large amounts. He started talking, so his girlfriend kept trying to get him to be quiet. And he kept talking and talking. And then he said, "That's why the President is trying to cut off welfare because of people like that!" I turned to him and I say, I say, "Well, you know something? I have worked in my time too. And I will work again. It's not like I'm asking you for anything. And I hope you don't come and ask me for anything 'cause with me and my five kids I couldn't give you none anyway!" And he stomped out of there when I told him that. But I was being honest with him. I have worked. I felt real bad that day, I really did.

Cashiers and others who are looking for evidence of fraud or abuse closely scrutinize the foods that women purchase. "Welfare mothers who purchase steak with food stamps" is a classic metaphor used by many people to illustrate the supposed fraud and abuse within the food stamp program. One woman in our study described how the fellow students in her class at the community college believed the stereotypes about women on welfare, and criticized them for buying "steaks or shrimp with food stamps." The assumption is made that welfare mothers live "high on the hog" at taxpayer expense and must be closely monitored to prevent irresponsible behavior and abuse of the system.

One woman told us about an actual experience purchasing a steak with food stamps. She described the critical responses she received by other shoppers in line who witnessed it. Acknowledging that she was feeding the stereotype, she tried not to let it bother her:

> I did have this instance where I was in the store, and I was buying groceries, and I got a thin three dollar steak, and this lady behind me said, "It

must be nice to be able to buy steak. I can't afford to buy steak with my money!" And the lady behind her said, "Well if you were on food stamps, you could afford to buy two or three steaks!" And I just shook my head. It really didn't bother me, because I was, like, as long as I can feed my kids, I don't care what people say. And if food stamps help me buy my kids a steak every now and then, then so be it . . . I don't look at what somebody else gets and say, "Oh look what they got? A steak or pork chops." That's their business.

Using food stamps or other stigma symbols requires women to give up their privacy and their choices. Their lives, their shopping habits, and their food preferences are closely scrutinized. We are quick to judge their spending habits as inappropriate and wasteful, and to look for examples of this to verify our assumptions. We look for women who buy steak with food stamps, and are vindicated when we find them. Yes, she purchased a steak, but in order to do so, what else did she give up? In what other ways did she scrimp and save during the rest of the month? Purchasing a month's worth of food on the food stamp allotment provided to families takes resourcefulness and ingenuity. At a funding level of about 75 cents per person per meal, wastefulness is unlikely.

The women we interviewed responded in a variety of ways to using food stamps. Some were embarrassed about using them, and preferred to shop only in specific stores where they felt welcome. It was generally common knowledge which stores have cashiers who are less sympathetic to food stamps, and women tried to avoid shopping there. Other women were more defensive, saying, "What do they want us to do, starve?"

Interestingly, in addition to grocery stores, another common context in which negative comments were routinely heard was the welfare office itself. Rather then being viewed as a place for help, the welfare office is viewed with disdain. It is run by people who are seen as self-serving, and who have contempt for their clients. The caseworkers are the gatekeepers to welfare, and many welfare recipients resent this. They believe that caseworkers take their function far too seriously: "They act like it's their own money they're giving away." Women commonly reported ill feelings toward their caseworker. Two women specifically suggested caseworkers should be community volunteers or representatives from churches to insure that case workers' first concerns were humanitarian, rather than simply viewing welfare and welfare recipients as a routine and boring job. Welfare recipients felt demeaned by their caseworkers: "They think you ain't much of nothing . . . ," "They try and make you feel bad and say little mean things . . . ," "Some of them talk to you like dirt . . . " were frequent comments. As one mother, a 41-year-old white woman named Denise, revealed:

Some of them treat you like you got to take this, "because I got your case in my hand and I'm the one who decides whether you get these stamps." And some of them talk to you like dirt and some of them are all right. It's like they have no respect for you, but you have to take it because you need it. You need that check, you need that Medicaid. It's like, if you make them mad, you can hang it up, because you ain't going to get it! One lady said, "I have thirty days to approve your case or not." It didn't matter if you had kids or not. I've heard some of the workers talk to the elderly people and some of them talk to the elderly people so bad. And they don't care, it's like, "I got my job."

Amy is a 23-year-old white mother of one child, who attends a university full-time and plans to go to graduate school. She will earn her bachelor's degree next year, and plans to get a master's degree in physical therapy. She told me about her experience going into the welfare office to meet with her case worker:

It's a very humiliating experience—being on welfare and being involved in the system. You are treated as though you are the scum of the earth. A stupid, lazy, nasty person. How dare you take this money? It's a very unpleasant experience. I'd avoid it at all costs. But unfortunately, I can't avoid it right now.

Recipients felt stigmatized and discriminated against in other ways as well. They felt mistreated by public health clinics, for example. Several women mentioned that they have to sit several hours in the waiting room before being seen, or that doctors and nurses talk "down" to them, as though they are too ignorant to understand basic medical or health terminology. Others talked about the stigma they experience when applying for a job and revealing that they currently receive welfare. They felt that they had been denied job opportunities because they were labeled as "stupid" for being on welfare. Kim, a 29-year-old African American mother of three children, is employed part-time, and told me that she is diligently looking for full-time employment. She talked about her frustration in dealing with people when applying for jobs:

Yeah, people in employment offices, when you go looking for a job and say you're on AFDC, they automatically look at you and assume you're a dummy, "here's another drop out." . . . If you put all this stuff down on your application they, like, double question you about the information, like you're lying. And I don't think that's fair. I don't think that you should be judged, just for being on AFDC.

Other contexts in which stigma and discrimination occurred were more personalized. Women told me that their friends, neighbors, boyfriends, or family members were sometimes extremely critical of their use of welfare. Many told me of their anxiety with telling certain people, or of the ways in which they tried to keep it a secret from them.

But perhaps the disapproval from family, friends or acquaintances hit the children the hardest. They don't understand the societal disapproval heaped upon their families. Dawn revealed a story in which her daughter, unsuspecting that food stamps were stigmatized, pulled one out of her backpack on the school bus. She was teased unmercifully by her school mates, "The kids picked on her so bad, she came home crying." Likewise, Sheila's daughter Melanie, who was introduced in Chapter 1, is shy and a loner, and Sheila attributes this to feeling self-conscious among her peers at school about being poor and on welfare. "That's why she, Melanie now, she's a loner too. When she comes in that door, she don't go back outside." Criticism from peers is especially difficult for children and teens; peers are an important reference group. Teens, especially, spend an inordinate amount of time trying to look, dress, and behave in certain ways that reflect those of the peer group. Criticism from them is a painful and blatant reminder of the stigma attached to welfare.

Managing Stigma

How do women on welfare feel about such sentiment levied at themselves and their families? Many of the women who were interviewed volunteered that derogatory comments were painful to hear, "It makes me feel bad," "It's just discouraging," "It's a humiliating experience," "Some days it kind of hurts your feelings. You think, oh they really hate us."

How do women cope with, or manage the stigma of being on welfare? As Goffman (1963) suggests, for someone with a known stigma the basic problem is managing the tension produced by the fact that people know of the problem. For someone who is effectively hiding the stigma, the problem is in managing information so that the problem remains unknown to the audience. But it is difficult to completely hide being on welfare. One can hide it in some contexts, such as with friends, family members, and with neighbors unless living in the housing projects. But it is revealed in other contexts, such as in grocery stores when using food stamps or in the welfare office when waiting in line for recertification or to pick up stamps.

During the course of interviewing women, it became apparent that they used one or more of four primary strategies for coping with the stigma attached to using welfare. These four strategies were (1) denial; (2) distancing themselves from other women who used welfare; (3) blaming external forces and thus denying that using welfare was their fault; and (4) extolling the importance of motherhood. Each of these is discussed below.

Denial

As is the case with other types of stigmas, some women denied that they had encountered negative sentiment against them. Ten women, including both African Americans and whites, said that neither they nor their children had ever experienced stigma or discrimination because of being on welfare. Denying that it occurred frees women from feeling bad, guilty, or embarrassed. However, half of these women followed their denial with statements such as "And I don't listen to it anyhow," indicating that they had indeed heard such comments, but chose to deny them or dismiss them as irrelevant to themselves. Kim told me how she dismisses and ignores the comments or innuendoes that she receives:

I'm trying to make it. So whatever opinion you have, just keep it to your-self. I don't, I guess I haven't ran into nobody who really said anything about it because it really don't matter to me. Right now, I know what I got to do, so just leave me alone.

Several women suggested that people had been especially kind to them when they revealed to others that they were on welfare. For example, one woman reported that clerks in stores steered her to special in-store savings or pointed out cheaper brands to buy.

Denial also took another important form. A few women seemed genuinely un-aware of the stigma levied at welfare recipients. They were perplexed when they were asked what kinds of things they had heard said about welfare recipients, and didn't quite know what was meant by the question because most or all of their social network of family and friends also received welfare. They didn't feel stigmatized be-cause they rarely interacted with people who weren't receiving welfare. These women likely lived in one of several large housing projects, they associated primarily with other women who receive welfare, and they shopped at the neighborhood store which is considered "user friendly" to welfare recipients by offering such services as quick check cashing and day-old baked goods at reduced prices. One mother with two chil-dren reflected upon her homogenous network:

> The majority of the black females that I hang around with are on welfare also. Except for one, and she doesn't have a child. She's my best friend, and her mother used to be on it, so, you know, it's all the same. Everyone is treated equal.

Comments such as these lend some credence to the Culture of Poverty per-spective. For these few women at least, welfare use was normative and ceased being stigmatized. They successfully avoided the stigma associated with welfare by avoiding people or places where stigma is likely to be encountered. It is important to acknowl-edge that, for a small number of women, welfare use may be viewed as common, rather than the exception. But unfortunately, it is this small group that receives the most media attention, despite their relatively modest numbers within the welfare population. It gives the general public the exaggerated and false notion, a racialized one, that the majority of welfare recipients live within a separate subculture, with val-ues that are at odds with those of hardworking Americans.

Distancing Themselves from Other Welfare Recipients

Drawing upon the individualistic and culture of poverty themes, a second strategy for managing the stigma associated with welfare use was distancing themselves from other welfare recipients. Some women made a concerted effort to identify themselves with higher economic classes, such as the middle class. Several women said they do not let other people know they are on welfare: "I tell people I receive aid from the state" leaving the source of the aid vague. One 42-year-old African American woman named Treena, who also received welfare as a child for a period when her father was in jail, told me:

> I don't really tell a lot of people that I'm on AFDC. Not that I'm getting anything much. But I don't, you know. Because I dress myself up and I look nice once I'm dressed up. And I carry myself in a professional manner, and I try to be professional and respectful and go about my business. It makes a lot of difference to other people, especially those that got something. It does. It makes a difference, it really does.

Women talked about buying their children expensive, popular-brand athletic shoes so that no one would know they receive welfare. One African American mother in particular, commented that dressing so as to appear middle class, such as buying name-brand clothing and shoes, was very important in keeping her sons away from drug dealers who are known to offer young children these items as a way to entice them to sell drugs for them. Although it takes a sizable chunk out of her monthly budget, it is worth it in order to "pass" as middle class. She and her son lived in the housing projects, and she commented that drugs and drug dealers were commonplace.

Others try to disassociate themselves from women on welfare by criticizing and blaming them for their own economic circumstances. I found that women on welfare sounded much like the more affluent; they blamed other poor women for their own economic circumstances. Drawing upon the Individual perspective, the narratives revealed that they attributed other women's poverty and use of welfare to that person's own (a) laziness; (b) drug use; (c) lack of human capital; (d) personal choice; or (e) other personal shortcomings or irresponsible behavior.

Janie is a 19-year-old white mother of a two-year-old child who characterizes the Individual perspective. She lives in an apartment that is not subsidized and has a roommate to share expenses. The apartment is in good repair, although her furnishings are modest and sparse. Despite being only 19, Janie has been living virtually on her own for years. She ran away from home as a young teenager, lived on the streets for a period of time, stayed in shelters, and more recently has shared apartments with one or two other people. Janie was gang raped several years ago, and she became pregnant as a result. She decided to keep the baby, and turned to welfare for help. Janie has received welfare since her daughter was born two years ago, but, like others I interviewed, is convinced that welfare is just a temporary step in her otherwise busy, confused, and complicated life. She hopes to be off the system within a year or two, after she pays off her bills and "gets established." But she feels that many others who receive assistance are far less motivated than she is:

> There are some people on welfare who don't need to be on welfare. They can go out and get a job. They have nothing better to do than to live off of welfare and to live off the system. I'm sorry. I have no sympathy. Look at all the signs on the road, "will work for food." Go down to Day Labor,

for crying out loud. They'll pay you more money than you can make in a regular day. It's by choice. Either (a) they don't want to work; (b) they are being supported by others; or (c) they don't give a damn about themselves.

Sheri is a 27-year-old African American with three children, who has been on welfare for seven years. She referred back to the idea that people on welfare are lazy. She clearly did not include herself in this category, despite the fact that outsiders may be concerned over her supposed long-term welfare "dependency."

> I think a lot of them are on it just to be on it. Lazy. Don't want to do nothing. Lot of them on it 'cause a lot of them are on drugs. Keep having kids to get more money, more food stamps. Now that's abusing the system. And a lot of women are abusing the system.

She, like other women on welfare, distanced herself from other recipients physically, emotionally, or both. Clear distinctions were drawn between "me" and "them." Many women believed that other women did not deserve to receive welfare, were bad mothers who neglected their children, or in other ways committed fraud or deliberately abused the system. Even Dawn prefers to distance herself from other welfare recipients:

> I think some people are lazy. Some people, umm, it's like passed down, and that's how they think. They think that's how it is supposed to be. Some people are lazy. Some people are uneducated, and you can't really get the—yes you can. Yes, you can get a job. I think some people are lazy and they just want some kind of income. Not everybody just sits around. But some people do. I think the people who are just sitting around are lazy, to tell you the truth.

Several women, both African American and white, admitted that they didn't know anyone who committed fraud or abuse personally, but claimed that "there are a lot of people like that out there." They subscribe to the common perception of welfare mothers, even though this perception contradicts their own personal experience, and contradicts the lives of other women they know personally.

Mary, 47 and white, expressed concern over the fraud she believes is committed by welfare recipients, African Americans in particular. Mary is separated from her husband, and receives welfare for one of her seven children who still resides in the home. She has worked most of her life as a waitress and cashier, but has several health problems that she feels prevent her now from working. She comments that she just "knows" people are being fraudulent, even though she acknowledges that she doesn't personally know anyone who is.

> **MARY:**   How can they afford to drive fancy new cars and fancy—excuse me, there's a lot of blacks wearing $100 shoes that I can't even afford to buy my daughter a $10 pair. Now, you tell me what is wrong with that picture.

INTERVIEWER: And you know these cases?

MARY: Not personally. But you can walk down the street, or go to the food stamp office or the welfare office and see who drives up in the fancy cars and the new fancy clothes and stuff. You tell me.

Concern about fraud and abuse of the system transcends racial prejudice and discrimination. Tamara, a 31-year-old African American woman with three children, voiced a similar, if less racially charged concern about fraud and abuse.

TAMARA: A lot of those mothers on AFDC get food stamps and stuff, and take the stamps and sell them. If not, they'll take the money and, you know, buy crack and leave the kids hungry, and they don't have clothes to put on, and shoes to wear. Once they're on drugs, they'll do anything to get them.

INTERVIEWER: Do you know of any cases where people are actually doing this?

TAMARA: I've heard of some people, but, uh . . . It's happening everywhere.

It appears that women on welfare subscribe to the popular Individual perspective to explain poverty and welfare use—at least to explain why other women use welfare. They assume that other women are poor and on welfare primarily through their own doing, and that they lack incentive and motivation to improve their economic circumstances. The women interviewed want to distance themselves as far as possible from other recipients.

I found that recipients also draw upon Culture of Poverty metaphors to distance themselves from other women who are on welfare. They invoked images of a separate subculture in which these other welfare mothers and their families live. It is a subculture with separate values, norms, and cultural milieu. The themes that emerged from the narratives revolved around such subcultural issues as (1) women who rely upon welfare for the long-term as a way of life; (2) intergenerational welfare use; (3) unmarried teenagers who have babies and assume that welfare will take care of them; (4) women who have additional children simply to increase the amount of their welfare benefits; and (5) the cultural milieu in the projects. Again, recipients distanced themselves from these cultural contexts, and in doing so voiced that they have little in common with other recipients.

First, Amy characterized the concern that some people see welfare as a way of life. Like the others, she sees her situation as unique and different from the norm, despite the fact that many welfare recipients are in school obtaining further education or vocational training to increase their opportunities for social mobility. Our sample was obtained in a region in which an experimental welfare reform program was being implemented. It provided educational opportunities and an extensive array of incentives, such as assistance with transportation and childcare, for the women who were randomly selected, and who agreed to participate in the program. Thus, an unusually high percentage of welfare recipients in the region, including 40 percent of the sample, were in school or vocational training. Yet, this young mother, working towards a college degree in a health field, insisted that her situation was distinctly different from the norm:

> Well, there are people like me who are using it as a means to make ends meet while they are preparing to support themselves. And I think we are a pretty small number. I think that there are those people for whom welfare and AFDC are a way of life. Their parents were on it, their parents' parents were on it, and this is how they live. I think they are not the majority, but I think they exist.

Second, many women, both African American and white, were alarmed by intergenerational welfare use. Some claimed to know families, in which the mothers and then the daughters received welfare, referring to it as "a cycle that keeps on going." They suggested that young girls need to be educated about the difficulties of raising children, and that they be told that welfare is likely to be changed in the future and cannot be relied upon to help them. In reality, the number of people who are affected by intergenerational welfare use is quite small. As shown in Chapter 1, national data indicate that half of all women on welfare have used it for two years or less, and fewer than one in five recipients uses welfare for five years or longer, continuously. Although there is considerable movement on and off welfare, it is likely that only a modest number of these women use welfare for decades and within multigenerations. Nonetheless, many welfare recipients, as is the case with the more affluent, exaggerate the frequency of intergenerational welfare use and are concerned that it is widespread.

Third, concern and anger were also expressed over young unmarried teenage girls who have babies and automatically assume that welfare will support them. A culture of poverty, of sorts, was alluded to—that young girls haven't been taught that reliance on welfare is not a good thing. Interestingly, older women who also had babies out of wedlock while they were teenagers often voiced this concern. For example, Dawn told me, "I think some girls have a certain amount of babies just to get a check. I'm not sure." Kim, a 29-year-old African American, expressed both disgust and concern over the epidemic of teenage pregnancy and their subsequent reliance on welfare. Yet, Kim had her first of three children when she was aged 17, a teenager herself. Despite being in similar circumstances, she distanced herself from the behavior of teenagers today. She expressed concern over the fact that many young girls want to get pregnant and rely on welfare. Kim saw herself as different from others: very ambitious and working hard to try to improve her situation for herself and her three children. She had recently finished a community college program, and was trying to secure full-time employment during the day while her children were in school. At the time of the interview, she was working at a part-time job with hours during the late afternoon and early evening, a schedule that she felt interfered with her responsibilities as a mother. She commented:

> These girls are having babies younger and younger, and I say it's more to having a baby than just getting a check and some food stamps. A lot of

people. I say they shouldn't even give them a check until they graduate. 'Cause a lot of them, that's all they are waiting for . . . and they just steadily having babies. They having babies at twelve and thirteen. They aren't even at a legal age to get a job.

Kim's concerns are not unfounded, at least in part. Births occurring out of wedlock have increased dramatically during the past few decades, increasing from 28 percent of all births in 1990 to 34 percent of all births in 2002 (Sutton & Mathews, 2004). The increase is particularly acute among white women, whose rate increased by about 40 percent during this period (while African Americans increased by only 3 percent). It is incorrect to attribute this increase in unmarried births solely to teenagers, however, as Kim and others were inclined to do, because the number of teen births has actually declined considerably, down to 43 per 1,000 births in 2002 from 60 per 1,000 births in 1990 (Sutton & Mathews, 2004). Instead, most of the unmarried births are occurring among older women, including women in their 30s and even 40s. Births to unmarried women of this age are generally seen as less problematic because the women are more likely to have completed their education, have work experience, and are less likely to need welfare to support themselves and their children.

Fourth, a controversial issue, with passionate arguments on both sides, was whether women continue to have children simply to increase the size of their welfare check. This is a prominent component of President Clinton's welfare reform, as it is popularly believed that poor women have additional children so that they will receive increased welfare benefits. Some women argued adamantly that a $50 a month increase in benefit level would not be enough to encourage a person to have additional children. For example, Molly, a white woman with three children, who also attends community college, disagreed with the widely held perception that women have children to increase their welfare check:

> When I was taking my sociology class at <Community College>, we had this talk, and it sickened me some of the things people were saying. They were not true. You can't generalize and say that everyone is the same, "She has babies so she can have this extra money to live on!" I don't think I've met anybody who wanted to be on welfare.

Many respondents, however, felt differently, and argued that other women do have additional children to increase the size of "the check," as it is routinely referred to. As a 28-year-old African American mother with four children claimed:

> A lot of people are saying that the only reason that they are having a baby is to get money from the system. And nine times out of ten it's true. Because I know a lot of young girls that are pregnant and having babies. I try to talk to them, and say in the future welfare is going to be cut out, it's going to be cut out for everybody. So why go out, why have a baby and risk getting the AIDS virus? Why risk all that, your life and health and everything just so you can get on welfare? I don't understand that.

A 42 year-old African American mother of two young children, Kate, voiced a similar sentiment:

> **INTERVIEWER:** I think some lawmakers think that women on AFDC have more children just . . .
>
> **KATE:** Just to get more AFDC. I believe that too. I really believe that too. But not me. No. Some women are just breeders.
>
> **INTERVIEWER:** They're just breeders? What does that mean?
>
> **KATE:** They like to have babies. If they don't go get themselves stopped, they'll just keep having them. If it were me, I wouldn't have no more babies just to get more AFDC. No.
>
> **INTERVIEWER:** But you do think some people do it?
>
> **KATE:** Yeah, I do. I really do.

Again, we can see how women on welfare distanced themselves from others who received aid. Kate, and others, distinguished between "me" and "them." Other welfare recipients are viewed as having deviant values and engaging in negative behaviors that fuel their dependence on welfare.

Finally, the cultural milieu in the housing projects was also of considerable concern. The majority of our respondents lived in housing subsidized by the government. There are several types of federal housing programs: (1) public housing, which generally consists of high rises and "garden apartment" rental units owned and operated by public housing authorities; (2) Section 8 certificates, which allow tenants to rent in the private market, with tenants paying 30 percent of their income and public housing authorities paying the remainder; and (3) Project-based Section 8, which are not administered by the public housing authorities (Barry, 1998). Owners maintain their own waiting lists, and within federal guidelines, decide who gets admitted.

There is a serious shortage of low-income housing for those who need it. Only 19 percent of TANF recipients in 2002 lived in subsidized housing (U.S. Department of Health and Human Services, November, 2004). Beginning in the 1990s there was a decline in subsidized housing units. Congress reduced funding to restore and refurnish older buildings, thus ensuring that more units will deteriorate, and eventually will be destroyed. Equally important, Congress also eliminated the "one-for-one" replacement rule, which required that a new unit be built for every unit demolished (Barry, 1998). Cuts in subsidized housing have continued. By 2004, things were so severe that some agencies raised rent burdens on low-income families that receive vouchers by reducing the maximum amount of rent a voucher can cover. Other agencies reduced the number of families assisted, by rescinding vouchers provided to families that are searching for housing but have not yet found a unit to rent with their voucher, and by "shelving" vouchers that become available when current voucher holders leave the program (rather than reissuing the vouchers to needy families on waiting lists as is the normal practice). For some agencies, the shortfalls created by the new HUD policy are so severe that the agencies have no alternative but to terminate assistance to some low-income families that currently rely on vouchers to help pay the rent (Sard & Fischer, July 15, 2004).

A few women who participated in this study, such as Dawn, lived in single-family homes, by far the most desirable of the subsidized housing available. Others lived in small apartment complexes, sometimes integrated with other residents who were not on public assistance. This too was considered a desirable alternative to the large housing projects. Generally, there were waiting lists for these types of arrangements. Instead, the most common type of subsidized housing, and the one in which over one-quarter of our respondents, primarily African Americans, resided at the time of the interview, were the public housing "projects." These large, often multilevel structures were home to hundreds of families, all of whom were on welfare. They were characterized by the women who live in them as noisy, lacking in privacy, in disrepair, full of loiterers, and as breeding grounds for drug use and other illegal activities.

Many respondents dreamed about the day they would be in a financial position to leave the project—"I'm saying to my boyfriend, if you love me, get me out of here." They expressed surprise, concern, and contempt that their neighbors often seemed to be satisfied living there. One African American woman, Coreen, who attends community college with the hope of someday being a teacher, described the cultural milieu she experienced in the projects. She currently lives in a very large multi-story housing project, moving there because her mother's house was too crowded for her and her baby. On the Saturday afternoon I was there, I noticed a large number of men hanging around in the breezeways and on the porches despite the fact that the housing was for welfare recipients, that is, women and their children. When I knocked on her door, she would not open it until I gave her complete information about who I was. She wasn't being unfriendly, just cautious. As she told me later, crime and drugs are commonplace.

> I live out here, and this place really puts you down. A lot of people don't realize about living in projects, it puts you down. I mean, because you have no one to encourage you to get out. If you try to accomplish or achieve anything, then you must think you are better than them and they won't like you. You have people here in the projects who always compete with you about how your house looks, but they won't compete with you about trying to get out of here. You know what I'm saying? Don't compete with me because of my apartment, compete with me with school, compete with me about trying to get out of here. Let's try to race to get out, you know? Some people just don't want to get out.

Because Coreen felt that she had little in common with the hundreds of other families in her project, she did not socialize with neighbors, usually kept her curtains closed, and generally did not allow her young daughter to play outside. This was a common strategy to cope with problems encountered with the high-density living in the projects. Other women told us that they also refused to socialize with neighbors: "They just some jealous-hearted people around here, they evil-hearted, and that's why I stay in my house."

What effects might this living environment have on a family? A team of researchers at Northwestern University found that when poor African American sin-gle-parent families were given the opportunity to move out of their crime-ridden urban housing projects and into white suburbs, the children's school performance improved dramatically, and mothers were more likely to become financially self-sufficient (San Francisco Chronicle, Feb. 22, 1993). Class position, and its resulting environment, affects one's opportunities, self-esteem, and achievements—both adults and children—in ways that we can only begin to know.

Women distanced themselves from other welfare recipients in a variety of ways, drawing upon both Individual and Culture of Poverty perspectives. Although recognizing in the abstract that there may be a multitude of reasons that bring women to the welfare system, most recipients were also quick to cite individual blame. Other women who receive welfare were often portrayed as lazy, unmotivated, or as cheating the system. They were described as living in a separate subculture with differing values and norms. These images are so strong that the women interviewed subscribed to them even if they don't personally know anyone who fits these profiles.

Blaming External Forces: "It's Not My Fault."

The third way in which women managed the stigma associated with welfare was by disregarding it because they believed that their present status was the result of social factors outside of their control. They generally felt that they were on welfare through no fault of their own, and therefore were not really to blame. They were more likely to invoke *Structural* or *Fatalist* perspectives to explain their welfare use. As will be shown in Chapter 4, their concerns with the social structure were based primarily on factors such as a lack of jobs paying a living wage; lack of good-quality and affordable daycare; lack of father involvement and child support enforcement; inadequate transportation systems; broader problems in our social structure such as racism or sexism; and a welfare system that penalizes women for their initiative by eliminating their welfare benefits. They also told me of needing welfare because of bad luck and unfortunate circumstances, such as a relationship gone awry. Sometimes, a relationship turned violent. Overall, women voiced that they simply couldn't help turning to welfare; structural problems were in their way, or they were a victim of unfortunate and unplanned circumstances, and "were between a rock and a hard place," "doing what I have to do" to survive. Some women were very articulate, and told us outright of racial or gender discrimination, for example. Others were more vague, and explained, "Something is kinda like holding me down."

In only a few cases did respondents fail to distance themselves from other women. In these few cases, respondents suggested that the social structure or unfortunate events are the primary reason why most other women also receive welfare. They defended welfare recipients as a collective group when they were being attacked, often referring to welfare recipients as "we."

However, most of the women interviewed distanced themselves from other recipients while simultaneously blaming their own welfare use on forces beyond their control. It appears that using these two coping methods were not mutually exclusive.

Overall, women generally felt that they were on welfare through no fault of their own, but other recipients were often responsible for their own economic plight.

Extolling the Importance of Motherhood

A fourth strategy for managing the stigma associated with receiving welfare was extolling the importance of their roles as mothers. This provided a personal validation of the work they do in the home as the sole caretakers of their children. When they were asked to name one of their "strengths" or something that they were particularly good at or proud of, the most common answer was "I'm a good mother." Being a competent mother, which was defined as someone who invested a considerable amount of time in the direct care of children, was a highly valued social identity. Dawn told us about the perplexing problem of how to be a "good mother" while going to school, and then being forced to work at the same time because of welfare reforms:

> If I go to school, and have to work, then what happens to my kids? Every time I'm taking from one, I'm taking from another. And my kids are very important to me. I don't want them to grow up on the system. I don't want them growing up on the streets and acting like little hoodlums, and not knowing that education is important. Even though what I did is different from what I want for them, I always want them to be a better person then me. So I want to be there for them. I want to be there to make sure they're doing their homework. I want, personally to be there. If I have to work, I'll work at night, I guess. It's not good at all.

The dominant cultural ideology of motherhood is embodied in two common images (Thurer, 1994). One is the full-time domestic mother whose primary job is taking care of her family's needs. She is solely responsible for the social, emotional, and physical care of her children. Others, presumably fathers, will provide for their financial needs. The second image is the employed professional "supermom" who successfully juggles her children's needs with the demands of full-time employment or with her own self-fulfillment. Her image is regularly featured on the covers of magazines—with briefcase in one hand, and baby in the other.

Both images are race and class-biased, despite the fact that, as cultural ideologies, they presume to reflect all women's experience. Both perpetuate the assumption that mothers are the primary adults responsible for child care. And finally, both images portray motherhood as an isolated, individual activity; even competing employment and family demands are handled privately. The United States, as compared to Canada, Western Europe, and many other countries throughout the world, has weak family support policies (Bergmann, 1996; Gornick & Meyers, 2003; Rainwater & Smeeding, 2003). Instead, mothers are encouraged to develop individual coping strategies to relieve stress.

It has been argued that a somewhat different ideology surrounding motherhood exists among many African Americans (Collins, 1990; 1994) and other minority groups (Segura, 1994). For example, motherhood among African Americans may be less privatized. "Mother" is a powerful figure; a leader in her community, her church, and among other children as well as her own. Motherhood may not be connected to simply one woman based upon a biological tie. Instead, "the boundaries distinguishing biological mothers of children from other women who care for children are often fluid and changing (Collins, 1994; p. 168). As we saw in the opening segment of this chapter, Dawn and her mother have a more collectivist orientation to parenting. Dawn's mother was raising one of her biological children, just as her grandmother had raised her. Grandmothers can also "mother."

I witnessed each of these three images among the women interviewed, both African American and white, although the supermom ideology emerged least often among both groups. Sometimes, these images occurred in conjunction with one another. Being a "good mother" involved different things to different women, but the common theme was putting children's needs first. Others report similar conclusions: like the more affluent, women on welfare adhere to the value placed on the importance of the family. Poor women usually place the highest priority on meeting the financial and emotional needs of their children (Berrick, 1995; Edin & Lein, 1997; Hays, 2003). Several of the women I interviewed bragged about not putting their children in daycare or turning them over to babysitters, especially those women who had young children who were not yet in school. Although many women simultaneously said that they wanted to work, they also praised the importance of staying home to care for their children. Being a "good mother" was the most important occupation of all. Becky, who is the mother of a four-year-old, commented about the guilt she felt at leaving her son with babysitters when she left the house for various housecleaning jobs:

> He cried when I left him in the morning, and I didn't like that. I felt like I should be home with him. I worked for about a year. It got too stressful—with trying to work and all the problems, and trying to, you know, be a good mother. So I gave up.

Working interfered with her attempts to fit the dominant cultural identity: To be a stay-at-home mother who devotes herself fully to her child's physical, emotional, and physical needs. But in this case there is no father or husband available to take care of their financial needs. She therefore turned to the state for aid.

When asked if she ever had a job, one African American woman curtly replied, "Yes, I take care of my children." Another told me that she felt no guilt in receiving welfare, "This is my paycheck," her remuneration for raising children. As Jarrett (1996) also found, our recipients believed that their ability to manage the challenges of single parenthood elevated their status. They proudly told me of nurturing and teaching young children, of helping older children with their school work, and of trying to keep their teenagers busy and out of trouble. They were hesitant to leave their children alone for any period of time. Most women and their children lived in sections of town with high crime rates. I was told that drug use and drug dealing was common in the large housing projects. Women did not trust their neighbors. Thus, being a "good mother" was defined by many as staying home to take care of their children themselves, including watching out the window for them to come home off the school bus safely. Although they said that they also wanted to work, women often saw their role first and foremost as providing direct care for their children. Being the family's breadwinner was secondary in importance.

This priority contradicts the changing norms regarding women's roles, as outlined in Chapter 2. Although programs like AFDC were originally created to allow single mothers the ability to stay home and raise their children, the norms about women's roles are in a state of flux. What does it mean to be a "good mother" in the twenty-first century? The old image of a stay-at-home mom in the kitchen, wearing an apron as she bakes cookies for her family, no longer fits the economic realities or personal inclinations of most families today. Most women have to, or want to, work outside the home. Our current ideologies suggest that you can be a "good mother" and also be employed. But, it is more difficult to be both a "good mother" and be employed when you are impoverished and therefore cannot buy the amenities that the more affluent families use in order to cope with dual demands. When you have no money for take-out fast food on the nights you are too tired to cook, when you must go to the laundromat twice a week because you cannot afford your own washer and dryer, when you have to leave young children home alone sometimes because you cannot always afford a babysitter or round up someone to watch them for free, and when you and your children must rely upon the bus for transportation because you cannot afford a reliable car and it takes two transfers to get where you are going, the glamour of both a career and motherhood begins to vanish. The stresses of being both a "good mother" and a full-time employee are compounded by not only poverty, but by being the sole parent—of having no one else to rely upon and share the burden and responsibilities.

Many of the tensions in the welfare debate revolve around our expectations of single mothers: should their priority be to earn a living, or should it be to provide direct physical and emotional care to their children? While the more affluent suggest that the former should now be the number one priority—that women who receive welfare should get a job—not all women on welfare see the issue so simply. Recognizing the dangers lurking in their neighborhoods, the stresses on children who have only one parent, and the restricted job opportunities and the subsequent low pay they will likely receive, it was common for women on welfare to, instead, glorify the virtues of motherhood rather than the virtues of full-time employment. This was particularly noted among those mothers with young children.

These four mechanisms for managing the stigma associated with welfare— (1) denial; (2) distancing; (3) blaming external forces; and (4) extolling motherhood— were commonplace. They occurred alone, or in combination with each other. Women used these strategies to regain a semblance of dignity and self-respect. They are well aware of the negative connotations associated with welfare use: that they are lazy, unmotivated, bad mothers, and that they have no desire to work or otherwise improve their economic circumstances. To keep from adopting these depictions, women on welfare invent ways to merge their "virtual" and "actual" social identities (Goffman, 1963).

Dawn, our previously introduced "stereotypical welfare mother," was very conscious of the stigma and negative sentiment surrounding women and families who receive welfare benefits. She coped with the stigma of welfare primarily by extolling the virtues of motherhood. She is proud of the fact that she stayed at home while her children were young—nurturing and socializing them. She shared "motherhood"—at least the care of her son—with her own mother. And she is a "good mother" herself. There is no ideological conflict here. Yet Dawn would probably evoke little empathy upon first glance. We are quick to blame her for her own predicament and wonder, "Why doesn't she go get a job?" We imply that she is lazy or not sufficiently motivated—she has been spoiled by welfare.

Yet our conversation revealed a depth and richness to her life and to her circumstances that are easily overlooked in the zealous quest to reform welfare. She told me of her appreciation and determination to one day be self-sufficient. Dawn wants to make it. Toward this goal, she attends school full-time to learn business and computer skills that she hopes will one day help her land a job as a secretary or an office manager. She is up at 6:30 A.M. every day, getting herself and her family organized for school. She has no car of her own, so makes the significant daily trek to school on the city bus.

> My grandmother, bless her heart. She was religious all her life. She died in subsidized housing. She didn't own nothing. She wasn't very educated, and I don't want to be like that. God knows I don't want to be like that. I want to have something to leave behind.

Dawn is 31 years old, has teenage children, and her youngest child is now 10. They are therefore more independent now and require less direct care from her. They can participate in cooking, cleaning and other chores so that Dawn may go to school. She feels that she's been on welfare too long already, but she insists that it has taken this long to get her family ready for her extended absences from home. She has been a "good mother," and is now ready for, and eagerly looks forward to, a life of employment. She hopes that by getting an education, she will be able to find more satisfying work, a job that she will stick with. She shares the same mainstream values as do many other Americans: education is important and will help you find a good job—but all in all, taking care of one's children is the most important job of all.

> I always say, "I don't want my kids to be like this." I was brought up as an AFDC kid. I feel like I've been on it all my life. I really do, and it's real depressing when you think about it. But I don't know. We might have been even poorer if it wasn't for it. It's not easy, and it's not much. I hear a lot of girls say, "They only give me this amount and I don't have enough to do this." But I don't feel like that. They're not supposed to be taking care of me. This is like a supplement. Appreciate what they give you. They don't owe us, you know? That's just how I feel about AFDC . . . That's why I'm trying to go to school and do this. I've put my mind to it. I know I've waited a long time. But I feel like I can still do this <get off welfare>.

CRITICAL THINKING QUESTIONS

1. How do you feel about Dawn? What feelings does her story evoke? How would your friends respond to her? How would your family respond to her?

2. What strategy or strategies did Dawn use to manage her stigma?

3. Have you ever personally experienced stigma? How did you feel? How did you respond? How did you manage the stigma? How might your experience be similar to, or different from, that of people on welfare?

4. What do you think about, and how do you feel, when you see someone ahead of you in line at a grocery store paying with food stamps?

5. Why would someone on welfare distance herself from other welfare recipients?

6. If a person said to you, "I'm on welfare but it's not my fault . . . " what would you think?

7. Women on welfare often extol the importance of motherhood. Do you think they do this more (or differently) from other women? If so, what ways are different and why are they different?

CHAPTER

4

Why Welfare?

Why do women use welfare? Given the stigma that surrounds welfare, and the negative perception of welfare mothers, we might wonder why women would choose to receive welfare. Perhaps they are lazy. Perhaps they lack motivation. Or do they seek welfare out of desperation?

As we saw in Chapter 3, women on welfare often disassociated themselves from other welfare recipients. They were critical of the reasons that other women received aid and often portrayed other recipients in a disparaging light. This chapter explores the reasons that women give for why they need welfare, and seeks to explain the discrepancy between these reasons and those they assign to other women. I found that recipients tend to attribute their own welfare use to circumstances that are largely beyond their control. When they told me why they needed welfare, they said things like, "there are no jobs"; "how can I take care of all my kids and work too?"; "I would be fine if he would just pay child support"; "I was raped"; "I was beaten and abused"; "he deserted us, and I'm trying to get my feet on the ground"; "I'm trying to better myself"; or "the welfare system penalizes me if I get a job." In the lives of women, these are not small or trivial reasons.

Like most women interviewed, Rhonda believes that she has little in common with other welfare recipients. She says that she knows many other women who receive welfare for their families whom they raise alone: her friends, her neighbors, and her son's father's family. She perceives that they "enjoy" being on welfare and "getting everything handed to them." But what about herself and her son? Why is she on welfare? She told me that her situation is entirely different; she elaborated on the circumstances that brought her to welfare: She can't find a permanent job and her son has a chronic medical condition. Exactly how is her situation different? Despite her belief that her circumstances are highly unusual, her story has a familiar ring.

Rhonda is a 28-year-old white woman with a 5-year-old son named Bobby, who is in kindergarten. She has been off and on welfare for four years since her son was born. Rhonda remains in contact with Bobby's father who lives out of state; he is a truckdriver and visits his son regularly once each month. During that visit, he will take

Bobby out, buy him clothes, and take him to dinner at McDonald's. He, however, does not pay child support. Rhonda and Bobby's father remain cordial, and she appreciates the monthly visits, clothing, and dinners for her son. She expects little else from Bobby's father, financially or otherwise, and receives little else.

Rhonda and her son's father never married. They were romantically involved, but the relationship ended shortly before Bobby was born. After the birth of her son, she lived with her mother briefly, but it was difficult having two families under one small roof. Rhonda wanted to be on her own, so she applied for welfare.

When I interviewed Rhonda, she and Bobby had recently moved from a trailer to an apartment within a subsidized housing project. They had lived there for six months, and she detested it. She told me neither she nor her son socializes with neighbors; they were abusive to him. She also believes that most of them are criminals, dependent on the system, and have no interest in "bettering themselves."

The apartment in which Rhonda and Bobby live is cramped, dingy, and rundown. There is no carpeting, just dark brown linoleum that is peeling in many places. Two chairs, one end table, and a television are about all that fit in her tiny living room. She stays in the projects because after losing her job, the $11 monthly rent is all she can afford. About $140 of her $241 welfare check goes for utilities because her apartment is poorly insulated. Heat and air conditioning (nearly a requirement in Florida's sweltering six-month summers) escapes through the windows and door cracks. After paying for car insurance ($22 a month), cleaning supplies, laundry soap, and other miscellaneous expenses, Rhonda has little money left over. When her budget permits, she buys clothes for her son who is growing rapidly, often from the Salvation Army or Goodwill. She has no opportunity to save money.

Rhonda does not see herself as dependent on the welfare system. During the four years she has been off and on welfare, she has held a variety of jobs. She has worked in the housekeeping department of a hospital, as a cashier, at a warehouse where she sorted lids for a printing company, and she recently ran a daycare center out of her home. She took great pride in her daycare center, and claimed it is her ideal job, and one that she would like to try again someday. She enjoys young children, although is quick to point out that she does not intend to have any more. Having children around the house taught her son Bobby responsibility, and her job did not take her away from Bobby for eight or nine hours a day. Like other women who were interviewed, and consistent with the views of women with greater financial means, an ideal job was seen as one that interfered as little as possible with her responsibilities as a single parent. Unfortunately, Rhonda was forced to close her daycare because many of her clients were considerably delinquent in paying their childcare bills. Unable to force them to pay the money they owed her, Rhonda wasn't able to keep up with her own bills, and thus was forced to close her business.

Rhonda told me that she "hates welfare." Then why is she receiving it? Like so many others before and after her, she told of having a very difficult time finding a permanent job that paid well enough for her to take care of her family. She had an easier time securing employment when she lived in Maryland. She moved to Florida to be near her sister and father, but has had a difficult time finding a full-time permanent job in a university town. Moreover, her job options are limited; Rhonda quit school in the tenth grade, eventually earning her GED after Bobby was born. She says she actively looks for work, but usually can only turn up temporary jobs that expire after several months. Rhonda told me that she desperately wants to work because she sees it as a ticket to a better life for her and Bobby. Since he's now enrolled in school she will not have to shell out the $200 a month for daycare as she used to do. A job, she believes, holds promise for a better life. She enthusiastically told me about a job lead she had from her sister. A nearby factory may be hiring over 20 new people, and she is hopeful that she will be one of them. She submitted her application last week. She knows that by securing a job, her rent will go up, her welfare check will be eliminated, and her food stamps will likely be significantly reduced. She acknowledges that these are "disadvantages" but she insists that she prefers "to be out working, meeting people, you know. Making it better for me and my son."

Rhonda sees herself as different from others on welfare. She described this difference to me:

> A lot of my friends are on welfare. But see, they enjoy getting the check, and I don't. They have a different view of welfare than I do. You know, they've been on it for 8 to 12 years, and I've only been on it for 4. They can go without things, and it don't bother them. Every time I go off welfare and go to work, it's like they condemn me for it. It's not easy going off and on. But it's like you got to face the real world. They don't look ahead. They haven't come to terms that they're going to cut welfare.

Rhonda is concerned about losing her medical benefits, however. As a welfare recipient she receives virtually free medical care for herself and Bobby. Finding a job that would provide medical benefits poses a challenge. But given Bobby's condition, medical benefits are of paramount importance, and she ranks them as her most critical welfare benefit. Bobby suffers from lead-paint poisoning. As a baby, he ingested paint peeling off a wall in a house they rented. Lead-paint poisoning is a serious and common problem in old, dilapidated structures that the poor often inhabit. An estimated 3 million poor children may be at risk of impaired physical and mental development related to ingesting lead-based paint flaking off the walls of older homes (Needleman, Schell, Bellinger, Leviton & Allred, 1990). Low-income preschoolers are three times more likely than children living in moderate-income families to have lead levels in their bloodstream of at least 10 micrograms of lead per deciliter of blood, a level at which harmful effects have been noted. Lead exposure damages the brain and central nervous system. Consequently, one study reported that second-grade children with high levels of lead in their bloodstream were six times more likely to have a reading disability, had significantly lower IQ rates, and lower scores on vocabulary tests. When researchers followed these children over time, they noted that the children were seven times more likely to drop out of high school (Children's Defense Fund, 1994). Bobby continues to suffer from the poisoning several years after ingesting it. He endures frequent pain, and during these episodes is lethargic and without an appetite. His flare-ups occur every few months, and physicians closely monitor him. He continues to be in and out of the hospital with regularity.

Despite what Rhonda may think, her situation is fairly typical. She receives no child support from her son's father. She has difficulty finding permanent work with pay sufficient to pull her above the level she would be at if she stayed home and received welfare. Moreover, a job necessitates that she will lose most of her welfare benefits, including Medicaid. Given the health problems in her family, losing medical benefits is a steep price to pay for a minimum-wage job. Despite her insistence that she will be off welfare very shortly, would we be surprised to find that she later returned to the system?

The truth is that Rhonda is on welfare more because of structural problems than personal shortcomings. She is not lacking in personal drive or initiative. Since having a baby, she has earned a GED and has opened her own business—fair accomplishments for someone who is the sole parent to a young child, a child with a serious illness. She describes one of her personal strengths as being "responsible. I've made accomplishments along the way." Rhonda ingeniously sought to combine work and motherhood so that she could excel at both, and neither would suffer. She struggled as a small business owner, as do many small business owners, until she was forced to close her business due to clients who refused to pay their bills. Rhonda is hardworking and is motivated to improve her circumstances in life. In these ways, she is quite typical of many women I met who receive welfare. Despite her thinking to the contrary, she was not the exceptional case.

As identified in Chapter 2, women on welfare, including Rhonda, largely point to two general explanations of their own use of welfare: They cite the problems inherent in our social structure, and they cite fate. Neither perspective focuses on the individual as much as on external forces largely outside of her control. A structural perspective attributes poverty and welfare use to economic or social imbalances that restrict opportunities for some people. Fatalism assumes that poverty and welfare use can be traced to bad luck, unpredictable quirks of human nature, or simply to chance. As we saw in Chapter 3, these explanations generally are not accorded to other welfare recipients. They are, however, used routinely by recipients to elucidate why they themselves receive aid.

The Influence of Social Structure

Women on welfare commonly attributed their reliance on welfare to problems and concerns related to the way our social structure is organized. Their concerns primarily revolved around (1) a lack of jobs paying a living wage; (2) the risk of losing health insurance; (3) lack of good-quality and affordable daycare; (4) lack of father involvement and child support enforcement; (5) inadequate transportation systems; (6) broader problems in our social structure, such as racism or sexism; and (7) a welfare system that penalizes women for initiative and eliminates their welfare benefits prematurely. Each of these concerns is discussed below. How many welfare critics think of all these hurdles when blithely putting down welfare recipients and welfare more generally?

Employment

Many women talked about the difficulty of finding employment, particularly a job that pays a living wage. Although the U.S. unemployment rate in February 2005 was a moderate 5.4 percent (U.S. Department of Labor, March 2005), many women told me of submitting application after application, to no avail. "You can't make someone hire you," they said. The reason for their difficulty becomes more apparent when we recognize that certain segments of the populations have extraordinarily high rates of unemployment, particularly young African Americans and other minority groups without a high school diploma. In February 2005, the unemployment among African American woman age 16 and over was 10.9 percent, over twice as high as among white women of the same age (4.6 percent) (U.S. Department of Labor, March 2005). Younger women, or those without a high school diploma, fare considerably worse. While the economy was strong in the mid-1990s when welfare reform was passed, many jobs were lost in the early 2000s. With higher rates of unemployment, it is not surprising that women have difficulty securing employment. Searching for work and coming up with nothing is a demoralizing experience. Consequently, some women quit looking for a job after many unsuccessful attempts.

One woman, Cassandra, told me of her frustration after applying for job after job with no luck at landing one. Her responsibilities related to caring for her home and her children were not considered legitimate work experience, even for service sector occupations. She described her frustration after applying for a job as a custodian.

> I even applied for custodial work at the University, and I know I'm qualified to sweep floors. And the lady even told me at the desk that I'd be competing with people who already have experience in this area. Now, I know I'm qualified to sweep floors. If I'm going to do it at home for free, I might as well get paid to do it.

Sarah is a white 30-year-old divorced mother who, after an extended job search, finally landed a part-time job at a fast-food franchise while also attending college in pursuit of an AA degree. She commented on her difficulty in finding even minimum-wage work. She has many years of experience, including as a manager in the fast-food industry. She wondered if her difficulty in finding work was due to the fact that she has been on Workmen's Compensation, and therefore was viewed as a high risk by potential employers. However, too many others voiced similar complaints for her case to be an isolated incident.

> It is very hard to find a job. Because people are picky and some of these places, you'll only get a job if you know someone. I spent a year looking for a job, and Colonel Sanders was the first place to hire me. I've gone places, because when you are on Workmen's Comp you have to fill out a list every month, and how many jobs you've applied in. I've applied for 20 to 100 a month. And this was the first place that even

contacted me in a year. It's not that I'm not qualified. I've had six years of management.

Moreover, when women do find work, most are employed in service-sector jobs, such as the fast-food industry, which generally pay minimum wage and offer no fringe benefits, such as health insurance. Fast-food franchises such as Wendy's, McDonald's, Burger King, Hardee's, and several others offer the most recurrent avenues of employment to women on welfare. They generally do not require a high school diploma or extensive experience. Yet despite their possibilities, these jobs do not pay enough to support a family or even pull them above the poverty line. At $5.15 an hour, the national minimum wage, working 40 hours per week yields less than $900 a month before taxes. Working 52 weeks a year, an employee would average around $10,700 per year. For even the smallest families who have only one child, living and surviving on minimum wage poses a challenge. Recognizing this, 12 states have set higher minimum-wage rates (U.S. Department of Labor, December 2004). However, in 2004 3 percent of hourly-paid employed African American and Hispanic women still earned $5.15 per hour or less (U.S. Department of Labor, April, 2005). About three in four workers earning $5.15 or less in 2004 were employed in service occupations, mostly in food service jobs.

Yet many women were eager to take on the challenge of finding work. They told me that they want to work, and enthusiastically told me about leads or tips that they had heard regarding which businesses were hiring, and at how much pay. Although most women did not shun minimum-wage jobs, jobs that paid $8 an hour or more were highly sought after. Women felt confident that they could live on the nearly $16,000 a year that such jobs would provide. Several women told me that they heard the postal service might be hiring—the postal service is notorious for paying "good money." Three other women told me about jobs in the nearby jails or prisons that also offer wages substantially higher than minimum wage.

> They are hiring and so I want to submit my application for this corrections job. They pay five dollars an hour to start out with the training. Then, when you get past the correctional course, then you go to the prison and you start working. But they don't pay five dollars an hour for being a correctional officer. They pay more than that. They pay you about nine or ten dollars an hour! Plus benefits. See, I'm looking for where the money is at!

In 1997, as welfare reform was implemented, there were 3,100 welfare recipients, in the region in Florida in which the interviews were conducted, on the list to move from welfare to work. One year later, the figure had dropped to about 2,000. The welfare rolls had been reduced. Some women found jobs, but there was no tracking system to find out if and where those individuals are still working, according to Richard Cunningham, Chair of the WAGES (Work and Gain Economic Self-sufficiency—Florida's welfare reform law) Coalition, which was responsible for implementing WAGES in the area (Chandler, January 8, 1998). It is easy to reduce the number of people on welfare; simply make them ineligible for benefits after two or three years, as federal law now mandates. In this sleight of hand, statistics can be pulled out and dangled to the public showing that welfare use, and presumably poverty, has declined. This, however, is incorrect. A study in Michigan found that by the fall of 2001, only one-quarter of TANF-leavers were working in good jobs, defined as full-time jobs that pay at least $7 per hour and offer health insurance, or full-time jobs that do not offer health insurance but pay at least $8.50 an hour (Johnson & Cochrane, 2003). Another study in Philadelphia found that the share of women who worked full-time in jobs that paid at least $7.50 per hour and offered health benefits increased between 1998 and 2001, but that only about two in five working women held such a job in 2001 (Michalopoulous et al., 2003). Indeed, one study with a national sample of women leaving TANF found that 42 percent remained poor five years after leaving welfare (Cancian, Haveman, Kaplan, Meyer & Wolfe, 2002). Explored more fully in Chapter 8, we see that the true extent of poverty will not decline until the poor are paid higher wages for the work that they do, and until working conditions change significantly to provide stable, reliable employment complete with critical fringe benefits.

The Risk of Losing Health Insurance

Concern about losing Medicaid was commonly expressed. Medicaid is a program designed to pay the health care costs of the poor. Not all poor are eligible for Medicaid, however. Like other welfare benefits, Medicaid has specific eligibility requirements, some of which are established at the state level. Each state is required to extend Medicaid to recipients of Aid to Families of Dependent Children (AFDC), and now Temporary Assistance to Needy Families (TANF), and to recipients of Supplemental Security Income (SSI), which covers the impoverished elderly and the disabled. However, it is up to state discretion whether to cover others who are impoverished, such as the homeless or the working poor. Medicaid benefits are a primary reason why women stayed on welfare as long as they have. If they leave welfare, they risk joining the ranks of the uninsured. According to estimates from the 2003 Medical Expenditure Panel Survey (MEPS-HC), 18.8 percent of people under age 65, or 47 million people, have no insurance (Rhoades, 2004). At least 52 million people were uninsured for at least part of the year (Cohen & Ni, 2004). About three-quarters of these individuals are employed or are the dependents of an employed adult, usually working at a low-wage, part-time, or temporary position. Over ten million of the uninsured are children under age 15.

It is well documented that persons without health insurance or with inadequate insurance use the health care system less frequently than do others, resulting in a variety of negative health outcomes (Hadley, 2003). The uninsured are more likely than both privately and publicly insured individuals to lack a usual source of care; to have fewer episodes of inpatient hospital care and lack preventive services; and to report delays in receiving health care. They typically seek care at hospital emergency rooms, which are increasingly turning people away and transferring the most serious cases to public hospitals. The uninsured are twice as likely to postpone seeking medical care, over four times as likely to forgo needed medical care, and are more than twice as likely to have a needed prescription go unfilled (Kaiser Commission on Medicaid and the Uninsured, 2003). Consequently, without health insurance, adults and children are more likely to experience unnecessary pain, suffering, disability, and death. Women on welfare know this. They fear joining the ranks of the uninsured or under-insured if they were to take a job.

Stephanie, in school to become a Registered Nurse, echoed this concern with losing Medicaid. Her daughter has several specific health problems:

> We gripe and we gripe about the fact that we are paying all this money for people who don't seem to be doing very much for themselves, but if you looked at the system from an insider's point of view, you would see that there are actually penalties built into the system for a person with initiative, going out to get a job, or doing something to try to bet-ter themselves. As soon as you earn a buck, they take it away from you. You are penalized if you have any kind of asset whatsoever. You have to be so damn poor that it's not even funny. . . . Next summer in nursing school there are no classes. Yet I can't work. And I will tell you why. I would like to work as a nurse's aide, and that is something I can do with my training that I have had. But I can't afford to lose my benefits, specif-ically my medical benefits. Because if I went to work, they would cut me off. Even though I would not be making enough to pay my bills, I would be cut off from Medicaid. And I can't afford that, you know? It's part-time. Usually a nurse's aide gets five–six dollars an hour, which is not that much above minimum wage. And you know, you work 20 or 30 hours a week. No health benefits, no nothing. So I can't work. It's not that I don't want to work. I'd love to work. But I can't.

Respondents in the Oregon study also considered health insurance to be im-portant to their families and worry about being uninsured. Of all welfare benefits, in-cluding food stamps, the TANF check, Oregon Health Plan (OHP), subsidized housing, or other benefit, respondents considered that OHP was the most important benefit that they received (Seccombe, Hartley, Newsom, Pope & Hoffman, 2005). This is indeed telling; respondents report that health benefits are more important to them than the TANF check itself. Moreover, 94 percent evaluated health insurance as of great importance to their family. Likewise, virtually all respondents who had lost their health insurance expressed concern about being uninsured.

Kelly is a case in point. She has Tourette's Syndrome, and is also being treated for Parkinson's disease, and obsessive-compulsive and bipolar disorders. Her son is also being treated for attention-deficit/hyperactivity. She worries about her future without insurance and his ability to care for her.

> It's really scary. For me, the only thing that I do worry about is . . . what's going to happen to me? Am I going to be able to get my medications? Am I going to be able to take care of myself? I know my kids would help me out, but why make it harder for your kids to have to deal with somebody

with mental health problems that can't take their medicine. I think about what kind of burden that's going to put on my kids or my community. That's kind of scary.

Childcare

The question of who will care for children is one of the most pressing and perplexing questions of our time. If we expect poor single mothers to be employed, who then will care for, socialize, nurture, discipline, play with, teach, and love their children? And, how much will this cost, both financially and socially? "There is no more important job than raising a child," claimed former President Clinton, as he insisted that parents should not have to choose between their jobs and their children. In 1998, he proposed a record investment in childcare—$22 billion over five years to make care more affordable, accessible, and safe. The money was requested to help parents and businesses pay for care through tax credits; to improve the quality of care by giving states money to improve safety inspections, conduct research, and provide scholarships to students training to be childcare workers; to expand Head Start programs to low-income youngsters, including doubling to 80,000 the number of infants and toddlers in a new program called Early Head Start; and to increase the availability of after-school care (Enda, January 8, 1998).

Recent studies confirm the importance of childcare to working women. A study of TANF recipients in Michigan found that women who received a childcare subsidy worked 50 percent longer than did women without a subsidy and earned more than double in wages (Danziger, Ananat & Browning, 2004). A national study found that 28 percent of TANF leavers who did not receive child care assistance returned to welfare within three months, compared to only 19.5 percent of welfare leavers who received assistance (Loprest, 2003).

Concern over the lack of safe and affordable childcare emerged as a common structural reason for why women turned to, or remained on, welfare. They know that children need more than custodial care in large and crowded daycare centers in order to thrive. Yet, for most poor and working-class families, childcare is often patched together in a fashion that leaves mothers anxious. Some told me that they did not feel comfortable leaving their children with strangers and preferred to depend on other family members. National data from the Survey of Income and Program Participation (SIPP) reveal that 53 percent of children whose mothers work and also receive AFDC are taken care of by a relative (usually a grandparent), 17 percent are taken care of by a nonrelative in a family-based care setting, and 20 percent are cared for in formal daycare settings (Burns, Ballew, Yi & Mountford, 1996). A significantly higher number of AFDC mothers who have childcare needs rely on relatives than do other low-income single mothers (53 percent versus 37 percent, respectively). While extended families are the preferred childcare provider, women acknowledged that their mothers, sisters, or other relatives could not always be counted on. They have their own family responsibilities and obligations, and cannot always provide daycare when needed. Living in high-density and high crime areas, they worried about the safety of their children in daycare centers or with other babysitters that they did not know well: "I'm not going to leave him with someone I don't know until he's old enough to tell me what happened." And they worried about the psychological effects of inadequate care—crowded, dirty, or impersonal conditions—upon their children. These concerns have largely been overlooked in quantitative studies that simply focus on the availability of daycare—are there enough daycare slots for the children who need them? These in-depth interviews reveal that an important reason that women elect to receive welfare rather than work is that they do not trust the care of their children to strangers. The availability of daycare slots is not the primary consideration, rather, it is the quality of daycare that is most imperative.

Moreover, mothers worried about the cost of daycare. Unless a program within the welfare office subsidized childcare, costs for childcare ranging from $400 to $800 a month, depending on the type of care provided. This could come to half of a full-time paycheck, obviously making paying for childcare an impossibility. The dilemma prompted many women to comment, "I had to quit—the money went to the babysitter." Childcare costs vary dramatically across the country, with costs in many communities in Florida being well below average costs in other communities, yet still beyond the reach of most poor and low-income families. On average, full-day childcare costs in a day care facility can cost over $10,000 a year per child (Schulman, 2000), which is higher than the costs of college tuition.

Moreover, Rhonda, who has a GED, reminded us that jobs in the service sector required evenings and weekend hours when childcare might not be available. Her son Bobby is only five years old, far too young to remain at home alone at night while she works.

> My hardest problem is—I can find a job—it's trying to work around my son. On weekends I ain't got nobody on weekends to watch him. Like my sister, she's busy with her own kids. And my dad, he's kind of a senior citizen, you know. And that's the only problem I have. It's like they always want nights and weekends. See I can do days while he's in school, you know. It's hard.

Research shows that Rhonda's concerns are well-founded (Presser, 2003; Presser & Cox, 1997). Women with only high school diplomas or less are disproportionately found working irregular schedules that include night and weekend shifts, and varying hours. Forty-three percent of women with a high school education or less, work at least some weekend days or have varying shifts, compared with 36 percent of women who have more than a high school education. Most women do not work these schedules out of personal inclination, but because these are the required working conditions of their jobs, such as cashiers, maids, nursing aids, cooks, and waitresses. Moreover, these occupations are likely to grow in the future. Working in these types of jobs has important implications for the availability and costs of formal childcare. It also affects the degree to which family, friends, and neighbors are able to provide childcare. Sociologists Harriet Presser and Amy Cox reveal:

To the extent that mothers who receive AFDC do not wish to work during nonstand-ard times, but find that it is their only job opportunity, many will have to find child-care arrangements that are complex and far from optimal. Reliance on grandmothers and other family members may be an option, but these relatives are often themselves employed, leading to complex split-shift arrangements that may be stressful or tempo-rary only. For mothers who have school-aged children, school cannot function as an alternative to childcare. Furthermore, the little we know about the availability of for-mal childcare during nonstandard times suggests that it is a rare option. Moreover, formal childcare during nonstandard times is likely to be more expensive than during standard times. In sum, the childcare issue is clearly problematic (Presser & Cox, 1997, pp. 32–33).

Childcare is not simply an issue for mothers of young children. Mothers with older, school-age children also face considerable dilemmas about how to juggle em-ployment and parental responsibilities. Low-income children are less likely to live in neighborhoods that have before- and after-school programs and are less likely to en-gage in after-school enrichment programs such as sports, clubs, or lessons (Fields, Smith, Bass & Lugaila, 2001). Yet these programs have been shown to help low-in-come students perform better academically, and they help improve student conduct and study habits (Posner & Vandell, 1994).

Some mothers interviewed suggested that parenting is more time-consuming and labor-intensive as children become teenagers. Peer pressure is strong, including pressure to act out and behave in destructive ways. They feared that their children would get into trouble with the law; that they might use, abuse, or sell drugs; that they may get pregnant or impregnate others; or that they may drop out of school. Mothers interviewed here, as well as those responding to nationwide studies, clamored for more organized activities for their school-aged children (Center for Research on Women, 1996; Meyers & Kyle, 1996). Moreover, because they are the sole parent to their children, they have no one to share the burden and responsibilities of childcare. They do not have a spouse, and generally they cannot rely upon the father of their children for assistance or relief from their duties.

Women on welfare juggle their employment and parental responsibilities in a variety of ways, but one aspect was very clear: their children are more important than any specific job. Their jobs were seen as "work"; they were not careers with the degree of commitment that careers entail. While "work" was considered im-portant psychologically and financially, under no circumstances should it interfere significantly with family responsibilities. Their first and foremost responsibility was perceived as being a "good mother" to their children. So how do women on wel-fare reconcile being good mothers with working? Many women did not want to work before their children were in preschool. Some women refused work that en-tailed weekends when their children were out of school. Others preferred to work the night shift so that they could be home in the afternoons to help their children with their homework after school. Some women wanted to work in the afternoons so that they could get their children up and off to school. Others insisted that they could only work part-time so that they could be available to their children in the morning and at night. And finally, other women pursued or dreamed of work that allowed them to stay at home, such as Rhonda's childcare center, or several other women's stated desire to be cosmetologists working out of their home. The structure of the desired workday or setting may differ significantly, but the underlying theme is that work should be built around their family schedule and important family events, rather than vice versa. This, however, is not easily accomplished.

One woman, Cassie, revealed a strong preference for working the night shift, leaving her children home alone at night despite the fact that they are only twelve, nine, eight, and six years of age. Although some people might abhor the thought of leaving children this young alone at night, she saw it as the best possible alternative because it allowed her to spend her days with them. She further explained that her oldest daughter had experience getting the kids up and ready for school. All her children chip in with chores and are very responsible.

> I'd rather work at night. I could be home with my kids when they get home from school. Yeah, I'd have the whole afternoon to be with them. It's from 12 midnight to eight. And at midnight I'd be gone to work, I'd come home at eight and get me some sleep. And when they come home I'll be fresh and ready to go again. . . . My daughter was getting them up when I worked at XXX <fast food franchise>, and she was not but nine. Eight or nine. I had to be at work at six o'clock in the morning, so I would call home and she would be up, and everybody would be up and ready to go to school. I taught her to help me, and that's what she's been doing.

Fathers' Involvement

A third structural problem cited was the lack of involvement on the part of the children's fathers. Fathers' participation in the emotional or financial upbringing of their children was noticeably absent in the vast majority of cases I interviewed. Absentee fathers represent a growing and alarming national trend. How frequently a father will visit his noncustodial children depends on many factors, including whether the child was born out of wedlock, the child's age, race and ethnic background, mother's level of education, and family income. Using data from the 1999 National Survey of American Families, Koball & Principe (2002) found that about two-thirds of children who were born out of wedlock reported having seen their father at least once during the previous year, compared with about 80 percent of those children who were born to married parents; (2) Hispanic children are the least likely to have seen their fathers during the previous year; (3) children who have mothers with higher levels of education are more likely to have seen their fathers; and (4) children who live in families with higher incomes are more likely to have visited with their fathers during the previous year.

As described more thoroughly in Chapter 6, since 1988 the government has stepped up its efforts to enforce court-ordered child support with the passage of the Family Support Act (PL 100-485). Yet, of the 13.4 million custodial single parents in 2002, only 59 percent had some type of legal or nonlegal support agreement for their children. Reasons for the failure to have a support agreement include sentiments such as "did not feel the need to make it legal" (33 percent), "other parent pays what they can" (26 percent), "other parent could not afford to pay" (23 percent), "did not want other parent to pay" (19 percent) (Grall, 2003).

To receive cash assistance, federal law requires recipients to assign their support rights to the state (Rowe & Russell, 2004) They must cooperate with the state in establishing paternity of a child born outside of marriage, and in obtaining child support payments. The women I interviewed were required to report the name and whereabouts of the fathers of their children, if known, when they signed up for welfare. When the children's fathers did pay child support, the money went to the welfare agency, and mothers were given an additional $50 per month in their check. This $50 is disregarded in benefit calculations, and is designed to serve as an incentive to provide information on the children's fathers to the welfare agency, just in case women are reluctant to do so.

Yet, despite the mandatory ruling that fathers be identified, the apparent eagerness of women to comply with this ruling, and the welfare agency's supposed vigorous search for the fathers, most women interviewed continued to received no, or very sporadic, child support. Some women resented this, in particular, the freedom that their children's fathers have, while they are stigmatized for receiving welfare. A divorced African American mother who received welfare for her two children responded typically to my question about whether she received child support.

> No, I don't. And with my ex-husband, he was court-ordered to pay child support. He works. But I don't get child support from him. They have money—they can go out and buy themselves cars and they can save money in the bank, but they're not supporting their kids. And I don't like it. I don't think the government should have to take care of a man's kids, especially if he can take care of his own kids. I don't understand it. They are so hard on us, but where is my child support? My kids deserve that money.

She and many others acknowledged that mothers on welfare are stigmatized for caring for their children, whereas fathers are rarely stigmatized for their failure to support their children.

Likewise, Pearl summarized the sentiment of many when she expressed that their father's resistance to paying child support has cheated her children. She is a 48-year-old African American woman who is divorced. Pearl has eight children, three of whom still reside in the home and receive welfare. They live in the housing projects where she has lived for 25 years. Pearl's life has been hard. She only finished the eighth grade of school, quitting so that she could work as a farm laborer and help support her siblings. She's been married twice, divorced because of her husbands' continual infidelity. She has worked on and off for most of her life—hard jobs, such as farm laborer and housecleaner. Now alone, she dreams about taking her younger children out of the projects to live in the country where she envisions a safer life for them, free from the pressures of drugs and dropping out of school. The likelihood of her dream materializing is extremely slim. She complained of health problems, and has not held a job in many years. The father of her oldest children is in prison, as are her two oldest sons. The father of the youngest children previously contributed to their support, but quit paying child support a few years prior to this interview. He remarried: "He figured he got a new wife and shouldn't have to pay," she told me. Pearl continued:

> All my kids' daddies owe child support. I used to talk to their daddies about that. I said, well, if you would have been willing to help take care of your kids, they would have had a living and wouldn't have had to been on welfare.

In Chapter 6, I elaborate on the reasons that child support enforcement policies have met with limited success and have not significantly reduced the number of children in poverty. Until the dismal trends in child support are altered through stricter enforcement, and through changing norms of greater paternal involvement, it will be very difficult for many women to fully support their children on their own without additional assistance.

Transportation

It also became clear in the interviews that transportation was a major structural barrier to women getting or keeping jobs. Past recipients of JOBS programs report that the lack of affordable transportation presents a barrier even more serious than the lack of childcare to securing employment (Kaplan, 1998). Women on welfare cannot afford to buy reliable automobiles. Those few women who owned newer models likely received them as gifts from family members or boyfriends. Often, they did not put the car in their name, hiding it from the welfare office even if they were the sole driver, because it would jeopardize their welfare benefits. The personal asset value of an automobile (value minus debt) varies by state, but in several states it cannot be worth more than $4,650 before it is counted against eligibility for assistance (U.S. Department of Health and Human Services, November, 2004). This poses a dilemma for a rational person—how can I find and maintain a respectable job, if I am not allowed to have reliable (e.g., more expensive) transportation? Most women who had cars, even those exceeding the maximum asset level, owned older models that were in a constant state of disrepair. Many cars guzzled gas. Car maintenance is expensive. One woman explained that her car, although a necessity in many respects, also assisted in keeping her poor: "It's either your tires, or extra gas, or a part tearing up on your car. No, I can never really get caught up." Obviously, women on welfare are not driving Cadillacs.

Public transportation and walking are the primary alternatives to the private automobile. While public transportation is available in the largest community in the area in which the interviews were conducted, women complained that it was expensive (one dollar, plus an additional 25 cents per transfer), unreliable, and inconvenient. They reported long waits and complained that they had to wait even longer to transfer to a second bus to get to their destination. Bus service was reduced or eliminated on weekends or at night. Moreover, even with all its logistical problems, public transportation was completely unavailable in some of the smaller communities within the county.

Bicycling or walking was the primary mode of transportation for some women. Tamela, a 23-year-old African American woman with two young children told me how she used to put them in a wagon and walk to the grocery store and to do other errands. But communities built since the 1950s are often spread out, not geared toward pedestrians or public transportation systems, but geared instead toward private automobile ownership. A strong, central, vibrant downtown area for work, shopping, and entertainment are memories of a bygone era in most communities. Instead, numerous strip malls are spread throughout the city limits and fringe areas. Sidewalks may not exist, traffic whizzes by at 45 or more miles per hour, and without a central core, walking, bicycling, or relying on public transportation becomes difficult. While offhand it is easy to say, "You can walk to work," reality may dictate something else. In many communities, walking to work can be more than just inconvenient, it can be dangerous or impractical. Walking through high crime neighborhoods or crossing highways, especially at night, poses special dangers. Walking can add an hour or two to childcare bills, and may necessitate being away from one's children for 9, 10, or 11 hours a day instead of the usual 8. Moreover, in inclement weather, such as heavy rains or snow, it is impractical to expect women to walk for miles and still appear freshly groomed and ready for work. Life without a car is difficult in most cities and towns in the United States. Even with the best intentions, it is not surprising that women without cars find it difficult to maintain steady work (Seccombe, Hartley, Newsome, Pope & Hoffman, 2005).

Several women revealed to us elaborate transportation logistics that allowed them to work or go to school, including commutes of an hour to an hour and a half each way. One African American mother, Dee, who is studying to become an accountant, lives five miles from campus and described her transportation ordeal using the city bus:

> I leave here by 6:45 to get to school at 8:00. So that's an hour and 15 minutes. I leave school at 2:00 to get home by 4:00, so that's 2 hours. So that's 3 hours and 15 minutes I spend. If I had a car I could leave here at 7:30 and be there by 8:00. And then I have three-hour breaks in between so I could be home relaxing or doing something.

Transportation problems prevent many women from seeking work altogether, and they inhibit other women from staying at their job. Several women told me that they quit otherwise "good" jobs because of inadequate transportation schemes. When they worked at night, after the buses stopped running, they were forced to rely on friends, family, or a taxicab service for rides home after work. Friends and family, although well meaning, were sometimes unreliable. Taxis were expensive. Consequently, the risk of job failure increases, often becoming an inevitability. Many might ask, why try?

> I just had a job in September where I worked six days. But I had to quit my job because I had to pay transportation. And transportation was costing me, like $40 a week. Sometimes at night it was difficult because the shift that I was working was three to twelve—three in the afternoon to twelve at night. And a lot of people don't want to get up and come get you. So, I had to quit the job because of the transportation costs that I had to pay.

In this instance, and several others like it, a recipient sought work despite the obstacles, explored alternative transportation with some optimism, and finally quit for personal economic reasons.

Women in Oregon were more likely to own their own cars, although they were often breaking down and caused considerable stress to their owners. Rates of car ownership for rural respondents ranged between 60 to 80 percent, as compared to about 40 percent in the metro area. For those respondents that did not own cars in the rural areas, or whose cars are unreliable, there are few options. Public transportation is nearly non-existent, thereby forcing people to prioritize buying a car despite their economic situation, to rely on friends and family for rides. A number of the respondents reported that family members or friends had to step in to help out with transportation if necessary, as Kristin expresses, "My car is my lifeline, and it is not going to last much longer, and I don't know what I am going to do . . . thank goodness for Grandma and Grandpa." But as another woman, Javita, was quick to point out, depending on others has limitations: "If you don't have a car you're completely dependent on someone else, which isn't that secure."

People who have always had reliable personal automobiles often overlook the magnitude of this issue for many would-be workers. Growing urban sprawl increases the likelihood of distance to the workplace, and therefore reduces the likelihood of regularly getting to a job without a personal automobile.

Racism and Sexism

Racism and sexism are unpleasant realities in our polarized society. The famous tennis star, Authur Ashe, before he died of AIDS in 1993, disagreed with a reporter who assumed that AIDS must be the heaviest burden he has ever had to bear. "No, it isn't," Ashe told the reporter. "Being black is the greatest burden I've had to bear. Having to live as a minority in America . . . because of what we as a people have experienced historically in America, and what we as individuals experience each and every day" (Ashe & Rampersad, 1994, pp. 139–141). Likewise, the social construction of gender permeates all aspects of life, and people continually distinguish between males and females and evaluate them differently. It is difficult to escape both racism and sexism.

Racism and sexism generally have three components: (1) negative attitudes toward minority group members or toward women; (2) stereotypical beliefs that reinforce, complement, or justify the prejudice, and (3) discrimination—acts that exclude, distance, or segregate minorities or women (Lott, 1994). All these problems can be blatant or more subtle. Blatant racism and sexism can take the form of not being hired in the first place, being passed over for a job promotion or a pay raise, or being fired prematurely. A few African American women told us directly that racism had hindered their ability to get, or keep, a good-paying job. One woman spoke of her neighbor in the housing project who "has a problem with, excuse my language, white people. They did her real bad."

Racism and sexism can also be more subtle, and this form is sometimes referred to as "institutional" racism or sexism. Patterns of inequality may be woven into the fabric of society, so that it becomes institutionalized, or normative. It may be imbedded in our culture or our social policy. It often goes unnoticed, and when pointed out, sometimes people will fail to grasp its significance. For example, job opportunities for women are limited in ways that men's generally are not, in part due to structural barriers, but also due to the ways women are socialized. Women may not seek training in the higher-paying skilled trades, for example, because they have been taught that these are unfeminine occupations.

Stephanie, a 26-year-old mother who is in the nursing program at the university, explicitly acknowledged that sexism as well as racism were likely to limit opportunities for social mobility. She is the mother of one young daughter and is attuned to issues of social inequality. Like many of the women I interviewed, she was married when she had her daughter, and assumed that her marriage would last forever. Instead, after a painful divorce, her husband has never once paid child support or contacted his daughter.

> Why are people on welfare? There have to be at least a thousand reasons why people are on welfare. Like I tell my daughter, life isn't fair. Things happen. And you have to do the best you can. There are lots of socioeconomic groups in this country, races, blacks, Hispanics, women who don't really have the same opportunities that most people consider normal opportunities. I mean, for myself, look who got stuck taking care of the child?

The Welfare System Breeds "Dependence" on the System

Finally, a recurring theme in the narratives was that the welfare system itself is responsible for their reliance on welfare. A few respondents felt that the welfare system can indeed make people get lazy, and lose their motivation to work, as some social conservatives have argued. A 29-year-old African American woman with three children who has been on and off the system repeatedly said:

> Sometimes I think people get a little too satisfied with it and stay on it a little longer than they should. Once you start getting this check the way we do, you get a little lazy sometimes.

However, the majority of women who expressed concerns with the welfare system did not say that it made recipients lazy per se, but claimed that the welfare system had built-in disincentives or penalties for work. Working, especially at minimum-wage jobs that usually lack health insurance and other critical benefits, would not achieve their goals of self-sufficiency, and in fact would jeopardize the health and well-being of their children because they would lose critically needed benefits. Moreover, as good mothers they said they would never want to jeopardize their children's well-being. From these interviews, it became clear that without continued assistance with (a) health insurance; (b) childcare; (c) transportation; (d) food stamps; and (e) subsidized housing, working not only becomes prohibitive, but sometimes was seen as downright dangerous. Many women claimed that they want to work, or that they could find a job, or even that they had a job previously, but felt compelled to quit because working, and the automatic reduction in their welfare benefits, actually lowered their standard of living or jeopardized their children's health. They expressed frustration that the welfare system, as currently structured, actually discourages them from working by raising their rent, eliminating Medicaid, and cutting them off from needed social services before they had a chance to establish themselves. Jo Lynn, a mother of two young children claimed:

> I've had a job before, and I know I can get a job. It's just really hard. It's like, I got a job at Hardee's (fast food franchise), and I had a friend take me back and forth. I was paying her 20 dollars a week for gas. I got off the system. I was honest about it and told them I had a job. They took my assistance away, and they raised my rent 200 dollars. And they said they weren't going to give me any Medicaid for them either, and I didn't have any health insurance. I had a baby at the time, and she was only a year old. She had to go to the periodic appointments and stuff, and I was like, "Okay, well I'm going to try to do it." And I had to work there six months to a year to get health insurance. I was really scared, like, what am I going to do? But I'm gonna do it. So I started doing it, and then I started realizing that, you know, that after about two months, I was *under* the welfare level. I mean, by making minimum wage I couldn't keep my bills up, and I could never afford to take her to the doctor. It wasn't getting me ahead. I was being penalized for trying to get off the system, and it's happened to all my friends that are on welfare. It's like a trap, and they don't help.

Jo Lynn did what our society expects of welfare mothers—she found a job. But with that job, her financial picture became even more bleak. She told me it caused her to be "under the welfare level." Jo's situation was not an isolated case. Therefore, without considerable change in the welfare system and the structure of low-tier work, what hope is there for her, and for other mothers trying to get off welfare?

Patrice is mother of two who works part-time as a nurse's aide, but continues to receive a partial welfare benefit, explains how her benefits were reduced when she began to work:

> The thing that gets me, being a single parent, once my income exceeds a certain amount, I'm in a project, and my rent goes up. It has been close to $300 for this <she laughs and sweeps her arms around the room.>

And then I have to end up paying expensive childcare, and the Medicaid stops for me and my children. You know, most jobs the health insurance is so expensive you can't afford it. Then, you pretty much be where you started from. You end up with nothing.

These interviews, which are grounded in the real-world receipt of welfare, suggest that the presumed link between social programs and welfare dependency touted by social conservatives is flawed. Yes, on a cursory glance, the welfare system does appear to reduce one's incentive to work, but a more thorough examination from an *insider's perspective* reveals that welfare programs do not encourage laziness or dependency. Both white and African American women talked about desperately wanting to work, but felt that employment reduced their already meager standard of living and often placed their children at risk because it eliminated or reduced their eligibility for critical medical and social services. They repeatedly pleaded that the welfare system be changed so as to not penalize them by cutting them off of critically needed services, at least temporarily, while they "pull themselves up by their bootstraps." Rather than being lazy or dependent on the system, they are making the most rational, intelligent choice they can, given their circumstances. These issues will be revisited in Chapter 8, when I further examine the obstacles to getting off welfare.

In sum, these women frequently cited concerns related to the social structure when explaining their welfare use. Problems with finding inexpensive or reliable childcare; a scarcity of jobs, particularly those that pay a livable wage; lack of father involvement with their children and ineffective child support policies; inadequate public transportation systems; racism and sexism; and a welfare system that prematurely reduces income and benefits were all recognized as factors that inhibited their upward social mobility.

Fatalism

Bad luck, poor health, and soured relationships—many women alluded to these when asked to explain why they are on welfare. They felt that they simply couldn't help it; they turned to welfare as a way out of a desperate, unplanned, and unfortunate situation.

Bad Luck

For example, many discussed their bad luck at becoming pregnant. Several who were unmarried teenage girls when they had their first child, told me that they were surprised at becoming pregnant—they didn't know that sexual activity caused pregnancy, or they didn't know that they could get pregnant the first time they had sexual intercourse. They were confused and unknowledgeable about sex. Many disclosed that they had intercourse as a way to please a boyfriend, or because of peer pressure from their girlfriends at school or in their neighborhoods. They rarely used birth control. Either they didn't know it was necessary, or their partner complained about wearing a condom, and they acquiesced to his wishes. When they discovered they were pregnant, they were surprised. How did this happen? Abortion was rarely a consideration among the women interviewed. Instead, these young girls accepted that they somehow got caught, and had their babies.

Terri Lynn, the young mother previously introduced who works at the bowling alley to support herself and her six-year old son, told me of her surprise at becoming pregnant. She did well in high school, and never suspected that it would happen to her.

> Sure, I don't want to be on AFDC, but I don't have a choice. You know, I didn't plan to get pregnant with him, but it just happened. You know? I don't want to be on AFDC. I'm going to get off it as soon as I put him in school.

An African American woman with four children commented on the bad luck that young women have in their encounters with young men. Her attitude indicated that teenage pregnancies are unfortunate, but that not much can be done about it. It's acceptable, or at least unavoidable. Her greater concern is with women who have multiple births out of wedlock, but having one child "just happens":

> I know a first baby is a mistake. You know what I'm saying? It happens. You go out there, you young, you have sex. It's a mistake. I mean, they got birth control methods, but guys are so persuasive about sex these days. Girls don't think about rubbers or birth control. They just think about impressing him, so they have sex. So they get pregnant. If they keep having babies, then they should get a job and help support the rest of those kids, but not the first child.

As both women allude to, peer pressure to have sex is powerful, and difficult to avoid. One recent study involving 1,000 girls in Atlanta found that 82 percent said the subject they wanted to learn most about in their sex education class was "how to say no without hurting the other person's feelings" (reported in Besharov & Gardiner, 1997). The average age for first intercourse is 16.9 years for men and 17.4 years for women. By their late teenage years, at least three-quarters of all men and women have had intercourse, and more than two-thirds of all sexually experienced teens have had two or more partners (Alan Guttmacher Institute, 2002).

One-quarter of teenage women failed to use contraceptives at first intercourse, and 20 percent failed to use them at their most recent sexual intercourse (Darroch, Singh & Frost, 2001). Adolescent childbearing is far more common in the United States than in other industrialized countries. Twenty-two percent of women in the United States reported having had a child before age 20, compared to 11 percent in Canada, 6 percent in France, and 4 percent in Sweden (Darroch, Singh, Frost, 2001).

Poor Health

Poor women are in considerably poorer health than other women, and these health concerns can interfere with their ability to look for, or keep a job, and thus they continued to rely on welfare (Centers for Disease Control, 2004; Corcoran, Danziger & Tolman, 2003; Seccombe, Hartley, Newsom, Pope & Hoffman, 2005; Wood, Smith, Romero, Wise & Chavkin, 2002; Zedlewski, 2003). For example, nearly one-third of women in the four counties that were part of the Manpower Demonstration Research Corporation's Urban Change Project had low physical well-being scores, compared to one-tenth of adults nationally (London, Martinez & Polit, 2001). Another study using data from the National Health Interview Survey (NHIS) reports that about 1 in 4 children enrolled in TANF during the study year had some form of chronic illness (Wise, Wampler, Chavkin & Romero, 2002). Likewise, in the statewide study of TANF-leavers in Oregon, the respondents were in poorer health than the national average on almost every indicator of well-known health scales. The respondents report poorer health, less vitality, more pain, and greater mental health problems. Related to these, our respondents report greater difficulty in social and physical functioning and in performing emotional roles (Seccombe, Hartley, Newsom, Hoffman & Pope, 2005). Nearly one-third of women interviewed complained of health problems, including asthma, depression, high blood pressure, or back pain.

Poor children are also more likely to suffer a wide array of ailments, both chronic and acute, than are more affluent children (National Center for Health Statistics, 2004). For example, they are more than three times as likely to be iron deficient; 1.5 times more likely to have frequent diarrhea or colitis; two times more likely to suffer from severe asthma; and 1.5 times more likely to suffer from partial or complete blindness or deafness. These are due to a variety of prenatal and postnatal factors. One important factor is that poor children are more often born with a lower birthweight than are other children, due to the mother's poor nutrition, lack of prenatal care, stress, youth, insufficient weight gain, or smoking or other drug use. Thus, the effects of poverty on the health and well-being of children, and adults are significant, long-term, and can cause considerable heartache, consternation, and chaos in the lives of families.

In the interviews, many women told us that their children were sickly or had emotional problems, and consequently they did not feel comfortable leaving their children with baby-sitters. Program and caseload data document the high proportion of welfare families with poor health, special needs, or disabilities. In reviews of case records conducted in Colorado, Iowa, and Utah, 15, 18, and 13 percent of the cases respectively included documentation noting a child medical or behavioral problem as a potential or actual barrier to participation in work training programs or actual employment (Pavetti & Duke, 1995). Mothers caring for children with health problems are less likely to be employed and work fewer hours when they are employed (Powers, 2003).

Parents whose children have serious or chronic health problems, disabilities, or behavioral problems must attend to a variety of needs, such as multiple doctor appointments, or meeting with school officials. Mothers expressed worry that, should they go off to work, their children would not get the physical and emotional attention that they might need because of their ailments. For example, Jasmine has a history of working full-time, often at several different jobs in order to make ends meet. She is divorced, and has a ten-year-old daughter who lives with her ex-husband's sister, and a five-year-old daughter and an infant to care for. Doctor's appointments are routine for Jasmine and her two young children, but they are stressful nonetheless. Both of her children have severe cases of asthma. She has been on welfare for four years, because of "the sickness of the children." She gives them breathing treatments on and off as needed. For Jasmine, as was the case with many other women we interviewed, being a "good mother" means being there physically to care for her sick or needy children.

Women routinely said that they did not feel comfortable leaving their sick children in daycare, with a babysitter, or even with family members for extended hours. They know that they may have to take time off from work to attend to their children. They see, first and foremost, that their job is to provide the direct care that they believe their child needs. Among the more affluent, these family values of placing children's needs before employment, would be applauded. Returning to more traditional family values is a popular theme espoused by Democrats as well as conservative Republicans. However, among poor women who receive welfare, such values are not applauded; instead, they are suspect.

Sarah is one of the Oregonians interviewed after leaving welfare. She has an eight-year-old son, Jake, who has a severe case of cerebral palsy and developmental delays that were likely caused by her complications during pregnancy. Sarah cares for her son by herself, in conjunction with his school. She receives a little babysitting help from her mother, but Jake's father is not a part of his life. In this interview, she describes the heartache of caring for a child who is seriously disabled, the struggles she faces in doing this on a near-poverty budget, her confusion over insurance procedures, and anxiety about this lifelong commitment that she undertakes virtually alone. Because he is so deeply dependent on Sarah, all of her own needs, desires, and aspirations take a back seat to his daily survival. Eight years later, what is her son, Jake, like today?

> He's eight years old. He doesn't talk. He makes sounds, more or less to indicate what he needs . . . He's in a wheelchair because he doesn't walk. So it's basically like having a three-month-old child that cries whenever it needs anything, and as a mom you do the same thing any mother would. You go down a little checklist: You've just eaten, you've had your diaper changed, so it's a matter of a guessing game of what he needs or wants. Sometimes you can see the frustration in his eyes because he can't communicate what he wants. His favorite sound is "uh" which sometimes means he wants a drink of water. But "uh" also means he can't reach his toy, "uh" means you're watching TV and not feeding me . . . My child is eight years old, and the plain fact, he's eight years old, and he can't do anything for himself, except play with his toys and his newspaper. He can't verbally communicate with me. He basically can't do anything for himself. If I set him here on the floor, he stays in this vicinity, he falls over to his side, he rolls on his tummy, he turns himself around a little

but, but he's subject to this part of the house because that's where I put him. Other than crying, I could leave him here all day long if I so desired and that would just have to work; there's nothing he could do about it. Not that I would, and let me tell you, that boy's got a great set of lungs (W1-90).

Sarah fears for her son and his future. She dreads the day when she is no longer able to physically care for Jake, who is still physiologically growing as would a normal eight-year-old. Additionally, she is deeply concerned that people he meets in his everyday life will mistreat him or ignore his needs. She does not have the money to buy the care he really needs and the security she craves.

You can't have somebody come over and babysit at your house for five dollars. You're not talking about a kid who can say, I'm tired, I want to go to bed, or can we watch this movie. Or I'm hungry now. My fear of having any other sort of daycare take care of him is because of the fact he doesn't complain about things. Does that mean he's going to sit in the corner for an hour and a half? There's no way of knowing, and in this day and age, God knows, he can't tell me if someone is doing anything unmentionable to him. I just pray to God every time he leaves the house that the person I'm sending him to school with is dependable and not some weirdo. Nowadays you hear about all that stuff on TV about how a child was molested in daycare. Good God, you're paying these people to do nasty things to your children (W1-90).

The Termination of Relationships

A primary reason that women turned to welfare was that a relationship ended, and they could not solely support their family. When married or living together, a spouse or partner may have provided an important source of income for the family. When a relationship ends, that income is abruptly halted. Some women find that they are unable to secure a job providing wages above the poverty line. Or they may have no experience working and do not know how to go about finding a job to support the family. The termination of a relationship was a primary reason that women turned to welfare. Patrice, an African American with two young sons explained to me the difficulty she experienced when relationships with her children's father ended:

I prefer to be in a stable family environment. You know, have a husband, and with my children, feel like a family. Because, I have always been pretty much alone after it ended with my children's fathers. One guy I was with for five years. When I got pregnant, he left. It was kind of a shock, and I knew he was financially able for a child because he had been in the military for like 11 years, so it hurt. And I was kind of depressed, moping over that, and, before I knew it, got in another relationship. The other guy just took up with me while I was pregnant and was kind of there for me while I was still depressed about my first relationship. And then, before I knew it I was pregnant again. It just happened so fast. At first he was there for me until I got real big, you know in my pregnancy. Then it seemed like when I started having problems in my pregnancy he wasn't anywhere to be found and I was stuck there by myself. And from that point on, I'm like, if he couldn't be there for me in time of need, he sure didn't need to be there for me once I got on my feet. So I got rid of him, and just stayed by myself for a year before I tried dating again. Tried to make sure that I wasn't vulnerable and that I had recuperated, you know, so I wouldn't be another target. And from that point on it has just been me and my boys ever since.

A 35-year-old divorced African American woman felt that her use of welfare was directly related to her divorce. She told me, "What made me get on was, I guess, my broken marriage. Because when I was married, I wasn't on AFDC. My husband was employed, and I was working."

The United States has the highest rate of divorce of any country in the world. Our divorce rate rose dramatically in the 1970s and 1980s, and has since declined slightly to 4 divorces per 1,000 total population (Sutton & Munson, 2005). Divorce is more prevalent among lower socioeconomic classes despite the economic hardships it creates. One national study of men and women between the ages of 25 and 34 found that people who had only high school diplomas were significantly more likely to divorce than were people who had bachelor's degrees (Glick, 1984). This is due to a variety of reasons including younger age at marriage; greater likelihood of premarital pregnancy and childbirth; and greater stress, crises, and disruptions in their lives related to economic vulnerability. When people marry young, for example, they are less prepared for marital responsibilities. They are more unhappy about their partners in terms of love, affection, sex, wage earning, companionship, and faithfulness. They also are more likely than their older counterparts to complain that their spouses are moody, jealous, spend money foolishly, or get in trouble with the law (Booth & Edwards, 1985; Teti, Lamb & Elster, 1987).

African Americans are more likely to divorce than are whites. According to the 2000 U.S. Census nearly 12 percent of African Americans were currently divorced, compared to less than 10 percent of whites (U.S. Census Bureau, 2001). The higher divorce rate is due to many factors, including that African Americans are disproportionately poor or have low incomes, and therefore face many poverty-related stresses. Moreover, they are more likely to marry earlier, have a premarital pregnancy, and have a child born out of wedlock. These factors increase their odds of divorce.

Women and men face different odds of remarriage after a divorce. Men are more likely to remarry, and they remarry more quickly than do women. In her famous book *Families on the Fault Line*, Lillian Rubin reinterviewed 32 working-class families twenty years after their original interviews, and found that 56 percent of them had divorced sometime during this period (1994). All but one of the men had remarried, and the lone exception was already in a serious relationship after being separated for only a few months. In contrast, Rubin found that divorced women fared differently. They remained single for a longer period of time after a divorce, and over half needed either welfare or food stamps during this financially difficult period. Over one-third of the women had not remarried. For most of these women, life continued to be a series of economic struggles.

Although both men and women go through financial adjustments after divorce, women's income declines more dramatically than does men's (Page & Stevens, 2002; Peterson, 1996). Women's standard of living declines over 20 percent after a divorce, while men's actually increases, on average. Most women have little experience being the primary breadwinner in relationships. When they are forced to do so, while taking care of the children as well, it can be overwhelming. Many women reported that receiving welfare was perceived as a method of regaining control over their lives. It allowed them the opportunity to take stock of their situation, to regroup, to assess their options, or to attend school or find a job. Some women reported that they were deserted by their partners, and left alone to care for their children. One such case was Dee, an African American woman with three small children under the age of five, who served five years in the Army. She had a career that she enjoyed. But her husband pressured her to quit, saying that her job was too hard on the family. She quit, and became a housewife at her ex-husband's insistence. Then, when she was dependent on him for financial support, he left her without warning. "My husband left us with no food. The rent was due. You know, when he left he just split. It was like he was never there, no clothes, nothing."

Stephanie, the nursing student at the University, spoke about the shock of having to raise her child alone. Since the divorce, her husband has never once paid child support, nor visited or contacted their daughter. Like all women, she thought that their marriage would last forever and that he would support both her and their child. She made a wrong choice, but she had no way of knowing it was wrong at the time. It was a choice that any woman could make. She never imagined that she would be on welfare.

> I gave birth thinking—he begged me to keep the child when I found out I was pregnant—thinking that we would be a couple, that we would always be together, and he would always want her. And now, it's four years later, and I am by myself, and I am doing this by myself. Even the best-laid plans sometimes go down the drain.

Both Dee and Stephanie, and many others that we interviewed, saw welfare as a critical, but temporary form of assistance, which enabled them to take care of their children immediately after a husband or partner disappeared, or when the marriage or relationship ended. Welfare made it possible for them to pursue further training so that they could be the sole support of a family, or it provided some base level of financial support while they reassessed their life options. They did not see themselves as being irresponsible. Instead, the temporary receipt of welfare was viewed more positively. It allowed them to take control of their lives and provide a better home environment for their children until they could provide it themselves.

Violence

Some detrimental relationships involved violence and abuse. Violence or its threat is a part of every woman's reality. No woman is really exempt. According to the National Crime Victimization Survey, there were 209,880 rapes and sexual assaults measured in

2004 (Bureau of Justice Statistics, 2005). A rape, for example, is reported in the United States every five minutes (U.S. Federal Bureau of Investigation, 1995), yet most rapes remain unreported. Two women interviewed told us that they bore children as a result of rapes. They credit welfare with giving them the opportunity to bear and raise their children, rather than forcing them to have abortions or give up the child for adoption.

Although no direct question about violence was asked, many other women volunteered that they were fleeing abusive relationships or had left an abusive relationship in the past. Violence in the home has reached staggering levels. It is a critical social problem affecting the lives of millions, poor or rich. The true rate of domestic violence can perhaps never be known as it often occurs behind closed doors, where a "man's home is his castle." Groundbreaking research by Straus and Gelles, referred to as the National Family Violence Surveys, was conducted in 1975 and 1985 with a nationwide sample of 8,145 husbands, wives, and cohabiting couples. They define violence as "an act carried out with the intention, or perceived intention, of causing physical pain to another person," synonymous with the legal definition of assault. The respondents of these surveys were asked about their involvement in violent acts such as: throwing something at the other; pushing; grabbing; shoving; slapping; kicking; biting; hitting with fists; hitting with an object; beatings; burning, scalding, or choking; threatening with a knife or gun; and using a knife or gun. Together, the two surveys found that in 16 percent of the couples, at least one of the partners had engaged in a violent act against the other during the previous year. In other words, these data reveal that, every year in the United States, about one in six couples have at least one act of violence in their relationship. Moreover, Straus and Gelles found that, over the course of the entire marriage, 28 percent of the relationships contained violence (Straus and Gelles, 1986; 1988).

Data from the more recent 1995–1996 National Violence Against Women (NVAW) survey also indicates that violence by an intimate partner is a relatively common occurrence. Nearly 8 percent of women have been raped, 22 percent have been physically assaulted by someone close to them, and nearly 25 percent have experienced either one or the other (National Institute of Justice and Centers for Disease Control and Prevention, 1998).

Although domestic violence occurs in all social classes, data indicate an inverse relationship between social class and likelihood of violence (National Council on Domestic Violence and Abuse, 2003). That is, women who have lower incomes and lower levels of education are more likely to be victimized than are more affluent or well-educated women. Some of this difference may be due to social class differences in the likelihood of reporting violence. Nonetheless, a Department of Justice report, for example, stated that women living in households with annual incomes below $10,000 are four times more likely to be violently attacked than are other women, usually by their intimate partners. When income and educational levels are taken into account, white, African-American, and Hispanic women have equivalent rates of domestic violence being committed against them.

Molly was one battered woman who fled violence, and turned to welfare for support after escaping while her husband was asleep. She has three young sons, the oldest of whom was four at the time she fled. They lived in a rural mountainous area, 30 miles from the nearest town. Her husband deliberately kept her isolated from family and friends, and put a block on the telephone. He was abusive to both her and the children:

> I left my husband when he was asleep. I stayed in a shelter. I grabbed some clothes for the kids and left. My mom came up and got us. I had no car, no nothing. No furniture. Zero. That was August of '92. So I had to start completely over from scratch. I got a few of my things back, but basically I lost everything that I had.

Molly has been on welfare for three years since leaving her husband. During that time, she had nearly completed an AA degree at a community college, and intends to transfer to the university to work on her bachelor's degree. At the same time, she cares for her three young children, the oldest of whom is now seven years of age. Two of her children have been diagnosed with Attention Deficit Disorder (ADD), a disruptive and challenging learning disability. They had difficulty in school until they were correctly diagnosed, and began to take appropriate medication. Working through these issues by herself, she cannot imagine what her life would be like without the help she received from welfare. She receives no child support, and doubts that her ex-husband will ever pay the tens of thousands of dollars that he currently owes.

Jessie, a 42-year-old African American woman reflected on the common problem of physical abuse:

> I would say that most women who are on the system, it's due to abuse, either from their spouse or something that happened in the past, like a sexual abuse, and they have low self esteem about themselves. And that's why they are on the system. Because they just don't have the willpower to go out there and fight to try to struggle or get a job. They just feel lonely, you know. Not highly of themselves.

The belief that poverty and welfare use are something that is not one's fault and is beyond one's control, something that was forced upon them, was commonly used to explain their own use of welfare. Because of bad luck with relationships, or being raped or victimized in abusive relationships, many women felt that they had no other choice but to turn to welfare to help them out of an unplanned, but potentially desperate situation. Many women implied that turning to welfare was the responsible and rational thing to do for their children, and for themselves. They indicated that they were not to blame, and in fact, for many, welfare was a source of empowerment. It allowed them to be independent of an abusive spouse, retain custody of their children, or to take care of their family when a husband or lover deserted them. These are laudable goals, ones that our society would support, at least in theory. Who would really suggest that a woman remain in an abusive situation, lose custody of her children simply because of money, or move her family to a homeless shelter? The women interviewed were likely to see welfare as short-term, a temporary helping hand while they planned the next step in their lives. With few exceptions, each woman interviewed was confident that she would be off welfare within five years. Yet, as we witnessed in Chapter 3, women were less optimistic about the lives of other women who receive assistance, and were quick to denigrate them as stereotypical welfare mothers, immersed in a subculture that tolerated indolence.

Why the Inconsistency Between Explanations of Their Own and Others' Use of Welfare?

These interviews revealed an important contradiction; *women perceived that their own use of welfare was due to structural factors, or fate, or to the idiosyncrasies of the welfare system itself. In contrast, welfare use by other women was often attributed to laziness, personal shortcomings, or other inadequacies.* This was the case for both the African American and the white women interviewed. They perceived the economic hierarchy in the United States as essentially fair, and that one's placement in the hierarchy tends to reflect work effort and motivation. They generally believed the popular constructions of the "welfare mother," but evaluated their own situation as distinctly different from the norm. When asked directly how their situation was different from other women, only a few women reported similarities. Instead, the majority claim that they are different because (1) they want to make something of themselves; (2) they don't abuse the system like other women do; (3) they make a concerted effort to live within their means; (4) they have health problems or some other serious difficulty that prevents them from working; and (5) unlike other women, they are on it solely for their children and not for themselves. They tended to segregate themselves from other recipients and saw structural constraints as applying uniquely to themselves: "I'm sure people look at me and say the same thing, but I really do have a legitimate excuse"; "my situation is different because I injured my back."

Rhonda, who opened this chapter, distanced herself from other welfare recipients:

> They have all these children. You know, they take it for granted. I mean, just like people in public housing take it for granted. That's why the neighborhoods are the way they are.

Mary, a 47-year-old white woman, who has seven children, receives welfare for her one child who still lives at home. Mary has received welfare sporadically for two years since she and her husband separated. She disassociated herself from other women on welfare:

> I may be on welfare, but I don't live in poverty. I think I got a pretty little home here. Anybody that's on welfare can do the same thing. They shouldn't be on welfare though if they can help it. You know, like me. If it wasn't for my back, I'd be waiting tables.

Janie, who has been on welfare since being gang-raped and giving birth to her daughter two years ago, denied being on welfare altogether:

I'm not on welfare. I don't even know exactly what welfare is. I'm just receiving AFDC, and that might be considered welfare, I'm not sure. As it
stands, most of them get on it because they don't want to work, they don't
want to take care of their kids. I've seen more people on welfare lose their
kids because of it, rather than to take care of themselves. Why they do that
is beyond me.

Given the strong negative messages about welfare and welfare recipients, perhaps it is not surprising that both white and African American women who receive
welfare also subscribe to Individual or Culture of Poverty blaming perspectives. An
enduring theme in the social sciences has been to explain the persistence of social inequality. Sociologists, political scientists, and others are interested in how legitimat-
ing occurs; that is, how do certain justifications become widely believed and taken for
granted? (Bourdieu, 1977; Dahrendorf, 1959; Della Fave, 1980; Habermas, 1973,
Marx & Engels, 1959). Critical theorists, such as Foucault (1980), suggest that our social structures produce views of truth and knowledge that are value-laden and disad-
vantageous to the less powerful. These views camouflage the self-serving interests of
the powerful by making them appear as though they are natural, normal, and serving
the interests of everyone. The views become "commonsense." The less powerful in
society, which include the poor, internalize these views of truth and knowledge and do
not see that they serve the powerful more than themselves. They come to identify
with the powerful and do not recognize that these views of truth and knowledge are
not in their best interests. Therefore, poverty and welfare use are relegated to the
realm of a *personal problem*, rather than a *social problem* (Mills, 1956). Consequently,
women on welfare agree that the popular construction of the "welfare mother" is just.
They accept the dominant ideology that stigmatizes welfare recipients.

However, it is important to note that my respondents infused Structural and
Fatalistic perspectives in their worldviews as well, constructed out of their own experiences. While they accept the dominant ideology, they also think of themselves as the
lone exception to the ideology. As far as their own experiences were concerned, their
need for welfare was due to circumstances over which they had little control.

Other studies have come to similar conclusions. A classic study by Briar (1966),
using a sample from 92 African American, white, and Mexican American families receiving AFDC, also found that the respondents almost never referred to welfare recipients as "we" but instead used the word "they." The tendency to view oneself as an
atypical recipient, disassociating oneself from other recipients was identified as a coping mechanism for dealing with stigma. More recently, interviewing 16 women in
focus groups, Davis and Hagen (1996) also found that welfare recipients had the tendency to view themselves as atypical recipients. For example, while they were quick to
condemn others for being welfare frauds, they did not see their own actions as fraudulent. Instead, they were merely "beating the system" by working to get extra money
to pay for necessary items that their checks could not pay for.

What then may explain why many women do not see the commonalties of their
experience? One explanation may be found in attribution theory, which proposes that
people have a tendency to overestimate the degree to which other people's behavior is

caused by individual traits or dispositions, and underestimate the degree to which it is caused by structural factors. In contrast, although we tend to attribute other people's actions to their own personal traits or dispositions, we are more likely to attribute our own behaviors to the social structure or situational factors over which we have little control (Jones & Nisbett, 1972).

Consistent with attribution theory, our respondents assigned individual traits or dispositions to other women to explain their use of welfare, ones that are well touted in the media and within the larger cultural milieu. Recipients were accused of laziness, of lacking sufficient motivation to improve their condition, of having deficiencies in human capital such as low education or few job skills, of having little desire to "better themselves," and of living in cultural surroundings that encourage welfare use. It appears that welfare recipients, just like the more affluent, overestimate the degree to which individualistic notions of very negative personality traits or dispositions shape welfare use behavior. Yet, when it comes to explaining the causes of their own welfare use, also consistent with attribution theory, they tend to blame it on structural or situational causes that are beyond their control. They assess little personal blame; it is simply not their fault. "There are no jobs"; "How can I take care of all my kids and work too?"; "I would be fine if he would just pay child support"; "I must have health insurance because my child is so sick"; "I was raped"; "I was beaten and abused"; "He deserted us, and I'm trying to get my feet on the ground"; "I'm trying to better myself"; "The welfare system penalizes me if I get a job"—all these explanations were frequently voiced. While all of these factors may be justifiable reasons why a woman would turn to welfare, they are reasons that can apply to all women, and indeed, they did apply to the majority of women interviewed. Women assumed they were exceptions to general trends; however, these exceptions were common and widespread. They were grounded in their experiences as women in a patriarchal society. Few women were nonchalant about welfare. Instead, most were embarrassed, pained, appreciative, or resigned, and applied for welfare as a last resort. As Rhonda bluntly told me,

> It's not what I want for me and my son. It's just that there are a lot of disadvantages to it. I just don't want to be on it. I'd rather be out working, meeting people—making it better for me and my son.

CRITICAL THINKING QUESTIONS

1. Rhonda does not see herself as dependent on the welfare system. Do you think she is? Why or why not?

2. Should Rhonda insist that her son's father play a more prominent role in his life? Why doesn't she? What might be the pros and cons of insisting that he be more involved?

3. The author found that structural reasons or fate were often used by women to explain why they need welfare. Which reasons do you think are the most valid, and why?

4. What kinds of structural changes are needed so that women can get along without welfare? What type of social policies should be enacted (or amended) to make some of these structural changes?

5. Evaluate the argument, "The welfare system breeds dependence on the system." Do you agree or disagree with this statement? Defend your position.

6. The author suggests that dominant groups in society can be successful in developing widespread ideas about truth and knowledge that really represent their own interests at the expense of the less powerful. Yet the less powerful groups in society come to accept these dominant ideas. Can you provide any other examples where this might be the case?

7. How can you ensure that you, your mother, your sister, your girlfriend, or your wife will never need welfare?

CHAPTER

5 Day-to-Day Living and Decision Making

"Officials May Gain Welfare Insight" declares a headline in a local newspaper soon after welfare reform had passed (*Gainesville Sun*, September 2, 1997). A group of Florida legislators and state policymakers voluntarily signed up to be paired with a welfare recipient for one month "to walk a mile in the shoes of a welfare recipient." For 30 days policy makers talked on the telephone with their welfare "match" at least once a week, and they did something with her related to her life, such as shopping with food stamps, visiting the welfare office, participating in training programs, or visiting a food bank. Perhaps most importantly, during this month they pledged to feed themselves and their families on a food stamp budget, although they used cash, rather than food stamps to purchase their food. Those legislators who volunteered for this experiment were applauded for their interest and sensitivity towards welfare recipients. It is considered a noble experiment.

While this was an important step toward understanding the daily experience of welfare recipients, it should not be confused with the actual realities of welfare existence. How was it different? The legislators' "welfare experience" was of short duration, took place weekly largely at their convenience, and had a fixed beginning and ending point. They did not have to use stigma symbols such as food stamps during this period. Furthermore, they knew that, at the end of 30 days, they could resume their upper-middle-class lifestyles, replete with expensive clothes, late-model cars, and dinners in lavish restaurants. Who can't rough it for 30 days? Finally, because the experiment was only temporary, there were no real decisions that needed to be made to cope with the monotony, struggles, or stresses associated with poverty.

For welfare recipients in Florida, living with a child on $241 in cash and $212 in food stamps is not an experiment. (Note: in Florida, a 2005 cash grant remains $241 and food stamps are increased to $274.) In addition, many recipients would argue that it is not truly voluntary and that they are on welfare because they are "between a rock and a hard place, doing what I've got to do." Moreover, for most recipients their stay on welfare is considerably longer than 30 days, and they do not have the security of returning to an upper-middle-class lifestyle afterwards. Women on welfare do not simply rough it. Instead, they actually must learn how to live and survive on meager amounts, knowing full well that their financial circumstances may never improve considerably. Their clothes come from the thrift shops and garage sales, their cars are old and in disrepair, and dinners out are likely to be monthly excursions to a fast-food restaurant. Their stays on welfare are not an experiment. Unlike state legislators, women on welfare are not considered noble for enduring poverty of this magnitude.

This chapter considers what daily life is like for someone who is poor. It examines the kinds of decisions and struggles that ensue, and asks if these are different from those faced by persons who are more affluent. Do the poor simply live a less affluent version of the middle-class dream and family ideal? Or have their lives been significantly reconfigured in order to survive?

Jana's life is a far cry from that of any state legislator's. She is a 28-year-old African American woman with four children. Her oldest child, a ten-year-old son, resides in a center for emotionally disturbed children, located over 120 miles away. Since Jana has no car, she relies on the county welfare office to take her to see him, but unfortunately, these visits are restricted to once a week. She calls him between visits on the telephone. "I miss him terribly," she told me.

Jana's other children are aged seven, four, and eighteen months, all of whom live at home with her. She has voluntarily been sterilized so that she will have no more children. Their home is a dilapidated house in one of the poorest sections of town. The small two-bedroom structure sits on a small dirt lot without grass or other shrubbery. Walking up to the front door requires one to hop a series of makeshift stepping stones to prevent falling into large deep holes in her yard. Several of these deep holes are adjacent to her front porch, a potentially dangerous situation for herself, her children, and visitors. From the front of the house, a broken living room window was visible. No apparent attempt had been made to fix it. Thus, her house would be an easy target to burglarize, if only she had something to steal.

The brightly painted, but chipping, lime-green exterior of the house sharply contrasted with the brown dark interior. The living room where we sat was very small and crowded. It was hot and stuffy, despite having the door wide open on a sunny 70-degree day in the middle of Florida's winter. The dirty, dark carpet and faded and well-worn furniture added to the dankness of the living room. A soiled blanket, tacked up in the doorway, separated off other rooms. Jana's home costs her $160 a month to rent, a sizable component of the $364 she received in welfare aid for her three children who live at home, and the $50 she received some months in child support. Utilities average another $70 a month. The rent for her house is not subsidized, and she has no roommate. Thus, she pays approximately $230, or over half of her welfare grant and sporadic child support, on living quarters that by most standards would be deemed unfit and unsafe. However, she tells me that her alternative is the housing projects, which she believes are even more stifling and dangerous for her children. So instead, they live month after month in their decaying house. Jana and her children will be there long after the Florida legislators have completed their noble month-long experiment and have gone back to their comfortable homes.

Jana has no telephone and no car. She says she cannot afford them. Unlike many welfare recipients I met, she does not have an extended family network to help her out. She moved to Florida ten years ago to distance herself from an unhappy home life, "trying to make a change for myself." She chose Florida because an aunt lived there, but her aunt has since died. Jana is on her own, raising her children with only minimal help from the children's fathers. She has cultivated a strong friendship network to help out when needed, not surprising given her outgoing and gregarious personality. However, for the most part, if she cannot provide something for her children, they do without.

Her daily living reflects both the tedium and struggle of being poor. It is tedious because it is predictable, month after month. There is little money for frivolous expenditures that add sparkle and interest to one's life. Jana takes no vacations, no shopping trips to the mall, and rarely goes to a movie or out to dinner. She stays home day after day, and takes care of her three children who live with her. She is up at 5:00 A.M. daily, awakened by her toddler who shares her bed; "He gets up at 5 o'clock every morning. I mean *every* morning. And when he gets up, he gets out of bed and walks all the way around the house," she tells me sourly. There are no breaks. She has no husband or partner whom she can turn to and say, "It's your turn. I'm tired and need a break." Instead her day is spent getting her seven-year-old daughter off to school, taking care of her four-year-old and her toddler, cleaning the house, helping her daughter with homework when she returns from school, fixing dinner, and getting her family ready for bed. There is no money to vary the routine. She cannot hire a babysitter so that she can spend an evening out without her children. The tedium is stressful. "Sometimes I just go in my room and close the door and lay down on the bed. That's about all I can do. I just try to relax myself the best way I can because I get so stressed out sometime that my head hurts. My head really hurts," she recounts.

Jana's life is also a constant struggle. It is not easy to pay the bills on time, to put food on the table, to pay for childcare, to nurse sick children, to find a job, and to locate donations and charities to help benefits stretch throughout the month. A task as simple and common as grocery shopping poses its set of challenges. Without a car and without a direct public transportation line near her home, how does she get to the grocery store? With only $367 in food stamps, how can she buy enough food to feed her family for a month? Since food stamps cannot be used for non-food items, how does she afford necessities like toilet paper, diapers for her baby, laundry detergent, cleaning supplies, and other toiletries and feminine hygiene products? "I use rags for just about everything, if you know what I mean," she winked.

For the more affluent, grocery shopping is a minor errand, conducted without much thought. For Jana, like other women on welfare, grocery shopping is a major ordeal, and one that has to be dealt with every month. She does not like to rely on others for transportation and then owe them something, so she often walks to the grocery store—which is over a mile each way—taking her four-year-old and her baby with her. She "borrows" a shopping cart to tote them and haul her groceries in. Unfortunately, there are no sidewalks in her neighborhood, and she therefore must take her family out on the open roadway. Because of the logistical hassles, and to prevent spending beyond her budget, Jana shops for groceries only once a month, a procedure I found to be relatively common.

Meals at the end of the month are "creative," usually involving a dab of whatever she has left in the house. Peanut butter sandwiches made on day-old bread for several days in a row are common. "I try to make them with different kinds of jelly," she told me. Jana tries to avoid spending her welfare grant on food, but usually finds that she runs short of food stamps, and must spend $30–$40 of her cash grant at the end of the month on food. When this is coupled with the additional $50 she spends on non-food necessities such as cleaning supplies, diapers, and toiletries, her meager welfare grant is virtually depleted for the month. When she first gets her check, she tries to squeeze out a family meal at a nearby fast-food restaurant that they can walk to, as a special monthly treat. Afterwards, there is little, if anything left for a telephone, a car, or many other conveniences of modern living.

As we all know, unexpected costs or emergencies often break even the most conservative budgets. Buying a simple pair of children's shoes can wreak havoc on Jana's budget for the remainder of the month. What does she do when these unanticipated needs arise? Like other women on welfare, Jana lives month to month in a precarious juggling of bills. Paying her rent is her first priority, but on a couple of occasions, the utility bill has gone unpaid, and her electricity has been turned off. She vows to never let this happen again, as the turn-on charge is more than she can muster. She sometimes turns to the children's fathers, and they occasionally will buy food or clothing. She is also well versed in the location of charities, particularly those that will donate food. "See, I can get food. Food is no problem because they have the Catholic Charities, and they will give you food when you need it. In addition, there is the Salvation Army and the Community Ministries. There are different places that you can go to and get help for food," she informs me. So she doesn't really feel that she or her children have ever gone to bed hungry. But without a telephone, and without transportation, even getting free help poses a difficulty. Therefore, instead, she usually ends up spending a portion of her cash grant on food. Jana's daily living, as is the case for the other women interviewed, is a shocking attempt at obtaining a standard of living that falls well below what most people in the United States simply take for granted.

Like many other poor women on welfare, Jana and her family live in substandard housing that poses a potential threat to their health and safety. The national median fair market rent for a modest two-bedroom unit is $720 a month, or nearly five times the cost of Jana's house (Manpower Demonstration Project, 2001). What does Jana's family, and millions of families like hers, receive for their modest rent? They must live in damp, dirty, crowded, dangerous, and disease-ridden conditions that may lack proper cooking or sanitation facilities (Joint Center for Housing Studies at Harvard University, 2003). Poor children are 3.6 times more likely to have signs of rats or mice in their homes during the past three months; are 3.4 times more likely to have family members sharing bedrooms; and are 2.7 times more likely to have spent time in a house that was considered by a parent or other survey respondent as "too cold" (Children's Defense Fund, 1994). Exposure to rodents, crowding, and cold can wreak havoc on a family's health and well-being. For example, manifestations of rats and mice, in addition to the more obvious concern associated with bites, can contribute to asthma and other respiratory problems by filling the air with rodent urinary proteins (Swanson, 1985). A study summarizing 100 anecdotes and articles in medical journals from doctors, nurses, and social workers, estimates that nearly 18,000 children are hospitalized each year because of asthma complications from cockroaches, rats, and mold. Another 1,400 are hospitalized from exposed radiators. Where children live can have a tremendous effect on their health, the authors conclude (*Gainesville Sun*, February 10, 1998).

The United States currently faces a severely limited supply of affordable housing units, which continue to deteriorate (Children's Defense Fund, 2005). Over 14 million households spend more than 50 percent of their income on rent, and three-quarters of these households are poor. Even full-time minimum wage workers cannot afford to pay fair market value in any jurisdiction across the country (Joint Center for Housing Studies at Harvard University, 2003). To afford a modest two-bedroom unit in 2002, a worker needed to earn $14.66 an hour, which is nearly three times the federal minimum wage of $5.15 an hour (National Low Income Housing Coalition, 2002). This is far more than families on welfare or families who leave welfare for work can realistically afford (Seccombe et al., 2005).

Living in poverty is more than simply an economic issue. While legislators, in their month-long voluntary poverty experiment, likely encountered some of the routine financial experiences that women on welfare face, they were able to gracefully sidestep many other important ones. They did not have to deal with the monotony of poverty, the stigma attached to it, and the hopelessness and despair that can accompany people who feel trapped in dire circumstances. Florida's legislators, in all likelihood, did not grapple with finding adequate childcare. They did not face the dilemma of finding a way to care for a sick child, while at the same time looking for a job. They did not need to search for small kernels of gratification to energize their spirits and keep their sanity, such as buying a steak or other such treats with their food stamps, only to then have even less money for the remainder of the month. The legislators may have missed the fact that there is more to being poor than simply not having enough money to live on. Decisions must be made daily, weekly, monthly, on how to keep your family's spirit alive.

Daily Activities: Wild Living or Depressing Routine?

It is difficult to understand the day-to-day struggles of women on welfare without considering the difficulties associated with single motherhood more generally. The interviews reconfirmed that many single mothers face difficult economic and personal situations that they cannot resolve quickly by themselves. Having no husband or partner forces them to be both mother and father to their children. They must be the sole provider, disciplinarian, nurturer, tutor, housekeeper, cook, and chauffeur despite having their own problems or difficulties to work through. Most women interviewed felt that being a good mother was their number one priority. Being a good mother meant, at a minimum, keeping their children safe and out of danger. They wanted their children to stay in school, and to stay off drugs. They wanted them to stay out of gangs, and to stay off the streets. They wanted their teenage daughters to avoid pregnancy. For their sons, "I just hope they do the right thing and not end up in jail." Their daily expressions reflected these goals for their children.

For most women on welfare, daily living is a continuous and depressing battle to keep the worst of poverty at bay. On one level, it appears that recipients lead largely uneventful lives: The drug use, alcohol abuse, and child neglect that is suspected by the more affluent is exaggerated. Certainly, drugs and alcohol are not unknown to welfare recipients. For example, one study found that 12 percent of women on welfare consumed five or more drinks in one sitting at least two times in the past month, defined as binge drinking, compared to 6 percent of adult women who were not on welfare (Center on Addiction and Substance Abuse, Columbia University, 1994). However, 44 percent of college students engage in binge drinking according to a Harvard survey of 18,000 undergraduates, a figure that is considerably higher than that among welfare recipients (Schlein, 1997). Moreover, 23 percent of welfare recipients used an illicit drug in the past year, compared to 12 percent of non-welfare women (Center on Addiction and Substance Abuse, Columbia University, 1994). However, a national sample from the 2004 survey *Monitoring the Future* reveals that about 39 percent of twelfth graders have also used an illicit drug during the past year (Monitoring the Future, 2005). It is likely that students and welfare recipients drink and take drugs for different reasons. While students may indulge because of peer pressure, several women told us that they used these substances as a coping strategy for their depression. Thus, while we may conclude that women on welfare are significantly more likely to be binge drinkers or use drugs than other women, it is incorrect to assume that the majority of women on welfare do so, or that problems with alcohol and drugs are restricted to poor women on welfare.

Instead, the vast majority of women interviewed were simply trying their best to be good mothers, caring for their children the best way they knew how. Heavy drug or alcohol use would conflict with this, and was avoided. Their daily activities largely consist of getting up early to get children off for school; taking care of preschool-aged children; housecleaning; cooking; socializing with extended family members, friends, or neighbors; helping their children with homework; and getting children ready for bed, "really, just being a mother. No spectacular anything, just taking care of my children, running a couple of errands, and then coming back and being a full-time mom." These are routine activities familiar to all stay-at-home mothers, regardless of income level. Yet, they rarely make the headlines. Those women who worked outside the home also had familiar lives; they held paying jobs while having sole parental responsibilities. Patrice, who works part-time at a nearby hospital, but continues to receive a partial welfare check because of her low earnings, told me how she spends her day. She has two young sons; one is four years old, and one is almost three. Her routine sounds hauntingly familiar to single working mothers everywhere:

> Well, usually my days start around 6:30 when my youngest child gets up. Then I'll start, getting up, assisting him with brushing his teeth and washing his face and showering. Then I take my bath. Then I fix him something for breakfast. Then my second child usually wakes up round about 7:30, so I assist him with brushing his teeth and taking his morning bath. I used to fix him breakfast, but this past Monday he started school, and gets breakfast there, so all I have to do is just get up, get him ready, and usually around by

8:00 we're out the door. I drop him off at school. Then usually I drop my
second child off around quarter to nine. Then I come back home, clean up
a little bit, and then I report to work around 9:30. My mom has to pick up
my oldest child at the end of the school day because I'm not off of work.
Then usually when I get off from work I have to immediately pick up my
second child. Then I start my routines of getting them settled, and start
cooking. Then I feed them, clean up, start giving them their baths, and
we'll spend maybe an hour together. Then it's usually time to go to bed.

Making Ends Meet with "The Check"

Despite the seemingly routine nature of their daily lives, making ends meet on the income provided by welfare requires ingenuity and creativity. I was told repeatedly that
welfare does not provide enough money to live on. I asked a young mother, Amy, a
university student with hopes of being a physical therapist, if welfare provided enough
money for her and her daughter to live on. Her eyes widened as she burst out:

> "*No!* In Florida? *No!* See, I was on it in New York, and in New York, it's
> enough money to live on. It's enough money to have a really low-rent
> apartment, maybe a shack somewhere, and pay these meager little bills.
> And you can survive, maybe by just a hair. But not down here. It's not
> enough to even subsist on at all. And I'd like to know everyone's story about
> how they are getting by. I have financial aid, but what about all the other
> people who don't? How on earth do they make it, without lying? Every se-
> mester I get about five thousand dollars. And I'm pretty frugal. I don't buy
> things. I don't go out and buy CDs. I don't go out and buy clothes. I spend
> my money on dishwashing detergent, soap, laundry detergent, and car
> brake lights and things like that. I don't have money for anything else.

She raises the important question, how are other women getting by on welfare?
I tackled this issue in a series of questions to respondents and, like other researchers
before me, found that welfare recipients usually run out of money well before the end
of the month (Mayer & Jencks, 1989; Edin and Lein, 1997). I talked with women
about their budgeting and spending. As Jana told me "sometimes it comes out right,
and sometimes it doesn't."

Eliza, an African American mother with four children, was typical in many respects. She is completely out of money before the end of the month, and has to scrape
by to provide food and material goods to her family.

> **INTERVIEWER:**   Let's say that this is the day you get your check. What do you
> spend your money on first?
>
> **ELIZA:**   My rent. My light bill. My phone. And then, whatever I have left I go
> and buy my kids what they need, like clothes. Then there's household goods,
> washing powder, bleach, and going to the laundromat. That's what I usually

do with the extra money. Once I get through, I won't have nothing. Paying bills, buying for them and buying stuff for the house—soap, toilet paper, and all that kind of stuff, and going to the laundromat to wash clothes, all of that.

INTERVIEWER: Do you ever run out of money?

ELIZA: I ain't got none now. That's why I need a job. A good paying job.

Eliza's consumption patterns were not exorbitant. They are at the low end of widely shared consumption norms. As was the case for most other women interviewed, she rarely bought clothes for herself, or spent very much on entertainment. Most women knew precisely what their monthly expenditures were. They spent the greater part of their check on basic necessities such as shelter, electricity, cleaning supplies, and clothing for their children, with very little, if any, disposable income left. Data from the 2003 Consumer Expenditure Survey found that poor households spend approximately three-quarters of their income on three items: housing, food, and transportation (U.S. Department of Labor, U.S. Bureau of Labor Statistics, 2005). This figure may be even higher for families on welfare, as food stamps alone constitute nearly 50 percent of their monthly income, particularly in low-grant states such as Florida. Even when presented with the fantasy of having an extra $50 this month, few mothers told me that they would spend it on themselves. Most commonly, I was told, "I would save it for a rainy day because something always comes up"; "it would go to pay bills"; "I'd buy my children clothes that they need." No woman had any significant savings stashed away for emergencies. "Savings? This is a joke, right?" Few women had a credit card, on which they could charge items, thereby allowing them to amortize their costs over the course of several months. They are largely removed from the spending sprees spurred by credit cards and accompanied debt that many Americans experience.

To make ends meet, women on welfare must do without basic amenities that many people take for granted. "Being on welfare, you can't have a lot of luxury," was certainly an understatement. Most commonly, they were without cars, telephones, washing machines, and clothes dryers—things most Americans now see as routine household appliances. According to a recent survey by the Federal Highway Administration, one-fourth of low-income households do not have a car, compared to just 4 percent of other households. Americans may make a billion daily trips to the store, school, work and other destinations, but for many low-income persons, particularly those who live on welfare, they make these trips by walking, taking public transportation, or by depending on the generosity of others (U.S.A. Today, September 16, 1997).

Similarly, I also noted that many women do not have a telephone. According to data from the 2000 U.S. Census Bureau, between 6 and 10 percent of poor households are without telephone service, more than twice the national average (U.S. Census Bureau, accessed 3/13/05). However, the percentage of families who have fluctuating service is considerably higher. Often families could not afford to pay their telephone bills and telephones were disconnected within months after having them hooked up. It may take many more months to get their telephones reinstated. Yet telephones are an important resource and can improve the lives of poor families in many ways. They provide greater access to routine and emergency services. They can also help mothers form a social network with other relatives, neighbors, and friends. Keisha, a 33-year-old African American woman with two children, who also works part-time to supplement her welfare check, still feels that she cannot afford a telephone. She uses a common strategy of relying upon a neighbor to deliver important messages.

> A phone? No. That's an extra bill I can't afford right now. I had one, and that was a bill I had to let go. My parents, especially my mom, say, "Why don't you get a phone?" Well, Mom, I can't afford a phone right now. "You need a phone! You need a phone! What if something happens to those children in the middle of the night?" she asks me. "You've got to go across the street and use the phone and wake the neighbors up." Well, Mom, let's just pray that doesn't happen.

Washing clothes, a routine task, also posed a major obstacle for the women interviewed. Because most women and their children had very small wardrobes, they washed clothes at least weekly. First, there is the cost associated with washing and drying clothes at a public Laundromat, since most women did not own their own washing machines. The $10 spent on laundry per week, or approximately $40 a month depending on family size, constituted a significant component of their income after their other bills were paid. Second, there is the difficulty of getting to a laundromat, particularly among women without their own cars. Women who lived in the housing projects or large apartment complexes were likely to have laundry facilities in their building, but other women did not. For these women without in-house facilities, getting to the laundromat to wash and dry their clothes was an all-day chore. Third, some women were nervous about the kind of people who hung out at laundromats, and they did not find them safe or respectable places to take their children. Yet, most needed to take their children with them anyway because of having no childcare. After witnessing, along with her children, a fight between two men, Lynda decided that finding a way to purchase a washing machine was one of her highest priorities. Even though she set her sights on a used machine, buying one was not easy:

> My washing machine causes me a lot of tears. Buying it. There were a lot of sacrifices I just had to make. I have no clothes. It's so sad, but I have no clothes. There were lots of things I had to sacrifice to get something as basic as a washing machine. And I sacrificed with my kids' school clothes. I have to go through the months when it's warm, and save money out of my check then, just to get my kids their school clothes. It was really hard when I had to try to get school clothes for all of them. My grant was a little more than what I get now. I think, with four kids and myself, I was only getting $426 in cash for a family of five.

Because money is so tight, even small fluctuations in monthly bills or monthly income, which would be trivial to the more affluent, can be disastrous to those who are trying to survive on a welfare budget. Every dollar is budgeted or set aside for something, so that when the unforeseen arises, or when the expected $50 in child support from the welfare office doesn't come, it is difficult or impossible to cover expenses. There is no money left over to fix the car, repair the washing machine, or purchase shoes for their children. As Alexandra, who lives in a subsidized apartment, continues to tell us, "They just raised my rent $15, and I'm like 'Fifteen dollars? That was my gas money!' I had everything so figured out, and then something changes." As she reveals, even small fluctuations in monthly income or expenditures can wreak havoc on the best-made budgets. Her daughter often comes home from school with notices in her backpack about upcoming school or community events that cost money. "If I see things in her backpack that need money, I'll just take it out of her backpack and throw them away. I won't even say anything to her. I mean, if she sees it, she's going to want it."

Holidays such as Christmas or birthdays posed tremendous obstacles. Poor children are not isolated from the consumerism that surrounds holidays. They are bombarded with commercials on television for expensive toys; they see their peers wearing expensive clothing and shoes at school; and they are frustrated by opportunities that are seemingly unavailable to them. How do families on welfare confront Christmas, and other holidays? Several women dealt with such holidays by making gifts themselves, justifying their homemade gifts as more meaningful than store-bought ones. Others comb the secondhand stores for clothing and other items that their children need. What their children "want," such as toys, is immaterial. Pearl, a 48-year-old African American woman, told me that her teenage sons smirk when they receive a used shirt from the secondhand store for Christmas or birthday gifts, but "I don't care; they'll wear them," she proudly told me. Another woman, Sarah, saved part of her food stamps each month, and bought her children food for Christmas. "I can't really afford anything else."

A common strategy among recipients is to try to begin saving for Christmas several months in advance. Beginning in October, after the back-to-school clothes have been purchased, recipients reported trying to save $10 or $20 a month for Christmas. This savings goal, while admirable, still did not provide much money with which to purchase gifts. And, more often than not, they were not able to set aside even this modest amount each month. Something unexpected came up, and they had to spend it. Many women reported using the layaway program at discount stores, such as K-Mart or Wal-Mart. They used layaway programs as a form of interest-free credit: they would pay a little each month, and then when the entire sum was paid, they received the item. Although discount stores are popular among the poor, some specific stores were criticized for their punitive layaway policies—at one store, you lose your entire deposit if the item is not purchased by a particular date. Your money will not be returned.

Living and Surviving on Food Stamps

In addition to running out of money before the end of the month, the majority of respondents interviewed in both Florida and Oregon also did not receive enough food stamps and therefore ran out of food (Seccombe et al., 2005). The food stamp program was created in the 1960s to increase the food purchasing power of low-income households so that they would be better able to afford a nutritionally adequate low-cost diet. Approximately 19 million persons in the United States received food stamps in 2002, representing a decline over the previous decade (U.S. Department of Agriculture, 2004). The food stamp program has various tests for eligibility, with income being a primary criterion. For example, a family of two in the continental United States in 2005 cannot have cash income exceeding $1,041 (net) and countable resources (i.e., a bank account) in excess of $2,000 (U.S. Department of Agriculture, 2004). TANF recipients are generally automatically eligible for food stamps in every state, yet not all recipients receive them (Zedlewski, May 19, 2004).

Stephanie was enrolled in nursing school in 1995 when she was interviewed, and was better off financially than most women on welfare because she received financial aid. (Note: After welfare reform she would no longer be eligible for welfare while attending school.) But in 1995, her grants and loans provided some extra money in addition to paying her tuition and books. She received the same amount of food stamps for herself and her child as other recipients: $212. When I asked her if she received enough food stamps every month, she answered emphatically:

> No! I eat out very rarely, so I find that food stamps rarely last the month for me. I eat very little meat. But I try to eat a lot of fresh fruits and vegetables. I try to be very healthful in my diet. I eat a low fat diet. And unfortunately, those foods are expensive. When it comes to the end of the month, I sometimes have to pay $20 or $30 until the next time I can get food stamps. Some months are four weeks, and some are five. Like, right now, it's tight. I only have 1 gallon of milk in the fridge, a half a loaf of bread, and some orange juice. I have to be real creative about what I make to eat. There haven't been any fruits or veggies this past week.

As Stephanie reveals, eating healthy can be more costly than filling up on junk food. The food stamp benefit level is derived from the U.S. Department of Agriculture's lowest-cost food plan, named the "Thrifty Food Plan." Its precise amount is varied for household size and is adjusted annually for inflation. In 2005, it allowed for less than $70 a week for two people (U.S. Department of Agriculture, 2004). Yet this modest amount is only half of that provided under the more generous food budget constructed by the USDA that is more in line with spending habits of middle-class America.

Poor households are expected to be able to devote 30 percent of their monthly income to food purchases. Food stamps, then, make up the difference between what the household can contribute, and the amount judged to be sufficient to purchase the Thrifty Food Plan.

The plan as a basis for food stamps can be criticized on several grounds. First, it was designed to be a temporary budget, "for temporary or emergency use when funds are low" (Peterkin, 1964), not a threshold at which families are to survive indefinitely. Later the USDA stressed that "the cost of this plan is not a reasonable measure of basic money needs for a good diet," and suggested it be increased by approximately 25 percent (Peterkin & Kerr, 1982).

Second, the Thrifty Food Plan is based on the poor's spending patterns 40 years ago—adjusted for inflation (Ruggles, 1990). But it does not provide for changing spending habits. For example, it still assumes that families will bake daily, cook foods from scratch, and that they will not buy prepared convenience foods. The plan fails to take into account important changes in cooking styles, family tastes, and women's lifestyles since its creation four decades ago.

Despite its claim of enabling poor households to buy nutritionally adequate diets, many recipients argued that this plan does not allow sufficient funds to buy nutritious foods. Therefore, it comes as no surprise that the lowest-income households consumed 27 percent less fresh fruit than the national average, while the highest income level consumed about 40 percent more than the national average (Lutz, Blaylock & Smallwood, 1993).

Because purchasing the necessary food to feed their families realistically costs more than their food stamp allocation, women on welfare are required to dip into their small cash benefit to make ends meet. How do women keep from having to use too much of their own money? Alexandra, a 29-year-old divorced white woman with one child, revealed a common strategy:

ALEXANDRA: They never last. I get $212. But when you go to the store, you spend at least $50 easily on food, a week. So usually, the last week of every month I have no more food stamps. It gets pretty bad.

INTERVIEWER: So, then what do you do?

ALEXANDRA: Rent money. I spend money from the rent that's coming up. I'll buy something like peanut butter and jelly. She'll eat peanut butter and jelly for a week. Breakfast, lunch, and dinner. But it's food. It works. If she complains I say, "Hey you can have grape or strawberry jelly. It's a choice today."

INTERVIEWER: Would some people say that you should just figure out how to budget better?

ALEXANDRA: I basically buy things that last a long time. Lots of spaghetti. You can make massive amounts for 63 cents. Lots of spaghetti, peanut butter and jelly. I like those frozen pot pies. At least there's a whole day's nutrition in just that. Five for a dollar.

Another commonly used strategy for making food stamps last throughout the month was grocery shopping only once. Many women claimed that they made all food purchases at the beginning of the month after receiving their stamps. They purchased foods designed to last the month—particularly pastas and canned goods. They bragged that they shopped the sales, and shied away from name-brand goods. As the weeks progressed, if they were running low on food, they cooked creatively and sparsely, they spent portions of their cash grant, they visited food banks or charities, or they ate meals with friends or relatives. Beth, a 27-year-old white woman, frankly told of her various jobs which go unreported to the welfare office so that she can make ends meet. She also has an extensive social support network:

> I usually spend all my food stamps at the first of the month, so if it doesn't last me all month, I don't have any more. So usually I'll go to my mom's and get some few groceries, or my church and get a few groceries.

Other women, particularly those without reliable transportation, shopped for many of their food items in convenience stores. These small neighborhood stores generally charge significantly higher prices for food than do the large chain grocery stores, but they are used nonetheless because they are located closer to home. It is ironic that those who have the least money often pay the most for their food because of where they shop (Rank, 1994).

Food insecurity—defined by the U.S. Department of Agriculture as households that were uncertain of having, or unable to acquire, enough food for all their members because they had insufficient money or other resources—and *food insecurity with hunger*—defined as households that were food insecure to the extent that one or more household members were hungry—are on the rise, and comprise about 20 percent of families with children (U.S. Department of Agriculture, 2002). In the study of Oregon families who had left welfare for work, 30 percent of respondents were food insecure, and another 22 percent could be classified as food insecure with hunger (Seccombe et al., 2005). Nearly 30 percent reported that they sometimes, often, or always worry about where their next meal is coming from. Thirty-eight percent reported cutting the size of their own meals almost every month, and 37 percent reported that they have cut the size or skipped meals for their children because of lack of money (or stamps) (Seccombe et al., 2005).

Juggling Bills

The women interviewed here revealed elaborate schemes in order to live on insufficient welfare checks. There is little financial leeway, so when the unexpected occurs, which it does often, it sets forth in motion a series of decisions that touch every aspect of women's lives. Unexpected events included broken appliances, unexpected medical or pharmaceutical bills, car repairs, and even outgrown clothing. Women wondered, "How can I cover these expenses?" A common method used was juggling these bills because they could not all be paid at one time. Almost every woman interviewed nodded "yes" when asked if she ever juggled bills. For some, it was a common occurrence. For others, it was rare, something done in emergencies only. While virtually all claimed to juggle their bills, they recognized that this was not an efficient way to stay afloat. Dee, a 24-year-old African American mother, in school with plans of becoming an accountant, told me:

> Oh, my electricity has been turned off, many times. That's because my bill has been so much higher than what I can pay after my other bills. I pay the rent, and then I pay the utility. Whatever is unpaid goes on the next bill.

But then the next bill is higher than it should be. And now I'm just wait-ing for it to go off again. But they will usually turn it on within a week. I stay at my girlfriend's or I stay at my sister's house. Or sometimes I stay here and just take my kids over there to give them a bath, feed them, and then bring them back over here. At night there isn't anything to look at anyway, so I just put them to bed. So, it works out, kind of.

When deciding which bill to pay, and which to let go in a particular month, few claimed that they would juggle something as important as rent. "Having a roof over my children's head is the most important thing," I was told. One woman admitted to living in a homeless shelter at an earlier period in life, and she shuddered when discussing it. Many others had doubled up with family members such as mothers, sisters, and cousins, or had shared housing with friends in order to make ends meet. They know, from first-hand experience, the anxiety of having little privacy, sharing beds, and living in cramped quarters not meant for their children. Despite detesting her home in a pub-lic housing project, Coreen is at least thankful to no longer sleep in a bed with both her mother and her two-year-old daughter. She moved out to the housing projects, where the rent on her small one-bedroom apartment is only $26 a month, so that she and her daughter could share their own bedroom, rather than also sharing it with Coreen's mother. The security of having a roof over their head was deemed all-important, and the women interviewed did not want to jeopardize this security. Thus, when asked what bill they pay first, I was repeatedly told, "My rent, absolutely." Kim, a 29-year-old African American woman with three children answered my query as to what she spends her money on first after she gets her check:

> Okay, first I have to get a money order to pay my rent—it's due on the fifth. I wait on my light bill, but basically I know about how much all my bills are going to be. So I know how much I'm going to spend and how much I have left over. Like a budget. I don't never go over my budget. Well, this month I bought my kids some clothes with the telephone money. You do what you have to do.

Utility and telephone bills are those bills that are most likely to go unpaid. Like many of the women interviewed, 35-year-old Lynda has had her utilities cut off sev-eral times. Utilities are a critical component to daily living, unlike a telephone, which some people might consider a luxury. Yet, utility companies do not hesitate to turn electricity or gas off, after what they consider sufficient notice. Women routinely complained that utility companies were not willing to "work with me" by accepting a partial payment, or by allowing a month's payment to lapse. Consequently, most women interviewed had at least one experience of having her utilities turned off, leav-ing their families without basic services. Yet, when turned off, women must find a way to muster not only the remainder of the bill, but also the money it costs to have them turned back on:

> I hate for my gas service to get disconnected because when they cut it off it's $15. And when they come back to turn it on it's another $15. So that's

an extra $30 right there, which is not a lot of money to a lot of people, but $30 is a lot of money to me. Three hundred and three dollars is not even covering my bills every month.

Coping with the Stress

Legislators, in their month-long experiment, did not have to face these issues. They bypassed the myriad of decisions that welfare recipients have to make for their families on a daily, weekly, or monthly basis. How will I pay the bills? What do I need to juggle this month? Do we have enough food in the house? Who will care for my children while I look for work? Can I afford public transportation, if I am lucky enough to find a job? If I get a job, will the wage cover my corresponding increase in rent, the decrease in food stamps, and will it provide health insurance for my children? How can I entice my children to do well in school, when they are being tempted to do otherwise by influential peers? Can I fight a well-established drug culture that preys off young, poor teenage boys? How can I get my daughter to understand that having a baby will not fulfill her needs for love, affection, and independence, which she so desperately craves from a man? How can I find the strength to motivate my family, when all around them they see images of consumption that we can never afford?

Irene, for example, knows the dangers and temptations facing poor children and poor teenagers. Compounding her financial difficulties are the innumerable struggles she encounters trying to keep her five children safe and out of trouble. She knows the dangers they face; she worked for a period of time as a school bus driver, and made it a point to get to know the children on her bus route; children who lived in some of the poorest neighborhoods in town. Poor children face multiple difficulties that are less likely to plague the more affluent, she believes. As one example, she describes witnessing elementary school-age children selling drugs:

> Little children in fourth, fifth, and sixth grade, you know what I'm saying? So I know it's out there. These grown men give it to the children to sell it because when police drive in an area, they'll never look at the child. And if the children do get caught, they ain't going to get no time. They'll probably just get community hours and that's that. So, that's what I'm scared of. I'm scared that, if I don't buy my kids the things that they want, somebody out there is gonna say to them, "You want them hundred dollar pair of Nikes? I know where you can make some easy." I'm scared they're going to influence them that way. So that's why I struggle and try to buy them those $70 shoes.

Irene also elaborates on her other fears for her children, and how she deals with them. For example, she is trying to share her religious values about sexuality with her teenage son—explaining that sex is appropriate only in the confines of a committed relationship, preferably marriage. She wants him to consider the benefits of abstinence, but recognizes her uphill battle:

I just talk to my children about sex, drugs, everything. I don't hide noth-ing from them because I rather for them to hear it from me than out there. Like sex. My oldest son was going through puberty, and the school was teaching him about rubbers. You know, condoms and stuff. And I thought that was bad. He had some, and was going to keep them, but then his con-science started bothering him because I'd read stretches from the Bible about how God don't want us to have sex until we're married. So we talked about it, and he still got some pressure on him. Because when his friends find out you ain't having sex—when you turn 15 and 16, if you don't done be having sex by then, people will pick at you. They think you odd. So he's trying to deal with it, but I know it's getting to him. I'm going to try to hang in there with him.

Irene also works hard to prevent her children from using the drugs that are com-monly passed around the housing project in which she lives:

The neighbor kids would wait until I go to bed, then they—we didn't have no screens on the window—they would slip cigarettes and reefers through the window to my kids. So I confronted them, and I went to confront the parents. She kept telling me no, that her child wouldn't do this, and so on. And I went and talked to some officer that I knew personally, right? And they told me that if I caught them again I could have them arrested. If you try to nip something in the bud, you have a better chance of stopping it than if you wait for it to go down. I think I got it under control. I don't want them smoking cigarettes and smoking reefers.

Given these many concerns, it is not surprising that welfare recipients are more likely to be depressed, and suffer from more psychological distress than do others (London, Martinez & Polit, 2001). In a recent evaluation of TANF in the District of Columbia, 21 percent of respondents faced serious mental health challenges to secur-ing employment (Acs & Loprest, 2003). Another study followed 833 African American mothers over time, some of whom were on welfare, and some of whom were not. The research found that women on welfare reported more psychological distress and anxious moods at the first time they were interviewed, and again ten years later, than did the other women who were not on welfare (Ensminger, 1995). Part of the ex-planation appears to be recipients' poorer health status, including higher rates of chronic conditions, and their lower levels of education, both of which significantly im-pact their chances of finding employment.

Adolescent mothers are particularly at risk for stress, depression, and psycholog-ical distress. The teenage years are difficult as it is, without the added responsibility of motherhood. It is a period of time when children are making the transition from child-hood to adulthood, and it is usually fraught with emotion, tension, quests for inde-pendence, and then recoiling back into dependence. Consequently, many young mothers are poorly equipped to handle parenthood, since they are still learning how to be adults themselves. Not surprisingly, then, adolescent mothers are more likely to report depressive symptoms, low self-efficacy, and low self-esteem than are older women, or those without children. In a longitudinal study of 2,079 teenage mothers on welfare, over half were at risk of clinical depression at the beginning of the study, and 43 percent remained at risk at the 42-month follow-up (Quint, Bos & Polit, 1997).

Much like Irene, and like Jana, introduced in the beginning of this chapter, women deal with these financial and social pressures in a multiplicity of ways. Some vent their frustration alone. How do they cope with these pressures? "I lay on my bed and have a good cry," I was told repeatedly. Other women reported physical ailments from the stress: headaches, insomnia, nervousness, exhaustion, and depression. A couple of women told me that they were seeing a counselor to help deal with their stress. Amy, a college student with a young daughter, told me:

> I get real bad stress, where I get to the point where I don't sleep at all. Or I sleep for two hours and wake up exhausted. I'll go to bed exhausted, but not be able to sleep and stare at the ceiling for six hours. When I wake up I'll have nail prints in my palms, from clenching my fists in my sleep. I've actually had some spine problems in my neck because of muscle spasms. It actually throws my spinal column out of whack. I never feel like I get a reprieve. I never really get a school vacation. As soon as I don't have school stuff to worry about, I have everything else.

Prayer and a belief in God helped many women cope with the stresses of being poor, raising children alone, and being on welfare. "I know the Lord is going to look out for me," symbolizes many women's beliefs. Recognizing that they have little control over their lives, they willingly turn over the control to someone else. "He ain't going to put no more on your shoulders than you can handle." Religion gives meaning to life, and provides guidance for seemingly unanswerable questions (Durkheim, 1947). Concerns about social injustice and inequality are often addressed by religion, and a belief in God and in an afterlife, make injustices easier to endure (McGuire, 1992). "I pray until I get an answer or something changes" characterizes the coping strategies used by many women.

Finally, a prominent strategy for coping with poverty and welfare use is holding steadfast to the position that this stay on welfare is only temporary, and that things will soon improve. Coreen is a young African American woman who lives in the housing projects with her two-year-old daughter. She works part-time at a fast-food restaurant to supplement her welfare check, and does not report her earnings to her caseworker. She is trying to save her money in order to move out of the projects and eventually get her own house.

> I hold on by knowing that I'm going to have something better someday. You know, my hopes are my dreams. It keeps me holding on, knowing what I can do, what I can accomplish. Knowing that this is going to be temporary for me.

Women were nearly unanimous in voicing their certainty that welfare was not going to be their permanent form of financial support. Each woman held on to a goal—from wanting a house, to wanting a high-paying job, to wanting to marry a man who would help take care of her. Coreen continued:

> I used to have a boyfriend, and he was abusive. And I used to say, "If you love me so much, then why do you let me live in <name of housing project>? If you love me, then get me out of here. I want to have my own home. I'm going to have a house, with or without having a husband. You know, I'm going to work that hard for me and my baby."

Affording Life's "Luxuries"

From these interviews it became apparent that many women made expenditures that some people would consider as unnecessary luxuries for their families. Quite commonly, the women I interviewed owned large television sets, VCRs or DVDs, and paid extra money each month for cable television to supplement the few channels received in the viewing area in which the interviews were conducted. Some people might consider these purchases extravagant. Welfare critics may be tempted to cite these purchases as evidence of fraud or waste within the welfare system. Other women spent part of their check on cigarettes or alcohol. Still, other women added fuel to the stereotypes about women on welfare by going into grocery stores to purchase relatively expensive foods with their food stamps, such as steak or seafood. This causes many people to wonder why and how do poor women make such extravagant purchases? Are welfare benefits too generous, in that recipients can afford luxuries that many middle-class families struggle to afford?

A more accurate explanation is that poverty is depressing. Affording some luxury helps ward off feelings of hopelessness, despair, and depression. The poor experience a cultural dissonance. They are painfully aware of the American dream, which is laden with heavy consumerism, and fueled by cash or credit. However, they are disconnected from it. They see the same advertisements as the more affluent, encouraging us to eat this; to shop here; to buy that; and to wear this. Despite being bombarded with these cultural images, they cannot consume like average Americans. They are, in many ways, removed from the cultural loop. Thus, in an attempt to allow themselves some degree of relative comfort, they may purchase something that makes them feel connected to mainstream America, but that welfare critics may argue is an unnecessary luxury: cable television, a VCR or DVD, expensive running shoes for their teenage son, a new dress for their daughter, a manicure or set of nails for themselves, or dinner out to a fast-food restaurant.

Are these luxuries? Certainly they are not necessities, in that they are not necessary for survival as are food, shelter, and clothing. In our modern society, we might add health care and education to the list. So, one could argue, that in the strictest sense of the term, all else is really a luxury. Purchases designed to enhance self-esteem, such as clothing or cosmetics, or those designed to keep children busy and off the streets, such as cable television or a VCR or DVD, could be designated as frills—nonessential items. But are they really? The vast majority of Americans, from rich to poor have their self-image and self-esteem tied up in material possessions: cars, clothes, stereos, jewelry, and the like. Can we expect welfare recipients and their children to feel differently? How important is it to enhance poor adults and children's self-esteem, or to keep children busy and off the streets? I suggest that many of these purchases are paramount to providing the psychological tools that enable both adults and children to help themselves. For example, teens that feel good about themselves are less likely to experiment with drugs, to get pregnant, or to impregnate others. They are more likely to stay in school and graduate. Adults who have a positive self-image are more likely to have a plan about their future, and are less likely to be emotionally crippled when it comes to implementing that plan. Thus, we should be encouraging self-esteem among welfare recipients and their families, not crippling its development.

Most splurges did not cost excessive amounts, and were a means of building and uniting a family. Meals out were usually to a fast-food restaurant or to buffets where children eat free. Women told me of taking their children to the "dollar movie" theaters, where prices for children under age 12 were only 50 cents. Or they splurged and rented a movie from the local video store and saved even more money. Irene's comments were typical:

> Me and my children used to go to the Dollar Movie on Tuesday. I mean, it was fifty cents for them. We would eat a lot of food before we go, because then I can afford it. We'll eat real good, and then we'll go there, and if there's two or three movies we'll watch them all. But then, they done raised the price, and now we can't afford it. On the weekend, instead, we'll rent movies and pop popcorn. Sometimes we'll set up like we be camping out. We get real comfy.

Molly, a white mother of three young boys agreed:

> I try to treat my kids at least once a month. We go to Shoney's where the kids eat free. Or to Ryan's. That's a big deal for them. I told myself, try to treat them at least once a month. And I would try to take them to a movie at the Dollar Theater. I would use my food stamps and go get whatever we wanted to eat and hide it in my purse. That's kind of sneaky, but that's the only way we could afford to go to the movies, you know? And they love to go to the movies—that's a big deal.

Likewise, the mother who buys expensive shoes for her teenage son may not necessarily be spending money foolishly. She may be trying to keep him out of the hands of drug dealers who like to flaunt expensive clothing and name-brand shoes to young boys as a way to entice them into the trade, as I was told on several occasions. Likewise, purchasing a large television set may also be a rational act if your goal is to keep children satisfied staying indoors. Many mothers, particularly those in the housing projects, did not want their children to go outside unsupervised. They worried about the crime, the drugs, and the peer group that would tempt their children. They did not want their daughters to have boyfriends. Therefore, after school many children came directly home, and were not allowed outside again.

Some teenagers even fear their own neighborhoods. Bowen and Chapman (1996) surveyed 207 middle and high school students in communities within Florida and North Carolina. They found that low-income youth were significantly more likely to report such neighborhood dangers as gunshots, murders, gang-related fights, or selling illegal drugs during the past 30 days than were their more affluent peers. Although these were not frequent occurrences among either group, it remains that low-income youth did not feel as safe in their neighborhoods as did others.

Low-income neighborhoods are less likely to offer after-school programs for children and teens, and are less likely to have parks or recreational facilities within them. Moreover, poor families are less able to afford the costs associated with extracurricular activities, such as uniforms, or dues. Children in middle- and upper-middle-class families are two–three times more likely than low-income children to be enrolled in extracurricular activities such as sports, clubs or lessons (Fields, Smith, Bass & Lugaila, 2001). Poor families cannot afford them and are instead forced to find ways to entice their children to stay at home and stay out of trouble.

Marissa, a 28-year-old African American mother, is concerned about her neighborhood, and she is typical in the way she likes to keep her children occupied. She has four children, the oldest of whom is twelve years old. They all have chores around the house every day after school and on weekends. Her goal is to keep them busy and out of trouble:

> There is nothing out in the streets but trouble. I talk to my children a lot, and I say, "Look, you see how people hang out in the street? It's not good for you." Because there are so many young kids hanging out on the streets. You walk down this main road, and that's all you see is young kids. Hanging out in the streets, I can't handle that. My daughter has a 14-year-old girl going to her school right now and she's pregnant. And it's like, man, I'm not risking that.

Purchasing a television, cable programming, and electronic equipment are ways to keep their children occupied. Without these items, home could seem confining, boring, and repressive. Therefore, purchases such as expensive athletic shoes or electronic equipment are arguably, not irrational acts that waste taxpayers' money. On the contrary, they exemplify the kind of rational decisionmaking that women on welfare must routinely face in order to keep their children safe and out of danger—decisionmaking that is absent from the month-long welfare experiment conducted by members of the state legislature. Buying $75 shoes for one family member or steak for dinner is not without its sacrifices. It means that there is that much less in the family budget for something else. It may mean not paying a utility bill in full this month, thus risking the family's well-being in other ways. It may take several months of sacrifice, using the lay-away system available in many stores. Or it may mean that the family will have to scrimp and save on food purchases made for the remainder of the month. And often, it means that mothers must find some other way to augment their incomes. They do it, however, to add a glimmer of sparkle and hope to their lives, and especially, to the lives of their children.

Supplementing Welfare

A perplexing discrepancy has been documented by other researchers between welfare recipient's self-reported income and their expenditures, a discrepancy that was also noted in these interviews. That is, welfare recipients report that their expenditures on food, housing, medical supplies, household supplies, and other incidentals far exceeded their entire income (Berrick, 1995; Mayer & Jencks, 1989; Edin & Lein, 1997). Edin and Lein found, for example, through detailed budgeting records, that welfare recipients covered only about three-fifths of their expenditures with their welfare benefits (1997). Their interviews with 214 welfare recipients revealed an average monthly expenditure of $876 for housing; food; necessities such as medical care, clothing, transportation, childcare, toiletries, and cleaning supplies; and other nonessentials such as entertainment, cable television, and cigarettes and alcohol. With an average family size of three people, respondents spent on average $213 a month on housing, $262 on food, $336 on other necessary expenses, and $64 on those nonessential items that some may label "luxuries."

Meanwhile, the welfare benefits given to poor women in every state do not come anywhere near these expenses. Not surprisingly then, their budgets revealed a constant shortfall of money. In the four cities in which Edin and Lein conducted their interviews—Charleston, South Carolina; San Antonio, Texas; Chicago, Illinois; and Boston, Massachusetts, the average welfare cash benefit was $307, the average food stamp allocation was $222, and the average SSI grant was $36, for a total monthly income of $565. Those who lived in subsidized housing came closest to meeting their monthly expenses with their welfare benefits, but still generally fell short by $200–$300 a month. Only one mother in eight came within $50 of covering her expenses using her welfare benefit alone.

Consequently, the women Edin and Lein interviewed had to generate additional money or in-kind benefits in order to make ends meet. With the exception of one mother, no welfare recipient interviewed lived on welfare alone. The single exception was a mother who was in danger of losing custody of her child because she failed to provide adequate food and clothing on a regular basis. Edin and Lein concluded that welfare benefits including food stamps, subsidized housing and other benefits, do not provide an adequate financial floor.

Introduced in the opening of this chapter, Jana is one of many women on welfare whose expenditures exceed her income. Unfortunately, in addition to ingenuity and creativity, making ends meet on a welfare check may also require one to manipulate the system substantially, otherwise known as fraud.

In a follow-up study of the "Walk a Mile" program, 172 Florida legislators, city and county commissioners, and agency heads around the state signed up for the program in which they were paired up with a welfare recipient for one month. One such legislator, State Representative Cynthia Chestnut, who represents the area in which the interviews were conducted, felt that she has gained valuable experience from the match. Yet, she could not abide by perhaps the most crucial component of the program—living on a food stamp budget for a month. "One part of the Walk A Mile project that many policy makers, including Chestnut, found it difficult to stick to was the agreement to live on a food stamp budget for the month of November," the news article stated. It features a picture of Representative Chestnut presiding over an elaborate and expensive traditional Thanksgiving meal, complete with all the trimmings. Meanwhile, her welfare "match" went without Thanksgiving festivities that year (Chandler, November 28, 1997).

It is ironic that while state legislators felt noble from their month-long experiment, welfare recipients must be fraudulent in order to be able to provide for, and thus keep, their children. Recipients are not given enough money on which to live and raise their families. In Chapter 6, I examine the formal and informal support systems that recipients draw upon to augment their welfare benefits for themselves and their children. How do women and their families supplement their welfare benefits to make ends meet?

Like other studies, I found that poor women and welfare recipients often share conventional, mainstream aspirations, yet harsh economic realities impinge upon their abilities to meet these conventional goals (DeParle, 2004; Edin & Kefalas, 2005; Hays, 2003). Consequently, they develop strategies that make sense to them and their families, given their economic constraints. They are not merely passive victims of adverse circumstances, but, rather, are active agents striving to better the lives of their families through negotiation and exchange. They evaluate each situation as it arises, rationally assess their options, and make decisions that provide some semblance of self-respect. Living and surviving welfare touches all aspects of one's personal life, not simply the economic realm. Some of the daily decisions and coping strategies may be alien, or difficult to comprehend, to those who are more affluent and thereby find themselves in different circumstances. Poor women on welfare make these decisions and develop these strategies because they work to mediate the deleterious effects of poverty on the human spirit.

CRITICAL THINKING QUESTIONS

1. Can you survive on a welfare budget? Make a realistic but lean budget for yourself and one child. Be sure to include housing, transportation, and entertainment costs for the part of the country in which you live. How much money do you think that you would need?

2. Now, pare that budget down so that your maximum is $241 in cash and $274 in food stamps for you and your child. What do you have to give up to make ends meet? Do you think you could live on this amount? For how long?

3. If you were Jana, what would you do to improve your situation?

4. What is so depressing about getting free money from the government? It sounds like a great deal, doesn't it?

5. Is there any truth to the stereotype that poor families on welfare splurge on extras such as large-screen televisions or fancy name-brand shoes? Please explain.

6. If there is a discrepancy between income and expenditures, how do you think that welfare recipients supplement their income?

7. The author claims that living and surviving welfare touches all aspects of one's personal life, not simply the economic realm. Provide some explicit examples of this.

6

Living and Surviving Welfare: The Importance of Family, Friends, and Formal Support

Women who receive welfare must find additional sources of assistance in order to take care of their families because they cannot survive on welfare alone. This is a well-guarded secret kept from caseworkers, but it is a well-known fact of life among recipients. It is also a deep suspicion on the part of the American taxpayer and elected policy makers (DeParle, 2004; Gilens, 1999; Hancock, 2004).

Women's accounts of their welfare experience indicate manipulation of the rules and regulations. However, few women label their actions fraudulent. Instead, most women on welfare have come to see their reliance on family members, friends, neighbors, boyfriends, their children's fathers, charities, and hidden jobs as normative. They could not feed, clothe, shelter, or enliven the spirits of their children without this aid.

Yet not all women have access to such help. Some have loving and devoted family close by who are able to help them out financially, offer babysitting, purchase clothing for their children, or provide the family with a large-ticket item such as a car. But other women do not have these family resources. Some women have friends and neighbors whom they have come to rely on for transportation or babysitting. Other do not trust or socialize with their neighbors, perhaps feeling rejected or let down by them too many times. Other women work part-time and keep the money hidden from their caseworkers. Yet others are unable or unwilling to work outside the bounds of welfare. This chapter examines, in women's own words, the sources of support that they draw upon to meet their financial and social obligations.

Assembling a system of social support is part luck, part skill, and part deception. *Lucky* are those women with family and friends who have the inclination and ability to help them out. Yet, even good fortune can be temporary and unreliable. A grandmother who can babysit today may be unavailable next week.

Second, it takes *skill* to seek out the needed services in a fragmented social welfare system. However, not everyone has the same level of tenacity or resources with which to develop those skills.

Third, it takes some *deception* to finesse and manipulate a system, sometimes illegally, to amass the resources needed to provide for one's children. Ambitious women—women with hope—may see that hiding resources from their caseworker is a rational, reasonable, and responsible way to care for their family, given the circumstances. But not everyone feels comfortable amassing pay from part-time work, or money from a boyfriend, and not reporting it when the law demands that you do so.

The system of aid and social support that a woman orchestrates, legal or otherwise, not only helps her live and survive on welfare, it is also crucial to helping her exit the system. Success in transitioning off welfare is due in large part to the formal and informal support recipients can muster. These supports help to build assets, relieve stress, provide transportation, perform babysitting, and in many ways provide the necessary boost that allows women to leave the welfare system, sometimes temporarily, often permanently.

If assistance of this nature is so crucial to women's success at leaving welfare, why do we leave it up to luck, skill, and deception—in other words, up to *chance*? For women to survive on welfare and to successfully leave the welfare system, they need access to a multitude of supportive services. I suggest that these must be institutionalized so that services (a) are available to all families; (b) are reliable; and (c) do not encourage welfare recipients to become fraudulent in order to receive them.

Kate receives welfare for herself and her two young children, but she could not make it without augmenting her check with the generous help of family, friends, and charities. She knows this, and sees it as a fact of life. Welfare is "okay," she said, but she gently asked that the President of the United States be reminded that it's not enough to live on, "to cover what we really need." She was quick to add that she doesn't want to complain. The last thing Kate wants to be identified as is someone who complains about the size of her welfare check. Rather, she is very appreciative of her small grant, even though it falls short of providing the basic necessities for her family. Like many other women, Kate pieces together her own package of economic aid. This aid comes in part from the government, but must be heavily subsidized by her siblings, her grown children, and her friends and neighbors. She receives aid from charities, and she augments her welfare check with the money she earns from working in the informal sector babysitting for her neighbor's children.

Kate is a 42-year-old African American woman with five children ranging in age from 6 to 25 years. Her three grown children have their own apartments, although she sees them regularly. She also has two young school-aged children, a boy, Kenny, age seven, and a girl nicknamed Pru, age six, for whom she collects welfare. She has been on the system for two years this time, since leaving an abusive boyfriend—Kenny's father—whom she lived with in a nearby rural area. After one of their frequent arguments, he tried to kill her and her young children by setting their house on fire when they were inside asleep. In a fit of rage, he doused the perimeter of the house with kerosene and lit a match to it. Luckily for Kate, Kenny, and Pru, the grass and leaves surrounding the house were wet, and the fire smoldered slowly and they were able to escape unharmed. Her siblings came to her rescue, and she moved to the city where the interviews were conducted to be closer to them, and to her adult children. Meanwhile, Kenny's father went to jail for his crime, although he has now been released and is living in a city about 75 miles away from Kate. She has a restraining order against him to ensure that he does not bother her again.

This is not Kate's first bout with an abusive boyfriend. The father of her oldest son was also physically abusive to her. The abuse was frequent and severe. One day, about 25 years ago, she fought back in an attempt to defend herself, "I had to get him off of me, and I hurt him." He was seriously injured and required hospitalization. He pressed charges against her, and at 17, she was charged with a felony assault. Kate doesn't understand the charges, and isn't even exactly sure what the specific charges were. She blames her vagueness on the time that has lapsed between then and now, but I'm not convinced that she ever quite understood why she was charged with a felony crime in the first place, and he was not. In part, her confusion seems to stem from her inability to articulate the injustice of what happened and the sexism in the courtroom 25 years ago, which treated battered women punitively. Her boyfriend had a history of assaulting her: "It was a weekend thing of him always beating me up." She said that she had called the police before, but the court did not forgive her for hurting a man who had repeatedly hurt her. There was little discussion in the court of self-defense and no discussion of "Battered Women's Syndrome." Twenty-five years ago our society spoke very little of domestic violence. Kate spent 30 days in jail: "But the jury told me I should have gotten 30 years."

Her felony record has followed her over the years, and has interfered with her ability to land or to keep a job. She tells me that this is why she has been off and on welfare since her first child was born. She has a strong work ethic and, not surprisingly, has held many jobs. She has worked in the fast-food industry, as a maid in a hotel, as a cook for the Head Start Program, in the kitchen of a hospital, and as a cook in the coffee shop of a chain discount store. She particularly likes cooking and working with food, and emphasized how much she would like to have a job of this nature. To upgrade her cooking skills, she contemplated taking a course at the local community college. Transportation barriers, however, prevented her from pursuing the course. She does not have her own car, and the city bus quits running before the class gets out for the evening, and therefore she would have no way home. The seven-mile trip home is too far to walk, and she has no bicycle.

Kate would love to have a job and is resentful of others on welfare whom she perceives as not wanting to work. She volunteers regularly at her children's school to pass the time. Despite her experience and her willingness to work, she tells story after story of being dismissed on the job or having her application ignored because of her criminal record. "I put it on the application. Any job I work on, they do a background check, and it always comes up. And then, that's the end of that," she told me. It has happened so often that she feels defeated. When asked about her plans to get off of welfare, she commented that she no longer had any "because any decent job I could get they'll do a background check on me. I'll probably end up babysitting when my kids turn eighteen. I'll do something." An act of self-defense against an abusive boyfriend has cost Kate dearly.

Kate's inner strength and sense of fortitude primarily comes from the large extended family and social networks that surround her. Along with her six brothers and sisters, she was raised in the countryside by an aunt after her mother, and then a year later, her father died. With the help of her aunt, she graduated from high school, even though she had her first baby during her senior year. Alongside her aunt, Kate helped raise her younger brothers and sisters. She was the oldest girl, and her role as caretaker within the family was important and highly valued.

> I had two sisters. One sister died, so now I have one sister and four brothers. There were seven of us, only six of us now. But we're still a close family. We all lived in the big house together, my momma, her sister, and my granddaddy, and us kids, all lived in the same house. And after my momma died, my aunt was there. So she took care of us. And I helped take care of the younger ones. It was a big family house, but later the wiring went out in it, and the taxes went up, so we had to tear the house down. So, my brother now has a trailer on the land where we grew up. I was living in the trailer for a while. And that's when my youngest boy's daddy started acting crazy.

Kate remained very close to her siblings as each one grew up and had families of their own. Together, they also remained in close contact with their aunt. Kate credits her aunt as being the "father" to her three oldest children in their early years. They lived together in her aunt's home while her children were young, and they shared a warm and happy home life. When her children were in middle school, they moved in with Kate's sister. This arrangement was considered by Kate and her family to be a natural extension of a warm and loving extended family. Kate had a full-time job as a cook with Head Start, and her sister could more easily care for the children. This sister always wanted children, but never had any of her own, so she welcomed them into her home. It was a living situation that worked out best for everyone, Kate says, nonchalantly. She seemed unaware that other people may find this arrangement unusual. From her perspective, an extended family is a blessing, and is not indicative of any dysfunction. She told me:

> I know where they were, and I didn't have to worry about them. About three or four years ago, before I moved to XXX <city>, they were still staying with her. She didn't want them to go. She bought a doublewide trailer so she'd have room for them. So it's like they have two moms.

This close extended family relationship continues today. Although her aunt is no longer alive, Kate continues to see her siblings, their children, and her own three grown children regularly. One brother and his family live across the street from her, and she sees them virtually daily. Many of her relatives hold middle or working-class jobs. One is a teacher in a nearby community. They provide her with a wide variety of financial assistance and informal social support. Since Kate has no car, they drive her to many of her errands, and they babysit for her when the need arises. Her extended family will buy her young children the clothing they need when her finances are low, and they will supplement the meager number of Christmas presents that she can afford to buy and have sitting under the tree. They assist her in both the routine and irregular aspects of living on welfare. She returns these favors when she can, usually by babysitting for them.

The stresses in Kate's life are mediated considerably by knowing that her family is available to take care of her should an emergency arise. She tries not to call upon them for help too often, but she knows that she can if need be. They not only have the resources to respond, but they are very willing to do so. While taking care of her two young children on a welfare-level budget is difficult, Kate is successful because she calls upon her extended family regularly.

Although Kate has lived in town only a few years since fleeing the abuse from Kenny's father, she has also developed a small, but crucial, social support network within her housing project. Not one to complain, Kate told of her dream of having a house for her children—a house where she could garden, and grow some of her own food as she did years ago in the countryside. She holds on to her fantasy, but she also has her feet firmly planted in the real-life daily struggles of trying to live and survive on welfare. Toward that end, she has cultivated several important friendships with neighbors who live near her in the housing project; these friendships help sustain her. For example, a neighbor has generously allowed Kate to use her telephone whenever the need arises because Kate cannot afford one. In fact, Kate gives out this phone number as "hers," when a number is requested. Another neighbor graciously shares her car with Kate and offers to take her to the store or run other errands when needed. "She's a real nice lady," Kate informed me.

The two people who do not assist Kate in any way are the fathers of her children. Neither pays child support nor visits his children with any degree of regularity. She has no knowledge of Pru's father's whereabouts. Although she would prefer to have no contact with Kenny's father, given the abuse and his attempt to set the house on fire, she said she would not try to stand in the way of visits between father and son. Kenny's father went to court to demand visitation rights, which Kate feels was in retaliation for being jailed on the arson charge, and for being identified to the welfare office as Kenny's father and thus pursued for child support payments. After going to court and being given visitation rights, Kate says that he has only come by to see Kenny twice during the past year. In addition, he only sporadically pays child support. When he does pay, the money goes to the welfare office and Kate receives $50 from them. But, she tells me, because he pays only sporadically, she is frustrated by her inability to plan on whether the $50 is actually coming each month. Her rent was increased by nearly $20 in response to the expectation that he would pay child support. Yet, according to Kate, he hasn't paid in five months. In a strange twist, her bills have increased, but she rarely gets the corresponding child support to pay those bills. She is worse off than she would be if he never paid child support at all.

Kate's assortment of formal and informal support is highly representative of other women I interviewed. They cannot makes ends meet on their welfare grant alone. They live month to month, piecing an existence together in an attempt to stay afloat: to put food on the table for their children; to ward off eviction from their landlords; to obtain furniture in which to sit and sleep; to find the transportation necessary to get to medical appointments and to look for work.

Like the other women interviewed, Kate had no savings account, no checking account, no assets of any real value, no credit cards, no individual retirement account, no life insurance, and no stocks or bonds. She has nothing of her own to fall back upon to cushion the blow when unexpected financial problems arise. How does she make it from month to month? Like the other women that were interviewed, Kate relies upon an assortment of people, community groups, side jobs, and other strategies to pay the bills each month. Most commonly, women depended upon their own mothers, sisters, or other family members to provide a wide array of financial help or important goods and services, such as providing them with an automobile, transportation, or free babysitting. Some women rely upon their children's fathers to slip them money occasionally, or to purchase their children's school clothes, Christmas presents, or a new winter coat. Others rely on the generosity of their current boyfriends to help support children that are not theirs. Still, many women took advantage of the offerings of private charities or churches to get help with food, clothing, or to get a subsidy for their utility bill.

Even with this type of assistance, many women also worked on the side. They babysat for neighbors, provided rides to the store for others without a car, fixed women's hair or nails, raked leaves, or worked in the fields. The work was generally sporadic and not particularly well paying. Usually, it was not reported to their caseworker, out of fear that their overall benefits would be reduced, and they would therefore be in a worse position than when they started. Other women took side jobs in the more formal sector, most often working in fast-food industries or as nurses' aides. Sometimes the jobs and their earnings were reported to their caseworker; other times they were not. These interviews support the growing body of research that indicates that having both informal support from family and friends, and formal support from agencies and outside employment is crucial to being able to live and survive on welfare. More importantly, however, these support networks are also crucial to getting off welfare. They provide the needed boost that makes it possible to work, collect some minor assets, and leave the welfare system.

The patchwork of help that women draw upon is not static. Instead, women continuously expend their energies piecing together a survival strategy. When that strategy no longer works for one reason or another, they piece together a new one. They substitute buying goods from the day-old bakery when they have worn out their welcome borrowing from a neighbor. They pay for taxicab rides when their brother can no longer pick them up from work late at night. They leave their children home alone when they can no longer pay the fee charged by the babysitter. They offer to rake leaves for neighbors when they cannot get their utility bill paid for by a local charity. They have sexual relations in exchange for clothing for their children when their grant runs low. As one woman told me, "everybody has a scheme, so let me tell you mine." Laura, a 29-year-old white woman with two young children, told me that some caseworkers are more flexible than are others toward recipients' attempts at supplementing their welfare checks so that they can have enough to live on.

> If you follow all the rules, then you don't get enough to live on. It's just scraping by, and it seems like some caseworkers are more aware of that

than are others. The first time that I ever applied for it I didn't know what answers to give or not, and the caseworker's not allowed to coach you or anything. But she did kind of say, if you did have this other situation I would be able to award you more. Oh, you mean, so if I went and got this other form filled out, I could get more. . . . But she couldn't directly tell me that.

People who have a dependable source of social support generally fare much better than those who do not, on a wide variety of mental health indices (Berns, 2003; Uchino, 2004). This support is so important because it can mediate the effects of the stresses associated with poverty. Stress can manifest itself in a variety of ways. Unfortunately, it sometimes influences negatively the way in which parents interact with their children. For example, poor families have been criticized for having a variety of maladies, including higher rates of violence toward, and mistreatment of, children, less nurturing of children, and more inconsistent discipline practices. Parents with incomes below the poverty line have the highest rates of violence toward their children, while upper-income families have the lowest; however, most studies fail to examine the role that social support from family, friends, and formal agencies may play in buffering the stresses that lead to greater frequency of abuse (National Council on Domestic Violence and Abuse, 2003).

In their study of parental behaviors, sociologists Hashima and Amato (1994) examined whether social support can help to minimize the mistreatment of children. They used data from the National Survey of Families and Households collected from a representative sample of 1,035 families in the United States. They found that in general, low-income parents were more likely to report behaving in a punitive and unsupportive manner toward their children. However, receiving some type of support significantly reduced the likelihood of these behaviors. Poor parents who reported a greater number of people they could rely on in times of crisis or when they were having problems were less likely to report that they frequently yelled at or slapped their children than parents who had few sources of support. Family, friends, neighbors, children's fathers, other individuals, and even social service agencies can be important resources to help alleviate, or at least minimize, the numerous daily tensions and unforeseen disasters that are commonplace when one lives in poverty.

Informal Support: Help from Families, Friends and Neighbors, and Children's Fathers

Assistance from Families

Most women interviewed expressed clear preferences about where they turn for help. They usually relied on women in their immediate family for help: mothers, sisters, cousins, or adult daughters. This help was commonplace, although it was not always easily given. Poor women sometimes come from poor families themselves, and therefore family members had little to offer. Other women had families who were in better financial circumstances and could offer greater amounts of assistance. But whether the amount received was large or small, I was struck by how frequently it was given. Even family members with meager resources of their own were willing to share what they had with their kin.

Kim is a 29-year-old African American woman who works part-time in the afternoons, while also taking care of three children aged twelve, nine, and seven. Kim is very ambitious, and is looking for a full-time job since completing a certificate program at a nearby community college. She spoke of the nice things she wants in life for herself and her children. She has been off and on welfare for ten years, and looks forward to making a permanent exit as soon as she secures a full-time job. While ideally she would like to work with computers as an office assistant, the area for which she was trained, in desperation she has extended her search into a variety of different fields, including the fast-food industry and custodial work. "Surely I can get a job doing this, I figured. Believe me, I have lots of experience mopping and cleaning for my family," she winced. Nonetheless, she has not been able to find a full-time job, custodial or otherwise. Her combined income for her family of four, with her welfare check and her earnings, is approximately $600 a month, significantly more than other women who receive welfare alone. She receives an additional $323 in food stamps. [Note: In 2005 she would have received up to $499 a month in food stamps.] Yet, for all practical purposes, this is not a lot of money to support a family of four. How does she make it? Kim's relationship with kin sustains her and her children:

> I have my mother and sisters. I had my first child at seventeen, so my mother has always been there. Thank God for her. My other sister, I see a lot because she picks me up from work because my car is broken. We do a lot together, like we go to the movies with the kids. We are close. Between my mom or sisters, someone is always there.

Kim continues to tell me how she relies on her mother:

> My mother bought me my dining room table. She's always there. She lends me money, or sometimes I wash my clothes at her house. Me and my sister drag our laundry over there, but you know, she basically takes me anywhere I want to go. My kids are the first grandchildren, you know . . . My mother helped me to make sure I did finish school. If you don't have that support, that's why a lot of girls don't finish school.

Kim's sister also provides innumerable types of aid:

> Most of the time my sister gives me money. She doesn't have any kids, and works at the university as a custodian. We are tight! She's there no matter what. If I needed money, I would go to my sister first. Most of the time, I don't like asking other people. I might have a problem with that. I'm one of those who tries to be independent. She has bought me outfits. She might say, "You want something, Kim?" because she knows most of the time I don't have the money. But, like when she picks me

up, I pay her $10 a week. And she eats at my house, because she can't cook <laughter>. She always comes here because I'm always cooking. So whatever she wants, she can have.

Kim's discussion of her relationships with her family is significant on several accounts. There are a number of themes here that are found in many other interviews.

First, it was common for respondents to feel most comfortable borrowing or relying upon their families for help, rather than friends or neighbors. Help from kin was generally a first resort, not a last one. It is deemed more socially acceptable. Borrowing items, cooking, cleaning, running errands for kin, or receiving this type of help from them is often normative and routine. Yet, at the same time, the borrowing, or favors needed, by would-be friends or neighbors were seen as troublesome or meddling. "She's always borrowing this or that, but not me, no," said one woman proudly, referring to her neighbor's borrowing habits. But when it comes to blood kin, the rules change drastically.

Second, family members often serve in the role of friends. Siblings, cousins, even mothers and daughters frequently reported spending their free time together, socializing with one another. I was often told about avoiding non-family members. "They ain't nothing but trouble," I was told repeatedly. Neighbors, an obvious potential source for friendships, were often viewed with distrust, particularly in the housing projects. Most often, women preferred the company of kin if they were available.

Third, although cash is sometimes exchanged, the assistance that welfare recipients receive is often in goods and services. Kim and others relied upon family members for transportation or for a place to do laundry. These goods and services are important to the women for several reasons. If purchased privately, services would consume a significant portion of the cash grants; they are logistically difficult to orchestrate; they translate into money saved for other items; and finally, goods and services are not reported to their caseworker.

Fourth, Kim maintains an illusion of trying to be independent. This was not uncommon. Few women acknowledged how much they rely upon family members for help. Although they acknowledged how indispensable this exchange is to them for sheer survival, many women did not view it as "assistance" or "help" per se, because of the strong norms associated with sharing among members of the extended family. Even Kim continued a facade of reciprocity by declaring she paid her sister $10 a week for gas. This reciprocity allows Kim and others to feel independent and thus maintain their dignity and self-respect. I was told in numerous interviews that they received little or no "help" from family members, but in further discussions, women would reveal receiving cars, free rent, babysitting, clothing for their children, or numerous Christmas presents. For example, Jo Lynn, a white woman with two children, reported that she received no financial support at all from her family. Yet, I noticed an expensive late-model car parked in her driveway. I probed further. She replied:

Financially they don't help me out. No. Well, they do, like on certain holidays. They always get the kids presents and stuff that I could never afford. They buy clothes. My mom always comes with a piece of clothing every time she walks in the door. Another thing my mom does for me is that she will come over here and bring me a present for my grandmother for her birthday and write my name on the card, and then I give it to her. And my dad gave me a car. If I didn't have it, I would be in a lot of problems just like everyone else around here. But he did give me that car. I didn't pay a dime for it.

These gifts, goods, and services from family members can tip the balance of the scale from the most dire to one of hopeful survival. I did not talk with anyone whose family support genuinely lifted them from poverty. Rather, many women, knowing they cannot survive on their welfare alone, turned to their families to maintain a decent, if minimal, standard of living for themselves and their children.

These four themes indicate the primacy of the extended family in the lives of many poor women on welfare. Extended families have been shown to provide critical resources for the poor and minority groups (DeParle, 2004; Glick & Van Hook, 2002; Oliker, 1995; Stack, 1974). They are important throughout the life course, but may play a particularly critical role for adolescent mothers (DeParle, 2004; Nitz, Ketterlinus & Brandt, 1995; Panzarine, Slater & Sharps, 1995). Although teen mothers are at significant risk for psychological distress, extended families, especially warm relationships with their own mothers, can buffer the stresses associated with teen parenting. Certainly, not all adolescents have good relationships with their own mothers, even if they are co-residing with them. One study based on 75 African American adolescent mothers found that one-third of them cited their mother as a source of conflict. But positive and supportive family relationships have been linked to higher levels of self-esteem, fewer depressive symptoms, greater likelihood of remaining in school, and avoiding repeat pregnancy and premature marriage (Panzarine, Slater and Sharps, 1995, Sun & Li, 2002). Kate and Kim, who were both seventeen when their first child was born, indicate that their female kin were instrumental in providing the conditions so that they could finish high school, while also raising their babies.

Extended families are more prevalent among certain racial and ethnic minority groups. African Americans, for example, are three times more likely to live in extended families than are whites. Moreover, this is not simply a survival strategy among the poor; significant racial and ethnic differences in the likelihood of living in an extended family exist at all income levels. In their review of the literature, Hatchett and Jackson (1993) note six features of the African American extended family system: (1) a high degree of geographical closeness; (2) a strong sense of family and familial obligation; (3) fluidity of household boundaries, with a greater willingness to take in relatives, both children and adults, if the need arises; (4) frequent interaction with relatives; (5) frequent extended family get-togethers for special occasions and holidays; and (6) a system of mutual aid.

Yet, despite the apparent benefits that an extended family can offer, the dominant ideology in the United States suggests that the extended family is a dysfunctional family. Sharing assistance or residing with kin is thought to reflect that something is wrong, rather than reflecting a normal, and even desirable, family exchange. For example, single mothers who allow other kin to raise their children, as Kate and Dawn have done, violate the conventional image of the normal American family. Extended families are associated with the Culture of Poverty—they are accused of imparting a deviant set of cultural values to their children.

These images reflect dominant cultural ideology by glorifying as normative the family that has a husband who is the primary breadwinner, and a wife who is devoted primarily to the care of her biological children, whether or not employed. Popular television often reinforce narrow conceptions about families and how families are supposed to behave. Family scholars note the dangers associated with the idealized "normal" American family, claiming that it is classist, sexist, and racist (Pyke, 2000a, 2000b; Smith, 1993; Baca Zinn, 1994). It ignores or even denigrates racial and ethnic minority families, poor families, single-parent families, and gay and lesbian families. By idealizing only one model of family life, it ignores the strengths and resiliency offered within a multitude of family structures and dynamics. Is it, after all, dysfunctional for children to have the warmth and love of two women—in essence, as Kate said, to have "two moms"?

Some readers might be tempted to argue that, if aid from family is so commonplace, then we can cut the amount of welfare cash grants accordingly. Can we expect family members to make up the difference between the amount of money needed to live on, and some smaller amount provided by the government? Just as social security benefits were not created to fund retirees in full, can we extend this same logic to welfare? I argue that we cannot. I found that some women received a tremendous amount of support from their families, while others received none. Women who received no assistance may have been estranged from family members or had family with little or nothing to give. Some women reportedly had very small families or none at all in the immediate area. Whites, in particular, were less likely to have a close-knit extended family upon whom to draw. Unlike retirement, for which people have years to plan, the need for welfare is often surprising and swift. A violent husband, an unplanned pregnancy, health problems that prevent work, a partner who deserts without warning, or a default on court-ordered child support, are all reasons that women turn to welfare—reasons that preclude planning. We therefore should not expect or mandate that poor families will rely on their kin for aid.

Assistance from Friends and Neighbors

Although family members were apt to be the preferred source of assistance for most women interviewed, some turned to friends and neighbors, rather than, or in addition to, asking their families for help. Some women had no immediate family nearby. Several of these women told of fleeing abusive childhoods and beginning anew. Others had moved from their home towns to the area where the interviews were conducted because of promised job prospects, to attend college, or to pursue a relationship that had now ended. Other women had family nearby, but preferred to turn to friends and neighbors for assistance because they felt that they were embarrassing their parents by being on welfare. One woman, who was raised in a middle-class household, refused to tell her parents that she was on welfare, fearing that she would be criticized. Instead, such women relied upon friends and neighbors to help fill in the significant gap between income and needs.

Stephanie, divorced with one daughter aged seven, moved away from her family to attend nursing school at the university. When I interviewed her in her third year of the program, she struggled to combine motherhood and being a full-time student. Her classes often last all day, and she was up at 3:00 or 4:00 A.M. most mornings to begin her studies or complete her household chores before her daughter awakens. She had no family nearby and has not seen her ex-husband since their divorce four years ago. Stephanie was able to make it this far because of student financial aid, which supplemented her welfare check by several thousand dollars a year, and by relying upon her network of other single mothers who live in the university-owned student family housing complex for a variety of goods and services. Together, they share babysitting, carpooling the children to school, clothing, and offers of help and assistance in a multitude of other ways on a regular basis. "We share. We have to," Stephanie revealed.

> I don't have any family here. But I do have—I've spent the last three years building up a network of friends that I could leave my daughter with in case of an emergency. I have a "made family." I don't think it would happen as easily if I wasn't in family housing. We are all in the same situation. We are either married and have children, or are single who have kids. I could name a half dozen single mothers around here right off the top of my head.

However, this aid would not be available to Stephanie today. With few exceptions, welfare can no longer augment financial aid for women who are attending four-year universities. Instead, any school assistance is limited to programs that help welfare recipients earn GEDs or other work-ready programs.

Women who live in the public housing projects also appear to have a wide assortment of potential neighbors to whom they could turn for help. Like Stephanie, they are not isolated in single-family homes. However, women in housing projects often would rather not associate with neighbors, and most struck up only a few, if any, friendships. Instead, they complained that their neighbors were jealous, nosy, suspicious, loud, and inconsiderate, or were bad mothers. Some women cultivated one or two friends that they could turn to for emergencies, or to share telephones or transportation. As shown in the opening section of this chapter, Kate, for example, relied on her two friends for a wide variety of services to supplement those provided by her large extended family. She routinely used one neighbor's telephone and relied upon another woman to take her to the store when her family was not available. Yet many other women in the housing projects remained inside their apartments; a self-made prison, as they tried to avoid their neighbors and carve out some privacy in an otherwise crowded world. They trusted few people; "I don't borrow from nobody. I just don't . . . " Many women proudly told me.

Only a few women indicated that they cultivated a wide circle of friends in the housing projects. They created a wide network in which to borrow, to lend, to support, and to be supported. My hour-and-a-half interview with Janie, a 19-year-old mother of a young daughter, was interrupted four times, as friends and neighbors called on the telephone or came by her house to visit, borrow an item, or to see if she needed them to pick up anything from the grocery store. Referring to her friends, Janie told me that she and her daughter are not alone: "We have an extended family of sorts."

Many women rely on their boyfriends to help pay the bills that welfare alone does not cover. These were men to whom they were not legally married and who were not the biological fathers of their children. Some of these men were, however, *social* fathers to the respondents' children. They provided additional financial support to augment welfare, although usually only sporadically—$25 towards food last month, nothing this month, and then a high-priced household item like a television next month. These "gifts" were an important resource to women and their families. Although not usually a steady and reliable source of income, they provided the unexpected treats that make the monotony of poverty easier to endure. Patrice is an African American woman with two children and works part-time for a nearby hospital. She explains how her boyfriend contributes financially to her family by buying her a car, although his contributions go unreported to the welfare office:

> Sure, my fiancé helps me out. He helps me because I try to maintain a good level. My boys need things, and we need a place to stay, and my money goes. I don't make very much, so therefore I run short. And that's how I got the car. He put the down payment on it, because when you get any kind of welfare assistance they don't like you to have anything valuable. So I can't have no accounts like a savings account. They want to know all that. So, I don't have access to money. My trade-in was almost ten years old, and kind of rundown, so I didn't get much for it. So I had to go to him for my down payment. And usually my monthly payments too. He pretty much helps me with those.

Boyfriends also sometimes provided emotional support to the entire family. While their level of involvement with children varied, some women claimed that their children called their boyfriends "Daddy," indicative of the active role boyfriends played within the families. However, it did not appear that co-residence was common. Instead, boyfriends usually lived elsewhere and were free to come and go as they chose. Coreen, an African American mother with one young daughter, told me the housing projects generally had rules against boyfriends co-residing—these units were reserved for welfare recipients and their children. Yet, I noticed many men lingering in the breezeways or the parking lots. When I asked Coreen about this, she responded, "They don't listen. These apartments are for women and their children, but they don't listen," intimating that boyfriends, although barred from living in the projects formally, are often invited guests of the residents and spend a substantial portion of their time there.

Yet boyfriends generally do not stay for free. Despite the popular media image that women on welfare support freeloading boyfriends, these interviews suggest that boyfriends are allowed considerable freedom to come and go at their own discretion because of the cash and in-kind contributions that they make to the household. As Edin and Lein note also (1997), women have an informal "no pay, no stay" arrangement.

Mothers were unwilling to sustain freeloading boyfriends in their homes for long. Moreover, they found, as I did in these interviews, that the exchange relationships sometimes made it difficult to distinguish between their serial boyfriends and prostitution. Several women expressed trading sex, or "being his woman" for money, food, or for clothing for their children. "Yeah, I'll be his woman. Hell, why not, he pays my rent." What distinguished them from outright prostitutes in their minds, however, was that they had ongoing relationships with "my man," or "my friend." Prostitutes were those who engaged in one-night stands for money or in-kind goods. I was told that some welfare recipients engage in prostitution, although none of the women I interviewed admitted to doing so. One woman told me that a friend suggested that she should turn tricks as an easy way to make money, but she proudly told me, "No, I don't want that. I'm being good, I'm doing my best, you know?"

Not all of the relationships with boyfriends were a positive influence, however. Some boyfriends were emotionally or physically abusive to the women interviewed or to their children, or attempted to use the women for their own financial or personal gain. Tamela was involved with one such man, and shared her story in an interview filled with emotion and pain. She is an African American woman, with two children aged six and seven. Although she looks younger than her 23 years, she has the experiences of someone far beyond her years. She grew up with a drug- and alcohol-addicted mother, and spent most of her life on welfare and living in the housing projects. As the oldest of four children, she was forced into the role of raising her siblings because of her mother's addictions and inept parenting. She has been on her own and collecting welfare since age 16 when she gave birth to her son. Because her mother has since been deemed an unfit parent, Tamela also has custody of her two teenage brothers. She is often thrust in the difficult role of family caretaker for an extended family that is fraught with personal, emotional, and financial problems. Aunts, cousins, brothers, and mother demand Tamela's attention. They continually ask for her help and support, but offer little in return. They cannot distract her from her ultimate goal, however, which is to be a nurse. She is in a student-nursing program at the nearby community college, but was taking a semester's reprieve from classes at the time of the interview. The tension caused by a demanding extended family, caring for teenage brothers, being a single parent of two young children on a welfare budget, and successfully attending college, is small compared to the stresses and anxiety induced by her ex-boyfriend. He was aggressive, controlling, and abusive. When she wanted to end the relationship, he beat her. When she threatened to call the police on him, he lied and told her the housing project would evict her, her brothers, and her children. Frightened, she believed him. She acknowledges now that she was young, naïve, and easily manipulated. When she mustered the courage to get a restraining order against him, he broke all the windows in her car. He threatened to call the welfare office and tell them that they had been living together while she collected welfare—a charge that is a serious crime—and one that she vehemently denies. When she called the police one final time to have him removed from her home, he was arrested and taken to jail. Upon being released the next day, he sought revenge. He immediately went to the welfare office and reported that they had been living together and that she had fraudulently collected welfare.

There was a two-year investigation, where all his friends said, yeah he was living with me. It wasn't true. It was stressful because here I am trying to do what's right: go to school, wanting to get off the system. Not wanting to abuse the system, but just to use it to my advantage. I had him removed from my house because he wouldn't go. I called the police and asked them to remove him, so he blames me for going to jail that night. So, when released, he walks from the jailhouse to the welfare office, and tells them that he was living with me. I felt in the beginning that the system was siding with him the whole time. No one listened to me; they just took sides with what he had to say. I tried to tell them what type of person he was, that he was lying, how he slit his wrist, he had to be in crisis stabilization twice, and how he was so abusive, and I just had enough. But nobody would listen to me. But he would call me up all the time and say, "How's the welfare office? I'll tell them I just made everything up because I was just upset for you putting me in jail, if you take me back." But I just said no, I'd rather . . . because I'm finally free of him.

Tamela refused to continue their relationship, and he refused to alter his story. She was assigned an attorney and attempted to fight the charge of welfare fraud. After a drawn-out court proceeding, and further action from the State Attorney's Office, the result is that Tamela was required to pay back nearly $8,000 to the state. To Tamela, the sum might as well be $8,000,000. Her attorney suggested that she could have another hearing, but acknowledged that her case is weak; it is his word against hers. She feels lost in the maze and confusion, and is worn down by her ex-boyfriend's lies and manipulations. Meanwhile, the welfare office has reduced her already small welfare grant as a means to repay the thousands that they deemed she collected fraudulently. Living on the reduced grant is difficult, yet she feels a sense of relief: "I'm finally free of him. I've learned an expensive lesson."

Assistance from Children's Fathers

Since 1988, with passage of the Family Support Act, the government has made greater effort to secure child support from the absent fathers of children. It requires states to increase the percentage of child support collection from those fathers of children supported by welfare who could be identified. Intended to be accomplished by a variety of means, the act includes withholding child support from fathers' wages; requiring states to adopt uniform standards for setting child support awards; and implementing computerized systems for locating delinquent parents. Some states take several further steps; they intercept tax returns, withdraw funds from bank accounts, suspend drivers' licenses, and, as a last resort, put fathers in jail if they fail to pay child support. Mothers are also affected. In order to qualify for welfare, mothers must provide the name and whereabouts of their children's fathers if known, and they are asked to provide a recent picture, if available. In return, the recipient receives an additional $50 each month in her cash grant if a child support payment is made directly to the welfare office. Refusal to provide this information is grounds for denial of assistance (U.S. Department of Health and Human Services, November 2004).

Despite these efforts, there has not been overwhelming improvement in the collection of child support. For millions of parents, there is no child support agreement at all. Among those who do have some sort of agreement, legal or nonlegal, less than three-quarters of custodial mothers received any payment at all, and less than half received their full payment. Among custodial fathers, receipt of child support was even more grim. The average child support bill due was $5,138 in 2002, but the average amount received was $3,198, nearly $2,000 short (Grall, 2003).

Why has the collection of child support not lifted families out of poverty more dramatically? One reason is that many poor women had children with men who are also impoverished. One of every four workers earns less than $8.70 an hour (Shulman, 2003). These parents are unlikely to be able to offer significant sums of money to their children. They may be unskilled workers earning near-minimum wage, or they may be cyclically or chronically unemployed. Unskilled workers generally have unemployment rates double the national average. Their situation has not improved in recent decades. Other absent fathers whose children are impoverished may be in jail or dead, and therefore cannot contribute any support. Leah, a 24-year-old African American mother with four children, was one of several women who told me that their children's fathers were, as far as they knew, in jail: "No, I don't socialize with my oldest child's father. He's in prison now. He walked out on us, and that was it. I didn't hear anything else from him."

A second reason that child enforcement policies have not put a significant dent into the numbers of impoverished children is that many fathers simply disappear, and government does not fund the massive effort that it may take to retrieve them. Women spoke of being owed thousands, even tens of thousands of dollars in overdue child support payments. Many women were very angry about what they perceived as the lack of child support enforcement. As one woman asked, "Why does he get to be out riding his motorcycle, while I'm being treated like a criminal?" Yet most knew that the chances of retrieving any of the owed support was small or non-existent. Many women are disgruntled with the welfare system's low success rate of securing support. The story of Marissa, a 28-year-old African American woman, was routine. Despite providing the necessary information to the welfare office, she still receives only sporadic child support from one of her children's fathers. She receives nothing from the other fathers.

> Where are the daddies? They need to kick in. I don't get child support. What I get is AFDC and try to live off that. We're trying to work on my son's dad, but I'm tired of going to court, and I'm tired of this bull crap. I have to go to court again on December 1. He missed three months. I think he only paid, like two months. And I only get $50 a month. When it's supposed to come to you, and then it's not there no more, it messes up your budget.

A third reason that child support policies have only met with minimum success is because some women adamantly do not want child support from their children's fathers. A recent study found that 19 percent of women who did not receive child support for their children said flat-out that they did not want it (Grall, 2003). I found that a significant number of women shared this sentiment. Two of the women interviewed bore children as a result of rapes. They wanted nothing to do with their attackers. Others were physically, emotionally, or sexually abused by their children's fathers and also did not want any further contact. They worry that, if forced to pay child support, these men will also demand visitation. Although most women complied with the welfare office's policy of identifying fathers, three women told me that they lied to their caseworker outright and claimed that they didn't know who fathered their child. One example is Laura, a 29-year-old white woman with a toddler named Jackie and an infant named Sam. She moved over 1,000 miles to get away from her abusive boyfriend—Sam's father. Her relationship with him is still very tense. Although her relationship with Jackie's father is less strained, it also involves virtually no interaction, and no child support payment.

> Jackie's father—he and I get along just fine. We don't speak. And I like it that way. We're both comfortable with that. I wanted to have a baby, and I guess he didn't. Sam's father is more difficult. He wants to be more involved, and I don't want him to because I don't trust him. We had a very difficult time. We lived together for a very brief period in Chicago and I got pregnant. Then I moved down here. It was too stressful to be there, and . . . I don't like this story. Hopefully we won't have too much to do with him. He is still in Chicago. I don't want him to send me any child support. I told the AFDC office that I don't know who the father is. Jackie's father doesn't pay child support either. I would be more flexible in dealing with him. But Sam's father? No. It doesn't feel right to me to take child support because it has strings attached to it, and I don't want to invite him in our life. I'd rather sever the ties completely.

Jasmine, a 35-year-old African American woman now divorced from her husband, believes that he sexually abused their daughter, and she therefore also wanted nothing to do with him. This includes forgoing the $50 child support check she would receive from the welfare office if he were to pay child support. Fifty dollars is not a large enough incentive to overcome the hatred and distrust she has of him.

> If he ever comes around, and we have to go to counseling again, the counselor will see the angry side of me because I'll tell her right then and there that I can't stand to be in the same room as that person. I wish he would admit to a particular incident that he did. That's all, and just let me have my daughter.

Some women on welfare would like to forgo child support payments altogether out of fear that the pursuit of support may lead to physical violence against them. Welfare recipients have high rates of physical and emotional abuse; it is estimated that 50–60 percent of welfare recipients have experienced domestic violence over their lifetime, and 20–30 percent report being recent or current victims of abuse (Welfare Information Network, accessed March 17, 2005).

Although violence among partners likely has many interrelated causes, one study at the University of Michigan indicates that many abused women reported arguments about such issues as child support (30 percent); visitation (23 percent); and child custody (15 percent) (Raphael & Tolman, 1997). A Massachusetts study also found that approximately 30 percent of abuses involved recent problems or arguments about child support (Allard, Albelda, Colton & Cosenza, 1997).

Thus, it appears that a large number of welfare recipients are using welfare as a way to flee an abusive home situation, such as Kate, who was profiled in the beginning of this chapter. They do not seek child support because they are trying to sever their relationship with their attacker. For many battered women, welfare is a critical alternative source of income to being dependent upon the man who abuses them. It can give them the opportunity and incentive to free themselves from their abuser—financially, physically, and psychologically.

Because the relationship between welfare use and domestic violence appears so strong, victims of violence may be exempt from several Temporary Assistance to Needy Families (TANF) requirements, such as work requirements, time limits, or the requirements of establishing paternity so that child support can be obtained (Rowe and Russell, 2004; U.S. Department of Health and Human Services, November, 2004). These requirements may be waived by individual states in those cases where the requirements would make it more difficult for women to escape domestic violence, would unfairly penalize them, or would put them at risk for further violence and retaliation.

But, a fourth reason that child support policies have not had a large impact is because some women appeared to be relatively indifferent to receiving child support. The number of women who had no expectations that fathers should be responsible financially for their children surprised me. Content with things the way they were, they were appreciative if their children's father occasionally gave them small gifts. The reasons for this indifference are not clear. Some women may have few expectations because of their own lack of self-esteem. Perhaps they did not feel confident rocking the boat with their children's fathers. Other women that I interviewed did not have fathers who supported them as children, and may therefore see this behavior as normative, supporting the tenets of the Culture of Poverty perspective.

Along with her young son Bobby profiled in Chapter 4, Rhonda is an example of a woman who does not expect a regular financial commitment from her child's father. She receives no regular child support from Bobby's father, despite the fact that he works as a long-distance truck driver and has a steady income. She did not express resentment. Rather, she was complimentary, and focused on the gifts he brings when he stops by to see their son approximately once each month. "He takes him to dinner and buys him shoes and stuff like that," Rhonda told me, with a tone that indicated that she holds no ill will toward him for failing to provide financially for Bobby on a regular basis. Likewise, Dee, a 24-year-old African American mother who is in school working towards a degree in accounting, referred to her ex-husband as "sweet" because he will buy his daughter items such as shoes or clothing when he is asked to do so.

These women complied with the welfare office's request for data on the children's father, but were not indignant when money failed to arrive. Instead, they seemed to be more concerned with the lack of emotional involvement on the part of their children's father, rather than the lack of financial support. Kim was typical in her response to my query about her expectations of her children's father:

> All I expect is, even if they don't give them any money or buy them anything, just spend some time with them. Because my daddy never did anything for me and my oldest sister. But he took care of two other boys from somebody else. He and my mother couldn't get along, and he took it out on us. And I don't want to do that. My first kid's daddy, he used to go with this girl in the other building, but he used to walk right past us. He would never even stop and say, "Hey, how you doing," or whatever. Even if he had problems with me, don't take it out on the kids, you know? They didn't ask to come here.

Twenty-year-old Mandy concurs:

> I really don't expect nothing from them. But they can help out in many different ways: Moneywise and clothing, or sometimes babysitting. There might be something I want to do, or something that comes up for me and I'm not supposed to bring a child along, or whatever. I don't go out that much, regardless. But I might have some luck and get a job one day. You know, things like that.

These four reasons suggest that, while pursuing fathers' support is a laudable and worthwhile goal and should be vigorously enforced, it is only one of many problems faced in reversing the plight of poor children and their mothers. Many poor families will need additional help as they struggle to improve their economic plight.

Formal Support: Help from Charities and Social Services

It was not unusual for women to turn to private or public charities and social service agencies to augment their welfare check. These agencies provided important and valuable resources, at least occasionally, for the majority of women interviewed. Some women used them only rarely. They turned to them as a last resort, generally preferring to turn to family first because of the lesser stigma associated with exchanging aid among kin. Often, there was a particular time in a woman's life when she was worse off than at the time of our interview and felt she had no other choice than to turn to charity; initially leaving an abusive partner; moving to a new community; getting the first apartment; or waiting to receive food stamps or a cash grant after a job was terminated. Doreen, a 31-year-old African American woman who is currently married but separated from her husband, turned to charities and social services when they were still together, because her husband had lost his job.

> Yes, I got help. That was before we moved in this house, when we were staying out on the place by the highway. My husband had lost his job, and the agency paid my light bill for me. And I couldn't get the kids nothing for Christmas, so I signed up for "Hope for the Holidays." My mom helped me sign up. They gave us bunk beds and stuff like that. And they gave us food. I have been down low. I've really been down low.

Certain charities or social services were mentioned frequently by women. Food banks were among the agencies mentioned most often, although few women used them on a regular basis. They felt that food programs were stigmatized; use of them indicated that they were poor mothers because they couldn't plan their family's food budget adequately. Irene, an African American woman with four children, commented upon the stigma associated with using charities, food banks in particular.

> About four months ago we went to Catholic Charities and got a referral for some food, but I didn't like to do that so good. I just felt like, there's people out there that might need it more than me. You know what I'm saying? So I said no. Then when I found out that drug addicts are going there and getting it, so I said no. Because they get their money and they use it for drugs, and then they go there and take advantage of that, and that ain't so good. So I try not to go there that much.

Like others, Irene did not want to be affiliated with a program servicing drug addicts. She created a hierarchy of needy people, and she, as a poor mother, was at or near the top of the hierarchy. Drug addicts, in contrast, were at or near the bottom.

My study of Oregon families who had left TANF for work revealed that hunger is a considerable problem. Fifty-nine percent of the 552 respondents from across Oregon claimed that they sometimes or often ran out of food by the end of the month and had no money to buy more. Thirty percent met the classification of "food insecurity," defined by the U.S. Department of Agriculture as households that were uncertain of having, or unable to acquire, enough food for all of their members because they had insufficient money or other resources. Another 22 percent suffered from "food insecurity with hunger" defined as households that were food insecure to the extent that one or more household members were hungry, at least sometime during the year because they could not afford enough food. These figures are higher than among the Oregon population more generally and higher than the national average.

How do families cope with insufficient food? Again, food charities were not necessarily the solution of choice. While 27 percent of the respondents reported having used food charities in the past, 32 percent reported cutting the size of meals because of lack of money, and 36 percent reported that they ate less than they should have because of lack of money. Eight percent also reported that they had to reduce the size of their children's meal, or skipped their meal altogether because they could not afford to buy food (Seccombe, Hartley, Newsom, Pope & Hoffman, 2005).

Instead of routine help with food, women tended to be more comfortable seeking formal help with their rent or utilities. Programs that paid a family's utility bill were very popular, despite the fact that they were limited to one payment per year. Nonetheless, respondents regularly mentioned these as an important source of help. They saw this as a program uniquely created for them. It was not viewed as a program for drug addicts and other less respectable needy people. In fact, some women reported using no charity other than one that would cover their utility bills. Several failed to even know of any other charities in the community to which they could turn. It is not clear how they knew of this particular type of assistance—whether this agency was mentioned formally by their caseworkers, or whether information was passed informally among family members and friends.

Another frequently mentioned set of programs were those that help to buy gifts for children at Christmas time (most likely related to the fact that these interviews were conducted close to the Christmas holiday season). "Hope for the Holidays" is a large-scale community event designed to provide Christmas presents for poor children. It was a dream to be selected for one of the "grand prizes," such as new living room furniture, a new bedroom set, or even a used car.

Women who are new to welfare, or new to the community, often reported difficulty in finding out what services are available to help them. I was told on several occasions that accessing "the system," as it was referred to, is not straightforward—"I had no idea where to go and just stumbled upon things here and there."

From these interviews, I surmise that most women use social services only occasionally, primarily to help them during a particular crisis or a financially difficult period. However, I did interview a small number of other recipients who relied regularly upon private and public charities and social services to help them through each month. Unlike other recipients, they tended to have few family members to rely upon. They regularly used food banks, shopped at thrift stores and day-old bakeries, and used programs to assist them in paying utility bills. Janie is an example of a resourceful woman who relies upon a variety of services to help her make ends meet. She is a 19-year-old white woman, with one young child.

> Before I found out I was pregnant, I was living in my car or living at different people's houses. Or the Covenant House, or shelters, you know. I had a list of resources, and I used every one of them. I still do. I've gone to the Salvation Army for dinner a couple of times when it got to the point where I didn't have enough food in the house. They always have a hot meal. Sometimes, I don't have to buy my diapers. There are agencies: Right to Life, Catholic Charities, and Crisis Pregnancy Center, where if you bring your clothes that you can't use, they will trade them in. So sometimes I don't have the extra bills. Look around my house. That box, that table, all of those came from the Salvation Army. This . . . that . . . and that table came from other people who knew I needed help.

Working Side Jobs: Is This Fraud?

Welfare recipients depend on multiple sources of assistance to supplement their welfare checks. They must piece together these important sources because their cash grant and food stamps do not provide enough money on which to live and raise their families. Those who live in subsidized housing can generally stretch their welfare assistance further than those women who pay full rent for their apartments, but even they usually have trouble making ends meet at the end of the month. Utility bills, clothing, diapers, school supplies, transportation, laundry costs, and routine household cleaning supplies are some of the many items that deplete meager cash grants. Two hundred and forty-one dollars a month, plus a few hundred dollars in food stamps, does not adequately cover even a low cost of living for an adult with one child. It also comes nowhere near lifting a family from poverty. I have shown here that women must turn to other relatives, boyfriends, friends and neighbors, and to the fathers of their children to help them out. Yet it is important to note that these sources of assistance are unpredictable, and are not available to all women. To round out their budget, women also turn to private and public charities and social service agencies for at least occasional assistance.

These interviews revealed that even charities and social services agencies did not completely fill the gap between income and needs. Consequently, some women on welfare also work on the side, and often do not report this income to the welfare office. About one-quarter of the women interviewed informed me that they had recently worked at least sporadically to earn enough money to allow them to meet their monthly bills, buy food for their children, purchase the diapers or washing powder that food stamps cannot cover, or buy their children a special treat to keep their spirits up. These findings echo those reported elsewhere. For example, Edin and Lein (1997) reported that 39 percent of the 214 women in their study said that they had worked jobs on the side during the past year.

Jasmine, who is divorced from her husband and has two children, bluntly explained the necessity of supplementing her welfare assistance so that she can maintain a reasonable standard of living for her family.

> I may have some extras, like my telephone or cable bill, or something like that, but living these days and time, children need those things. We need a phone for emergencies and things, instead of having to walk to a neighbor or use a pay phone. To tell you the truth, I've been working little odd jobs on the side, like cleaning somebody's house or something like that to make ends meet. Also, there's a neighbor around the corner, and I've been taking him to the grocery store. He pays me $10 to take him up there to the grocery store, and I make money that way. Then, I also may go out in the fields, or something. You just have to do that to survive.

Sarah's story also reveals the necessity of side jobs in order to make it. Sarah is white, has three children, and is divorced from their father. The divorce was emotionally and financially complicated, and the difficulties are continuing as her husband attempts to gain custody of all their children. The children divide time between Sarah and her ex-husband, who lives in a larger city 70 miles away. Sarah currently works part-time at a fast food restaurant, and has informed her caseworker of her job. Her welfare benefits have been reduced accordingly, given her employment earnings. Sarah told me that it took her considerable time to find this position, despite having several years of experience working in the fast-food industry, including as a manager. Before she found this position, and during a period when only one of her children lived with her, they relied on a variety of other odd jobs to make ends meet. These were not reported to her caseworker. She and her daughter could not survive on welfare alone. Her rent for her trailer, which is subsidized through a program at the community college, is $250 a month. Sarah's utilities average $100 a month, and she has a telephone and a small car payment. Therefore, her bills run approximately $500 a month, yet her cash grant for herself and her daughter is only $241. How did she make ends meet? First, she relied on a neighbor. Mrs. Janson let her stay at her place for a few months, rent-free, while Sarah saved her welfare checks. This allowed her to eventually move into her trailer.

> If it wasn't for the school, and for my neighbor, me and my daughter would have been in the streets. But, between the school, AFDC, and Mrs. Janson letting me stay at her place, we could get this trailer. Otherwise, we had no money, and we would have fallen right through the cracks. But a lot of people don't have that extra help. And so that's what they do, they slide right into them cracks because there is nowhere else to go. They become homeless and draw inward because there is nowhere else to go.

Once in her trailer, Sarah faced the difficulty of trying to earn enough money on the side to continue to pay her recurring bills each month. She and her daughter, who wasn't yet in her teens, worked together to earn enough money to live. Her daughter's after-school hours were not spent in school sports, in clubs or organizations, or playing with friends. Rather, they were spent helping Sarah earn money to pay the utility bill.

> We cleaned houses; we raked people's yards. We did everything to get that extra money so they wouldn't turn off the utilities. We didn't have any money left over. If we had $5 or $6 at the end of the month we went bowling. That was our one thing we did together. If we didn't have any money we went to <a specific park in town> because if you're on welfare you can get in for free. We did a lot of walking. For holidays, birthdays, or Christmas they got food.

The dilemma that many women face is whether to report these earnings to their caseworker. Legally, they are required to do so. In reality, only some do. I was told that caseworkers vary in the rigor with which they pursue such information, and vary in their likelihood of documenting temporary earnings. Some women told me that caseworkers were aggressively searching for evidence of fraud. Other women told me that some caseworkers will "let you get away with it." Leah told me how she handles trying to get additional money for Christmas or other special occasions:

> Most of the time I try to do some temporary work. If I'm not employed, I try to get a lot of hours doing temporary work. Sometimes, AFDC will let you get away with it. And sometimes, if you work during holidays, then come January and February, when you're not working anymore, they cut your AFDC and food stamps. So, if you do it, it depends on the caseworkers. They might just say, "Hey, since it was only a couple of months we won't add it." And then again, some people add everything.

Some women are not willing to gamble with the generosity of a caseworker, who may or may not break the rules to allow a woman to keep her earnings. Recipients know that if they earn something and report it now, it may take a month for the paperwork to go through the proper channels and reduce their grant. But, more importantly, if they are laid off, or if the temporary employment ceases, it may take another month for the paperwork to go through the system to allow their benefits to resume. During this time they will have no aid, and may experience considerable financial hardship. Therefore, women are well alerted to the fact that reporting employment, especially if it is unstable or temporary employment, can leave you and your family vulnerable. Many women choose not to tell their caseworker about extra income. I was frequently told about side jobs involving babysitting, hairstyling, doing nails, and providing transportation to others. A few other women worked in the formal sector, holding part or full-time jobs in the fast-food industry, or at a nursing home, and did not report the income to a caseworker. This is risky, as Dawn, who was profiled in Chapter 3, found out. She was caught and convicted of welfare fraud. Yet, Jo Lynn, a white woman with two children, believes working in the informal or formal sector, or receiving benefits from friends or family that go unreported, is commonplace. She said this is due to the restrictive requirements and the low benefits afforded to recipients. They simply cannot live on what they are given, and therefore must find a way to augment it:

> The system makes us fraudulent. It makes us fraudulent. I can tell you right now it makes everyone that is on the system fraudulent. They might as well tell you. They might as well tell you the truth. I'm fraudulent, and everybody else that I know is. Because to get by, you have to do things that they're not going to allow.

Some women reported receiving extra income from boyfriends, or children's fathers, and most failed to report it to their caseworker. Legally, welfare recipients are required to report such "gifts," but most did not, especially if they saw the gift as a one-time or infrequent occurrence. They told me they could not afford to survive and raise their children without these gifts—they were one of the many ways to subsidize their meager cash grants. Some acknowledged, sheepishly, that they were breaking the rules: "I just hope they never catch up with us." Others rationalize it as a smart survival strategy. Coreen is a bright and ambitious 21-year-old African American mother of a toddler, who "never thought I'd be on welfare." Her pregnancy was unplanned, and she lived with her mother, even sharing her mother's bed, until the crowded conditions became intolerable. She applied for welfare, and moved into a small subsidized apartment, where she has resided for only a few months. Unknown to her caseworker, Coreen also works 30 hours a week at a fast-food restaurant. Why is she cheating the welfare system? "I want to get ahead, and make something of myself," she tells me. She sees her "double dipping" as the only way to get off of welfare, permanently. It will allow her the financial cushion she needs to continue college, with the goal of being a teacher. It will allow her to move out of the housing projects, which she desperately detests. It will allow her and her boyfriend, who plan to marry soon, to save money so that they can have a fresh start. Welfare, she tells me, doesn't allow for this.

> As long as they give you money, they don't want you to better yourself, that is to say, have a job. This is how I truly feel. They cut your money as soon as you get a job. You can't have a bank account; you can't save money. I feel the system traps women. But I'm in school, and I'm not dropping out until I finish . . . And I haven't told them I'm working yet because I feel like, it's not enough. With the money I make at <restaurant> that will only be enough for me to pay my bills and buy Pampers for my baby. That's not including clothes, socks, and stuff that she needs. They give you ten days; the last time I had a job they gave me ten days to report that I had a job. And then I lost my job, and I couldn't get a check for a whole month. That's not good. Me and my baby had to borrow, borrow, borrow. If they knew I was working, they would take away the whole thing. And I have a boyfriend, and we are trying to move and get married and stuff. I mean, I feel good, because I know I have a future.

Coreen is clearly committing welfare fraud. She is taking money that she is legally not entitled to. Yet, despite the seriousness of her crime, many readers will not be very angry with her. As will be shown in Chapter 7, one of the major concerns with the welfare system is that it does not allow women the opportunity to amass the assets needed to truly exit welfare. Assets can cushion the difficulties that may seem to be minor irritants to the more affluent, but become unbearable on a minimum-wage budget. Having assets can soften the blow when initial wages are held for a pay period; a car needs to be repaired; clothing or a uniform needs to be laundered or dry-cleaned regularly; or when a sick child cannot go to daycare or school, and a babysitter must be hired. Coreen, like others, knows that exiting welfare will be difficult. She feels that committing fraud by double dipping will at least give her a shot at it.

Kate, introduced in the beginning of this chapter knows that she and her children cannot survive on her welfare assistance. She is not alone. Each day millions of welfare recipients piece together a broad array of strategies that allow them to meet the basic necessities of life. A fortunate few, like Kate, have extended families who give help generously and graciously. Others are not so lucky. Living month to month, they resort to a variety of legal and illegal tactics to support their children. They live a tenuous existence between hope and despair.

CRITICAL THINKING QUESTIONS

1. Kate has no savings account, no checking account, no assets of any real value, no credit cards, no individual retirement account, no life insurance, and no stocks or bonds. How common do you think this situation is among the poor?

2. If you were on welfare, how much assistance would you receive from your family? Your friends? Whom would you feel more comfortable asking for help? Would you be able to make ends meet with what they would realistically give you?

3. Could you imagine life without a credit card or a checking account? How would you pay your bills, make expenditures, or manage your money?

4. What are the pros and cons of living in an extended family? Why do so few Americans live in them, particularly white Americans?

5. Why do many fathers not pay child support? Are these individual or structural reasons? How do the women interviewed feel about the lack of support?

6. Have you ever used charities or social services for food, shelter, or clothing? What was that experience like?

7. Some women make ends meet by working side jobs, but often do not report their earnings to their caseworker. Isn't this fraud? How do you feel about this?

CHAPTER

7

Insiders' Perspectives on the Welfare System

"We gripe and we gripe about the fact that we are paying all this money for people who don't seem to be doing very much for themselves. But if you looked at the system from an insider's point of view, you would see that there are actually penalties built into the system for someone with initiative, going out to get a job, or doing something to try to better themselves; I speak from personal experience," Stephanie told me, her eyes and voice full of spark and passion. When talking, she released a flood of pent-up emotions about the welfare system. She knows the system well; she has received aid for four consecutive years. This is now considered to be too long according to recent welfare reform mandates; she is wasting taxpayers' money. People like Stephanie must be removed from the welfare rolls. "People like Stephanie?" Who is Stephanie, anyway, and what exactly is she "like?" And why is she so critical of a welfare system that she has benefited from?

This chapter explores recipients' views of the welfare system. Contrary to popular belief, they have a passionate disdain for the system. Although recipients are often criticized as lazy and unmotivated, glibly taking free money from hard-working taxpayers, this research uncovers a far different portrait. Women are grasping at ways to get off welfare. They are virtually begging for help and begging that the system be reformed in such a way to help them get off welfare once and for all. To onlookers, it may appear that welfare recipients just want a free handout from the government. It appears that way because so many types of assistance are needed for them to be able to permanently exit the system. Their needs exceed what the public and politicians are often willing to pay.

Stephanie is a university student who lives with her seven-year-old daughter Megan in a student apartment on campus. The complex in which she lived had a generic army-base look to it, with row after row of identical and drab cinderblock apartments. The sidewalk was cluttered with children's toys, and grass areas were well worn from children playing and riding their bicycles in their safe and sheltered "yards." The directions she gave me were good, and I found her apartment quickly, even though it was indistinguishable from all the others. I knocked, and when she opened her door and smiled at me, I was startled. I knew her—fairly well as a matter of fact. Yes, her name had a familiar ring to it, now that I thought of it. Stephanie had been a student in one of my courses several semesters prior. I remember her because she was outspoken, vocal, and passionate about issues pertaining to social inequality. So it was with some surprise, and some understanding, when I saw who it was who had agreed to be interviewed.

Being on welfare was very unexpected, 26-year-old Stephanie told me. She grew up in a middle-class family, and although there were some lean years after her mother's divorce, her mother's subsequent marriage to a man of some wealth ended those difficult times. Stephanie had been taught about hard work and motivation; she called it "the Protestant work ethic." She had been a good student, and was a hard worker at the several jobs she had as a teen. She was promoted quickly and given increased responsibility. She met her husband-to-be while working at a hotel as a cashier. In her youthful idealism, and with a quest for adventure, she eventually left this job to join him and work for a circus. "This is the part of my life that I just hate. I actually joined him—the idiot that I was. I actually ran off and joined the circus" Stephanie chided herself. With the circus, they traveled all over the western United States.

It was soon thereafter that Stephanie discovered, or "acknowledged" as she put it, that she was four months pregnant. As she prepared for the birth of their child, she began questioning their lifestyle. "How in the hell are we going to raise a child in this atmosphere? I had no health insurance, nothing."

Her soul searching led her to leave the circus, and to move back home to live with her mother. Because neither she nor her husband had health insurance, and because they were separated, she received Medicaid to cover the birth expenses of her daughter. As it turned out, her daughter Megan was born with a congenital abnormality of her kidneys. She needed corrective surgery at birth, and has had several surgeries and other kidney treatments since, at costs that Stephanie could never have afforded without some assistance.

Eventually, she and her husband divorced. She has neither seen nor heard from him in four years, and has no idea where he is living. "It's as though he is dead, although I presume he's still alive. I don't really know." During his absence he has not contributed to the support of Megan whatsoever, nor has he ever contacted her.

Since their divorce, Stephanie has taken considerable measures to ensure that she and Megan will eventually have more financial security. These measures, for the time being at least, have been difficult. She moved over 100 miles away from her family to enroll in a state university and work towards a Bachelor of Science degree in nursing. At the time of the interview, she had finished all her prerequisites, and was taking coursework in the demanding nursing program. She looks forward to being able to support herself and Megan within the next couple of years without assistance from welfare.

Stephanie and Megan's financial situation is difficult, although they are considerably better off than are other recipients who are not in school. Stephanie receives a $241 cash grant for Megan and herself, $212 in food stamps, and receives several thousand dollars in grants and student loans each semester to cover the costs of tuition, books, and some of their living expenses. "I'll practically owe the costs of a house when I'm finished with school," she told me. In addition to receiving no support from Megan's father, she receives no regular financial support from her family either, except for a car they bought and keep in their name, but which she has in her possession. As I found to be relatively common among welfare recipients, the car is registered in her parents' name to circumvent stringent asset limitations imposed by the welfare office. Her parents pay for the insurance on the vehicle, an arrangement also undisclosed to the welfare office, while Stephanie provides the gas and maintenance.

Stephanie does not have the leisurely lifestyle that so many of her fellow students are able to have. She told me that her day normally begins about 3:00 or 4:00 A.M. so that she can do her laundry, housework, get herself and her daughter ready for school, and drop off Megan at before-school care, so that Stephanie will be on time for her 7:00 A.M. classes. Her classes, and the work associated with them, often last all day. On her open afternoons, she does her homework or library research. She tries to squeeze in a workout at the school's athletic club three times a week, her only real "mental health break—I get rid of a lot of stress that way." She picks up her daughter from school at 6:00 P.M., after she has been there for at least eleven hours. Stephanie spends much of her student loan on tuition for a private Christian-oriented school for Megan. The safe environment, small student-teacher ratio, and the more personalized attention at the school helps soothe Stephanie's fears that she is neglecting her child, or is in other ways a "bad mother" by having Megan stay at school for so long each day. Indeed, she is grateful and relieved that her daughter enjoys school and does not complain about the long hours away from home. She scarcely minds that the $300 per month tuition precludes her from ever buying new clothes or spending money on herself.

Evenings are spent making dinner, working on homework, watching a little television, bathing, and then, by 8:30 it's time for Megan's bedtime story. Stephanie usually falls asleep soon afterwards, only to get up again the next morning at 3:00 or 4:00 A.M. to begin the routine all over again. She does it though because she feels that a college education is her ticket out of poverty. She hopes that her nursing degree will provide her with the job security needed for a brighter future. Consequently, she studies diligently, and receives top grades. In many ways, Stephanie is a "model" student.

Because so many students in her student housing complex do not have parents or other relatives nearby, Stephanie and her neighbors have developed their own social support network and exchange babysitting and carpooling regularly—"You have to." Although she rarely goes anywhere socially without her daughter, this help from neighbors is especially important on weekends when she needs to study or when she has an important exam or paper due.

After being on welfare for four years, Stephanie knows the system well, and detests it. She told me it does little to help women help themselves and their families. With such low-paying benefits, "some live in squalor," and she is particularly concerned about the effects of this on children. She wonders if they can grow up to be physically and mentally healthy, without appropriate food, shelter, and clothing. "I fail to understand how we can allow people to suffer like this, without a second thought," she said.

It is a popular belief that benefits must be kept low as an inducement for women to get a job; the general public doesn't want women to get too comfortable on welfare. Yet, ironically, Stephanie suggests that the welfare system itself penalizes women who try to "better themselves" by seeking work. "Go get a job," it is decreed, but unless women are able to land high-paying jobs for themselves—jobs that include benefits such as health insurance—they will continue to need some help from somewhere. If the assistance will not come from the fathers of their children, then it must come from the government. But, instead, if a woman gets even a low-paying job, she will have her benefits reduced or completely eliminated. Their food stamps and housing subsidy, if they have a housing subsidy to begin with, will be reduced or eliminated, and they will likely lose their Medicaid. As Stephanie put it, "You can't survive on minimum wage. That's ridiculous!"

Little did Stephanie know that welfare reform would soon make most persons like her—e.g., college students—ineligible for aid anyway. She may be a model student, but she is no longer a model welfare recipient, despite working hard to gain the education she needs in order to exit welfare for good. Instead, "people like Stephanie" are seen as burdensome, and are no longer welcome on the welfare rolls. Paying for a four-year university degree is considered extravagant and a drain on our public resources.

Yet, as we pause to reflect on Stephanie's case, and the millions of women like her, we should ask, "Who benefits from welfare reform?" Are the recent changes designed to benefit poor women and their families? Or are they instead designed to benefit the rest of us? Perhaps they are designed to give us a sense of security—albeit a false one—that poverty has somehow been reduced simply because fewer families receive aid.

Imbedded in the current Temporary Assistance for Needy Families (TANF) program created in the 1990s are two critical philosophical undercurrents. *First, we apparently no longer believe that children, especially those with only one parent, are best cared for in the home by that parent.* Apparently we now believe that a single mother's priority should rest in the economic realm; she should be a wage earner first, a caretaker of her dependent children second. We now claim that it is better for a child to be physically cared for by strangers and financially supported by its mother, than vice versa. This is contrary to the well-touted "family values" discussion dominating much of the media, which extols families in which women stay home to care for children. Women on welfare are a subset of the undeserving poor, are suspect, and we question their right to care for their own children at taxpayer expense.

Second, we assume that women on welfare did not want significant changes made in the structure of the welfare system, and therefore, we needed to force these changes upon them. The Individual perspective suggests that the poor are largely responsible for their economic plight through their own laziness, immorality, or lack of human capital, as indicated in Chapter 2. Considerable concern is expressed over what "to do" with these women—women who seem satisfied living on the public dole and apparently do not want more for themselves or their children. Thus, welfare reform was based on the idea that we must force change upon recipients of the system, since they will not embrace reform efforts on their own.

These philosophical underpinnings are at the root of both federal and statewide initiatives, such as work requirements, time limits, and family caps, which will deny additional assistance for a child if the mother becomes pregnant while receiving TANF. Although all states have implemented welfare reform somewhat differently, here I will use Florida as a case example to provide a glimpse of the government impact on the lives of poor women and their families.

Florida WAGES: A Case Example

Following the leads of Wisconsin and Michigan, Florida was the third state to receive federal clearance to carry out its own welfare reform plan. On October 1, 1996, Florida implemented its own welfare reform law known as Work and Gain Economic Self-Sufficiency (WAGES), replacing the former federal Aid for Families of Dependent Children (AFDC) program. Like other state programs that followed, WAGES is a "welfare-to-work" rather than a "human-capital-investment" program. WAGES generally does not provide case management services designed to coordinate broad services to meet the physical, social, educational, or emotional needs of recipients. As a "welfare-to-work" program, its stated purpose is to "end entitlement, require work, support individual initiative, and protect children" (Florida Legislature, 1996, 1), but many onlookers suggest that the supportive and protective functions are secondary to simply ending entitlement and requiring work.

Closely following the federal mandates, or at other times becoming more stringent than new federal requirements, WAGES initiated several critical changes (The Florida Legislature, 1996). First, participants, with few exceptions, were limited to 24 months of benefits in any 60-month period, and set welfare total lifetime limits at 48 months (one year less than federal mandates). This requirement was based on the fear that large numbers of women chose to remain on welfare for extended periods, rather than secure employment. Yet the research shows that most women are on welfare for short periods of time. Nonetheless, it is true that many women who leave welfare returned to it within a few years. They worked outside the home, then, due to low pay, inadequate childcare, lack of medical benefits, and other constraints, they often returned to the welfare system (Edin & Lein, 1997; Hays, 2003; Seccombe, James & Battle-Walters, 1996).

Second, WAGES required able-bodied adults to work or engage in activities leading to eventual employment. The assumption is that they must be forced to obtain employment, since most would not do so willingly. However, as will be shown in Chapter 8, finding a job is not always an easy proposition, and when found, a near-minimum wage job is not necessarily a ticket out of poverty. Equally important, many of these jobs fail to provide health insurance, which is considered to be a valuable fringe benefit. My 2002–2003 study in Oregon showed that more than half of recent TANF leavers who hold jobs work in positions that do not offer health insurance (Seccombe et al., 2005).

Third, WAGES required teen parents to go to school or find a job, and they must live with their parents or another responsible adult. Unmarried mothers who head a household and who are without a high school degree must now get their diploma or GED in order to continue receiving assistance. This change stemmed from the concern that there has been an increase of young unmarried women who have children. These women likely find it difficult to complete their education, thereby reducing their job prospects. However, the teenage pregnancy rate has been declining significantly over the past 10–15 years among all racial and ethnic groups, particularly among African American teens. Overall, the teenage birth rate has declined 30 percent since the early 1990s (Centers for Disease Control, December 17, 2003).

Fourth, the WAGES program in Florida placed caps on benefits for children born after a mother begins receiving cash assistance. This is predicated on the widely held assumption that women on welfare have large numbers of children irresponsibly and may have a child simply to increase the size of their welfare check. However most studies on this topic do not support this conclusion (Wise, Chavkin & Romero, 1999). For example, Rank (1989, 1994) reports that fertility rates for women on welfare are actually lower than the national average (45.8 per 1,000 women on welfare versus 71.1 nationally). Moreover, an additional birth increases a welfare check by 24 to 147 dollars, depending on the state, with a national average of only 60 dollars. Moreover, why is there no similar public outcry against other anti-poverty programs, such as the Earned Income Tax Credit, that they too may induce women to have children beyond which they can afford?

Donovan (1995) examined the fertility rates among welfare recipients in New Jersey and Arkansas, two states that initiated family caps, and found no difference in their fertility rates compared to those states without caps. Initial findings, which implied that caps on aid for additional children did reduce fertility rates was later explained by a delay in the reporting of additional children. Many women on welfare had no incentive to rush and report a new birth under family cap policies, or feared that they would lose already existing benefits with an additional child.

Fifth, although WAGES does not offer the comprehensive services of Florida's previous program, WAGES allows "bootstrap" training to upgrade skills for up to two years after a participant leaves the program as long as it is directly related to employment. However, most women are no longer allowed to go to school full-time without working at least part-time. The WAGES program limits full-time education without simultaneous employment to 12 months for any person and to no more than 20 percent of the welfare caseload at any given time. This will undoubtedly slow women's progress towards their college degrees and stifle real hope for securing jobs providing a living wage. Thus, people like Stephanie who are pursuing a bachelor's degree would lose their eligibility for assistance if they remained in a four-year degree-granting program. Seemingly little consideration is given to the fact that finishing her degree program would virtually guarantee success at leaving welfare, and that over the course of her life she would pay back in taxes far more than she received in welfare.

Several additional features of the Florida WAGES program are particularly noteworthy. These include the provision of transitional childcare for two years after recipients leave the program, and transitional Medicaid for up to one year. Adult men aged 21 or older who impregnate girls aged 16 or younger are charged with statutory rape, regardless of the romantic feelings shared by both partners within the relationship. Moreover, given the increased emphasis on child support obligations, welfare benefits are reduced by one-quarter if the father of the child is not identified. As indicated in Chapter 6, women sometimes avoid seeking child support from non-contributing fathers at times in order to minimize conflict-ridden interactions between themselves and the children's fathers.

This is but one example of the ways in which welfare reforms have been implemented at the state level. One can clearly detect the underlying currents that we do not value the maternal labor of welfare mothers; and that we think they are swindling the American taxpayer and will continue to do so until they are forced to stop.

It is important to note that those who drafted the welfare legislation generally had little direct experience with the welfare system, and most likely never will. One notable exception is Lynn Woolsey, who received welfare many years prior to serving in Congress (D-CA). She told the New York Times, "I know what it's like to lie awake at night and worry about not having health insurance. I know how hard it is to find good daycare. I had thirteen different babysitters in one year. I know what it is like to choose between paying the rent and buying new shoes. Like so many American families, we turned to AFDC" (Woolsey, 1994). Ms. Woolsey notwithstanding, the representatives who spearheaded welfare reform efforts largely represent white, upper-middle-class males, the group least likely to ever need or use welfare. The participants of social welfare programs, primarily poor or working-class women, have had little input into the welfare reform process. Their needs, desires, and suggestions have not been uniformly sought. I suggest that the stigma associated with welfare and the dominant paradigm of Individualism have prevented fruitful discourse from occurring in critical national or statewide contexts.

But women who receive welfare have numerous ideas about how the system should have been changed to better meet their needs, and they enthusiastically shared their ideas with me. Several themes emerged. First, they discussed their attitudes toward government responsibility and the role that government should take in improving the lives of poor families. Second, they comment specifically on several key features of the reformed welfare system: (a) time limits on welfare; (b) work requirements; and (c) family caps that limit or deny additional benefits for children born to mothers on welfare. Third, they shared their own visions of meaningful reform, which require changes in the structure of work in our lowest tiers as well as changes in the welfare system.

The Role of Government

Most people, rich or poor, believe that our government owes its citizens some degree of protection and care. But it's not clear exactly how much, and of what nature this care should be. Nonetheless, many people are feeling abandoned by their government—their jobs and wages are vulnerable, they cannot provide health insurance for their family, and they cannot afford the down payment on their first home. These concerns are not spread evenly throughout the population; they are felt most acutely by the working class and the poor (Ehrenreich, 2001; Shipler, 2004; Shulman, 2003). For example, in *The Working Poor*, Shipler (2004) examines the "forgotten America" where the American Dream is out of the reach of millions despite their willingness to work hard. Struggling to simply survive, they live so close to the edge of poverty that a minor obstacle, such as a car breakdown or a child's illness, can lead to a downward financial spiral that can prove impossible to reverse. His interviews with the working poor reveal what it is like to be trapped in a cycle of dead-end jobs without benefits or opportunities for advancement. Even the poor themselves are confused about what government should do about it.

My interviews reveal that many poor women on welfare also feel confused and abandoned by our government. Respondents were concerned that politicians did not care about them and their children because politicians did not really know of their experiences. Stephanie commented on the distance between those on welfare and those who make the laws about welfare:

> It's very easy up in Washington to sit on their throne, as it were, to say, "Oh, they're lazy" and this and that. But, it doesn't hit home until you are in this situation. I think it would do them good to go and visit these people themselves, and see what kinds of houses people are living in. It's about compassion.

Politicians were seen as a far-off group of people who make policies to meet their own needs, and are generally unconcerned about the plight of the poor. Government was seen as "run by white males. White males have the status." Women didn't feel that their voices were given an avenue for expression, and suggested that the government was generally unaware or uninterested in their needs. Both African Americans and whites shared this opinion: Government is run by a distant and far off group of people who do not represent them.

Laura, a well-educated woman with three years of college behind her, expressed this sentiment that the government does not reflect her interests. Despite the fact that she resembles her state legislators more closely than most other welfare recipients, at least in terms of education and race, she feels little kinship with them as she tells me, "I think it would be nice if the government were totally different. Yeah. It would be nice if the government helped people. The government needs to shift entirely to being less for the politicians and more for the people."

Marissa stands in stark contrast to Laura. She has a tenth-grade education, and has given birth to four children, the first of which when she was only sixteen. Yet, like Laura, she echoed this concern that the government was generally unaware or uninterested in average families, particularly those who are poor and who receive welfare. She suggested that, while the government complains of deficits and high welfare expenditures, the tax structure favors wealthy Americans. They pay very little in taxes, while the middle classes are forced to subsidize the poor.

> The rich people, they ain't kicking in enough damn taxes, if they even is kicking in some. Like I told you before, it's the middle class that is doing it all. The middle class can't take care of their families and us, and the prisoners, and all that too. The rich people just sit there and try to

donate, but really not giving up nothing. But the government has a lot to do with it. Look at minimum wage. I thought it was going up? The government has a lot to do with it. They're not really helping. When you get off AFDC, you're still going to be poor because the jobs around here aren't paying too much.

Despite their educational differences, Laura and Marissa join the other women interviewed here, and the countless others among the working poor, who feel that our government has abandoned them. Their concern about the tax structure is not un-founded. Data published by Citizens for Tax Justice, a non-profit organization that monitors the tax system, indicate that in 2003, the top 1 percent of Floridians, with average incomes of $1,026,000 get 35 percent of the Bush tax cuts that go to Floridians. Their tax cut averaged $70,327. Moreover, by 2006, this group will get 41.5 percent of the tax cuts. In contrast, the poorest 20 percent of Florida residents, with average incomes of $10,000 get an average of $114 from the Bush tax cuts in 2003. This is only 1.1 percent of the total tax cuts for Floridians (Citizens for Tax Justice, November 19, 2003).

But, notwithstanding the concerns of Marissa and Laura, like Shipler (2004) I found tremendous diversity of opinion on the role and responsibility of government. Not all recipients believe that the government has a responsibility to help the poor, or that it has shirked that responsibility. Some recipients subscribed to Individualist philosophies themselves, and therefore not surprisingly, believed that the poor are ul-timately responsible for helping themselves and should not be reliant on public aid. Several women forcefully argued that people are responsible for their own economic plight, and the government is doing enough, or perhaps even too much to help women on welfare. These sentiments were reflected in my conversations with Kim. She is an African American mother of three, and has been on and off welfare for ten years. She now works part-time, and is diligently searching for full-time work. Kim is ambitious, and is focused in her plans for a better life. It just hasn't quite happened yet. She replied to my query as to whether the government should do more to help poor people:

> I don't think so. Because I say you got to want to help yourself. A lot of people don't want to help themselves. Why should the government keep helping them? Because a lot of them keep getting this handout, and aren't going to help themselves.

Others said that the responsibility ought to be shared by government and fami-lies. "It should be fifty-fifty," according to Tanya, a mother of five. She has been on welfare off and on for five years, and also received welfare as a child. Her need for aid notwithstanding, she feels strongly that individual initiative is important, and the role of government is to help people help themselves. She continued, "The government should subsidize, and people should try to help themselves. With all the opportunities out there, people can help themselves."

These interviews expose the diversity of opinion among welfare recipients. While most do indeed feel that their families have been abandoned and left behind by the federal and state governments, a significant number expressed opinions that differed substantially with what we would first expect. That is, opinions on government responsibility represent a spectrum that we might find with a survey from any other part of the population. Welfare recipients are not demanding that government should design policies to help them stay on welfare. They are, instead, asking that government be concerned about poverty and the problems associated with trying to raise a family on a welfare budget, and provide a helping hand in solving these problems.

Opinions of the Welfare System

I asked that women describe, in one word, what life is like on welfare. "Hell," "difficult," "miserable," "challenging," "degrading—very degrading" were just a few of their choices. Comments such as these contradict popular folklore, which suggests that women on welfare enjoy being on the system, are purposefully lazy, and enjoy the free ride that they receive at taxpayers' expense.

These interviews revealed a considerably different and contradictory impression of welfare recipients from the popular opinion expressed in the media. Welfare recipients do not like welfare. They described life on welfare as "a strain," "depressing," "rough," "a struggle," "aggravating," "a trap," and "scary."

Patrice, who receives a small check for $91 to augment her income from a part-time job, describes life on welfare as "a challenge." Prior to her employment, she received $305 per month for herself and her two children. Now, with her job, her check was reduced and her food stamps were reduced from $276 to $167 per month. Yet, despite the difficulty of living on reduced aid while raising her two young children, she told me that she would rather work than be on welfare. What is life like on welfare, I asked her? "A challenge. You have to try and budget every little thing, trying to survive with a minimum. It's a challenge, and it's really pitiful."

Strengths of the Welfare System

I asked women to describe the specific strengths or the positive features of our current welfare system. I wanted to know what aspects of the system worked well for them, and should be retained. Elected officials fail to ask the users of the system these crucial questions when they design social policy.

Few women had quick or enthusiastic answers to my query about the positive aspects of welfare. Most respondents tended to laugh at my question, grimace, shake their head in disbelief, stare back blankly, comment that they need more time to think about an answer, or curtly retorted, "There are none!" Despite the initial shock with the question, some women eventually conceded that there are some positive virtues with the welfare system. Three themes emerged in our discussion: (1) it provides services, even if minimal; (2) some programs were particularly applauded, such as Medicaid; and (3) several features of welfare reform were seen as extremely helpful.

First, a number of women commented that welfare provides an important floor for poor families, if only a marginal one. Without welfare, several women told me that they would have no recourse other than to be living out on the streets, in a homeless shelter, or remain married to a physically or emotionally abusive spouse. "It keeps me out of dumpsters," I was told. Welfare may not be much, but at least it's something. Janie, who bore a child conceived during a rape, has experience living out on the streets before her daughter was born, and is thankful that those days are over. Janie has been on welfare for a little over a year since her daughter was born, and sees welfare as a lifesaver. It gave her the opportunity to bear her child rather than having her pregnancy aborted. She elaborated on its importance in providing a stable home environment:

> It's been really helpful. Because of my current situation, without it, I would be highly lost. I really would be. Because without it, I've got nothing. I'd have no house, I'd have no money, and I'd have no baby. They could take her away from me for not being able to take care of her. My daughter and I would probably be on the streets.

Second, several specific programs were repeatedly mentioned as being particularly helpful. Medicaid was mentioned most often as a highlight of the welfare system, "because poor people, they can't afford all these high-priced doctor bills." When they were asked to prioritize their benefits, and which they would choose if they could have only one, Medicaid emerged most frequently as the benefit of choice. It was followed by food stamps, and then "the check" itself. My 2002–2003 study in Oregon, based on interviews with 552 people throughout the state also revealed that Medicaid—known as the Oregon Health Plan in that state—was the most valuable benefit, followed by food stamps, and then the cash grant (Seccombe et al., 2005). Interestingly, Medicaid is also the service that women used least often. Most women do not need Medicaid daily, weekly, or monthly, as is the case with food stamps, their cash grant, or subsidized housing. Nonetheless, it appears that women are acutely aware of the catastrophic results that could happen if they were without health insurance, and one of their children needed medical attention. Having health insurance of some sort appeared to be synonymous with being a good mother, as shown by Dawn's comments. Her four children have not been particularly sickly over the years.

> Medicaid. My kids' health has always been more important to me than anything else I ever did. And we had a couple of periods where we didn't have health insurance, Medicaid and stuff, and the kids didn't get their checkups like they should have. And that bothered me. Medicaid is definitely the most important.

Unlike Dawn's relatively healthy children, Stephanie's daughter Megan has not been so lucky. Megan has required extensive medical treatment over the past several years. To Stephanie, Medicaid is a lifesaver.

Oh, I've never had to use my Medicaid myself, but my daughter couldn't do without it. So, yeah, Medicaid is the most important benefit to me. I tend to not think about the Medicaid all that much; I think about food stamps because it puts food on my table. I see that everyday. But if I didn't have my Medicaid, I don't know what I would do. And it's an ad hoc thing. You never know when you are going to get sick. I may not use it for the rest of the time I'm on welfare, but at least for my daughter, I don't know what I'd do without Medicaid. There would be absolutely no way that I could pay for the medical care that she has received.

However, when these families leave welfare for work, they may lose health insurance that was a critical part of their welfare benefit. Their incomes generally preclude them from qualifying for Medicaid, and employers often do not offer insurance as a fringe benefit, yet their incomes are so low that they cannot afford to purchase insurance privately. Moreover, the recent drop in TANF caseloads has been accompanied by declines in funding for Medicaid programs. In 2002, 49 states and the District of Columbia took Medicaid cost-containment actions for FY 2003 (Singh & Peacock, 2003). In 27 states, the cost-containment actions included reducing or restricting Medicaid eligibility. In other words, at a time when more people may need Medicaid because of leaving welfare, funding has declined.

The third strength noted with the welfare system is the favorable review given to several reform efforts. In particular, programs designed to assist women's transition off of welfare, such as childcare assistance, or transportation vouchers, were applauded by many recipients. Dee, for example, describes her experiences. There are a lot of strengths.

They have programs for single parents. They have programs for teen parents. The system tries to help those who help themselves . . . they are paying my childcare. They give me my bus passes for free. So they help me out right there.

Although several positive features of the welfare system were identified when probed, many weaknesses remain.

Weaknesses of the System

Criticisms of the welfare system were vast and widespread. Women spoke with a heightened sense of concern and passion as they relayed their firsthand experiences with a system they called frustrating, demoralizing, and in need of considerable change and repair. The women interviewed here were anything but complacent about the system. They had firm ideas about the dysfunctions of the welfare system, ideas that had been fermenting since their introduction to it. Three critical themes emerged from these interviews: (1) welfare simply does not provide enough money to live on; (2) services are delivered inappropriately; and (3) benefits are eliminated prematurely.

First, many women lamented that the welfare system provides benefits at such a low level, that it is virtually impossible to maintain a decent standard of living for their children. An AFDC grant in the region where the interviews were conducted was $241 dollars a month for a parent with one child, $303, $364, and $426 for a parent with two, three, and four children, respectively, where it remains in 2005. In other words, the check did not increase between 1996 and 2005 despite a significant rise in the cost of living.

Jasmine, a 35-year-old African American mother of two children is employed part-time, but continues to receive a partial welfare benefit because of her low earnings. She would prefer to work full-time, as she has done in the past, but when her two children began having severe asthma attacks, she cut back her hours so that she could take care of them. She told me that she feels uncomfortable leaving them with a babysitter. Luckily, she has relatives who can watch them during her reduced work hours; they are knowledgeable about asthma, and how to treat it, in case an attack were to occur. Like others, Jasmine is frustrated by the size of her welfare grant and her reduction in food stamps, believing that they are inadequate for taking care of children:

> I simply don't get enough food stamps. And the cash. . . . are you kidding? They keep asking me, "How are you paying your rent, how are you paying your rent?" It's like, hey, if you'd give me more money, I could answer that. And she's like, "But this doesn't add up. Your income and your outcome don't add up. You just don't have enough money." And I'm like, why do you think I'm here? Yes, I don't have enough money. They are implying . . . what? That I'm selling my body, or what? You know? I bounce checks, there's your answer.

Stephanie expressed anger that a country as wealthy as ours spends so little to take care of its children. She began this conversation with a discussion of substandard housing that low-income people may reside in:

> Is something going to come out and bite me? This is the equivalent of the Black Plague, with all the rats. How can anyone grow up normal, intelligent, and become a productive member of society living like that? I don't understand. And when you're hungry at night, or when your child goes to bed cold, how can you expect them to go to school the next morning and learn anything? You know, Maslov's hierarchy of needs. If you don't meet the very bottom ones, how are you supposed to be anything on top? We're humans, and will resort to survival skills. And I'm sure that's what many people are doing. Just surviving. I've known a lot of women who live in these villages [student family housing at the university] who are not as fortunate as I am. I mean, I had a house full of stuff when I moved in here because I already had a house. I mean, how can any child grow up and be stimulated in an environment where they may or may not be able to heat the house, or be able to afford the extra

20 or 30 dollars that I hand over at the end of the month to buy food? Or they may not be able to go out and buy the clothing that their child needs when they outgrow it, or the shoes. Most of the time I can swing it. But, like I said, if it wasn't for family housing and living on campus, and my financial aid, there would be no way.

When mothers on welfare complain about the amount of money they receive, they are not just whining for the sake of it. Children who are deprived of adequate financial support suffer long-term consequences (Children's Defense Fund, 2004). McLanahan and Sandefur, in their award winning book, *Growing Up With a Single Parent* (1994), report that income is a significant factor, although certainly not the only one, in explaining the deleterious effects of growing up in a single-parent household. Using several data sources from nationally representative samples across the United States, they found that children in single-parent households are less likely to graduate from high school; they are less likely to enroll in and graduate from college; they are more likely to be out of work; and girls are more likely to become teen mothers than are those children who have grown up in two-parent households. Income itself accounts for approximately half of the differences between the two groups. Thus, our government's tradition of supporting children inadequately has serious long-term consequences.

A second concern with the welfare system was over the way in which services were delivered. Women repeatedly described many problems: They complained that the system is far too impersonal; caseworkers are unhelpful; the push is on to find a job, any job, regardless of the quality of it; there should be more one-on-one help; child support payments should be more closely enforced and monitored; and the delivery medical services through the Public Health Unit were problematic. Moreover, women repeatedly told me that the system is cumbersome and complicated.

Alexandra, a 29-year-old white woman who has been on welfare for four years, describes the maze she encountered when she lost her job and turned to welfare for help:

I mean, when you start on welfare, you have to start depending on people that are already on welfare to get you into the system because nobody is there to help you, and there are no guidelines to go by to tell you how. I just needed some assistance at the time, and I wanted to go back to school and stuff, but I couldn't get assistance because I couldn't figure out how. I kept going down for appointments, and I couldn't get in there. It's just like you have to know somebody to be able to get on it and get through it. It's like a maze; it's like a puzzle, and you have to fit the pieces together, and you have to start learning how to work the system, basically. It's like a job learning how to do it, and I was real naïve. I never saw a food stamp in my life. I never saw a WIC check, you know. I didn't even know what an AFDC check looked like. I had never even known a person who used them.

Becky, a 23-year-old white woman who works nearly full-time cleaning houses, summarized the concerns of many when she complained that services are delivered without individuals' needs in mind. If people are on welfare because of varying circumstances, then their needs are likely to differ as well. They may need different things in order to help them get *off* welfare.

> There needs to be more individual one-on-one help. Meet the individual's need, instead of forcing them to conform to some generic lot and saying take it or leave it. I feel like a hypocrite being on AFDC because I don't agree with it and its way of treating people. It treats everybody the same, but it needs to stop and look at the individual and try to help each individual person according to what they need. No patch solutions.

The third weakness of the welfare system that was repeatedly emphasized is that welfare benefits are significantly reduced or eliminated prematurely when a recipient acquires a job. Given the options of low-paying work for welfare recipients, their incomes are not sufficient to pull them out of poverty. Moreover, when working, they face a new host of challenges and difficulties, such as needing transportation, childcare, or requiring additional clothing or frequent laundering of uniforms. Many women would be willing to take on these extra challenges, but with their cash grant, food stamps, housing subsidies, and Medicaid cut, they are in a worse financial predicament than they were while they were home receiving welfare. Is it worth it, they ask themselves? This issue is addressed further in Chapter 8, which explores why some women are apparently hesitant to take jobs.

Welfare Reforms

No woman interviewed was opposed to reforming the welfare system because all recognized that it does little to improve life circumstances. Dee questions whether welfare, even in the aftermath of reform, even tries to help women.

> They give you just enough money to keep you going with helping with rent and the utility bill, just enough to keep you going and looking forward to that next month's check. So therefore, you look forward to next month's check. In a sense, they baited the hook and you done took a bite out of it, and now they are fighting you there.

In this next section, I examine how respondents felt about three particular reforms: (a) time limits on welfare; (b) work requirements; and (c) family caps that limit or deny additional benefits for children born to mothers on welfare. These three features are some of the more controversial changes made in welfare law. They illustrate our uneasiness with appropriate roles for single mothers, and our underlying contempt for welfare recipients who, we think, are smugly satisfied with the public dole and would like to remain on it.

Time Limits

Time limits impose a limit on the number of years that recipients can receive welfare, both consecutively and overall. The majority of women interviewed either opposed time limits or suggested that they supported them reluctantly, with specific conditions. Women who opposed time limits generally suggested that they are arbitrary, and that they fail to take personal needs into account. They believed that there are a variety of legitimate reasons why women, including themselves, may need to rely upon cash programs for longer than two or three years: "too many things could go wrong once the two or three years passed" or "you can be up on your feet one day, and down the next." Because they often felt that they were on welfare due to circumstances that were beyond their control, many felt that they also had little control over the circumstances that would get them off welfare. An example of this sentiment was expressed by Jasmine. She is employed, but her income was not enough to pull her above the poverty line. When asked if she thought time limits of two to three years should be imposed, she responded:

> No, I don't. Because sometimes it takes people a little longer than that to get on their feet. Like me with my children. Like I say, it's pretty much medical problems that will keep a person on. . . . There's got to be a reason why the person is on the system in the first place and there's got to be a reason why that person is still on the system later on down the line, maybe four or five years later on down the line. There's got to be a reason for that.

Stephanie also strongly opposed time limits. She also argued passionately that they are arbitrary and unfair, and further she suggests that they would ultimately increase the crime rate. Several respondents echoed this idea:

> Oh God, that is amusing. How can you put a timeline on someone's life? I see what they are trying to do. They are trying to get those individuals who they feel aren't making efforts to get off the rolls. But I don't agree with that. Setting an arbitrary time limit on a system that is so dysfunctional to begin with that, you know, it's amazing that anyone gets off it. . . . It's very easy up in Washington to sit on their thrones, as it were, and to say "Oh, they're lazy" and this and that. But it doesn't hit home until you are in this situation. I think it would do them good to go and visit these people themselves. It's about compassion. Even with the current system, we are suffering, and now they want to cut us off after three years? What do they think that is going to accomplish? Yeah, it will accomplish an incredible rise in crime because that is what people are going to resort to in order to survive. I mean, hell, if it was me, I'd probably push drugs

too. Even though it is totally against my beliefs. Or I would rob. I mean, if it means the difference between me eating and having a halfway decent place to live or not, I'd do it. So, if that's what they want to accomplish, then, hey, go ahead.

This concern that crime may increase as welfare eligibility becomes more stringent was alluded to by both white and African American women. They felt that strict time limits could result in considerable hardship for many families, and at least some of these families would resort to crime to make up for the lost income, "and they can't put people in jail forever, you know? They're going to have to take care of people some kind of way."

Amy, a 23-year-old white mother who has been on welfare for two years, elaborated on this theme:

> Once you start having people that are poor, or homeless, or hungry, you're going to have a lot more crime. We're going to see a lot of crime because they are going to do what it takes to support the family, whether it's drugs, or stealing, or burglarizing. We're going to see a lot of this if we yank people off. What are they going to do, you know? People say you can get a job anywhere, but you can't. And a lot of people aren't qualified to work. So, you know, we can't just say "we're taking this from you and next month you're not going to have a check, you're not going to have food stamps— go out there and find a job." They can't go out there and find a job. They have no job skills. They've been on welfare for ten years taking care of children and their home, or sitting home doing nothing. And, nobody's going to hire them right now. So it's just going to cause problems.

Other women supported time limits reluctantly, and only if allowances were made for specific circumstances and needs. These most commonly included allowing additional time for women whose lives are especially difficult or disorganized, giving women additional time for schooling or training, ensuring that women are guaranteed a job above minimum wage. Women on welfare experience a high degree of disorganization in their lives. Daily living is a challenging attempt to pay the bills on time, to put food on the table, to juggle childcare, to find a job, to locate donations and charities to help benefits stretch further, to nurse sick children, and to earn additional income that can be hidden from one's caseworker. Time limits make many women nervous: How can they ensure that their lives would smoothly progress through the stages necessary to be off welfare in two to three years, when their lives are a constant struggle today? Women referred to the concern they have in trying to find a job or their ability to keep a job. How can they really guarantee that they will be able to secure a well-paying job for themselves with medical benefits during this relatively short time period and not need any further aid? Many women reported that they have submitted numerous applications, but to no avail.

Doreen is a 31-year-old woman who receives $241 a month for herself and her 15-year-old daughter Latasha, who is seven months pregnant with her first child, and requires complete bed rest after going into early labor. She is being home schooled so that she can continue high school. Doreen said that she would like to get a job, and has earnestly looked for work in the past, but usually can only turn up part-time pay in the fast-food industry. So, instead, she babysits occasionally for extra money, but does not report this income to her caseworker. And now, without a car, with Latasha needing full-time care, and with a new grandchild on the way, finding a job seems a near impossibility. She summarizes the concerns of many regarding time limits when she says:

> If they can get a job within that time, then yeah. But if they can't get a job within that time period, then allow another three or four years until they can. Because if you go out and put out applications, that doesn't mean that person is going to hire you. You know, you can get out there and do it, but there's no guarantee that the person is going to hire you. They might hire the next person, or the next person. . . . You know, actually it would be really good if they guaranteed that you would get a job. It's my opinion that if they can go and guarantee you a job, then get off welfare. But if they can't guarantee that they're going to get you a job, then leave them alone because it's going to hurt the kids in the long run.

Other women voiced concern that they should be allowed to continue their education, and they recognized that doing so may take more than two or three years, "because when you got five kids, there's no way you can sit down and study all the time." One example is Dawn, introduced in Chapter 3. She has been on and off welfare for most of her childhood and adult life and had recently begun an educational program at the community college. She was enthusiastic about her future possibilities, but recognized that her training may take more than two years, given her other family and household responsibilities:

> I guess if somebody just sat around those two or three years and didn't do something, then cut maybe those people. But a person like me, you are going to cut it when I'm not through with my education? Wait, hold on, give me a few minutes, you know? I don't think you can say, "Just cut everybody at the same time. Just cut it off." . . .

Not all women opposed time limits for receiving welfare. A few women that I interviewed voiced their support, suggesting that time limits would prevent young teenage girls from getting pregnant and subsequently relying upon welfare. Others believed that two to three years was ample time to develop the skills to become self-supporting or to find a job. Not surprisingly, these women usually had been on welfare for one year or less, and were optimistic that their financial situation would improve very shortly. They maintained that welfare should be a short-term helping hand, and therefore it was reasonable that aid be discontinued after this brief amount of time. One mother, Janie, aged 19, who had been on welfare for one year after giving birth to a daughter conceived during a rape, candidly told me:

The reason they are stopping it is because they are providing ample time for school, for work, and they are giving you all the opportunities you need, and by then you should be able to take care of yourself. . . . Two years makes sense. It gives people long enough to get their programs, to figure out exactly what they want to do, exactly what they need, and can go from there.

In conclusion, most women who were interviewed opposed time limits, or only supported them reluctantly with significant clauses attached, because strict time limits were thought to be arbitrary and would not take into account personal need. Only a few welfare recipients felt that they were necessary to stop the abuse and fraud that is assumed to occur with the system. Most welfare recipients did not see time limits as a useful way to reform welfare because they did not perceive that they themselves were abusing the system or that they were careless in looking for work or trying to get off welfare. They felt that time limits would increase their stress level, potentially harm their children, and that it would make their attempts to get off welfare more difficult, not easier.

Work Requirements

Unlike time limits, work requirement reforms received overwhelming support among welfare recipients. Despite the persistent idea that recipients must be forced into work, I found that most women enthusiastically supported work requirements. Furthermore, they suggested that if recipients could not find jobs, they should do volunteer work in their community in order to be eligible to receive a check. Most women contended that requiring work would improve women's self-esteem, would provide them with needed skills and experience, would serve as an important role model to their children, and last but certainly not least, would get them off welfare. Carrie, a white 39-year-old mother of three, summarized the views of many women when she commented:

I think they ought to do something. Either like volunteer work at a hospital, or go out and help old people, or there's a lot of work to do. I don't think that people ought to just sit around and do nothing. Unless there's something wrong with them, people who are incapacitated in some way. . . . There's no reason why they should sit home and watch soaps all day. I think everyone should have something to do outside the home. Even people who have little kids. There should be some kind of group daycare for kids so that mothers can get out and have some kind of outlet.

Carrie was not alone in her ideas. Leah agrees with her. Leah is a 24-year-old unemployed African American mother who has four children, ages ten, eight, six, and her youngest not yet a year old. On first glance she looks like an unlikely candidate for work. Although she has a high school diploma, she has never held a job. Leah has been on welfare since she turned 18. Yet, even she concurred with the vast majority of women interviewed; women on welfare should have some sort of job, even one that does not pay wages.

> At least, if they can't get a paying job, they should have volunteer hours. They should have to go somewhere and volunteer so that if there are small children in the house, so the children can see the person do something— leave the home and go be involved in something. That they aren't always just surrounded by people who don't leave the house and who aren't doing anything. Hopefully it will be a better role model to see your parents get up and do something.

The majority of women—regardless of age, race, level of education, or number of children—embraced work requirements for women on welfare. However, in conjunction with their enthusiasm, women also felt that children should be over the age of three or should be in school before their parents are required to work; that recipients should be allowed to finish school if they were already enrolled; that the job should pay above minimum wage; and that benefits should not be automatically and immediately eliminated, "or else it just wouldn't work." Jo Lynn expressed the sentiment held by many who support work requirements, but only if these other conditions are met. Otherwise, she suggests, working becomes prohibitive. She tells us of her dilemma, of wanting to work, but wondering if work will enhance or detract from her meager standard of living. She is frightened by the prospect of working, and worries that employment will reduce her already meager standard of living.

> Yes, depending on the situation. Depending on your youngest child's age. Maybe on how long a person has been on AFDC, and depending on how much money that person gets from a job, or what benefits are going to be cut. I think a lot of people would be willing to go to work, even want to work. It's a scary thing, where, like me, okay, I have $241 a month, and I want to get a part-time job. And they say, "Okay, you can take the job, but we're going to start cutting everything off." You know, it takes a little while to establish yourself. I think if they would help establish people, like give them six months to keep their AFDC check and their work check, where they could put some money aside maybe or build up for their own apartment, or whatever they need to build up. With health insurance, if you get a job and make over a certain amount of money, you lose your Medicaid completely and everything. And I think that's a really serious situation for a lot of people.

Yet these criteria have not been met. For example, women with young children are not necessarily exempt from work unless their children are very young—perhaps only three or six months of age (Department of Health and Human Services, 2004). Women worried about their children. First and foremost, the women I interviewed wanted to ensure that work would be compatible with motherhood and would better their family's lives. If it did not, either financially or psychologically, then work was less enticing.

Alexandra is divorced and has one child. She has been on welfare for several years, although she anticipates being off welfare shortly. She has an AA degree from a community college, and would like to transfer to a four-year university for a bachelor's degree in art. The walls in her home were decorated with her own art work, revealing keen talent. Alexandra also suggested it is unrealistic to simply expect women to go to work without some assistance from the government. She questioned the benefits of putting infants and toddlers in daycare for nine or ten hours a day. She also brought up the cost of childcare, and questioned whether or not a job would even cover these costs. While she supports work requirements in theory, she does not believe it is desirable to work full-time when her child is young, nor is it even possible to work unless her childcare needs are taken care of:

> Work or go to school is good. I wouldn't mind having a part-time job or something. But how much money can I make at a part-time job? And how much does a sitter charge? A lot, you know? Is your entire paycheck even going to be able to pay for a week or a month's babysitter? So, I don't know. It's a good idea, but they would have to pay childcare. You see what I mean? Otherwise, it just wouldn't work.

Several women opposed work requirements outright, primarily because they felt that women who are single parents should not be required to work and leave their children to strangers for care. While opportunities for employment were applauded, they opposed mandates that apply to all women *carte blanche*. They adhere to the adage that it is better for children to be taken care of by their own parent than by a stranger. They expressed concern, as did several other mothers, about leaving their young children to be cared for by strangers in an impersonal daycare setting. Relying on their own kin was a common strategy for childcare. But many women indicated that even relatives could not be relied upon to provide full-time childcare on a regular daily basis.

Furthermore, they acknowledged that they did not *want* to relinquish the care of their children. They wanted to care for and nurture their own children, and they felt that they should not be denied this experience simply because they are poor and receive welfare. Although they may not be familiar with the nuances of the multiple scientific studies that indicate the importance of parental social support and interaction for the resiliency and adaptation of at-risk youth (Bowen & Chapman, 1996), somehow they knew intuitively that as sole parents, their physical presence and nurturing are critical to their child's social development. Stephanie, eager to work as a nurse, nonetheless referred to work requirements as "indentured servitude." Another woman, 29-year-old Laura, who has two children, a toddler and an infant, said:

> I think that it's more beneficial for my family that I be home than to compromise our lives in other ways, in sending them out to be cared for by

somebody else. I would rather have a system that helped people take care of their kids and take care of their kids well. To teach them to grow up and to have more of a community aspect of people helping each other than this "for each his own" kind of thing.

Despite the concerns expressed by these few women, the vast majority of welfare recipients enthusiastically endorsed work requirements. However, although largely supportive of work requirements, many women also exercised caution. They were concerned about the kinds of jobs would they get—whether their benefits would be immediately affected—and they worried most of all about their children. They were adamant that work should not come in the way of motherhood—after all, they are the only parents that their children have to rely upon.

Family Caps

Family caps are designed to limit or deny additional benefits for children born to women on welfare. This policy is based on the assumption that women have additional children carelessly, or perhaps even purposely, in order to increase the level of welfare benefits received. It is assumed that women will cease having children if they are no longer "rewarded" for it.

The majority of women interviewed opposed this reform effort. They believed that family caps unfairly penalize innocent children "from something that they need." Yet there is significant disagreement as to whether women on welfare deliberately have children to increase the size of their benefit level. Some women argue that yes, other recipients will be influenced to have more children if their welfare benefit is increased. However, even some respondents who believe that women do have additional children to augment their welfare check still opposed family caps, arguing that children should not be punished for the decisions made by their parents. Jessie, a 42-year-old mother, spoke for most women when she said, "Increase. You shouldn't jeopardize a woman for having a baby or make children suffer because of their parents."

Reference was often made to the additional costs associated with having a child, and that the current benefit probably could not realistically be stretched to cover these costs. Again, the child would ultimately suffer as a result. Marissa spoke of inflation, and that a child's needs cannot be squeezed out of an already low welfare grant.

There's inflation, you know, and prices go up. I think it should be increased. You know, the basics of buying clothes and stuff. That's another family member, and you can't live off the amount it is. Well, you can live, but as far as buying Pampers and stuff like that, you couldn't do it without an increase.

Other women were more ambivalent regarding whether or not benefits should cover an additional child born to women while on welfare. They may oppose family caps in principle, but they conceded that caps may be necessary if women continue to have many children while on welfare. The threshold at which caps should be implemented varied. Some claimed that if a woman had one or two additional children while on welfare she should still receive benefits for that child, but caps should be imposed for subsequent births. Others were more tolerant and allowed three or more additional births. Not surprisingly, their tolerance closely mirrored their own experience with out-of-wedlock births. For example, one woman, who had one child while receiving welfare, maintained that caps should be applied only to the second pregnancy:

> I feel that if they do it this one time, okay. I don't see to give them more money if they have more than one child on AFDC. Because one time, it could have been an accident, or whatever the case may be. But if they have more than one child when you're on AFDC—if you see a pattern there—you shouldn't get any more.

A few women endorsed family caps wholeheartedly and without any qualifiers. They believed that women have additional babies simply to receive a greater level of benefit, and felt that this reform would curtail this behavior. Tanya, who herself recently had a child while on welfare, felt that caps are fair and reasonable. She felt that it not unusual for other women on welfare to have a child for the sole purpose of increasing their check, unaware of the empirical evidence indicating that women on welfare have lower fertility rates than other women. She subscribes to the stereotype nonetheless, and believes that family caps will stop women from having additional children. Distancing her situation from these other women, she says that their benefit level should not increase:

> I would say, stay the same. A lot of people out there are saying, "The more children we have, the more money we'll get." I would say, after two or three years, it should stay the same, whether they have another child or not. They should know that the system can only do so much for them and their children.

These few women's concerns notwithstanding, the majority of women interviewed opposed family caps, which would deny or limit additional aid to women who have children while on welfare. They felt that the costs associated with having another child could not easily be absorbed within the previous benefit, and that the child would ultimately suffer as a result. Most felt that caps would not reduce the birth rate significantly, and that this program would do little to really help women exit from welfare.

Ideas for Reform

What reforms then do recipients perceive to be in their best interest? Soliciting ideas about how to really improve welfare generated spirited conversations. Women expressed a desire for a system that is proactive rather than reactive; one that supports and encourages women rather than punishes and threatens them; a system that provides incentive for self-help rather than one that discourages women from trying to help themselves; one that protects children and doesn't harm them in either the short or long term.

The interviews revealed several specific ideas for reform, falling into two broad themes. The first focused on how the welfare system itself could be improved so that women would have more security in raising their children on it. For example, they suggested that benefit levels themselves should be raised, because they are simply not enough to live on. Contrary to the rhetoric espoused by welfare critics, they told me that raising a benefit level would not encourage women to remain on the public dole. Instead, they suggested that it would help them terminate welfare more quickly by providing an opportunity to save money and acquire a few additional assets, such as a reliable automobile, that would ultimately make it easier for them to seek and maintain employment. The paltry benefit levels keep them impoverished, while the ambitious often resort to fraud so that they can realistically improve their financial status.

They also asked that the welfare system more vigorously enforce the collection of child support from fathers. Although some women clearly stated that they wanted nothing to do with the fathers of their children, often because of physical or emotional abuse, they generally did want the government to intervene on their children's behalf. Many expressed resentfulness that they alone shouldered the burden of childcare while fathers were off playing, working, in jail, or had the luxury of simply disappearing from sight. Some women preferred the fathers' absence because they would then not have to hassle with visitation schedules, engage in custody battles, or put up with sexually or emotionally harassing visits. One woman likened herself to a prostitute—providing sex to her son's father so that he would give her occasional child support money. Overall, the women wondered why the system treats them with suspicion and contempt, while apparently doing little to chase down fathers who do not financially support their children.

Recipients also told me that they wanted a system that was more customized to individual needs. Despite the exemptions that are written into the welfare reform legislation, they felt that it is a "one size fits all" model that does not work. They suggested an expanded case management approach where, ideally, case managers have a real personal interest in the needs of recipients and assist them in finding meaningful employment. I was reminded that not all women have the same needs, come from the same background, or have the same reasons for needing welfare in the first place. One woman, Sarah, suggested that recipients be allowed to choose from an array of benefit options in order to customize their welfare package to what they truly need. She told me that she received far more food stamps than she needed, for example, and used them as Christmas and birthday gifts for her family and friends. She acknowledged the waste, felt badly about it, and suggested that what she really needed instead was help with her rent. The unsubsidized rent on her small and rundown trailer consumed nearly all of her $241 welfare grant. Another woman told me that she would rather not have a cash grant at all, but she wouldn't be eligible for Medicaid without it and so continues to receive her check.

Recipients also clamored for a system that distinguished between those who want to work hard to improve their economic circumstances, and those who do not. They asked for a system that recognized that some women (themselves in particular) do not fit the stereotypes of welfare recipients that are so prevalent. Although they exaggerate the differences between themselves and other recipients, their concern that the system tends to punish those who are trying to improve their circumstances does have merit. For example, educational programs for welfare recipients are significantly curtailed under recent reforms. Women asked that the system allow those who are making strides toward self-sufficiency to continue to receive needed benefits. Benefits should be ended for those who are cheating or manipulating the system or who are making no effort to improve their economic circumstances through school or work. But those who want to pursue college, and who are making satisfactory progress in school, should not be arbitrarily dropped from welfare after some predetermined two- or three-year time limit. In other words, a woman like Stephanie, working towards a BSN in nursing, was viewed as a model welfare recipient, not as someone who should have her benefits eliminated.

The second set of suggestions for ways that the welfare system could be improved, surprisingly, had little to do with welfare itself. Rather, recipients pressed for changes in the way that our society structures low-tier work, and asked that policymakers reexamine the interplay between work and welfare. Women asked that low-tier work be made less tenuous and more secure so that they could get off welfare once and for all. Changing the structure of low-tier work so that they could exit welfare permanently was considered the best reform of all. For example, they asked for help in finding jobs, particularly jobs that paid sufficiently so they could support a family. They know that the 2005 minimum wage of $5.15 an hour will not allow them to take care of their children adequately; it leaves them in a more desperate situation than they were in while on welfare. They suggested that jobs in and of themselves were difficult to get, and finding jobs paying at least $8 to $10 an hour were nearly impossible to locate on their own. Many told of submitting job application after job application without ever being called for an interview. They asked for help finding employment, particularly jobs that would lift them above the poverty level. Several suggested that it was high time to raise the minimum wage so that they could support their families on it.

Recipients also suggested that, when they do get jobs, they should be allowed to keep part of their welfare check and part of their benefits, for a short period of time at least, to enable them to accumulate the capital necessary for stability. In a synthesis of 30 studies of welfare-leavers, the Department of Health and Human Services found that although many were employed, at least 25 percent experienced food insecurity and had trouble paying rent and utilities (Acs & Loprest, 2004).

My respondents acknowledged intermittent employment and welfare use, but attributed it to the vulnerability associated with suddenly having a huge housing bill, or startling food bills, or expensive childcare, or the need to buy an automobile for transportation, while earning wages that were only slightly higher than they made while on welfare. They found that their financial security did not improve when leaving welfare. Their lives became even more difficult and disheartening as they tried to juggle a new job paying at or near minimum wage with the newfound bills they were required to pay—all while they were trying to locate dependable and affordable childcare. They asked for interplay between work and welfare. They suggested that if they could keep part of their check and part of their benefits, such as housing subsidies or food stamps, for at least three to six months, they could begin to accumulate the capital needed to cushion themselves when the unforeseen emergency inevitably occurs. This would improve their confidence that they would not, once again, have to return to welfare.

Moreover, they asked that educational benefits be continued and strengthened. Many noted that their ticket out of welfare and minimum-wage jobs was through greater education and job training. Although over half of our sample had at least a high school diploma, most recognized that this is simply not enough to compete in today's job market. Moreover, they felt that teenage women on welfare must be encouraged, or perhaps even forced, to finish their high school education. It was commonly expressed that in order to receive benefits, teenagers should remain in school. Or they suggested that wages be tied to education; those with high school diplomas or GEDs would earn higher wages than would those without degrees. Some women requested remedial help in basic skills such as reading, writing, and arithmetic, believing that their skills were deficient. But more often, women asked for substantial training that would be directly tied to higher-wage work and job opportunities. They were suspicious of short-term training programs; many had experience with them already and still felt ill-prepared for the labor market. They know that there are higher-paying opportunities beyond the service sector, but many women do not yet have the skills to compete for these jobs, and they hoped that a component of welfare reforms would be devoted to helping them acquire work-related skills.

Finally, they asked that their medical benefits be continued beyond the one year of transitional benefits. They expressed fear and trepidation that future jobs were unlikely to offer health insurance to themselves or to their families. The need for medical benefits kept many women on welfare longer than they would like. But accepting a job without medical benefits was seen as behaving irresponsibly, by jeopardizing their children's health and well-being. The Oregon study of TANF-leavers revealed that health insurance is of great importance to their family because more than half worry that without it their families cannot get the health care that they need (Seccombe, Hartley, Newsom, Pope, & Hoffman, 2005).

We can conclude from these interviews that welfare recipients want a welfare system that is based on incentives rather than on a punitive approach. They asked for both a welfare system and an economic system that supports families, encourages them, invests in them, makes them more secure, and reinforces their duty and motivation to provide for their children. They wanted welfare to be a temporary helping hand—not a permanent fixture in their lives.

These in-depth interviews with women on welfare reveal a complex set of beliefs with respect to the welfare system. They want the government to help them off welfare; they do not simply want handouts. Moreover, recipients are not opposed to many features of the welfare reform legislation that was passed nearly a decade ago. They expressed eagerness to work, but they needed assistance in finding well-paying jobs. They needed enhanced support mechanisms such as education, childcare, and medical benefits that would enable them to continue working. Most importantly, their children's needs come first, and they were not willing to jeopardize their children's well-being by inadequate daycare. Recipients were less unanimous in their enthusiasm over strict time limits and caps denying additional benefits for children born to mothers already receiving welfare. They pleaded for a system that takes personal needs into account and suggested that a one-size-fits-all model cannot work. They want a system based on positive incentives, one that provides support and encouragement and strengthens the security of work for those employed in jobs within the bottom tier of our economic system. They don't want help to stay on the system; they want help to get off it.

Why does Stephanie, introduced at the beginning of this chapter, despise welfare, despite seemingly benefiting from the system for years? She suggested that its supposed help is really a facade. Because of our society's heavy emphasis on individual personality traits as the root cause of poverty, many people do not respect poor women. Consequently, lawmakers are not really motivated to create policies to help them. Welfare's policies and programs are punitive in nature. Welfare critics lament about women who are "dependent" on the system. The unspoken but inherent view is that people are lazy by nature, and thus welfare must be kept low to prevent women from getting too comfortable on the system and to serve as a warning to others who may be looking for an easy handout. But, Stephanie suggests, in the quest to cut costs, policymakers refuse to make the initial investments needed in both the welfare and economic systems to help women successfully jump from welfare to work—a jump that most recipients undoubtedly want to make. She reminds us that these things may be costly, but as a society we can pay now, or we can pay later in terms of increased crime and other social problems:

> The only thing I see with many of these things that they are trying to do today is that they are trying to cut their costs—in the short term. What they don't realize is that, in the long term, sooner or later it's going to end up costing more in lost property, crime, and you know, drug abuse and drug selling. Sooner or later, it is going to come out in the wash. I understand that they are trying to reform the welfare system. It needs it. It really does. From a person who is on it, it really needs it. They need to do something so that people can get off welfare. People need to think about investing in women and children. Give people the opportunity to work or give them an education. Do not penalize them. Give them a little extra for childcare. Help them make the transition from being on welfare to getting off. We need to make sure that people are living in decent, clean housing, with clean water, and decent air and good food. You can't do anything if your body is undernourished and you're living in a bad environment. I think that's the way we need to go.

CRITICAL THINKING QUESTIONS

1. People in Stephanie's situation who attend school full-time are largely ineligible for aid today. Why is that? Describe the pros and cons of offering welfare assistance to persons going to college for a four-year degree, or beyond.

2. What do you think are the strengths of the welfare system? Can you name any strengths that recipients themselves did not offer?

3. Welfare recipients claimed that the welfare system had several weaknesses. Do you agree with their assessment? Did welfare reform address those weaknesses?

4. Do welfare programs offer too much money, or too little? Defend your answer. Then take the opposite opinion and craft an argument to support that point of view.

5. Why was welfare reformed with so little input from recipients themselves?

6. What are the pros and cons of time limits, work requirements, and family caps? How do you think your opinions differ from welfare recipients' opinions, if at all?

7. Do welfare recipients have realistic ideas for welfare reform? Which seem realistic, and why? Which do not seem realistic, and why?

CHAPTER

8   Getting Off Welfare

It is likely that virtually all of the women who were originally interviewed in Florida in 1995 for this study have left the welfare system, most for low-wage work. Between 1994 and 2004, the number of families who receive welfare has been reduced by 60 percent, from about 5 million to under 2 million families (U.S. Department of Health and Human Services, February 9, 2005).

Some exemptions are granted to those who cannot work because of their health status, the age of their children, or special problems or conditions that may require additional assistance such as domestic violence, but these exemptions generally do not exceed 20 percent of those currently on welfare. Instead, for the vast majority of "able-bodied" recipients, the 1996 welfare reform legislation—Personal Responsibility and Work Opportunity Reconciliation Act (PRWORA)—mandates that they find jobs and become self-supporting—quickly.

This chapter explores the outlook for women who are on welfare. What kinds of jobs are they likely to find, and at what pay? It asks whether communities can absorb this many new workers, and looks at the obstacles women may face in finding and holding onto jobs. Unable to move back and forth on and off welfare, as recipients often have done in the past, how can we ensure that women will not need the extra assistance from welfare? Politicians, along with the public, measure the success of welfare reform by the rate at which recipients are eliminated from the welfare rolls and are put into jobs. Whether women and children remain impoverished in their new jobs is of less concern.

Welfare recipients are often lumped together into one large homogenous group. In reality, many different kinds of persons receive welfare, and they receive it for different reasons. Passell (1997) highlights three types of recipients, all of whom have different backgrounds and needs, and who will fare differently under recent reform legislation. The first group consists mostly of women who are impoverished because of bad luck, temporary illness, or divorce. These women often need a short-term helping hand to boost themselves back up to independence. Their stays on welfare are often short, especially if they have family, friends, and other social supports to draw upon. Their lives are temporarily disorganized, and usually are sorted out enough to leave welfare fairly quickly. Stays of only a few months are not uncommon. These women would find jobs on their own quickly without the prod of welfare reform legislation.

The second group of recipients, and the most numerous, are on welfare for an interrelated set of individual and structural reasons. Some are on welfare because they lack job skills, experience, education, literacy skills, or other types of human capital. A study in California demonstrated that welfare recipients have substantially lower basic literacy skills, including understanding prose, documents, or quantitative material. Almost 80 percent of welfare recipients there have either low or very basic skills, compared to 34 percent of full-time workers in the state. Their study found that the average welfare recipient had difficulty following simple written directions to perform a single mathematical operation such as addition (Johnson & Tafoya, 1999).

As it stands now, these women may not be desirable employees, except perhaps in the lowest-tier service sector positions where turnover is high, wages are low, and benefits are virtually non-existent. Women in this group can have their marketability enhanced with further training, counseling, and financial incentives in a strong job market. Although it is acknowledged that in a weak market their chances of finding work will be more difficult, the importance of the labor market itself is sometimes downplayed. Yet it is of critical importance in understanding the plight of these recipients. Lawmakers assume that with additional training or with a GED in hand women in this group will find employment to support themselves and their families. But can the labor market absorb all of these additional workers, even with their newly earned GEDs, and additional job training? It is this group of welfare recipients that will be most affected by welfare reform legislation. They potentially stand much to gain, and, realistically, will have much to lose by federal and state reforms. Whether they are winners or losers depends on whether they are allowed to attend, or remain, in school long enough to learn high-paying marketable trades, or are processed through superficial job training programs quickly and then turned loose to compete in a saturated service-sector labor market that pays minimum wages and offers few benefits that higher-paid workers have come to rely upon.

The third group faces even more severe obstacles to employment. Their physical health may be extremely poor. They may have severe learning disabilities and simply not be able to learn to read, write, or understand written instructions well enough to obtain or sustain employment. They may also have deep rooted psychological problems that simple short-term counseling or job training cannot overcome, and therefore they are of little interest to most employers. For example, while the national average of depression hovers around 5 percent overall, and about 12 percent for women, my study of TANF-leavers in Oregon revealed that over one-quarter of respondents suffered from depression (Seccombe et al., 2005).

In all likelihood, some individuals on welfare who suffer from depression or who have other severe problems may be exempt from work requirements, particularly those with physical ailments, because they will be certifiably unemployable. However, many of these women, particularly those with mental or emotional problems that are less visible, will not be exempt. They will be forced to compete with thousands of other individuals for low-wage jobs—jobs that they will have difficulty obtaining in the first place, jobs that they will have more difficulty keeping. In addition to their below-average general skills, national data indicate that about 15–25 percent of welfare recipients face barriers to employment in two or more of the following areas: physical disability or health limitation; mental health; health or behavioral problems in their children; alcohol or drug use; domestic violence; child welfare; housing instability; or a very young infant (Acs, Loprest & Roberts, 2001; Johnson & Tafoya, 1999; Olson & Pavetti, 1998; Zedlewski, 2003). Despite what we would like to believe, not all adults are psychologically, intellectually, and physically capable of financially supporting themselves and their families, given the demands and challenges that poor families face regularly.

Pearl is one of the women who will face profound obstacles to finding and keeping employment to support herself and her sons, yet her disabilities are largely psychological, and therefore will likely go unnoticed by officials. It took several attempts before I could reach Pearl at her home. She had no telephone, so I could not call in advance. Maybe it was her beautiful flower garden that drew me in, and encouraged me to return time and again. Beautiful and well-kept gardens are not common sights in the housing projects I visited. The second time I stopped by her house, and she was still not in, I wrote her a note, and stuck it in her door. I introduced myself in writing, briefly explained about this book, and told her I would stop by again. On my third attempt, I still did not catch her in, but two boys who were playing outside told me that she was their mom, and they indicated that she had my note, and wanted to talk with me. On my fourth visit I found Pearl at home.

After so many attempts to locate her, after seeing her lovely and well-tended garden, and after talking with her children, I felt that I knew her even before we met. I envisioned a young, vibrant African American woman, frequently off visiting friends or running errands. I was wrong. Pearl was very different than I expected. First, she was older than I had imagined. She was 48 years old, but looked considerably older than her age. Her teeth had all been recently pulled, adding to her aged looks. As it turns out, Pearl has eight children; the two I met were her youngest boys, ages 9 and 12. Two more boys, ages 14 and 17, also live at home, and one 18-year-old girl comes and goes at her own convenience. Pearl's oldest three children are grown and out of the house. Pearl looked tired and worn out. According to her own account, that's exactly how she feels.

> I have a lot of pressure. It's like a bruise, you know, all my life. By staying down and worrying about kids. I've had to raise them all myself. Stress. I've been under a lot of stress for a long time. They put me on Prozac. Sometimes I have so much pressure sometimes I don't take them. I just sit there and let the pressure worry me. I had fainting spells, and the doctor said, "I can't see anything, just get it together." Like I want to. But I tried, but with the kids, it was like, throw me back. It's hard being with such pressure all the time. I let myself go down by worrying about them.

Pearl's children have been a constant source of tension for her, especially since the divorce from her second husband due to his frequent infidelity. He is now in prison. She tells me that she loves her children dearly, but acknowledges that she has little control over them. On the weekday morning that I interviewed her, two of her boys were home from school; the 14-year-old was home because of a "cough," although I didn't hear him cough once during the 90 minutes that I was there. Her 12-year-old son was home because he had been suspended from school for two weeks because of a sex-related offense, of which he claimed innocence.

As she tells it, her life has been terribly disappointing: "I feel like I've been mistreated, held down, you know?" Her two oldest sons, aged 28 and 26, have been in and out of prison for drug-related offenses and burglary. One stole money from her—nearly $100, which represented a major savings effort on her part—so that he could buy crack cocaine. None of her children have graduated from high school; all dropped out in the ninth or tenth grade. "They just quit. I think it's because of drugs. You know, in this neighborhood, they get with other kids, and they are doing drugs, so they want to do the same thing," she told me. Nor does the future look bright for the boys who are still in school and living at home; "I've got one kid suspended out of school for ten days. And the 17-year-old is giving me lots of problems. He doesn't want to go to school. I've got a whole bunch of pressure," Pearl says. All she really wants, she tells me, wistfully, is to be able to move out of the housing projects—away from the crime, the drugs, the noise, and to keep them in school. She wants to move out of the city to the countryside, where she envisions a slower and more relaxed pace of life, and a more positive environment in which to raise her three remaining teenage boys. "I've been trying to get money to get out of here," she reveals. "I want to move far out of the projects. There is too much drugs. They're messing everywhere you go. Lots of drug dealers in this neighborhood." But sadly, a move is not likely to happen. Pearl has lived in the same public housing unit for nearly 25 years.

Pearl is no stranger to hard work. She's cleaned houses, has worked as a maid in hotels, and worked in a meat packing plant. She quit these various jobs because of problems with her children, or health problems related to the stress her children cause: "The kids really worry me. They call me on the job, one of them is in trouble, and the police are here. So I get so upset I give up. I'm too easy to give up." But Pearl is not a quitter. She has worked very hard over the years, including as a farm laborer off and on during much of her life, spending hours hunched over picking vegetables so that she could earn $20 for her family. "I've been working all my life like a boy." She left school in the eighth grade to help support her family by picking vegetables during Florida's long growing season. As a mother, Pearl has tried to teach her children the value of hard work and the rewards that can be reaped from it by taking them with her to work in the fields. "I try to teach them how to earn a dollar, you know?" She suggested that they could keep all of the money they earned, and put it towards the high-priced sneakers or other clothing that they have been begging for. However, they scoff at the idea of toiling for hours of backbreaking labor only to make less than minimum wage at the end of the day. "Those drug dealers put ideas of easy money into their heads . . . " she tells me. From her sons' perspective, why not sell drugs? It is glamorous, easy, and profitable work. Working in the fields, in contrast, is none of these.

If Pearl has worked before, why do I anticipate that it will be difficult for her to work again? Pearl suffers from a wide variety of physical ailments, but probably none of these are severe enough to excuse her from work requirements. She had recently broken her foot, although it has since healed. She has back problems that she claims prevent her from doing any heavy lifting. She gets tired easy and has asthma. She also has arthritis, and experiences pain when using her hands. She has applied for Supplemental Security Income (SSI), but has been turned down twice because her physical health problems have not been evaluated as serious enough for disability insurance.

More serious, perhaps, are Pearl's emotional and psychological limitations. She is under so much stress from her children, "pressure" as she repeatedly called it, that she would have extreme difficulty finding or holding a job. She told me that she would like to have a job, or go back to school after her children grow up. And, over the past few years, she has started working towards her GED several times with the assistance of the welfare office. But she quits because of the pressures associated with her children, and because of the numerous household chores that come with five children living in the home. Trying to keep them out of drugs, keep them in school, and cleaning up after them, is a full-time job in and of itself. It is, for all practical purposes, more than she can manage on many days. Adding a work requirement to her life would seem to be an impossibility:

> I wash clothes 24 hours a day, hang them up, fold them, and put them in the room. I mop the floor and clean up the house all the time. When I broke my foot, I had a cast on to my knee. And I couldn't get them to mop up the floor, pick up paper, keep the yard clean, or fold clothes. They don't want to do nothing like that. If you don't have any money, your children don't want to help you nowadays. I feel so much pressure that I can't go to sleep at night. If I lay down early, I might go to sleep. But in 30 minutes I'm up. At three or four or five o'clock in the morning, I never go back to sleep. I might go out there in the yard and work and rake.

Pearl is one of the most difficult cases I witnessed, in terms of her employability. She faces tremendous obstacles to finding and keeping a job. Short-term training programs will be of little real benefit to Pearl. She is not on welfare simply because she lacks job experience or a GED. A quick-fix job training program, or enrollment in school for a GED will not, miraculously, make Pearl significantly more employable than she is today. Pearl is on welfare primarily because of deep-rooted emotional and psychological problems that are caused by, or at least exacerbated by, the arduous task of raising eight children in a meager poverty-level existence. She was poor whether or not she was employed. Living in poverty is not a trivial event, and some families experience more noxious problems than others do. Moreover, some families have better coping skills, or more social support in times of crises. Pearl's coping skills are not well developed, and she has no friends or extended family to turn to for social support— support that I found to be crucial to the improvement of the lives of most women on welfare and their families, as noted in Chapter 6. Instead, her aging mother, siblings, and adult children make incessant demands upon her. She receives only a sporadic $50 check from the county welfare office as a child support payment for her youngest children. Without the material, financial, or emotional assistance that most other women reportedly had from extended families, neighbors, friends, boyfriends, or from the fathers' of their children, Pearl is poorly equipped to handle the stress of daily living, even without the added dimension of paid employment.

While perhaps Pearl's case was more extreme than it was for other women interviewed here, her limitations and concerns were not entirely unusual. I saw several other women whose sense of self-worth and self-determination had been eroded to the point that I wondered how they would possibly find the inner strength to leave welfare, despite telling me that they desperately wanted to do so. Their wounds and disabilities are on the inside, not on the outside. As such, they will likely go unnoticed by welfare authorities. They will be forced into a labor market that they are, to put it mildly, poorly equipped to handle. Who will be there to help the many who fail and fall through the cracks?

My guess is that there are thousands of women like Pearl all across the country. They do not represent all women on welfare, or even the majority of women on welfare. They are however, a sizable population that must be recognized and treated with fairness and dignity.

Amy represents the other end of the spectrum. In contrast to Pearl, her employment options look bright, and her future contains tremendous optimism. Amy has one five-year-old daughter who was conceived during a rape. She has been on welfare for three years. At the time of the interview, she was also attending a university and had nearly completed the requirements for a Bachelor's Degree in Occupational Therapy. Her intention was to enter a Master's Degree program in Physical Therapy. If she is successful, which I had every reason to believe she would be, Amy would earn $50,000 a year at her job within a few years. No more welfare, ever. Over the course of her working career she will pay in taxes far more than she ever received while on welfare.

Amy did not feel defeated when I interviewed her. She received financial aid to augment the $241 she received in welfare, and consequently had a somewhat higher standard of living than do others who receive welfare alone. Equally important, she has a very strong extended family that helps her out emotionally and financially, which is not known to welfare officials. Amy's mother and father tend to many of Amy's daily uncertainties: they watch their granddaughter every weekend so that Amy can study; they have loaned her a reliable automobile; they give Amy money at the end of the semester when her financial aid is running low, so that she will not have to live solely on welfare; they buy virtually all of their granddaughter's clothing, toys, and pay for her weekend entertainment when she is at their house. Amy's parents also support her emotionally in her endeavor to earn a college degree. They provide the praise and the moral support that is so necessary for her to continue the frantic pace that comes with a demanding course of study, required internships and volunteer hours, and single motherhood. Moreover, Amy has no particular health problems, has only one child, and is highly intelligent. Given her circumstances, she will undoubtedly be a success story. Nonetheless, even for Amy, life is far from easy. She suffers from a number of stress-related disorders, including panic attacks, in her quest to juggle school, motherhood, and paying the bills.

The Women in the Middle: Why Increasing Human Capital Is Not the Only Answer

Most women on welfare are neither as successful as Amy, nor as despairing as Pearl. Instead, they are somewhere on the continuum between these two cases. It is likely that these other women, too, will find it difficult to locate work. Of course it is correct to assume that increasing human capital—such as, education, literacy, and job experience—are important to improving the lives of many recipients. Many welfare recipients lack high school diplomas, marketable skills, and work experience. They cannot read, write, or perform arithmetic at a level that allow them to succeed in a job. These problems have a bearing on their employability and opportunities. Persons with more education, literacy, marketable skills, and work experience will have an easier time finding a well-paying job than will someone without these assets. Programs designed to enhance levels of human capital should be enhanced for those who so desperately need them.

But the challenges that women on welfare may face are not solely related to a lack of human capital, as we are led to believe. After all, many women leave welfare, permanently or temporarily, while doing nothing to improve their human capital standing, per se. While additional job training, particularly if the training was to come in the higher-paid skilled trades, such as carpentry, nursing, or electronics, would be useful and enthusiastically endorsed, this alone is not enough. Instead, other problems in the employability of women on welfare are more *structural* in origin. These major structural difficulties include (1) not enough unskilled, semi-skilled or skilled jobs to go around for all the women who want them or will need them; (2) jobs that do exist for welfare recipients are largely low paying and do not provide critical benefits; and (3) job training programs are not designed to significantly improve women's job prospects. These three work-related concerns are rooted in limitations of our social structure, and the full array of quick-fix job training or motivational programs in the world will not resolve these fundamental problems. Even if we successfully raised every former welfare recipient's educational level to a GED or beyond, the reality is that there are not enough jobs to go around in many regions of the country, and the wages and benefits of existing jobs do not permit the job holder to be lifted from poverty. Yet despite these structural obstacles to welfare reform, policymakers continue to draw upon the age-old notion that the problem with women on welfare is that they are personally deficient (Gilens, 2001; Hancock, 2004). Their deficiency in human capital, along with their lack of motivation and a socially acceptable work ethos, are blamed as the primary factors associated with welfare use and the primary obstacles to getting off the system.

The preoccupation with deficiency in human capital and a concern with a poverty subculture—major premises of Individualism and the Culture of Poverty perspective—dominated reform efforts during the War on Poverty of the 1960s, as shown in Chapter 2. Programs were created to enhance the skills and opportunities of the poor. Likewise, the Job Opportunities and Basic Skills (JOBS) programs in the late 1980s allowed welfare recipients to attend college while on aid. An emphasis on education and job training as a route to self-sufficiency—a "human capital enhancement model"—dominated the political ethos (London, 2004).

Today, although we still see individualistic and cultural concerns as the dominant drive behind reforming welfare, this time around fewer dollars are being put into significant human capital training programs. Instead, programs are of shorter duration and less comprehensive. The approach has changed from a human capital approach to a "work first" approach (London, 2004). The concern is that welfare dependence is bad, work is good, and we can solve our welfare dilemma by giving people some quick, rudimentary training and putting them to work, forcibly, if necessary.

Education and Employment Training

In spite of the real value of education and job training, changes to the welfare laws actually make it more difficult for welfare recipients under TANF to get quality training than in the past under AFDC. Although states may modify federal mandates, in general, only 30 percent of the caseload can pursue vocational training or education full-time, counting these activities towards work requirements, and they can do so for only up to 12 months (Strawn, February, 2004). However, most programs, even from a community college, take two years for welfare recipients to complete because they are juggling multiple demands of part-time work, parenting, and often must take remedial reading, writing, and math courses (Mathur, Reichle, Wiseley & Strawn, 2004). Nonetheless, most families do not even receive one year of education, and instead must settle for "bootstrap" training—short-term courses on resume writing, interviewing skills, and other how-to-get-a-job tips that are directly related to employment.

Two- and four-year college programs used by many of the respondents, such as in nursing, accounting, teaching, occupational therapy, and computer programming are discouraged by federal TANF provisions and are not a part of the 12 work activities designated by PRWORA (London, 2004). Yet the benefits of postsecondary education are clear. A four-year degree results in at least a 50 percent increase in earnings for women, shorter welfare spells, increased employment, and better educational outcomes for children (Gottshalck, September, 2003; London, 2004; Magnuson & McGroder, 2002). Therefore, some states skirt federal guidelines and allow postsecondary education to meet the state work requirements for a short period of time—22 allow postsecondary education for more than 12 months. Two states, Maine and Wyoming, allow use of mandatory state TANF contributions so that they are not counted as recipients of federal money (Greenberg, Strawn, and Plimpton, 2000; Butler and Deprez, 2002). However, even in those states that allow postsecondary education, it is up to case managers to promote it, and many do not. Many states report that their programs are underenrolled (Butler & Deprez, 2002; Coalition for Independence through Education, 2002).

What are the educational and job training needs of welfare recipients? My analysis reveals a complex situation. Certainly, additional education and more extensive employment training opportunities are better than less education and training. Most recipients—including those who are without a high school diploma or GED—would benefit from more extensive education and training, including in the skilled trades, such as auto mechanic, welder, or electrician.

But, it is important to recognize that not all welfare recipients are deficient in their education level and job training. While the average education level of recipients is lower than for the population as a whole, nearly 55 percent have at least finished high school, and some have attended or graduated from college or vocational school. Dee was at a community college studying accounting; Amy was at the university studying occupational therapy; Stephanie was at the university preparing to become a registered nurse; Molly was finishing her prerequisites at a community college so that she could transfer to the university to study to become a registered nurse; and Coreen was taking her prerequisites at the community college so that she could enter the college of education at the university. Several other women were in two-year programs at the community college studying business, computers, or nursing. These women are apparently bright, motivated, and have important literacy skills.

Several women had completed training programs in the for-profit schools located in the community. However, these were often problematic because few felt that their "diplomas" helped them get jobs for which they were trained. These proprietary schools are often built in poorer neighborhoods and court an impoverished clientele with offers of training that will lead to high-paying jobs, "and all I actually got was about a $4,000 student loan that now I need to pay." Their training did not lead to a permanent job that paid wages high enough to support their families.

Treena, a 42-year-old African American mother, earned her GED, and then attended a for-profit school where she studied to become a secretary. It did not lead to a job. She is now back at the local community college to further her studies in business. She was one of four women interviewed here who had attended a for-profit proprietary school. Like the others, she felt that their program had been a waste of time. She told me that she was led to believe that her degree would lead to a high-paying clerical job, perhaps earning $7 to $8 an hour. Instead, she found that potential employers did not value her degree from a for-profit college without work experience in that field. She now owes several thousand dollars in student loans, and blamed the school for encouraging her to borrow money for deficient job training.

> I was going to business classes, but I had just injured my back. That was in early '87, '88, '90. But I couldn't continue to walk there because of my back. You know, I fell, and reached out, and I could hear the pinch. I was in a neck brace and everything. So I transferred to <proprietary> College. It was closer. I completed college. It took a year. And that was in word processing, secretarial word processing, but I could never get a job in it. Everywhere you go to fill out an application, they said you haven't had any experience on the job. But you know, if you're just getting out of school, I

can't understand why people can't give you a chance to try and show them what you can do. No one gave me that chance. Nobody. <Proprietary> College didn't give me any help at all. No, no help in finding a job whatsoever. None. So I spent a lot of money. I'm still paying them back.

Women revealed that they valued education and training through local welfare programs, the community college, or university. However, many intimated that it was not clear that education and training by themselves would lead to a job. They had high hopes, but then found that it was very difficult, if not impossible to find a job in their field because of the high numbers of other qualified applicants.

Latasha, a 29-year-old African American mother, has been diligently looking for full-time, permanent employment. She did not complete high school, but recently went back and received her GED through a program sponsored by the welfare office. She's been off and on welfare since her first child was born nine years ago. She has worked a variety of low-wage jobs, primarily in fast-food restaurants, and then quit when her hours were cut, or work seemed to particularly interfere with her role as a mother. She's concerned about "the perverts" in her housing project neighborhood, and therefore refuses to let her children, ages nine, eight, and six, outside alone. Latasha doesn't like welfare. She is very ambitious, and hopes to have a full-time job soon and be off welfare completely. But despite her newly granted GED, she has not been able to secure the employment she desires:

> I'm trying hard, but it's like I'm kinda held down or something. I'm not sure the more education you get will necessarily get you a job. So I might need to move out of state. I might need a new start. It's extremely hard to get a job, there are so many students here. I'm really praying, and hoping the man up above is looking out for me.

Are the short-term classes designed to help women find employment helpful? For the most part, they appear to be doing very little to significantly help women in the arduous search for well-paying work. Instead, training programs are generally short-term and superficial attempts to teach women how to "market themselves" to an employer. Others are designed to teach women the academic skills necessary to pass a GED. But training programs overall do not provide the vocational or academic education that would give women the skills needed to command higher-wage work. Women commonly told me that they wanted real training and real education—not simply a GED or training in resume writing. A GED does not translate into a good-paying job, they told me. They wanted vocational training that would teach them a specific set of skills, and would eventually lead them to a specific well-paying job. The skills and jobs most sought after were in nursing and working with computers.

Some respondents were busy working toward these goals at the time of our interview. Nonetheless, I was struck by the alarming number of persons who had no real firm grasp on how to get from here to there. For example, some had no idea that they would be eligible for financial aid such as Pell grants if they went to college. Since they had no savings and no credit cards, they believed that college was not an option.

Other women luckily stumbled upon a path toward their goals, but admitted that they needed extra help in following it. Beth, a 27-year-old white woman with one daughter, has her high school diploma, but was not finding the type of job that would lift her and her daughter out of the depths of poverty. Given the additional problems of finding adequate childcare, affording transportation, and the risk of losing her Medicaid, she found it more productive to sit home and collect her small welfare check than work in the low-paying service sector. But Beth, like most other women I met, had a dream. She wanted to be off welfare, and specifically, she wanted to be a nurse. She happened to discover a program at the community college designed to help women like herself turn her dreams into realities. But, again, like so many of the other women I met, Beth was scared, and needed extra assistance:

> I went to <community college> for one of their classes—it was just like for a week. Like career opportunities. And I liked it. I started to, you know, go through the process of taking tests and everything. But it was like, they rush, rush, rushed me, and I got scared. My life was stressed out at that time, and I didn't need no more stress. I just quit. I was going to go for nursing. I've always wanted to go for nursing, but I kind of feel like if I can't have somebody right there helping me through it, instead of rushing me and pushing me, I just don't feel like I can do it.

Will job-training programs provide the training and moral support that many women transitioning off welfare are likely to need? "Welfare Mothers Prep for Jobs, and Wait," the headline in the *New York Times* read soon after welfare reform legislation was implemented (Swarns, 1997). The four-week job training program in New York City, known as Job Clubs, was helping women "learn to dress professionally, to write resumes, to give an employer a firm, confident handshake and to believe in the prospect of financial independence and newfound self-respect." Yet, of the thousands of women who completed the short Job Club program and were turned loose to find jobs in New York City, the vast majority were still unemployed months later (Swarns, 1997). Moreover, former welfare recipients who did find jobs most often found them in a small number of relatively low-paying industries, such as in retail, eating and drinking establishments, or in manufacturing. Although these industries were booming in the mid-1990s, unfortunately they have not performed well during the economic recession in the early 2000s (Boushey & Rosnick, April 2004).

Work Experience

Proponents of both the "welfare-to-work" and "human-capital-enhancement" approaches to welfare reform suggest that recipients' lack of work experience is a primary obstacle to finding quality employment. But the vast majority of women interviewed had held multiple jobs over the course of their lives. National data also suggest that most welfare recipients have been employed, often weaving employment with their stays on welfare. So, at first glance, welfare recipients do not lack work experience, *per se*. Unfortunately, if we look at the types of jobs recipients have held, we find that their jobs tend to be low-paying ones in the bottom tier of the service sector, are often temporary, and do little to improve their financial circumstances over welfare. For example, government data indicate that the retail jobs classification that includes many former welfare recipients pays an average hourly wage of $11.90, and food establishments averaged $7.77 (not including tips), both of which were much lower than the $15.47 an hour for the private sector as a whole in 2003 (Boushey & Rosnick, April, 2004). However, it is likely that many former recipients earn significantly less than the average in these industries because of their below-average basic skills and less seniority. They are generally taking the entry-level positions.

Like many other women on welfare, 23-year-old Tamela has worked in the fast-food industry. She had two children while still in high school, and it was at this time that she also tried to work at McDonald's. She earned minimum wage, and like so many others, found the stresses of juggling work and family outweighed the small wages she received:

> When I was in high school and had my two kids, I worked at McDonald's, and didn't see that I was benefiting by working. I mean, I liked working with the public and everything, and I had a lot of fun doing it. I could say, "I have a job," and that gave me pride, but it was not beneficial by no means. At the time, I did not have transportation, so I had to find my mom to keep my kids, making sure she could do it or finding someone else, then finding a way to work and getting back home. It's stressful. I think it's crazy for the simple fact that you don't benefit from it, from work, unless you have a job that's going to pay you more than minimum wages and the system would help you with childcare.

Amy's employment history is also not unusual:

> I worked in an electronics factory assembling little electronic things, parts, like resistors and transistors and things. It was for minimum wage. It was really nasty work. It was terrible. And when I was in high school, I worked as a secretary-stenographer type person in a medical records office. I did well. But, it also was pretty dead-end, you know, minimum wage.

Molly describes her work experience:

> I've done all kinds of things. I've worked at a hardware store; I've worked at department stores, at restaurants, I've waitressed, I've ridden a mobile munchies truck to construction sites and sold food out of a truck. Lots of different things. But when I had Jeffrey, my first child, we talked about it. And my husband Tom wanted me to stay home with Jeffrey. And I had William 15 and a half months later. So I was a stay-at-home mom. I took care of them. Sure, I could go to work now. I can work. But it would be pointless if I'm making minimum wage. Who is going to take care of my

kids? I might as well go to school and further my education so when I do go to work I get paid something decent so I can take care of my family the way they should be taken care of. Not from a minimum wage job.

Rhonda tells me about her employment history, which again, is familiar:

> In Maryland I had a lot of jobs. I wasn't on welfare. I worked at the hospital back home in Maryland, and I've done cashiering and housekeeping. But then I came down here to help my sister because she got sick and had two kids. But there are no jobs. I've done whatever temporary jobs that agency gave me, like housekeeping at the hospital and a warehouse where I sorted lids for a printing company.

Americans cherish the belief that hard work pays dividends. If one simply works hard enough, one will prosper. Each year of continued effort will yield progressive economic improvements, the theory holds. Unfortunately, for many people this is not the scenario that they encounter. Despite a vast array of work experience, the women interviewed here generally found that hard work rarely leads to anything better. Their past job experience, even when they worked diligently, did not lead to advancement. At best, their pay increased only slightly, even after years of employment. Moreover, their employment did not significantly increase their level of human capital by giving them additional education or training. Neither did it significantly increase their "social capital" by allowing them to make connections with others that could eventually lead to better-paying or permanent jobs with fringe benefits attached to them. No matter how hard or diligently they worked, they remained within the lowest-tier jobs. There was very little upward mobility into the kinds of jobs where higher pay and benefits were standard. These findings are similar to those by Edin and Lein, who, in their study of 214 welfare recipients, also report:

> In short, these women were unable to build careers; if they chose to work, they were much more likely to move from one dead-end job to another. Thus, women learned that the kind of jobs available to them were not avenues to success or even to bare-bones self-sufficiency; they were dead-end jobs (1997, p. 70).

Yet, despite hard work rarely leading to anything better, women repeatedly had high hopes for work. Those with less experience were the most hopeful: they were still holding out that they would find the job that would let them move out of the housing projects, buy them a car, provide daycare for their children, allow them to buy name-brand clothing for their children, and offer some semblance of a middle-class lifestyle. Older women, or women with extensive labor market experience were often more cynical; some had lost their hope because of one dead-end job after another. Yet, even among this group, I was intrigued with the high interest in employment, despite the likelihood that their jobs will not significantly improve their standard of living. Most continued to be hopeful despite the odds against them. They hoped for practical jobs that they felt were within their reach: nursing, daycare, and secretarial work. Dee, who is attending school to become an accountant, told me, poignantly: "I've always wanted to go to college. My goal is to get my CPA license. My dream is to open my own firm. And my fantasy is to be bigger than H & R Block."

Several factors increase the likelihood of women finding work, according to research by the Institute for Women's Policy Research. The most significant factors, according to national data from 1,181 single mothers who received welfare, are: (1) the ability to work (e.g., not having a work-preventing disability); (2) availability of jobs (e.g., living in states with lower unemployment rates); (3) not having toddlers or infants; (4) family supports (e.g., receiving child support or earnings from other members); and (5) having greater amounts of human capital (e.g., having past work experience, and having a high school diploma). Meanwhile, factors that were found to have no association with the likelihood of finding work include (1) average state benefit levels; (2) the amount of time spent looking for work; (3) the mother's age; (4) mother's welfare history; and (5) race.

Several of these findings are critical to our discussion here. First, human capital factors are only one of several relevant considerations in explaining the propensity of welfare mothers to work. Second, despite arguments to the contrary (Murray, 1984), according to these data at least, the relatively higher benefit levels in some states do not deter women from seeking employment; instead, a more important factor in the likelihood of procuring employment is the statewide unemployment rate. Third, these data suggest that structural factors are critical to understanding how and why women leave welfare, and why they do not.

The Importance of Our Social Structure

If increases in human capital, such as in education, job training, or job experience are not enough to ensure that women leave welfare and find quality jobs with which to support themselves and their families, what else is needed? I suggest that limited human capital itself does not necessarily cause one to turn to or remain on welfare. Rather it makes one more *vulnerable* to needing assistance when faced with other circumstances such as job layoffs, seasonable employment, illness, employer cost-cutting devices, and changes in family structure. Women with lower levels of human capital have a more difficult time navigating beyond these daunting personal and structural barriers to self-sufficiency and well-being. Therefore, they may have to turn to public welfare programs in the interim. Their stays on welfare may be short, or they may be long, depending on a variety of conditions, including their level of human capital, the severity of the event or structural condition, and their degree of social support. Reliance upon welfare is not simply the result of individual choice or personal failure. Instead, this reliance is largely a consequence of vulnerability to factors imbedded in our social structure. Some of these structural factors are more specific to women—such as dependence on men for financial support and negotiating childcare—while others transcend gender—such as too few jobs paying living wages and an inadequate set of social service programs designed to provide a safety net for low-income families. It is the interaction and failure of human capital, structural factors, and social support that prompt the need for welfare assistance.

A thorough discussion of the many aspects of our social structure that contribute to poverty and welfare use is obviously beyond the scope of this book. I will, however, focus on issues pertaining to employment—both the amount and types of jobs that are being generated in our economy, and relate these to the plight and needs of poor women on welfare.

Not Enough Jobs

In large cities and small towns across the nation, there are not enough jobs available to absorb the influx of people looking for paid work because of the cessation of their welfare benefits. With the recession in the early 2000s, not all citizens can find work easily. Some groups are experiencing dizzying rates of unemployment. Although the U.S. unemployment rate averaged 5.2 overall in April of 2005, it was double that for blacks (10.4 percent). The unemployment rate was more than triple the national average for teens (17.7 percent), and significantly higher yet for black teens (35.5 percent) (U.S. Department of Labor, May 6, 2005). In this era when Affirmative Action programs are criticized for giving minorities and women supposedly unfair advantages, it is unfashionable to allude to white privilege. But it is undeniable that in a society such as ours, which is so heavily focused on race, being white has its advantages in many realms.

Between 2001 and 2004, the economy had 7.9 percent fewer jobs because of the recession. Employment is down in manufacturing by 14.5 percent, temporary help by 22.3 percent, accommodations by 11.3 percent, child day care by 7.3 percent, and retail trade by 6.6 percent (Boushy and Rosnick, April, 2004). Moreover, the experiences of former welfare recipients within these sectors are likely to be worse than that of the average worker because they are among those with the least seniority—"last hired, first fired." Not surprisingly, research by the Urban Institute indicates those employment among welfare leavers fell from 50 percent to 42 percent between 1999 and 2002 (Loprest, August 2003). Moreover, the share of all families that have left welfare, but are not employed, do not have an employed partner, and are not receiving income from Supplemental Security Income (SSI) increased from 10 percent in 1999 to 14 percent in 2002 (Loprest, August, 2003).

What does it feel like to look for work week after week, and turn up with nothing? When even the lowest-tier jobs in our economy have stiff competition, many people feel psychologically wounded. What is the point, they ask themselves? The real faces behind the statistics reveal the hurt and frustration that comes with being unemployed—wanting work, but not being able to find it, let alone maintain it.

Illustrating this scenario is Sheila, a 40-year-old woman who is supporting her 12-year-old daughter on her monthly $241 check. At the time of the interview, she was working on her GED and applying for jobs. She acknowledges that her math and reading skills are not very strong. "I can do some math—I'm not real good at fractions yet, and I don't read real well, but I'm hoping to find a job." But her search is not going well. Despite submitting numerous applications, she has not landed an interview, let alone a job. Yet, for her the clock was ticking. At the time of the interview, she had only five months of welfare left. "It's depressing," she tells me. "You can apply and apply, but you can't make someone hire you."

This should come as no big surprise. It was becoming evident even as early as 1997, when the economy was booming, that there might not be enough lower-skilled jobs to go around. "Welfare Job Needs Worry Officials," declares the headline of a newspaper in North Florida where the women interviewed for this study reside (Rausch, February 19, 1997).

> Alachua County will need more than 3,100 new jobs to employ local welfare recipients as a result of Florida's welfare reform rules, state officials say. That has local officials worried. "And they're not there," says Commissioner Brown. More than 90 percent required to work are women, 40 percent have less than a high school education, and 38 percent have no work history in the past two years.

Likewise, a study by a Pennsylvania economic forecasting firm also reported as early as 1997 that nationwide, there were only enough net new jobs to employ about half (54 percent) of welfare recipients who needed work. Some states had considerably fewer jobs: California would be able to employ only 42 percent of recipients, Maine only 25 percent, and New York only 13 percent. Florida was expected to do comparatively well; it was estimated that they would be able to employ 93 percent of welfare recipients due to its growing service-sector economy. (Children's Defense Fund, 1997b). The competition for jobs becomes fierce as wages increase. A study conducted in Ohio by the Midwest Job Gap Project found, in that state, there were 23 would-be workers for every job that paid poverty-level wages; 66 job-seekers for every job that paid wages at 150 percent of poverty, and 100 contenders for every job that paid $25,000, the amount estimated as a livable wage for a family with children, residing in Ohio (Children's Defense Fund, 1997b).

Types of Jobs Available for Women on Welfare

Typically, what types of jobs are available to welfare mothers? American industries have undergone rapid restructuring in the past few decades in response to technological changes and global competition. Social scientists establish broad occupational categories by distinguishing between primary, secondary, and tertiary sectors in the labor market. The primary sector consists of jobs in which raw materials are harvested, such as in timber, agriculture, or mining. Jobs in the secondary sector transform raw materials into manufactured goods. The tertiary sector, or service sector, is the fastest-growing sector of our economy and focuses on providing a wide variety of positions, such as salesclerk, attorney, cashier, and waitress. Within each sector, we can distinguish between tiers of workers. The "primary labor market," is characterized by having relatively high pay, benefits, and job security. Relatively low pay, few benefits, and little job security characterize the "secondary labor market." Within this labor market, women leaving welfare usually occupy jobs within the lowest tier.

In recent years, the number of workers needed in manufacturing, has declined considerably. These disappearing jobs tended to pay relatively higher wages because of union protections. Instead, our economy is experiencing an explosion of jobs in the service sector. But compared to manufacturing jobs, those in the service sector, particularly within the lowest tiers, are generally without union protection, and tend to be poorly paid, and offer few fringe benefits to workers. The protections offered by unions are well established; for example, union workers receive higher pay than their nonunionized counterparts, and are more likely to have retirement and health insurance benefits (UAW, 2002).

Many families on welfare earn the minimum wage or only slightly above it. The minimum wage in the United States, at $5.15 per hour in 2005, comes nowhere lifting even a small family out of poverty. More than 7.4 million workers earn at or near the minimum wage. This includes 5.3 million adults (age 20 and older), and 1.8 million parents raising children. About 18 percent of African American workers and 14 percent of Hispanic workers earn at or near the minimum wage (Interfaith Worker Justice, 2005).

The minimum wage has not been increased since 1997 and continues to lose value because of inflation. Its real value fell to $4.82 by 2004 and continues to decline. It is not a living wage. Even if increased to $6.65 an hour, full-time minimum-wage earnings would come to only $13,832 a year, or 15 percent less than the poverty guideline for a family of three in 2005 ($16,090) (U.S. Department of Health and Human Services, March 23, 2005). Many onlookers suggest that the minimum wage level must be raised by several dollars per hour in order to pay a living wage. This would have the benefit of aiding welfare recipients and non-recipients alike.

However, when discussions of raising the minimum wage surface, business leaders often cry foul. They argue that increasing the minimum wage will harm the poor by raising prices and destroying entry-level job opportunities, and that it will cost consumers and workers billions per year as the higher cost of entry-level jobs is passed on through higher prices and lower real wages:

> Proponents defend a minimum-wage increase by declaring it to be a moral issue and moral imperative—not just an economic or political consideration. The minimum wage, however, epitomizes government paternalism as its worst. It presumes that politicians are morally justified in destroying some people's jobs in order to inflate other people's wages. The American principle of economic freedom has been replaced by the principle of "government knows best." . . . Government must share the blame for stagnant wages. . . . Employers, as well as workers, operate within a competitive labor market in which wage rates broadly reflect the productivity of workers—less the costs of government-imposed mandates and taxes associated with employing a worker. But instead of addressing the impediments to wage growth imposed by government, proponents prefer to blame employers for stagnating wages and curry favor with voters by proposing another hike in the minimum wage (Wilson, 1996, pp. 3–4).

But these complaints have been used against all minimum wage increases, including the creation of the minimum wage itself. Instead, many economists and other social scientists argue that the income gains from a minimum wage hike would outweigh the job losses and price increases, and would be an important component of reducing poverty (Economic Policy Institute, March, 2005). A 1998 Economic Policy Institute (EPI) study failed to find any systematic, significant job loss associated with the 1996–1997 minimum wage increase. In fact, following the most recent increase in the minimum wage in 1996–1997, the low-wage labor market performed better than it had in decades (e.g., lower unemployment rates, increased average hourly wages, increased family income, decreased poverty rates). Economic models that look specifically at low-wage labor markets find that employers are able to absorb some of the costs of a wage increase through higher productivity, lower recruiting and training costs, decreased absenteeism, and increased worker morale. Moreover, a recent Fiscal Policy Institute (FPI) study of state minimum wages found no evidence of negative employment effects on small business (Economic Policy Institute, March, 2005).

The concept of paying a living wage is taking hold. A living wage ordinance requires employers to pay wages that are above federal or state minimum wage levels, usually ranging from 100–130 percent of the poverty line. Only a specific set of workers are covered by living wage ordinances, usually those employed by businesses that have a contract with a city or county government or those who receive economic development subsidies from the locality. The rationale behind the ordinances is that city and county governments should not contract with or subsidize employers who pay poverty-level wages. Boston, Baltimore, Denver, Los Angeles, and Portland, Oregon, are among nearly 100 cities around the country that make particular companies pay their employees wages that are more in line with the cost of living in the area, usually $3.00–$6.00 above minimum wage.

In addition to pay, another concern is that many of the jobs that are being developed are part-time, sub-contracted, temporary in nature, or occur at night. Many offer irregular work schedules. Employees working in these types of jobs, referred to as "nonstandard work schedules" represent the fastest-growing category of workers in the United States (Presser, 2003). Since 1982, temporary employment has increased several hundred percent. In other words, millions of women and men begin the workday not knowing if, and for how long, their jobs are likely to continue.

Some part-time and contingency workers prefer this arrangement, especially highly paid professionals who value their freedom and independence on the job. Physicians, accountants, attorneys, and financial planners are among the professionals who can make a lucrative business in part-time consulting. But most Americans, particularly the financially insecure, likely prefer the assurance of a steady job with an established pay scale and fringe benefits.

There is also a growing trend towards jobs that require weekend, evening, or variable nonfixed schedules, particularly those found in the lower-paying service sector, which many welfare recipients will look towards for employment (Presser, 2003; Presser & Cox, 1997). Recent analyses of national data indicate that women with a high school diploma or less are most susceptible to nonstandardized work hours. Most women with children do not want this arrangement; over half of women surveyed whose youngest child was between ages 5 and 13, reported that the main reason they worked these shifts was because it was a requirement of the job, and that they could not get any other job (53 percent). Only 30 percent of women listed beneficial reasons for working these shifts, such as it allowed for better childcare arrangements (18 percent); it allowed better arrangements for care of other family members (7 percent); it offered time for school (2 percent); or it provided better pay (3 percent). Sociologists Harriet Presser and Amy Cox summarize the conclusions from their study and pose an important dilemma for getting women off of welfare:

> The results . . . show that low-educated mothers are disproportionately represented in occupations with high rates of nonstandard schedules, that many of these women who work nonstandard hours do so primarily for labor market rather than personal reasons, and that job characteristics are stronger determinants of employment during non-standard times than are family characteristics. To a substantial extent, then, low-educated mothers appear drawn into working nonstandard hours by a lack of options. Finally, the study shows that these trends are likely to increase given current occupational projections, thereby increasing demand for childcare during evenings, nights, and weekends. Accordingly, to achieve the primary objective of welfare reform—moving mothers permanently from welfare to employment—childcare will need to be expanded markedly during nonstandard times, including evenings and weekends. Generating new jobs and expanding childcare will go a long way toward meeting that objective if the scheduling of both can be better synchronized (1997, p. 33).

We all clamor for more good jobs at good pay for workers. Rhonda is one of many women who is looking for one of these jobs. She would like to raise her young son Bobby without welfare, and recognizes the need for a permanent full-time job. Instead, however, she has been stymied by the tremendous growth in part-time, temporary positions.

> Hopefully I can get me a job. A permanent job. My sister's trying to get me a job where she works. I put my application in last week. And it would be a permanent job. When you go through those agencies, it's just temporary work. It's just whenever they need you, and it's unfair too. Every job I've found is through this temporary agency, like Manpower, but it's only temporary. And they cut my check and my food stamps, and when my job ends, it's like you're stuck again. So I'm trying to find a permanent steady job. But it's hard around here. I've been out looking for work, and hoping that something comes through.

Rhonda may be surprised to learn that Manpower is one of the largest private employers in the United States, ranking 140 in the Fortune 500, employing 2.5 million workers a year (Manpower, 2005). Every morning, its workers scatter into factories and offices around the nation, looking for a day's work. As other industrial giants shrink their payrolls, Manpower, and many other temporary agencies, such as Kelly Services, are booming.

Turnover rates in many low-tier jobs are high, even those considered to be permanent. Sometimes, women quit work in hopes of finding something better or to return to welfare. However, women in these jobs are also considerably more likely to be laid off than are other workers. They are the expendable workforce. They work in the service industry, in clerical work, and on assembly lines performing routine tasks. To the management, people in these largely unskilled or semi-skilled jobs are interchangeable. A high turnover rate is not a problem for management, and in fact may even be considered desirable so that health insurance premiums and payments of other benefits can be avoided. These disposable workers generally earn less than those on the regular payroll, and must live with the uncertainty that their jobs may permanently end today when they clock-out at 5:00 P.M. Their anxiety is high, and for many, unemployment insurance is not an option. One recent study reports that only 11 percent of welfare recipients with substantial work hours were eligible for unemployment insurance (Spalter-Roth, Hartmann & Burr, 1994).

Eliza, a mother of four children, epitomizes the plight of many women who are looking for work, but find that they are at the mercy of employers who care more about profits than in providing stable employment, reliable and sufficient work hours, and benefits for their employees. Eager to work, she was delighted to find a job in a fast-food restaurant. She told them up front that she was looking for 30 to 40 hours of employment per week. Knowing this, they hired her, but instead of meeting her needs, they routinely ask her to leave work early, unpaid, during the slow periods. She was hired to fill an organizational need, and released as soon as their need for her labor abated. Because her income was so much less than she anticipated when being hired, Eliza found that the job did not pay her bills. In addition, she felt that the long commute was not worth her while, so she quit to return to welfare.

> That's something I need is a job. I've been looking. I just can't find the right one. I used to work at <fast-food industry>, but I wasn't making much money. By the time I caught the city bus, went out there, by the time I got to my kids, I spent all the money that they gave me. I liked the job, but it was just that I had to pay 75 cents to get to work, and paid 75 cents to get back. If I missed the bus I had to give somebody $3.00 or $4.00 to take me. And they wouldn't give me enough hours. I told them when they gave me this job that I needed at least 30–40 hours a week. I just can't afford to work less. But I was wasting my time going out there. I had to be at work by 11 o'clock, but they would send me home by two o'clock. I didn't even get 20 hours a week. You hear what I'm saying? Ten or 12, maybe. I think what they was doing was hiring you for the busy hour, and once the busy hour passed, you was sent out of there. I had to quit because it was costing me too much to go way over there.

Eliza's frustration with businesses that put profits above employee well-being was not unusual. Many others expressed this frustration, including Patrice. By most welfare recipients' standards, Patrice is a success story. Although still receiving a small welfare check at the time of the interview, Patrice was also employed 20 hours a week by a hospital in the community, and earned a wage of $7.00 an hour. She has some training in nursing, but failed to get a degree when she became pregnant and quit college. Despite her relatively high wage compared to others in similar circumstances, she has more trouble getting off welfare than one might imagine due to the piecemeal nature of the job. She provides home personal care, and travels extensively from client to client each day, but she does not get paid for her travel time. Thus, a considerable portion of her workday goes unpaid.

> I do personal care through the hospital. I'm not a nurse. I was attending LPN school and I became pregnant so I had to withdraw. But I do personal care. I usually go in and take vital signs and assist them with their shower, and if they need any assistance with feeding I'll do that. Usually, I'm only there for an hour or so. I comb their hair, and pretty much that is it. I get paid usually for 20 hours a week. Usually I get seven dollars an hour. But I don't get paid for time between clients. My driving time is really blank time, as far as they are concerned. It doesn't really exist. But in my job I have to commute from one side of town to the next and to different little cities. But without a job I'll be pitiful again with that fixed welfare income.

The new low-tier and low-wage jobs created in the service sector that welfare recipients fill provide few, if any fringe benefits. Research indicates that, in addition to lacking health insurance, women who received welfare in the past are less likely to work in jobs that provide paid sick leave or paid vacations. These are important benefits that help families recuperate from illnesses, provide the time needed to seek medical care, meet demands made by children, or to re-energize. Yet, barely half (51 percent) of workers have paid sick leave. Differences across wage levels are acute. Persons in the highest wage quartile (the 25 percent highest-paying jobs) are three times more likely to have paid sick leave than are persons in the lowest wage quartile, at 68 percent and 23 percent, respectively. Moreover, only 16 percent of part-time workers receive paid sick leave (Institute for Women's Policy Research, 2004).

The Value of Health Insurance

As noted in Chapter 4, Medicaid, or health insurance, is considered by TANF recipients and TANF-leavers to be the most valuable of all welfare benefits (Seccombe, Hartley, Newsom, Pope & Hoffman, 2005). Why is health insurance of such interest? Having health insurance can make a tremendous difference in the amount and type of health care that people receive. Without insurance, both adults and children use the health care system less often, are less likely to have a regular source of health care, rely on emergency rooms for their treatment, and often experience unnecessary pain, suffering, and even death. The uninsured are far more likely than persons with insurance to postpone seeking medical care, to forgo needed medical care, and to fail to fill a needed prescription (Kaiser Commission on Medicaid and the Uninsured, 2003). Consequently, uninsured adults and children are more likely to suffer a wide variety of chronic and acute ailments compared to the insured. Extensive review of research published over the last 25 years indicated that having health insurance could reduce the mortality rate of the uninsured by at least 4 percent, and possibly by 25 percent (Hadley, 2003). Despite its importance, over 47 million Americans were uninsured in 2003.

When families leave welfare for work, it is likely that most will lose the health insurance that was a critical part of their welfare benefit. Recognizing this, PRWORA allows their families to receive 12 months of transitional Medicaid assistance if they would otherwise lose eligibility because of their earnings. After the 12-month period, TANF leavers must find health insurance on their own. However with employment virtually disqualifying them for Medicaid, with few employers providing health insurance to their workers, and with costs out of reach of most low-tier workers, many TANF-leavers become uninsured. The Oregon study revealed that 40 percent of adults and 22 percent of children were uninsured 18 months after leaving welfare, after their one year of transitional medical benefits expired (Seccombe, Hartley, Newsom, Pope & Hoffman 2005). How do families deal with this?

Chris has three children, all of whom have health concerns, but her daughter's severe dental condition and need for surgery were her primary concerns during the interview. Eighteen months after leaving TANF, the entire family was uninsured. Chris' employer did not offer her insurance and she said that she and her children were cut from Medicaid (Oregon Health Plan [OHP]) after their transitional benefits expired. Here Chris was asked how it has been being uninsured:

> It's been terrible. . . . They need their shots, Scotty missed his shot, and we never got our dental work done. We had appointments. . . . I've got letters saying you have to finish your appointments, yet I don't have the coverage. . . . When I call and say I need some help with my kids [to get them insured], I want somebody to get it in motion, not send me somewhere else or refer me, give these people a call. I'm asking for the help.

When asked what she will do about her daughter's need for care for her serious gum condition, she says:

> I wasn't given no suggestions on where to go for help. They say they got all these funds out there. I'm just asking for one time to help my daughter. It's not like it's just to milk them. I believe I should have a chance, but people don't want to offer information or resources where to go. . . . That's how it is, nobody has a heart.

As the interview continues, Chris begins to cry. When asked what she would have liked to know a year ago, before her Medicaid (OHP) expired, she says:

> I don't know, how can you prepare for it? . . . My main priority was getting as much work as I can to keep a roof over my head. I have to do without

medical right now. I'm going to work my butt off and do whatever they need me to do and have myself available so they will hire me permanently so I can get medical through my employer. That's my goal, but now all these months gone by and I see give and take, and now they hire more temps. . . . I know I've proven myself. I feel like I'm being used right now through my work. . . . I was willing to give up part of my pay to be able to be permanent and have medical. I don't care about vacation or sick leave. What have I got to fall back on? What have my kids got to fall back on?

In the United States we assume that the right way to get health insurance is to get a job—this is "playing by the rules" (Seccombe & Amey, 1995). We mistakenly assume that an employer will automatically provide insurance to employees. However, this is not the case; only 41 percent of workers earning less than $10 have access to employer-sponsored health insurance (Collins, Davis, Doty & Ho, 2004). In the Oregon study of TANF leavers, we found that only 7 percent of respondents received insurance from an employer 18 months after leaving welfare. Among those who were employed, only about one-third received their insurance on the job. Others claimed that it was not offered at their worksite; was not offered to them because they worked only part-time (often at the insistence of management); that they were on a probationary period; or that it was offered but it was too expensive to purchase (Seccombe et al., 2005).

Michelle, who lives in Oregon, is a typical example of someone who falls through the cracks of the safety net. As a diabetic, Michelle is well aware of the importance of having health insurance and expressed great concern about this when we first met. Though she understood the need to comply with the complex medical management of her disease, she knew she would not be able to afford this care without insurance. Medicine alone can cost over $300 a month. Doctor appointments and visits to specialists are far beyond what Michelle could afford. Michelle enrolled in her employer-sponsored insurance through her job at Wal-Mart when her transitional Medicaid (OHP) expired. However, her policy has an 18-month waiting period on pre-existing conditions. Her type I, insulin-dependent diabetes is considered a pre-exisiting condition so her medications and her endocrinology visits are not covered by her insurance. Consequently, Michelle had ceased her regular visits with her endocrinologist at the time of the interview, despite the fact that care providers insist that patients be followed closely to minimize the complications of the disease. "They don't cover pre-existing conditions. Not at all. The doctor really wants me in every two months, but I told him that I can't afford to just come in for my diabetes."

Why Some Women on Welfare Are Hesitant to Take Jobs

In Chapter 7, I indicated that one of the criticisms of welfare is that benefits are significantly reduced or eliminated prematurely when a recipient acquires a job. Given the low wages of their work, recipients cannot support their families with so little disposable income. They often find that they are in a more precarious financial situation when employed than when they receive welfare. Work does not provide security. Instead of proving a secure economic base, women who are employed in low-wage work report that they get further and further behind in their bills. Low-wage work cannot sustain a family, yet at the same time, welfare benefits such as food stamps, subsidized housing, and Medicaid will be severely reduced or eliminated completely. In the quest to be a "good mother," leaving the security of welfare voluntarily for the insecurity of low-wage work is considered to be risky and even irresponsible, too risky for some. This is one important reason why some women on welfare are hesitant to accept these jobs.

Patrice purposefully limits the number of hours that she works so that she will not become ineligible for various forms of welfare assistance. She is willing to have her cash grant reduced, but wants to ensure that she will continue to receive food stamps, housing subsidies, and Medicaid. Is she simply greedy? Not really, since she knows that her job, even if full-time, and even at $7.00 an hour, will prohibit her from purchasing these things on the open market. Her salary would be below what she would need to pay full rent, pay all her own food costs, and purchase health insurance for herself and her two sons.

> Pretty much, the bottom line, being on the system, everything depends on your income. While you're on welfare, everything works for you. You got free Medicaid. You got free food because you get plenty of stamps. Then, you get your check once a month, which once you pay your rent, utilities, and buy Pampers for your baby, or whatever, your money pretty much be gone and you're broke. But once you start working, your [welfare] check depends on your income, and it may stop. Then your Medicaid becomes a question—depending on your income they'll cut it. Then your stamps be decreased or either cut off. Then, being in the projects, like me and many other welfare moms, your rent depends on your income, and your rent goes up. Then, usually I end up paying so much for childcare that I don't have nothing left. So, I have a harder time than when I'm not working! And therefore, you don't really benefit any. The majority of people out here [in the projects], they found that it's better to stay home and do nothing and receive welfare.

But when asked further why she doesn't then stay home full-time and receive welfare, she commented upon her conscious choice to work to augment welfare. She has found, for her family, the delicate balance between trying to survive on minimal welfare benefits, and having all her benefits eliminated without a job that pays enough to make up the difference. Finding this balance improves her self-esteem, and makes her feel that she is a good mother to her sons. She continues:

> Sometimes I used to think, I'd say, "Maybe I do better off staying on welfare." You have plenty of food to eat. You can sit home all day and play "mom." But, me, I have a certain, you know, look at life. I believe

in prospering because I like nice things, so I don't think welfare will work for me very well. So I just feel more, you know, secure about myself and it builds my self-esteem when I can be more independent, you know, do for myself and my children. I look out for them. They didn't volunteer to be here. So they're my responsibility. Things didn't work out with me and their father, so they are totally my responsibility. So I want to provide the best for them that I can.

Remaining on welfare is not an irrational choice. Rather, women weigh the costs and benefits associated with employment. If they believe the benefits outweigh the costs of employment, whether psychological or material, they are likely to choose work. But, if they believe that the costs outweigh the benefits, or begin to believe this during a spell of employment, they are likely to quit. For example, women who work full-time will receive significantly more money each month than if they received welfare. Earning $5.15 an hour for 40 hours a week, 52 weeks per year, would bring in approximately $900 a month before taxes. This is considerably more than a $241 monthly grant for a family of two, the $303 dollars received from welfare for a family of three, or the $343 received for a family of four in Florida in 2005. It would seem that it is in the best interest of welfare recipients to find, and keep, even low-wage work. However, the financial picture is more complicated. Earning $900 a month before taxes, a family would no longer be eligible for cash assistance, they would have their food stamps reduced, they may have to pay childcare costs, and would likely lose all, or at least part, of their low-income housing subsidy. Moreover, they would lose their Medicaid after one year. To purchase these items on the open market is expensive. This family would be eligible for the Earned Income Tax Credit (up to $4,200 for two or more qualifying children in 2004), but most of that would be offset by the new financial costs associated with childcare, transportation, clothing, and laundry needed for work. Since most welfare recipients do not have the skills or education that allow them to find and retain well-paid jobs, even relatively modest expenses associated with employment, such as a three-dollar daily bus fare, may represent a formidable obstacle to working. Families would have a difficult time supporting themselves on $900 a month, or $10,800 a year. For a three-person family—a mother and her two children—this income would be $5,000 *below* the 2005 poverty guideline of $16,090 (Department of Health and Human Services, March 23, 2005). Unless a woman locates incredibly cheap and well-insulated housing, free babysitting, has family or friends willing to share food with her, finds a job that provides medical benefits, and can easily walk to work, the odds are that she will not be able to earn her way to self-sufficiency. Carrie, a 39-year-old white woman with three children, told me:

> You know what ticks me off? I know you want to know. If I go out and get a job, it's going to about kill me to work because I'm already about to die because of the stress and responsibility I have. But, in order to get a little bit more money I would go and get a job. But then they take away my grant. It's like dollar per dollar that they take away. So what's the point of killing yourself?

Lynda has worked many jobs, but agrees wholeheartedly with Carrie.

> I have been on the system, off to work, on, off to work, and on again my whole life. I'm not one of the people who just raised my kids constantly on welfare. I always try to show them that you can do better. But every time I come up with a perfect plan to get off the system, I only find out the system is there to work against me. I had plans in September to get off the system again. But then, as soon as I got a job, I find out my food stamps are fixing to get cut to virtually nothing. That happened when I worked at the <convenience store>. When I worked there I started in January, and they allowed me to get my grant in February. But then in March my grant was cut off. And my food stamps was cut from almost $400 to around $170, which means I had to start taking money to buy food for the rest of the month. And then my rent went up. It was just too much.

Twenty-seven-year-old Roseanne who also has had a number of different jobs, reveals:

> And then like, okay, if we get a job and start working and stuff, they just want to drop everything. But you still got your bills and stuff. So that's kind of a strain, and that makes some people say, "I shouldn't bother." Because everything goes up too. Your rent goes up, like maybe a hundred and something dollars. Maybe two hundred; it depends on how much you're making. And then they want to drop you from stamps. So things are hard when you just have that one income coming in.

But as shown here, many workers today have trouble even securing full-time permanent work. Consequently, their earnings are likely to be considerably less than $900 per month. Eliza, for example, was routinely sent home during the slow periods in the fast-food restaurant where she worked. She could barely assemble 20 hours a week, despite repeatedly asking management for increased hours. Financial security crumbles when women earn sporadic wages. Their welfare benefits will be reduced or eliminated based on the initial wages earned, and it may take a month, or longer, for benefits to be reinstated when the earnings fail to materialize. This is a very dangerous period for families. If they have family or friends to rely on, they often move in with them or borrow money and food to get by. Some rely on food banks or other social services. Most women interviewed experienced at least one episode of being between a job and welfare benefits, and firmly said they want to avoid this predicament again.

In addition to the financial costs and rewards associated with work, there are also psychological ones. Work can enhance one's sense of self-esteem and self-efficacy. Women had dreams of returning to work when their children were older, when their schooling or training was completed, and when their lives were more orderly. But, at this point, even if they could earn adequate wages and benefits, they worried about the implications of leaving their children to strangers, or worse yet, leaving them home alone. They are keenly aware of the possible dangers lurking in their neighborhoods: molestation, drugs, vandalism, truancy, delinquency, and unprotected teenage sex, to name just a few. As good mothers, they want to protect their children from these seemingly common occurrences, and feel that they, rather than strangers, are in a better position to do so. As single mothers, the responsibility is on them; it generally cannot be shared with their children's fathers. The interviews revealed that they take this responsibility very seriously. Dawn, for example, told me of her concerted effort to warn her pre-teenage daughter about the dangers of teenage sex. Other mothers refuse to let their children outside after school. If they are at work, they wanted to know who will so strictly supervise their children.

Some welfare critics interpret recipients' rational choice to mean that welfare is a luxury; welfare policy was amended to make welfare less desirable by reducing benefits or denying them to women altogether. They further suggest that welfare programs breed dependency upon the system.

I suggest a different interpretation. Welfare is not a luxury or a frivolous program for mothers who are too lazy to work. Instead, it provides some degree of *predictability and security*, or at least it did in the past, compared to the turbulent irregularities and poor pay of work within the lower tier of the service sector. If we, as a society, value and care about the well-being of children, we correspondingly should value a more stable economic and social environment in which to raise them. Like Edin and Lein (1997), I found that women were "less interested in maximizing consumption, than in minimizing the risk of economic disaster" (p. 63). Add to this, their concern with "social disaster" as well.

I began this chapter by introducing Pearl. She is one of the many women who will, in all likelihood, not have a choice about whether to find and accept employment. With the overhaul of the welfare system, her benefits will likely run out shortly. Will Pearl, and the other women on welfare, be able to sustain themselves and their families, given the human capital and structural constraints that they face?

The number of families receiving welfare has declined to less than 2 million families by the end of 2004. Yet the data reveal that many families are not doing well when they leave welfare for work. For example, as shown in Chapter 6, about one-third of TANF leavers experience food insecurity and about one in five experience food insecurity with hunger (Acs, Loprest & Roberts, 2001; Seccombe, Hartley, Newsom, Pope & Hoffman, 2005). Many families must skip meals or cut the size of their meal portions because they cannot afford to buy more food.

In addition, more people are finding themselves unable to pay their rent. In their review of several studies of TANF-leavers, Acs, Loprest and Roberts (2001) found that between one-quarter and one-half of families who left TANF fell behind in paying their rent or mortgage. Homeless shelters face more requests for emergency services and are turning people away because they lack the beds and money to meet the demand, according to the National Student Campaign Against Hunger & Homelessness. Their surveys, based on 900 agencies in 32 states, found a 27 percent increase between 2004 and 2005 in requests for emergency shelter (Armas, 2005). Many people are hampered by rising housing costs that force them to spend much of their income on the rent or mortgage, but they find that they can no longer make the payment when an unexpected crisis occurs, such as an illness or a bout of unemployment.

What does Pearl want from welfare and welfare reform?

> I hope they can help me find a job. I need to go to job training. I've been through job training, but then you fall behind when you don't get a job. Because I know now that you've got to have the education, you know, to get a good job. Because you need writing. Okay, I'm 48. I'd rather be out there on a job if I had my health and strength like I used to. So I'd be able to accomplish something, you know, instead of sitting around here worried all the time. I can look back at myself and say I've been working since I was 14. I learned to work. Learned to earn money. And I look at my young neighbors, 20, 26, and never had a job. And I look at them and they say, "Pearl, you old." They say, "Pearl, you old now." And I say, "no, I'm not exactly old. This pressure is just getting me down."

CRITICAL THINKING QUESTIONS

1. Compare and contrast Pearl's and Amy's situation. What aspects of their personalities or situations will help or hurt their quest to leave welfare?

2. Who do you think is a more typical welfare recipient, Pearl or Amy?

3. The author claims that increasing human capital is important, but it is not a panacea. Why does she feel that increasing women's education and job skills is not enough to really help women leave welfare?

4. Are there enough jobs for welfare recipients? What is the nature of those jobs? Will these help pull women and their children out of poverty? Why or why not?

5. If welfare recipients really want to work, why are they hesitant to take jobs?

6. Welfare recipients and people who have recently left welfare for work report that Medicaid is the most important welfare benefit—more important than the check or even food stamps. Why do they value health insurance so highly? What should the welfare reform policy be regarding health insurance?

7. The author suggests that remaining on welfare is not an irrational choice. What does she mean by this? What evidence does she use?

CHAPTER
9 Conclusion: Lessons Learned and Visions of Change

Women who receive welfare have a longstanding history of being suspect or discredited as unworthy of assistance. Recipients are depicted as lazy, and responsible for their own economic circumstances through immoral behavior and irresponsible choices. They are criticized for living outside our idealized two-parent nuclear family form, and are accused of doing this voluntarily and flagrantly. Consequently, they are routinely denigrated, and they feel the burning stigma of welfare as though its identification were etched on their foreheads. Individualistic beliefs about the causes of poverty are so widespread that, ironically, even many poor women believe them. As these interviews revealed, many were quick to berate other welfare recipients as indolent and as not interested in "bettering themselves."

Despite the popularity of these individualistic explanations, I found that personal attributes were not sufficient to explain why a woman is poor and on welfare, and in some cases were largely irrelevant. Women's lives are more complex than Individualist, Structuralist, Culture of Poverty, or Fatalist explanations allow. Social policy, as well as common discourse that adopts these perspectives, often ignores the unique aspects of women's poverty and assumes that the causes, consequences, and experiences of poverty are the same for men and women. Poverty and welfare use are viewed as a personal problem rather than a social problem that reflects women's participation in the devalued caregiving roles and exploitation within a capitalistic economic structure. Ideological hegemony operates here—people have come to accept individual explanations as divine truth, which serves the interests of the more powerful members of our society. Yet, gendered differences in the causes and consequences of impoverishment and public aid should not be ignored.

The women that I interviewed shed new light on several important ways in which our explanations must become more inclusive of women's experience. Certainly, on first glance some women did look "lazy," in the sense that they had not looked for, or located, a job in recent months or even years. Some women, for example, were on welfare for five years or more, and it is easy to understand welfare critics who question whether these recipients are sufficiently motivated to look for work to improve the financial circumstances for their families. They also note, correctly, that a substantial number of women on welfare have low levels of education, poor job skills, and lack the human capital that employers would find attractive.

However, most women who had been on welfare for lengthy periods did not intend to remain on welfare this long. The women interviewed here did not enjoy the impoverishment and difficulties associated with living on welfare. They wanted the system changed and wanted to improve their situation with paid work. Yet many remained on welfare for significant periods of time because they believed that they are already working—they are taking care of their children. Being a "good mother," in impoverished conditions, is a full-time and very difficult job. As single parents, they knew that they have sole responsibility for raising their preschool-aged children, and that they needed to be available to their school-aged children before and after school to keep them safe, off the streets, and out of trouble. They scoffed at the idea that they were lazy, and instead saw themselves as working diligently to ensure that their children would have a better life.

The Gendered Nature of Welfare and Welfare Reform

It is a profoundly sexist assumption that taking care of children rather than searching for work is evidence of immorality or a lack of initiative. It reflects the low value that is accorded to caring for children—work that has been traditionally defined as "women's work." Our society discredits caring for children, despite pronatalist values that pressure people to have them. We now suggest that it is better for strangers to care for children at a minimum wage while their mothers work at other minimum-wage jobs, than it is for mothers to care for their children themselves.

These sexist values are unfortunate and unintended outcomes of the broader struggle for gender equality. As more women have successfully fought for the right to work outside the home for equal wages and opportunities, our society has begun to perceive women working outside the home as normative or expected. Most women with children, including infants and preschool-aged children, now work outside the home for pay. National data indicated that 53 percent of mothers with infants under 12 month of age are now employed, including 53 percent of whites, 57 percent of African Americans, 40 percent of Hispanics, and 51 percent of Asians (U.S. Department of Labor, May, 2005). Some work out of choice, some work out of necessity, and many can no longer distinguish between choice and necessity—they go hand in hand. Young women in high school and college today assume that they will work outside the home when they are married, and they intend to continue working if they become mothers. It is now part of our culture to expect mothers to have paid jobs, and when they do not, they often whisper defensively or with self-deprecation, that they are "just housewives."

Yet working women and their families often complain about the stress that dual employment causes in their lives (Douglas, 2004; Warner, 2005). It is not easy balancing two full-time jobs and children. Forty percent of full-time working parents report that balancing work and family is the biggest challenge they face as a parent, twice as many as voiced the number two concern of instilling moral values in their children (Rankin, 2002). Another study found that 45 percent of working parents report that work and family responsibilities interfere with each other "a lot" or "some" (Galinsky, Bond, Kim, Backon, Brownfield & Sakai, 2004). Perhaps because of the stress most parents report that they would prefer to stay home with their children when they are young (Farkas, Duffett & Johnson, 2000).

Consequently, if most women and men come to see mothers' employment as expected yet difficult, there is bound to be widespread resentment when others "choose" to buck the general trends, especially when these individuals are subsidized through taxes by those who are working. If most women work, then why can't welfare recipients work too, some people ask. Many middle-class mothers who are employed outside the home do not necessarily have an easy time juggling employment and parenthood. They describe having role overload and role strain, and they experience considerable guilt that they aren't doing enough for their families. But if they work, why are other women allowed a free ride, they wonder.

Yet, as these interviews reveal, poor mothers face additional burdens as they care for their children compared to middle-class mothers. Without minimizing the stress that middle-income families experience, it is simply more difficult for low-wage earners, especially single-parent low-wage earners, to muster up the personal, structural, and psychological resources that are needed to maintain a job and balance their family demands. There is no extra money for any of the mechanisms that might help alleviate the stress, from a washer and dryer in the home to an occasional night on the town. They also know that in all likelihood their job will not significantly improve their meager standard of living and that their family will continue to be impoverished despite the work. Not surprisingly, some women conclude that holding a job is virtually impossible—at least until their children grow older, their job opportunities improve, other structural impediments are eliminated, and their self-confidence is enhanced.

While there are always exceptions that feed our misconceptions, I generally found that women want to work, and that most are not lazy or satisfied with living on the public dole. Women who participated in the studies in Florida and Oregon were depressed about their economic circumstances. After weighing the costs and the rewards associated with work, many women, particularly those with large numbers of children, children under the age of six, or those with few skills and job prospects, glumly concluded that work does not currently provide the security necessary to make it a rational choice.

In addition to these constraints, I found that many women were poor, and in need of welfare because of issues far beyond their control, especially labor market conditions. Historically, women's labor has often been a reserve force under capitalism. Women workers are expendable; they are called out when needed because either not enough men are available for work (as in wartime), or because men do not want to do the type of work that needs to be done (as in nursing), or the pay is low (as in teaching). When the number of available men is once again sufficient to meet employment needs, or when the pay increases, or unemployment increases and men therefore begin to seek out the type of work they have been avoiding, women are then encouraged to leave their jobs on the grounds that men need these jobs to support their families. Women may be pushed out of the labor market altogether, or relocated into other more "feminine" jobs that men still do not want to fill (such as clerical positions). In contrast to men, women have never been taken seriously as breadwinners. Historically, they have been trivialized as working for "spending money," or extra money to pay for family vacations or to upgrade the family's standard of living. Men's breadwinning role within the family has been used against women to deny them jobs, to pass them over for promotion, and to pay them less.

Only three or four decades ago major newspapers in the country separated out their employment ads into "help wanted male" and "help wanted female" job categories. Men's jobs and women's jobs were not considered interchangeable, since men's had higher pay, better benefits, and greater chances for promotion. As the old saying goes, "Men have families to support." Women who also support families have never been able to amass these same types of public support, promotions, or wage increases because of their breadwinning needs. If they have to support their families, it is expected that they will do so with the wages of "women's work."

Today, occupations are still highly segregated, pay remains low, and the work is less prestigious than men's (U.S. Department of Labor, May, 2005). Women are likely to be found working as secretaries and other administrative support occupations, elementary school teachers, nurses, or service workers. To eliminate sex-segregated jobs in the United States, about half of all men or all women workers would have to change occupations. However, even within specific job categories—such as registered nurses, elementary school teachers, or cashiers—average wages for men virtually always exceed those for women. Moreover, the jobs in which women's salaries are the highest—such as managers and administrators, or registered nurses—have some of the largest gaps in men and women's earnings. This results in women age 16 and over earning only 80 percent of what men earn in 2004, which is an increase of only about 15 percentage points in over 50 years (U.S. Department of Labor, May 2005; Infoplease.com, 2003). The pay gap is higher for older workers, as the wages of men tend to increase as they age more quickly than do those of women. The pay gap is also higher for minority women. African American women earned only about two-thirds and Latinas earned only about half of what male workers earned. However, if working women earned the same as men (controlling for the same number of hours, education level, age, union status, and living in the same region of the country), their annual incomes would rise by about $4,000, and poverty rates would be cut in half (Infoplease.com, 2005).

In the 1990s when welfare was reformed, the U.S. economy was in another cycle of expansion. The service sector was rapidly expanding, unemployment was relatively low, and there were not enough men willing to fill the millions of low-wage jobs that were being generated. Not surprisingly, policymakers cut back the welfare rolls so that poor women would take these positions. This is an age-old maneuver. However, as we saw in Chapter 2, in the past not all women were eliminated from welfare, primarily African Americans or never-married mothers who were deemed as providing unsuitable homes had their benefits terminated. This time, however, the termination is more widespread. With few exceptions, all welfare recipients are subject to time limitations, work requirements, and family caps.

A significant problem has been created. Despite the rise in service-sector jobs, today there are simply not enough stable and permanent jobs for all the welfare recipients who need and want them. There is tremendous competition for semi-skilled and unskilled jobs, particularly those few that pay higher wages or offer health insurance benefits. Few of these jobs provide crucial fringe benefits. However, these benefits are not "fringe" in the sense of being peripheral to workers' needs. They are an important part of any remuneration package, and are critical to being able to raise a family off of the welfare system.

Part of the reason that pay and fringe benefits are so crucial to exiting welfare is because a significant number of women on welfare face tremendous personal hardships that they often did not choose and are, in an important sense, beyond their control. They need welfare's security because their lives have become sadly insecure otherwise. As revealed here, some women are on welfare because of being deserted by their spouse or partner, or because they left an unfaithful or violent partner. They need time to regroup, to assess their options, to build their self-esteem that poor relationships so often erode, or to acquire skills to support themselves.

Certainly, no woman asks or deserves to be beaten, or should have to live with her partner's continued infidelity. Her physical and mental health and well-being, and those of her children, are at stake. But women with fewer job skills, who have deficits in their education, or who have low self-esteem may find it difficult to endure the ending of relationships. They need assistance from somewhere to leave an intolerable situation and thrive afterwards.

Still other women turned to welfare because of poor health or the poor health of their children. Those who are impoverished are more likely to suffer from a wide variety of ailments than do others. Poor children are particularly vulnerable and may suffer long-term health effects such as stunted growth or learning disabilities. To voluntarily leave welfare, and risk losing health care benefits, was seen by these mothers as being grossly irresponsible.

Given the vice-like impoverishment that results from an inadequate welfare system or low-wage work, the mothers I interviewed turned to others to help them make ends meet each month. Most women had developed an intricate and elaborate web of assistance among family, friends, neighbors, boyfriends, social services and charities, and perhaps even with their children's fathers. This assistance was invaluable; without it, they would be out on the streets, and unable to provide any semblance of a decent living for their children.

Some critics have suggested that the welfare system is thus creating, or at least perpetuating, a culture of poverty. I witnessed that a subculture of sorts had developed among many of the respondents. Some held values that were somewhat distinctive from those of the middle class. They placed a high value on sharing, on the primacy of the extended family, and on the importance of women-centered aid. But rather than this subculture creating or keeping them poor, it instead served to keep them from being poorer than they would otherwise be. Women without this network or subculture of support—and many were without it—tended to have the most overwhelming circumstances. They lived in the poorest housing; their children were more likely to be in trouble with the law or involved in a pregnancy; and they had the fewest episodes of work. Given paltry welfare benefits, and the low minimum wage, having a supportive network on which to rely is the primary method of escaping poverty. Without this assistance, often coupled with unreported side jobs, few women would really be able to pull themselves up by their bootstraps, as our society seems to insist upon.

Our hostility toward welfare recipients is widespread and is deeply rooted in class divisions in our society. We draw sharp class lines around ourselves, rather than looking for the interconnectedness of our lives. I have shown that most poor mothers share many of the same concerns about raising their children as do middle-class mothers, but their struggles are exacerbated by not having enough money with which to provide for them adequately. As is the case with mothers everywhere, they want to provide for their children, they want them to be safe and secure, and they want their children's lives to be better than their own. The commonalities with other women are straightforward and obvious from these interviews. I expect their stories to enhance gender consciousness among women, while at the same time not negating the importance of social class. Our position in the class structure, independently, and interactively with gender, shapes both our objective existence, and subjective conceptions of our surroundings and ourselves.

Expectations for women with respect to work and family are in a state of flux, and women at all income levels are feeling tensions that result from rapid social change. It is not clear what our society expects from women anymore. The work/family tension is usually portrayed as something that can be alleviated individually by adjusting work schedules, managing time more efficiently, or paying for services that women used to do, such as hiring a housecleaner. Fathers' time in household tasks and childcare has increased in recent decades but still does not come close to the amount of time women spend on these activities, even when both work full-time (Coltrane, 2000).

Women often feel guilty for working and worry that they are ignoring their children or their spouses' needs. Women "cover" for their absence in the family by trying to maintain household and childcare standards similar to non-working mothers. This takes a great toll on their lives. Nearly 80 percent of mothers who work full-time claim that they do not have enough time for themselves (Rankin, 2002). Fathers, in contrast, are far less likely to feel these tensions or guilt over their work. This is because we have created an unresolved moral dilemma between motherhood and work. It is not clear to women that they can be good mothers and successful workers at the same time, whereas for men, being good fathers and successful providers are defined as virtually one and the same. There is no cultural ideology that suggests that fathers split their energies, time, and loyalties between work and family, as there is for mothers (Walzer, 1998). Childrearing experts do not suggest that fathers take years off of work to care for their new babies, nor do they remind fathers that raising a child is more worthwhile than any job. These messages are reserved for mothers, yet they too live in a culture that equates work with virtue, power, morality, and personal fulfillment.

Hays (1996) describes the "ideology of intensive motherhood," as having three key components. First, a child should have one central caregiver, and it should be the mother rather than the father. Second, children and their needs should be at the heart of childrearing, and mothers should lavish their time, energy and material resources on their children. Third, the child is sacred, so that comparisons of worth between childrearing and any other activity are morally impossible. Ironically, this ideology of intensive motherhood persists in a society where most women work, and those who do not are intimidated to report that they are "just housewives." Yet, it persists, she concludes, because its high value on love and self-sacrifice is a way of actively rejecting the selfish and materialistic market logic inside the family.

The moral confusion over women's appropriate roles is particularly blatant in the banner of family values carried by traditionalists who blame working mothers for society's ills. Juvenile delinquency, crime, drug addiction, and teenage pregnancy are pinned on mother-absence from the home. Underlying the theme of family values is the belief that a mother should stay home to raise her children, at least when they are young. But if poor mothers stay home, they are viewed as freeloaders. Mothers are damned if they work, and damned if they do not. Society is confused about what it expects from women, and the expectations seem to vary according to the mothers' social class—apparently only privileged mothers should stay home. Society asks that poor mothers work and work harder; we ask them to be better mothers and intervene to stop these social ills; we ask them to become mothers less often; and we ask them to put off becoming mothers until they can be good providers themselves or are able to marry one.

Welfare policy now invalidates poor women's right to stay at home with their children. Reforms dictate that the primary responsibility of single mothers is to provide for their children's financial needs rather than their emotional ones. They should be wage earners first, caregivers to their dependent children second. This represents a major change in orientation towards women's roles. Welfare was originally created so that single mothers could stay home, since caring for children was considered to be more important than working outside the home. Although the assumptions about women's appropriate roles vary historically, reforms continue the dogmatic tradition of defining for women what is, or what is not, in her best interest. Single mothers no longer have the authority to make their own decisions about their family's needs.

Ironically, many welfare recipients were happy to see the welfare system change substantially. Unlike the imagery we may have of the Cadillac welfare queen, they want to be off welfare altogether. Yet the negative sentiment towards recipients as freeloaders is so strong that we assume the system must be made punitive for them to leave. The misconception is that, since they cannot be shamed to get off of welfare, we need to force them off. Recent policy reforms of PRWORA have created a system that is far more punitive than helpful in nature. It is a welfare-to-work program—e.g., the focus is on getting women off welfare and into jobs, rather than a human-capital approach, where the goal is on meaningful job training. Scarce resources must now be devoted to enforcing the welfare-to-work policies.

I suggest we evaluate the cost of enforcement versus the value of reinforcement—that is, reinforcing the ability of women to adequately support their families. Forcing a change that is not helpful, but simply appeases a political goal, results in manpower and financial costs. We have created another welfare bureaucracy that does little to really help those who are impoverished.

Has Welfare Reform Been a Success or a Failure?

In the first edition of this book I predicted that welfare reforms would meet with minimal success because policymakers did not take into account the specific needs that poor women articulate. What have we seen since 1996 when PRWORA was passed? What happens to families when they leave welfare?

The unusually strong economy of the 1990s hid some of the consequences of welfare reform. However, the number of people living in poverty began to rise in 2001 among all racial and ethnic groups and among all age categories for the first time in nearly a decade, and the upward trend has continued. In 2004, 11 percent of families (12.7 percent of the population, or 37 million people) lived below the poverty line, calculated as $15,067 for an average family of three in 2003 (DeNavas-Walt, Proctor & Lee, 2005; U.S. Census Bureau, August 26, 2004). Children are the age group most likely to be poor, with nearly one in five children classified as impoverished (17.6 percent). In comparing racial and ethnic groups, African Americans and Hispanics are the most vulnerable, at 24.4 percent and 22.5 percent, respectively. Although non-Hispanic whites had a lower poverty rate than other racial or ethnic groups (8.2 percent), they account for 44 percent of the people in poverty.

Since 1996 poverty has increased, unemployment rates are higher, and most former welfare recipients are not faring particularly well. Several trends have become well documented by research and are noted throughout this book: average wages are low—minimum wage or only a few dollars above, few work in jobs that provide critical benefits such as health insurance, and most are stuck in temporary, dead-end jobs with little chance of advancement. Many former welfare recipients work nonstandardized schedules that can be extremely difficult while caring for children. An increasing number are unemployed, and the number who are without a job and any apparent income at all has risen by 40 percent between 1999 and 2002. Families leaving welfare have trouble paying their bills, keeping a roof over their head, and keeping food on the table. How then can policymakers call welfare reform a resounding success?

The Reasons for Its Failure

Why has welfare reform been so unsuccessful in improving the lives of families? The reason is that it was reformed with little or no direct input from its participants. It is critical that we understand poverty, and the welfare experience, from those who have direct, first-hand exposure to the system itself. Programs created by upper-class policymakers, who have little real empathy towards the interplay of structural, individual, cultural, and fatalistic reasons why women may need aid, are unlikely to be tailored to meet the needs of poor women. Despite the best of intentions, it is easy to misunderstand what is needed to improve the lives of poor single women who are trying to care for and protect their children.

What are they looking for? First and foremost, poor families are looking for *security*. Welfare is not just about money, really. It has been repeatedly shown that the cash is not considered the most valuable benefit. Welfare is about offering the security of knowing that one's family will, at least at a minimum level, be cared for. Like most women everywhere, poor women regard having a home, stability, and protection as essential comforts. But as poor single mothers taking care of children, with minimal or no help from their children's fathers, they feel vulnerable. They turn to the government for short periods, or perhaps for longer periods, because they hope that it can provide them and their children with the security that is sorely lacking in their lives. Their marriages and relationships did not provide this security—husbands walked out on them, partners abused them, and even the best-laid plans sometimes do not work out. Their jobs do not provide security either—hours are sporadic, work is temporary, the pay is low, few benefits are included, and they could be fired or laid off with little notice.

Some women have supportive extended family or close friendship networks, and rely on them extensively, but even they acknowledged that these were not secure— maybe grandmother could babysit today, but that does not necessarily mean that she can babysit tomorrow. Finally, children's fathers did not provide security—child support was sporadic, if given at all. Visitation was irregular, if there was any. I asked one woman with three children why she relied on welfare rather than the $600 child support her children's father was court-ordered to provide. Instead of keeping the child support for herself, it was turned over to the welfare office, and she was given only $50 of it. Her welfare check, coupled with her extra $50, was still $200 less than she would have received if she took the child support instead. I questioned her: Wouldn't the child support at $600 a month and a part-time job be the more rational way to go? She let me know, in no uncertain terms, that she was appalled by my illogical suggestion because there was no security in it.

> Absolutely not. Yeah, he paid $600 last month, and $600 the month before. But what about the month before that? And what about next month? He comes and goes. I can't be keeping track of him. He ain't been by to see his kids in months. He don't care. But I've got these children, and I got to feed and clothe them. I'm all they got, and I've got to do them right. And what if they got sick? I need to be able to take them to the doctor. I can't be counting on him. Yeah, it's less money, but it's steady money. And I can count on it.

The "problem with welfare" lies not within the welfare system. *The real problem lies with the structure of low-wage work in the United States.* Indeed, the welfare system actually works well compared to low-wage work. It offers the security that is sought by vulnerable families, and provides for their basic needs with food, shelter, clothing, and medical care, if only at a minimal level. However, poorly paid work within the lower tiers of the service sector does not necessarily provide a basic floor for any of these necessities. Welfare works, and that is a problem to many critics. It is a government program that provides the protection for families that low-wage work does not. The real way to eliminate the welfare problem is to restructure or enhance jobs in the lowest tiers of our labor market, rather than trying to force people off a system that, even with its faults, is a recipient's logical refuge.

These interviews and findings from other researchers using both qualitative narratives and quantitative data from large national data sources, find a considerable movement on and off welfare, and in and out of work. Women become discouraged and frustrated with work that demands so much and returns so little in terms of security for their family. It would be poor mothering to jeopardize the well-being of their children. In fact, women take their parental responsibilities so seriously that they are willing to put up with the stigma associated with welfare; they are willing to live on a "thrifty food plan" that was designated by our own government to be for emergency and temporary use only; they are willing to live in undesirable and sometimes substandard housing; and they are willing to live on a few hundred dollars a month.

Rather than lacking in motivation, women on welfare know first-hand that the conditions of work in the lowest tiers—the pay, benefits, hours, and uncertainty—are appalling, and so they opt for the security of the welfare system. Families who rely on these poorly compensated jobs lack back-up emergency reserves for when something goes wrong. They are families at risk. They live check to check, day to day, hoping that nothing occurs to trip them up again. But something invariably does.

At the same time, there is nothing inherently wrong with these jobs that would suggest why they are so poorly compensated. Picking tomatoes, working in the laundry of a hospital, serving food, or mopping floors at the local school are important jobs. Our society could not do without these services; they are vital. Therefore, if the services are important and necessary, then workers in these jobs should be paid wages and provided the health insurance benefits that allow them to continue working in them. Austria pays its service workers wages with which they can support themselves. So does Australia. Why does the wealthiest country in the world, the United States, refuse to pay living wages to its workers?

Our government has a responsibility to intervene in capitalism's free-market approach. We see this intervention occur at times when it behooves our moral conscience, or when it would be in the best interests of the masses. Certainly, these two qualifications apply here. It is moral, just, and fair to pay people a living wage in which they can support themselves and their families. Moreover, it may be less expensive in the long run for taxpayers to diminish a large welfare bureaucracy based on enforcement and allow former recipients to become contributing participants in the national economy. If jobs in the lowest tiers were enhanced—made more secure—then welfare would be unnecessary for most families who seek its safe and secure confines. According to these and other data, most poor women would flock to employment that paid a living wage, if benefits such as health care and childcare were included. Those who remained on welfare would be those who could not, for one reason or another, support themselves. Welfare has a role in any compassionate nation, as there will always be some small segment of the population who need assistance in meeting their basic needs.

Some readers may question how the United States can afford to offer poor people these types of services, or even whether we should offer them. Workplace and family policies are controversial because they reflect moral values and cultural ideologies. Not everyone agrees about where the responsibility for individual well-being lies. Compared to many other industrial nations the United States has wallowed in a laissez-faire approach in which selective policies for a few predominate, rather than universal policies available to all citizens. A look at how other countries, similar to the United States, manage their social welfare needs could serve as a powerful example as to what is feasible and can shape our notions of what is desirable (Bergmann, 1996; Rainwater & Smeeding, 2005; Smeeding, 1992).

Insights from Other Countries

It is an interesting, although challenging exercise to compare the rates of poverty in the United States to those of other industrialized countries (Rainwater & Smeeding, 2005; Smeeding, Rainwater & Burtless, 2000). Historically, precise comparisons have not been easy or straightforward, because measures of poverty vary from one country to another. However, the Luxembourg Income Study, initiated in the 1980s and which continues to the present, has standardized variables across 70 data sets to allow for some comparisons of poverty across a limited number of countries. Using several different measures of poverty across 18 developed nations, researchers are now able to make relatively valid cross-national comparisons within these countries.

All measures of poverty show a similar pattern: the U.S. poverty rate exceeds those of the other 17 comparable countries. For example, using one method that defines poverty as the percentage of persons living with incomes below 50 percent of the median income, Smeeding, Rainwater, and Burtless (2000) found that 17.8 percent of Americans were in poverty, far exceeding the 8.6 percent average for the other 17 countries. The percentage of American children who live below 50 percent of the median income is also greater than any of the other countries. Among the aged, only Australia has a higher proportion of seniors living in poverty. Comparative data such as these indicate that high rates of poverty in a wealthy industrialized nation such as the United States are not inevitable.

Most industrialized nations have an interrelated set of proactive and universal programs to help families with children escape poverty. These programs are not means-tested benefits available only for those people poor enough to qualify. They are universal and therefore available to everyone.

For example, *family allowances*, which are cash benefits provided by the government to families with children, are common worldwide and are provided to parents on behalf of children as a universal right of citizenship (Kamerman & Gatenio, 2002). Currently 88 countries provide child or family allowances to parents. In some countries, family allowances may be supplemented by birth grants, school grants, child-rearing or childcare allowances, adoption benefits, special supplements for single parents, guaranteed minimum child support benefits, and allowances for adult dependents and disabled children. By providing these cash benefits, governments are directly helping families with the costs associated with raising children and indirectly helping to lower the rate of child poverty.

Typically, family allowances have one or more of the following objectives: (1) redistributing income from childless households to families with children, in recognition of the heavier financial burden incurred by childrearing; (2) supplementing the incomes of poor and modest-income families with children as a means of reducing or preventing poverty; (3) strengthening labor force attachment, as in some countries benefits are only available to families with children who have at least one parent in the work force, or higher benefit levels are offered to families attached to the labor force; (4) increasing feelings of social cohesion and progress among people—this is particularly of interest to the European Union as they move toward greater unity among its member states.

For the most part, family allowances are modest benefits worth a little less than 10 percent of average wages for each child, but they can contribute a significant component of family income to large or low-income families. Family allowance benefit levels vary in different ways. Several countries provide a uniform rate per child, regardless of the number of children in the family (Australia, Spain, Norway, and Sweden), while in other countries, benefits increase with each additional child or are larger for later children, such as the third, fourth, or fifth child (Italy, Belgium, France, Germany, and Luxembourg). In still others, such as the United Kingdom, the benefit is higher for the first child, while in France a family is only eligible for the allowance after the second child is born.

Many countries provide higher benefits for older children (Austria, Belgium, France, Luxembourg, and the Netherlands). Some countries provide a higher or special benefit for families with very young children (Austria, France, Germany and Portugal) to make it possible for a parent to remain at home during a child's early years (until the child is age three, age one in Portugal). In Finland and Norway, parents have the option of a subsidized place in childcare or a cash benefit of equivalent value making it possible for a parent of a very young child (under three) to stop working and provide care. Benefit levels may also be reduced as income rises or by including the benefit in taxable income, as in Spain and Greece. In some countries, benefit levels vary by geographic regions. Austria, Germany and Spain offer national benefits that vary by state, due to differences in the cost of living. Norway, too, supplements the family allowances of families in the Arctic region.

Coverage is generally extended to children from the time of birth to the age of majority or completion of formal education, provided other eligibility criteria are met. In almost all the industrialized countries, the universal cash allowance is awarded to the mother, or to the person caring for the child (or lone parent). The income-related cash benefit is more likely to go to the wage-earning parent or to either parent.

In recent years, some countries have begun to deliver their family allowances through the tax system or have substituted targeted benefits for family allowances, or supplemented their allowances by targeted child or family tax benefits. Ultimately, the issue is how much reaches families with children. Given its child poverty rates and evidence of deprivation, the United States might want to consider enriching its package (Kamerman & Gatenio, 2002).

Other benefits are also available to all residents as a right of citizenship. Day care is often subsidized so that it is free or available at a very low cost. Virtually all industrialized countries have universal health insurance systems that are financed by progressive forms of taxation—those who earn more, pay more in taxes. They have these programs because residents favor structural explanations for inequality over individual explanations by a wide margin. For example, when asked, "Why are there people in this country who live in need," 35 percent of Swedes claimed it was due to societal in justice, and only 16 percent claimed it was because of personal laziness. The results in France were even more telling: 42 percent of those surveyed blamed societal injustice as compared to only 15 who believed it was due to personal laziness. In the United States the explanations are reversed: 33 percent invoked structural explanations, while 39 percent blamed personal laziness (World Values Survey, 1994).

France is one country out of many that can provide a rich contrast to the United States. In the book, *Saving Our Children From Poverty*, economist Barbara Bergmann notes that there are many demographic and economic similarities between the two nations. The annual rate of growth is comparable, and both countries have similar rates of female labor force participation and births outside of marriage, and have minority populations of comparable proportions. France has a 50 percent higher unemployment rate, yet their poverty rate is considerably less than that of the United States. The child poverty rate is 6 percent in France compared to 22 percent in the United States. Moreover, about a quarter of single mothers in France received welfare-type benefits, compared to two-thirds of single mothers in the United States. The reason for these differences is that France has made a successful commitment to enhance low-tier work. They have improved the conditions surrounding these jobs so that they are no longer necessarily associated with low wages, and they do not automatically reduce the array of benefits that are vital to an individual's and a family's well-being.

This investment in low-tier work is not only monetary, but is reflected in their entire orientation to caring for their citizens. French parents at all income levels get a great deal of government assistance with childcare and health care, for example. Childcare is provided by an educated work force, and it is considered valued and important work. Free public nursery schools are available for children ages two-and-a-half through six, and by the time they are three years old, virtually 100 percent of French children attend. There is also a well coordinated before- and after-school care program for a nominal fee. Likewise, free health care is available to everyone by right of citizenship, and it is not lost when a person loses a job, develops an illness that is expensive to treat, or leaves welfare. The French government supplements the income of families with children by providing family allowances, housing assistance, and cash payments to pregnant women. These programs are not limited to poor families, unemployed families, or single parents. Moreover, because most of these programs are universal and available regardless of income, they have little or no stigma attached to them. They are considered to be normal facets of their social structure, much in the way public education is in our country. These programs are rights of all citizens, not privileges, and therefore there is no shame in receiving them. In contrast, in the United States we have families who need assistance, but either do not know what is available, do not know how to access it, or have been so absorbed by the Individualist perspective that their ego or guilt prevents them from seeking help that they qualify for and need.

Workers in France with low wages get even more help from these and other programs. For example, a single mother in France who moves from welfare to work retains $6,000 in government cash and housing grants. She would continue to receive free health insurance and would pay a negligible amount for childcare, as do all

French citizens. She would not have to face the hardships associated with low-tier work as do her sisters in the United States. Thus, despite the fact that the welfare programs in France are more generous than are ours, women are still more likely to leave them to pursue jobs. They can do this because of the security that the French government provides to all its workers. It is wrong to assume that we must have a punitive approach and keep benefits low so that women will not abuse the welfare system. Here, as in France, women would prefer employment, and they will work, if they continue to have the security that they need to care for their families.

Critics may scoff that the costs for these programs are prohibitive. According to data compiled by Bergmann, the United States would need to spend approximately 59 percent more than its current level to increase our spending on programs for child well-being to that of the French. As the richest country in the world, with one of the lowest tax rates, investing in our families in this fashion is not an impossibility. Instead, our money is being spent in other ways—it is a matter of priority. For example, the United States spends over twice as much money on defense as it does for programs that promote children's well-being (e.g., childcare and development, income supplements, income tax reductions, medical care for low-income children), whereas in France, the opposite occurs. We also spend an inordinate amount of money on the enforcement of our new punitive policies. That money would be better spent reinforcing the security of the vulnerable members of our society, which, despite our comfort in thinking to the contrary, could be any one of us.

Our society needs to reevaluate, from the ground up, how and why we should reform welfare. The welfare system is not full of irresponsible adults living high on the hog at taxpayers' expense. This hostile image is off target in many respects. Most importantly, perhaps, is that the primary beneficiaries of welfare are children. These children generally live with their mothers who, alone, are trying to take care of their children's physical, emotional, and spiritual needs. Pushing single mothers and their children off government assistance and forcing them to accept low-wage and insecure work will not eliminate poverty. It will likely increase the number of people who are poor, and increase the myriad of social ills that are associated with economic insecurity. Children turn to drugs, girls get pregnant, boys impregnate others, and steal, to ease the despair and hopeless of impoverishment—the feeling that there is no real ticket out to a better life. They know what the bulk of Americans seem to forget: that there is very little social mobility in the United States. Most people die in or near the same social class in which they were born.

The United States, with its alleged compassion and sense of justice for all, coupled with its vast resources, could tackle the real "welfare problem," because the real problem is not the welfare system. The predominant problem is the insecurity associated with jobs in the lowest tiers of the American economy. Our government could enhance the feasibility of employment for millions of families by partnering with the private sector. Enhancing work by increasing the minimum wage by several dollars an hour to allow for a living wage; providing benefits such as medical insurance to all families who do not have it, and family-friendly leave policies that allow for care of a sick or needy child; subsidizing childcare to make it affordable; and allowing workers to keep a portion of their food stamp and housing benefits when necessary, would go a long way toward shrinking the welfare rolls. True and meaningful welfare reform is best seen as a "work problem" and approached as "work reform."

As welfare reform ages, we see impressive data and persuasive statistics proclaiming the politically successful reduction in the number of welfare recipients. When we do, we should remember that a decrease in families on welfare does not mean a reduction in the number of families living in poverty; it means a corresponding increase in the number of families at risk. With the passage of welfare reform in 1996, the welfare rolls have indeed declined, and at first look, all seems well. It is easy for our attention to shift to other social problems that are in vogue. Meanwhile, poor families are left to cope with enduring roadblocks, only to have added social pressure to conform to America's ideals of individualism and independence.

The truth of life within our lower economic classes is often not revealed. As long as unrestrained capitalism, still incumbent patriarchy, and cultural hegemony hold sway, welfare reform's public appearance will remain highly polished in the dominant media portrayals. Reducing welfare reliance is wonderful for all concerned, but we should be aware of the consequences of eliminating a valuable safety net without enhancing the structure and pay of the jobs that recipients are likely to hold. We should continue to examine closely how these working, but poor and at-risk, families are faring. We know, deep down, that when reform is politically rather than morally motivated and constructed, the cruelty in the reforms will inevitably emerge.

CRITICAL THINKING QUESTIONS

1. Women's roles in society are changing. The majority of women with children now work outside the home. Therefore, what argument would you make for allowing welfare recipients to collect cash assistance while they stay home to take care of their children? What argument would you make against allowing them to collect assistance for staying home?

2. Describe the moral confusion over women's changing roles? Is there any confusion over men's roles?

3. The author suggests that the problem with welfare is really a problem with low-tier work. What does she mean by this? Evaluate the evidence that she offers.

4. How can jobs in the lower tier be made more secure? Is it our government's responsibility to intervene to make them more secure? List the pros and cons of government intervention.

5. How do other industrialized nations deal with the issues associated with poverty and welfare? What lessons could the United States learn from other countries?

6. Summarize what this book has taught you. Has it changed your opinion or reinforced it? What can we learn from a study of 47 women in Florida and 552 families in Oregon?

7. Has welfare reform been a success or a failure? Defend your answer.

Websites of Interest

Listed below are websites that contain up-to-date and relevant information related to the many issues discussed in this book, including poverty, welfare, welfare reform, occupations, pay, health insurance, and other fringe benefits. Despite my attempt to provide active websites that are currently in use, please be advised that website addresses change frequently.

Administration for Children and Families
www.acf.dhhs.gov

This federal agency funds state, local, and tribal organizations to provide family assistance programs to improve economic and social well-being. This website provides critical details about many specific programs, including Head Start, TANF, child support programs, and programs for energy assistance.

Alan Guttmacher Institute *www.guttmacher.org*

The Alan Guttmacher Institute is the research arm of the Planned Parenthood Federation. The website provides extensive data on many sexual and reproductive topics, including teenage pregnancy. It also provides an index to the research journal, *Family Planning Perspectives*, a periodical that presents current research and policy related to sexuality and reproduction.

Center for Nutrition Policy and Promotion
www.cnpp.usda.gov

The Center for Nutrition Policy and Promotion was created in the U.S. Department of Agriculture and is the research branch of USDA where scientific research is linked with the nutritional needs of the American public. The Center publishes the Dietary Guidelines for Americans, and also maintains and updates the Thrifty Food Plan, which serves as the nutritional basis for determination of Food Stamp Program benefits.

Children's Defense Fund
www.childrensdefense.org

The mission of the Children's Defense Fund is to "leave no child behind," and to ensure every child a good start in life and successful passage to adulthood. The website
offers many reports, fact sheets, and summaries containing useful statistics
on social problems such as poverty, hunger, violence, and abuse that some children
experience.

Child Welfare League of America *www.cwla.org*

The Child Welfare League of America is a national organization designed to develop
and promote policies and programs to protect America's children and to strengthen
American families.

Center on Budget and Policy Priorities
www.cbpp.org

The Center on Budget and Policy Priorities works at the federal and state levels on
fiscal policy and public programs that affect low- and moderate-income families and
individuals. The Center conducts research and analysis to inform public debates over
proposed budget and tax policies and to help ensure that the needs of low-income
families and individuals are considered in these debates. Research findings are available on their website.

Citizens for Tax Justice *www.ctj.org*

Citizens for Tax Justice (CTJ) is a public interest research and advocacy organization
focusing on federal, state and local tax policies and their impact upon our nation.
CTJ's mission is to give ordinary people a greater voice in the development of tax
laws. Against the armies of special interest lobbyists for corporations and the wealthy,
CTJ fights for fair taxes for middle and low-income families, requiring the wealthy to
pay their fair share, closing corporate tax loopholes.

Economic Policy Institute *www.epi.org*

The Economic Policy Institute (EPI) conducts original research on economic issues,
makes policy recommendations based on its findings, and disseminates its work to the
appropriate audiences. Its research is focused on five main economic areas: living

standards / labor markets, government and the economy, globalization and trade, education, and retirement policy. According to their website, the EPI "seeks to broaden the public debate about strategies to achieve a prosperous and fair economy."

The Gallup Organization *www.gallup.com*

The Gallup Organization takes polls of people in the United States to assess their opinions on a variety of issues related to families and poverty. Recently the Gallup Organization began charging a subscription fee, so not all information they gather is available for free.

Head Start *www.acf.dhhs.gov.programs/hsb*

Head Start and Early Head Start are comprehensive child development programs that serve children from birth to age five, pregnant women, and their families. They offer child-focused programs that have the overall goal of increasing the school readiness of young children in low-income families. The website offers statistics and fact sheets describing the educational needs of poor children, and evaluates the effectiveness of Head Start.

Henry J. Kaiser Family Foundation *www.kff.org*

The Henry J. Kaiser Family Foundation is an independent philanthropy focusing on the major health care issues facing the nation, including reproductive and sexual health, health insurance coverage, and access to health care.

Heritage Foundation *www.heritage.org*

According the website, The Heritage Foundation is a "research and educational institute—a think tank—whose mission is to formulate and promote conservative public policies based on the principles of free enterprise, limited government, individual freedom, traditional American values, and a strong national defense."

Institute for Women's Policy Research *www.iwpr.org*

The Institute for Women's Policy Research (IWPR) is a public policy research organization dedicated to informing and stimulating the debate on issues of importance to women and their families. IWPR focuses on such issues as poverty and welfare among women, employment and earnings, work and family issues, and the economic and social aspects of health care and domestic violence.

Joint Center for Poverty Research *www.jcpr.org*

The Northwestern University and University of Chicago Joint Center for Poverty Research (JCPR) supports studies that examine what it means to be poor and live in America. JCPR concentrates on the causes and consequences of poverty in America and the effectiveness of policies aimed at reducing poverty. The website provides useful statistics and relevant articles.

MDRC *www.mdrc.org*

MDRC (formerly known as the Manpower Demonstration Research Corporation) was created in the wake of the Great Society antipoverty programs of the 1960s to evaluate the effectiveness of the social programs. MDRC's founders sought to establish a new kind of organization that would build a compelling body of evidence about whether social programs improve the lives of low-income individuals and families and are a cost-effective use of taxpayer dollars. Their research focuses on education, children and families, welfare and barriers to employment, and workers and their communities, and is available on their website.

The National Center for Health Statistics *www.cdc.gov/hchs*

The National Center for Health Statistics website provides data on demographic issues such as births, deaths, marriages, divorce, and abortion.

National Marriage Project *http://marriage.rutgers.edu*

This is the website of the National Marriage Project. The mission of the National Marriage Project is to provide research and analysis on the state of marriage in America and to educate the public on the social, economic, and cultural conditions affecting marital success and child well-being. They conduct research and make it available on their website. They are particularly interested in the values that young adults hold toward marriage and relationships.

Statistics on Children *www.childstats.gov*

This website, Statistics on Children, offers easy access to federal and state statistics and reports on children and their families, including population and family characteristics, economic security, health, behavior and social environment, and education. International comparisons can also be found.

The Urban Institute *www.urban.org*

The Urban Institute is an economic and social policy research organization that conducts research studies related to many important issues facing our nation. They have conducted extensive research related to the working poor, welfare reform, and urban poverty. Many of their studies are cited in this book.

U.S. Bureau of Justice Statistics *www.ojp.usdoj.gov/bjs*

The U.S. Bureau of Justice Statistics provides government statistics on domestic violence, including intimate partner violence, rape, and child abuse.

U.S. Bureau of Labor Statistics *www.bls.gov*

As part of the U.S. Labor Department, this bureau maintains data on workers and their employment conditions. They publish the *Monthly Labor Review*, which often contains articles related to working families.

The U.S. Census Bureau *www.census.gov*

The U.S. Census Bureau website contains data on a wide range of social and economic issues, including income, earnings, unemployment, and occupational characteristics. It also contains data on family and household topics, such as fertility, household composition, and marital status.

U.S. Department of Health and Human Services *www.dhhs.gov*

The U.S. Department of Health and Human Services is the government's principal agency for protecting the health of all citizens and providing essential human services, especially for those who are least able to help themselves. It is a large umbrella organization, and its website provides important links to other specific agencies within it.

REFERENCES

Abramovitz, Mimi. 1992. "The Reagan legacy: Undoing class, race, and gender accords." *Journal of Sociology and Social Welfare*. *19*: 91–110.

Abramovitz, Mimi. 1996a. *Regulating the Lives of Women: Social Welfare Policy from Colonial Times to the Present* (Revised Edition). Boston: South End Press.

Abramovitz, Mimi. 1996b. *Under Attack, Fighting Back: Women and Welfare in the United States*. New York: Monthly Review Press.

Acs, Gregory, & Pamela Loprest. 1995. "The effects of disabilities on exits from AFDC." Paper presented at the 17th Annual Research Conference of the Association for Public Policy Analysis and Management, November 2–4.

Acs, Gregory, & Pamela Loprest. 2003. *A Study of the District of Columbia's TANF Caseload*. Washington, DC: The Urban Institute.

Acs, Gregory, & Pamela Loprest. 2004. *Leaving Welfare: Employment and Well-Being of Families that Left Welfare in the Post-Entitlement Era*. Kalamazoo, MI: W.E. Upjohn Institute for Employment Research.

Acs, Gregory, Pamela Loprest & Tracy Roberts. 2001. *Final Synthesis Report of Findings from ASPE's Leavers Grants*. Washington, DC: The Urban Institute.

Alan Guttmacher Institute (AGI). 2002. *In Their Own Right: Addressing the Sexual and Reproductive Health Needs of American Men*. New York: AGI.

Allard, Mary Ann, Randy Albelda, Mary Ellen Colton, & Carol Cosenza. 1997. *In Harm's Way? Domestic Violence, AFDC Receipt, and Welfare Reform*. Boston: University of Massachusetts, Center for Social Policy Research, McCormick Institute. February.

Allison, Dorothy. 1993. *Bastard Out of Carolina*. New York: Dutton.

Amnesty International. February 17, 2004. *Female Genital Mutilation: A Human Rights Information Pack*. [Online] Available: www.amnesty.org/ailib/intcam/femgen/fgml.htm.

Anderson, Martin. 1978. *The Political Economy of Welfare Reform in the United States*. Palo Alto, CA: The Hoover Institution.

Armas, Genaro C. February 15, 2005. "Study: Homeless shelters, food in demand." *Contra Costa Times*. [Online] Available: www.mercurynews.com/mld/cctimes/1-0905033.htm.

Armey, Dick. 1994. "Public welfare in America." *The Journal of Social, Political And Economic Studies*. *19*: 245–250.

Ashe, Arthur, & Arnold Rampersad. 1994. *Days of Grace: A Memoir*. New York: Ballantine.

Axin, J., & H. Levine. 1975. *Social Welfare: A History of the American Response to Need*. New York: Harper and Row.

Bandler, Jean Taft Douglas. 1975. "Family issues in social policy: An analysis of social security." Unpublished Dissertation. New York: Columbia University of Social Work.

Barry, Skip. 1998. "City families face housing squeeze." *Dollars and Sense*. *215* (Jan.–Feb.): 32–36.

Beeghley, Leonard. 1989. *The Structure of Social Stratification in the United States*. Boston: Allyn and Bacon.

Belenky, Mary Field, Blyth McVicker Clinchy, Nancy Rule Goldberger & Jill Mattuck Tarule. 1986. *Women's Ways of Knowing: The Development of Self, Voice and Mind*. New York: Basic Books.

Bergmann, Barbara R. 1996. *Saving Our Children from Poverty: What the United States Can Learn from France*. New York: Russell Sage Foundation.

Bernades, Jon. 1985. " 'Family ideology': Identification and exploration." *Sociological Review. 33*: 275–297.

Berns, Roberta. 2003. *Child, Family, School, Community: Socialization and Support*. Belmont, CA: Wadsworth.

Bernstein, Aaron. 1997. "Off welfare—And worse off." *Business Week*. December 22, p. 38.

Bernstein, Jared. 1993. "Rethinking welfare reform." *Dissent*. Summer, 277–279.

Berrick, Jill Duerr. 1995. *Faces of Poverty*. New York: Oxford University Press.

Besharov, Douglas, & Karen M. Gardiner. 1997. "Sex education and abstinence: programs and evaluation." *Children and Youth Services Review, 19* (65/6), 327–339.

Bianchi, Suzanne M., & Daphne Spain. 1996. "Women, work and family in America." *Population Bulletin*. Vol. 51, No. 3, Washington, DC: Population Reference Bureau.

Blank, Rebecca. 1995. "Outlook for the U.S. labor market and prospects for low-wage entry jobs." In Demetra Smith Nightingale, & Robert H. Haveman (Eds.) *The Work Alternative*. Washington, DC: The Urban Institute Press and Cambridge: Harvard University Press.

Blank, Rebecca & Patricia Ruggles. 1996. "When do women use Aid to Families With Dependent Children and food stamps?" *Journal of Human Resources. 31*: 57–89.

Bloom, Dan. 1995. *The Family Transition Program: An Early Implementation Report on Florida's Time-Limit Welfare Initiative*. New York: Manpower Development Research Corporation.

Bloom, Dan, James J. Kemple, & Robin Rogers-Dillon. 1997. *The Family Transition Program: Implementation and Early Impacts of Florida's Initial Time-Limited Welfare Program*. New York: Manpower Development Research Corporation.

Blumer, Herbert. 1969. *Symbolic Interactionism*. Englewood Cliffs, NJ: Prentice Hall.

Bobo, Lawrence, & Ryan A. Smith. 1994. "Antipoverty policy, affirmative action, and racial attitudes." In *Confronting Poverty*. Sheldon H. Danziger, Gary D. Sandefur, and D. Weinberg (Eds.). Cambridge: Harvard University Press and New York: Russell Sage Foundation.

Booth, Alan & John N. Edwards. 1985. "Age at marriage and marital instability." *Journal of Marriage and the Family. 47*: 67–75.

Bose, Christine E., & Peter H. Rossi. 1983. "Gender and jobs: Prestige standings of occupations as affected by gender." *American Sociological Review. 48*: 316–330.

Bourdieu, Pierre. 1977. *Outline of a Theory of Practice*. New York: Cambridge University Press.

Boushey, Heather, and David Rosnick. April 2004. *For welfare reform to work, jobs must be available*. Center for Economic and Policy Research. [Online] Available: www.cepr.net/labor_markets/welfarejobshit-2004april01.htm.

Bowen, Gary L., & Mimi V. Chapman. 1996. "Poverty, neighborhood danger, social support, and the individual adaptation among at-risk youth in urban areas." *Journal of Family Issues. 17*: 641–666.

Briar, Scott. 1966. "Welfare from below: Recipients' views of the public welfare system." *California Law Review. 54*: 370–385.

Bristo-Brown, Gloria. 1991. "Letter to the Editor," *Oakland Tribune*. February 18, 1991.

Broder, John M. 1997. "Big social changes revive the false god of numbers." *New York Times*, August 17, 1997.

Bronars, Stephen, and Jeff Grogger. 1995. "The economic consequences of unwed motherhood: Using twin births as a natural experiment." *American Economic Review. 84*: 1141–1156.

Brownmiller, Susan. 1975. *Against Our Will: Men, Women, and Rape*. New York: Simon and Schuster.

Bureau of Justice Statistics. (2005). *National Crime Victimization Survey: Criminal Victimization, 2004*. Washington, DC: Office of Justice Programs. Retrieved October 3, 2005 from www.ojp.usdoj.gov/bjs/pub/pdf/cv04.pdf.

Burns, Jodi, Meredith Ballew, Hsiao-Ye Yi, & Meaghan Mountford. 1996. *Child Care Usage Among Low-Income and AFDC Families*.

Washington, DC: Institute for Women's Policy Research.

Burton, C. Emory. 1992. *The Poverty Debate*. Westport CT: Praeger.

Butler, Sandra S., & Luisa Deprez. 2002. "Something worth fighting for: Higher education for women on welfare." *Affilia*. 17: 30–54.

Cancian, Maria, Robert H. Haveman, Daniel R. Meyer, & Barbara Wolfe. 2002. "Before and after TANF: The economic well-being of women leaving welfare." *Social Science Review*. 76: 4.

Carney, Eliza N. 1995. "Taking over." *National Journal*. June: 1382–1387.

Castro, Janice. 1993. "Disposable workers." *Time*. March 29, pp. 43–47.

Cauthe, Nancy K., & Amenta Edwin. 1996. "Not for widows only: Institutional politics and the formative years of Aid to Dependent Children." *American Sociological Review*. 61: 427–449.

Center on Addiction and Substance Abuse. 1994. "Substance abuse and women on welfare." New York: Columbia University, Center on Addiction and Substance Abuse, p. 3.

Center for Research on Women. 1996. *School-Age Child Care Project—"I Wish The Kids Didn't Watch So Much TV": Out-of-School Time in Three Low Income Communities*. Wellesley, MA: Wellesley College, Center for Research on Women.

Center on Hunger, Poverty, and Nutritional Policy. 1995. *Statement on Key Welfare Reform Issues: The Empirical Evidence*. Medford, MA: Tufts University; p. 20.

Center for Law and Social Policy. 1997. *Welfare Changes Enacted*. [Online] Available: www.igc.apc.org/handsnet2/welfare.reform/Art icles/art.876261804.htm.

Centers for Disease Control. December 17, 2003. "Births: Final data for 2002." *National Vital Statistics Report, Vol. 52, Number 10*. Washington, DC: U.S. Department of Health and Human Services.

Centers for Disease Control. 2004. *Early Release of Selected Estimates Based on Data from the 2003 National Health Interview Survey*. [Online] Available: www.cdc.gov/nchs/data /nhis/earlyrelease/200406_11.pdf.

Chandler, Doris. January 8, 1997. "The shifting focus of welfare: Reforms hurt some recipients." *The Gainesville Sun*. Pp. 1B–2B.

Chandler, Doris. November 28, 1997. "Relationship to outlast walk a mile." *The Gainesville Sun*. Pp. 1A, 10A.

Chandler, Doris. November 22, 1997. "Housing concerns also prompt many calls to service agencies." *The Gainesville Sun*. Pp. 1B, 3B.

Chandler, Doris. 1998. "Workshop calls for challenge to welfare." *The Gainesville Sun*. January 8, 1998. Pp. 1B, 3B.

Cheng, Tyrone. (2002). "Welfare recipients: How do they become independent?" *Social Work Research*, 26(3), 159–170.

Children's Defense Fund. 1994. *Wasting America's Future*. Washington, DC: Children's Defense Fund.

Children's Defense Fund. 1997. *Key Facts About Child Care and Early Education: A Briefing Book*. Washington, DC: Children's Defense Fund.

Children's Defense Fund. 1997b. *The New Welfare Law: One Year Later*. [Online] Available: www.childrensdefense.org/fairstart_oneyr.htm.

Children's Defense Fund. 2004. *The State of America's Children, 2004*. Washington, DC: Children's Defense Fund.

Children's Defense Fund. January 2005. *Bush Administration Policies Exacerbate Growing Housing Crisis for Families with Children*. [Online] Available: *Childrensdefense.org*.

Citizens for Tax Justice. June 26, 1996. *State and Local Taxes Hit Poor and Middle Class Far Harder than the Wealthy*. [Online] Accessed October 21, 2005.

Citizens for Tax Justice. November 19, 2003. *CTJ Issue Brief: The Bush Tax Cuts in Florida*. Washington, DC: Citizens for Tax Justice.

Clark, Ann L., & Andrew F. Long. 1995. *Child Care Prices: A Profile of Six Communities-Final Report*. Washington, DC: The Urban Institute. P. 54.

Clinton, Bill. 1997a. "Welfare should be reformed." In C. P. Cozic (Ed.). (pp. 26–27). *Welfare: Opposing Viewpoints*. San Diego: Greenhaven Press, Inc.

Clinton, Bill. 1997b. "Welfare Reform Must Protect Children and Legal Immigrants." In *Welfare Reform*. C. P. Cozic (Ed.). (pp. 40–44).

San Diego, CA: Greenhaven Press, Inc.

Coalition for Independence through Education. 2002. *Access and Barriers to Post-Secondary Education under Michigan's Welfare to Work Policies: Policy Background and Recipients' Experience*. [Online] Available: www.umich.edu~/cew/CFITErep/CFITErpt.pdf.

Cohen, R. A., & H. Ni. 2004. *Health Insurance Coverage for the Civilian Noninstitutionalized Population: Early Release Estimates from the National Health Interview Survey*. Retrieved January, 2004, from www.cdc.gov/nchs/nhis.htm.

Colletta, Nancy Donohue, & Diane Lee. 1983. "The impact of support for black adolescent mothers." *Journal of Family Issues*. *4*: 127–139.

Collins, Patricia Hill. 1990. *Black Feminist Thought: Knowledge, Consciousness, and the Politics of Empowerment*. Cambridge: Unwin and Hyman.

Collins, Patricia Hill. 1994. "The meaning of motherhood in black culture." In R. Staples (Ed.) *The Black Family*, 5th ed., Belmont, CA: Wadsworth.

Collins, Sara R., Karen Davis & Michelle Doty. 2004. *Wages, Health Benefits, and Workers' Health*. The Commonwealth Fund. [Online] Available: www.cmwf.org/usr_doc/Collins_workers_IB_788.pdf.

Coltrane, Scott. 2000. "Research on household labor: Modeling and measuring the social embeddedness of routine family work." *Journal of Marriage and the Family*, *62*, 1208–1233.

Committee on Economic Security. 1985. *The Report of the Committee on Economic Security of 1935 and Other Basic Documents Related to the Social Welfare Act, 50th Anniversary Issue*. Washington, DC: National Conference on Social Welfare.

Community Food, Hunger and Nutrition. 2005. *Food Stamp Information*. [Online] Available: http://www.senseny.org/CFN/fs1.htm.

Conger, Rand D., Katherine J. Conger, Glen H. Elder Jr., Frederick O. Lorenz, Ronald L. Simons, & Les B. Whitbeck. 1992. "A family process model of economic hardship and adjustment of early adolescent boys." *Child Development*. *63*: 526–541.

Congressional Digest. 1995. *Welfare Overview*. Washington, DC: U.S. Government Printing Office, June–July, pp. 163–165.

Cook, Judith A., & Mary Margaret Fonow. 1986. "Knowledge and women's interests: Issues of epistemology and methodology in feminist sociological research." *Sociological Inquiry*. 56: 2–29.

Corbin, Juliet, & Anselm L. Strauss. 1990. *Basics of Qualitative Research: Grounded Theory Procedures and Techniques*. Newbury Park, CA: Sage.

Corcoran, Mary, Sandra Danziger, & Richard Tolman. 2003. *Employment Duration of African-American and White Welfare Recipients and the Role of Persistent Health and Mental Health Problems*. Ann Arbor: The Michigan Program on Poverty and Social Welfare Policy.

Coven, Martha. 2003. *An Introduction to TANF*. Center on Budget and Policy Priorities. [Online] Available: www.centeronbudget.org/1-22-02tanf2.htm.

Dahrendorf, Ralf. 1959. *Class and Class Conflict in Industrial Society*. Stanford: Stanford University Press.

Daly, Mary. 1978. *Gyn/ecology*. Boston: Beacon Press.

Danziger, Sandra K., Elizabeth Oltmans Ananat & Kimberly G. Browning. 2004. "Childcare subsidies and the transition from welfare to work." *Family Relations*. 53: 219–228.

Danziger, Sheldon. 1994. *Researchers Dispute Contention That Welfare Is a Major Cause of Out-of-Wedlock Births*. Press Release. Ann Arbor, MI University of Michigan School of Social Work. June 23, 1994.

Darroch, Jacqueline E., Susheela Singh, Jennifer J. Frost, & the Study Team. 2001. "Differences in teenage pregnancy rates among five developed countries: The role of sexual activity and contraceptive use." *Family Planning Perspectives*. 33 [Online] Available: www.agi-usa.org/pubs/journals/3324401.html.

Davis, Liane, & Jan Hagen. 1996. "Stereotypes and stigma: What's changed for welfare mothers." *Affilia*. *11*: 319–337.

Davis, Nancy J., & Robert V. Robinson. 1991: "Men and women's consciousness of gender inequality: Austria, West Germany, Great Britain, and the United States." *American Sociological Review*. 56: 72–84.

Della Fave, Richard L. 1980. "The meek shall not inherit the earth: Self-evaluation and the legitimacy of stratification." *American Sociological Review. 45*: 955–971.

DeNavas-Walt, Carmen, B. D. Proctor, and R. J. Lee. 2005. "Income, poverty, and health insurance coverage in the United States: 2003." *U.S. Census Bureau, Current Populations Reports, P60-229*. Washington, DC: U.S. Government Printing Office.

DeParle, Jason. 2004. *American Dream: Three Women, Ten Kids, and A Nation's Drive to End Welfare*. New York: Viking Books.

Donovan, Patricia. 1995. "The family cap: A popular but unproven method of welfare reform." *Family Planning Perspectives. 27*: 166–171.

Douglas, Susan. 2004. *The Mommy Myth*. Riverside, NJ: Free Press.

Dowd, Maureen. December 15, 1994. "Americans like G.O.P. agenda, but split on how to reach goals." *New York Times*. P. A1

Durkheim, Emile. 1947. *The Elementary Forms of the Religious Life*. New York. The Free Press (originally published in 1912).

Economic Policy Institute. March, 2005. *Minimum wage: Facts at a glance*. [Online] Available: www.epinet.org/content.cfm/issuesguides_min wage_minwagefacts.

Economic Policy Institute. 2005. "Living wage." *EPI Issue Guide*. [Online] Available: www.epi.org/content.cfm/issueguides_ livingwage_1wo-table.

Edin, Kathryn. 1991. "Surviving the welfare system: How AFDC recipients make ends meet in Chicago." *Social Problems. 38*: 462–474.

Edin, Kathryn, & Laura Lein. 1997. *Making Ends Meet*. New York: Russell Sage Foundation.

Edin, Kathryn, & Maria Kefalas. 2005. *Promises I Can Keep: Why Poor Women Put Motherhood Before Marriage*. Chicago: University of Chicago Press.

Ehrenreich, Barbara. 2001. *Nickel and Dimed: On (Not) Getting By in America*. New York: Henry Holt and Co.

Ellwood, David T. 1986. *Targeting "Would Be" Long-Term Recipients of AFDC*. MPR Reference No. 7617-953. Princeton, NJ: Mathematica Policy Research.

Ellwood, David T. 1988. *Poor Support: Poverty in the American Family*. New York: Basic Books.

Enda, Jodi. 1998. "Proposal expands child care." *The Gainesville Sun*. January 8, 1998. Pp. 1A, 7A.

Ensminger, Margaret E. 1995. "Welfare and psychological distress: A longitudinal study of African American urban mothers." *Journal of Health and Social Behavior. 36*: 346–359.

Farlie, Robert W., & Rebecca A. London. 1997. "The effect of incremental benefit levels on births to AFDC recipients." *Journal of Policy Analysis and Management. 16*: 575–597.

Feagin, Joe R. 1975. *Subordinating the Poor: Welfare and American Beliefs*. Englewood Cliffs, NJ: Prentice Hall.

Feagin, Joe R. & Clairece Booher Feagin. 1994. *Social Problems: A Critical Power-Conflict Perspective* (4th ed.). Upper Saddle River, NJ, Prentice Hall.

Fields, Smith, Bass and Lugaila. (2001). *A Child's Day: Home, School and Play: Selected Indicators of Child Wellbeing*. Washington, DC: U.S. Census Bureau. Retrieved February 27, 2001 from www.census.gov/population/socdemo/child/p7 0-68.pdf.

Florida Legislature. May, 1996. *A Plan to Reform Welfare in Florida: WAGES*. Conference Committee on Welfare Reform, CSSB 1662.

Forrest, Jaqueline Darroch, & Susheela Singh. 1990. "The sexual and reproductive behavior of American women, 1982–1988." *Family Planning Perspectives. 22*: 206–214.

Foucault, Michel. 1980. *Power/Knowledge: Selected Interviews and Other Writings, 1972–1977*. Collin Gordon. (Ed.). New York: Pantheon.

Fraser, Nancy, & Linda Gordon. 1994. "A geneology of *dependency*: Tracing a keyword of the U.S. welfare state." *Signs: Journal of Women in Culture and Society. 19*: 309–336.

Freidan, Betty. 1963. *The Feminine Mystique*. New York: Norton.

Fremstad, Shawn. September, 2003. *Falling TANF Caseloads Amidst Rising Poverty Should be a Cause of Concern*. Center on Budget and Policy Priorities. [Online] Available: www.cbpp. org/0-4-04tanf.htm.

Fremstad, Shawn. January 30, 2004. *Recent Welfare Reform Research Findings: Implications for TANF Reauthorization and State TANF Policies*. Center on Budget and Policy Priorities. [Online] Available: www.cbpp.org/1-30-04wel.htm

Gainesville Sun. December 2, 1996a. "Florida's welfare rolls drop." Pp. 1A, 5A.

Gainesville Sun. December 2, 1996b. "GOP resists changes to welfare." P. 5A.

Gainesville Sun. December 15, 1996. "Welfare debate doesn't vanish with latest law." P. 4A.

Gainesville Sun. January 22, 1997. "Sun's welfare article insulting, irresponsible." Letter to the Editor.

Gainesville Sun. February 23, 1997. "Requirements vary in states' welfare plans." P. A1.

Gainesville Sun. August 13, 1997. "Boston will require companies to pay a 'living wage.' " P. A7.

Gainesville Sun. September 2, 1997. "Officials may gain welfare insight." Pps. 1B, 2B.

Gainesville Sun. November 22, 1997. "Report: Poor seek help with rent, bills." Pp. 1B, 3B.

Gainesville Sun. February 10, 1998. "Home life affects children's health." P. 10A.

Galinsky, Ellen, James T. Bond, Stacy S. Kim, Lois Backon, Erin Brownfield & Kelly Sakai. 2000. *Overwork in America: When the Way We Work Becomes Too Much*. New York: Families and Work Institute. Retrieved July 9, 2005 from www.familiesandwork.org/announce/workforce.html.

Gans, Herbert. 1995. *The War Against the Poor: The Underclass and Antipoverty Policy*. New York: Basic Books.

Garfinkel, Irwin, Sara S. McLanahan & Philip K. Robins. 1994. *Child Support and Child Well-Being*. Washington, DC: The Urban Institute Press.

Gelles, Richard J., & Murray A. Straus. 1979. "Violence in the American family." *Journal of Social Issues*. *35*: 15–39.

General Accounting Office. 1994. *Families on Welfare: Teenage Mothers Least Likely to be Self-Sufficient*. Washington, DC: U.S. Government Printing Office.

Geronimus, Arline, & Sanders Korenman. 1993. "The costs of teenage childbearing: Evidence and interpretation." *Demography*. *30*: 281–290.

Giddens, Anthony. 1973. *The Class Structure of Advanced Societies*. New York: Barnes and Noble.

Gilder, George. 1981. *Wealth and Poverty*. New York, Basic Books.

Gilder, George. 1995. "Ending welfare as we know it." *American Spectator*. June. Pp. 24–27.

Gilens, Martin. 1999. *Why Americans Hate Welfare: Race, Media, and the Politics of Antipoverty Policy*. Chicago: University of Chicago Press.

Gillmore, Mary Rogers, Steven M. Lewis, Mary Jane Lohr, Michael S. Spencer & Rachelle D. White. 1997. "Rapid repeat pregnancies among adolescent mothers." *Journal of Marriage and the Family*. *57*: 536–550.

Gingrich, Newt, Dick Armey, & the House Republicans. 1994. In *Contract with America*. E. Gillespie and B. Schellhas (Eds.) New York: Times Books.

Glaser, Barney G. 1992. *Emergence Versus Forcing: Basics of Grounded Theory Analysis*. Mill Valley, CA: The Sociology Press.

Glaser, Barney G. & Anselm L. Strauss. 1967. *The Discovery of Grounded Theory*. New York: Aldine de Gruyter.

Glick Jennifer E., & Jennifer Van Hook. (2002). "Parents coresidence with adult children: Can immigration explain race and ethnic variation?" *Journal of Marriage and the Family*. *64*(1): 240–253.

Glick, Paul C. 1984. "Marriage, divorce, and living arrangements: Prospective changes." *Journal of Family Issues 5*: 7–26.

Goffman, Erving. 1963. *Stigma*. Englewood Cliffs, NJ: Prentice Hall.

Goldfield, Michael. 1987. *The Decline of Organized Labor in the United States*. Chicago: University of Chicago Press.

Goodban, Nancy. 1985. "The psychological impact of being on welfare." *Social Service Review*. *59*: 403–422.

Gordon, Linda. 1994. *Pitied But Not Entitled*. New York: The Free Press.

Gornick, J. C., & M. K. Meyers. 2003. *Families That Work: Policies for Reconciling Parenthood and Employment*. New York: Russell Sage Foundation.

Gottschalk, A. O. September, 2003. *Dynamics of Economic Well-Being: Unemployment Spells 1996–1999*. Washington, DC: U.S. Census Bureau.

Gottschalk, Peter, & Robert Moffitt. 1994. "Welfare dependence: Concepts, measures, and trends." *The American Economic Review*. *84*: 38–42.

Grall, Timothy. 2003. *Custodial Mothers and Fathers and Their Child Support: 2001*. Current

Population Report P60-225. Washington, DC: US Census Bureau.

Gramsci, Antonio. 1971. *Selections From the Prison Notebooks of Antonio Gramsci*. Edited and Translated by Quintin Hoare and Geoffrey Nowell Smith. New York: International Publishers.

Greenberg, Mark, Julie Strawn, & Lisa Plimtpon. 2000. *State Opportunities to Provide Access to Postsecondary Education under TANF*. Washington, DC: Center for Law And Social Policy.

Greenhouse, Steven. 1994. "State department finds widespread abuse of world's women." *New York Times*. February 3, p. A1.

Gubrium, Jaaber F., & James A. Holstein. 1990. *What is Family?* Mountain View, CA: Mayfield Publishing Co.

Habermas, Jurgen. 1973. *Legitimation Crisis*. Boston: Beacon Press.

Hadley, J. 2003. "Sicker and poorer—The consequences of being uninsured: A review of the research on the relationship between health insurance, medical care use, health, work, and income." *Medical Care Research and Review*. 60(2): 3s–75s.

Hancock, Ange-Marie. 2004. *The Politics of Disgust: The Public Identity of the Welfare Queen*. New York: New York University Press.

Handler, Joel F., & Yaheshel Hasenfeld. 1991. *The Moral Construction of Poverty: Welfare Reform in America*. Newbury Park, CA: Sage Publications.

Harp, Sharon. 2003. *Flat Broke with Children: Women in the Age of Welfare Reform*. New York: Oxford University Press.

Harrington, Michael. 1963. *The Other America: Poverty in the United States*. New York: Penguin Books.

Harris, Kathleen Mullan. 1993. "Work and welfare among single mothers in poverty." *American Journal of Sociology*. 99: 317–352.

Harris, Kathleen Mullan. 1996. "Life after welfare: Women, work, and repeat dependency." *American Sociological Review*. 61: 407–426.

Harvey, David L., & Michael H. Reed. (1996). "The culture of poverty: An ideological analysis." *Sociological Perspectives*, 39, 465–495.

Hashima, Patricia Y., & Paul R. Amato. 1994. "Poverty, social support, and parental behavior." *Child Development*. 65: 394–403.

Haskins, Ron. 2001a. "Liberal and conservative influences on the welfare reform legislation of 1996." In *For Better and For Worse: Welfare Reform and the Well-Being of Children and Families*. Greg J. Duncan & P. Lindsay Chase-Lansdale (Eds.). (pp. 9–34). New York: Russell Sage Foundation.

Haskins, Ron, 2001b. "Effects of welfare reform at four years." In *For Better and For Worse: Welfare Reform and the Well-Being of Children and Families* Greg J. Duncan and P. Lindsay Chase-Lansdale (Eds.). (pp. 264–289). New York: Russell Sage Foundation.

Hatchett, Shirley, & James S. Jackson. 1993. "African-American extended kin system: An assessment." In *Family Ethnicity: Strength in Diversity*, Harriete Pipes McAdoo (Ed.). Newbury Park, CA: Sage.

Hays, Sharon. 1996. *The Cultural Contradictions of Motherhood*. New Haven, CT: Yale University Press.

Hays, Sharon. 2003. *Flat Broke with Children: Women in the Age of Welfare Reform*. New York: Oxford University Press.

Herbert, Bob. 1996, April 26. "The real welfare cheats." *The New York Times*. P A31.

Herbert, Bob. 1997, November 20. "The game is rigged." *The New York Times*. [Online] Available: www.nytimes.com/1997/11/20/oped.

Heritage Foundation. 2004. "Poverty and inequality." *Issues in Brief*. [Online] Available: www.heritage.org/research/features/Issues2004/poverty-and-inequality.cfm.

Herrnstein, Richard, & Charles Murray. 1994. *The Bell Curve: Intelligence and Class Structure in American Life*. New York: Free Press.

Heymann, S. Jody, & Alison Earle. 1997. *Working Conditions: What Do Parents Leaving Welfare and Low Income Parents Face?* Working Paper H-97-01. Cambridge: the Malcolm Weiner Center for Social Policy in the John F. Kennedy School of Government, Harvard University, June 1997.

Holcomb, Pamela A., Karen Tumlin, Robin Koralek, Randy Capps & Anita Zuberi. 2003. *The Application Process for TANF, Food Stamps,*

Medicaid and SCHIP: Issues for Agencies and Applicants, Including Immigrants and Limited English Speakers. Washington, DC: U.S. Department of Health and Human Services Office of the Secretary, Office of the Assistant Secretary for Planning and Evaluation, and the Urban Institute.

Hope, Corman, Nancy E. Reichman & Kelly Noonan. 2003. *Mothers' labor supply in fragile families: The role of Child Health.* Working Paper #03-20-FF. Washington, DC: Center for Research on Child Wellbeing.

Hotz, V. Joseph, Susan Williams McElroy & Seth G. Sanders. 1996. "Costs and consequences of teenage childbearing." *Chicago Policy Review.* 1: 55–94.

Hunt, Matthew O. 1996. "The individual, society, or both? A comparison of Black, Latino, and White beliefs about the causes of poverty." *Social Forces.* 75: 293–322.

Information Please Database (2005). *The Wage Gap.* Pearson Education. Retrieved September 25, 2005 from http://www.infoplease.com/ipa/A0763170.html.

Institute for Women's Policy Research. 1995. *Welfare to Work: The Job Opportunities of AFDC Recipients.* [Online] Available: www.access.digex.net/~iwpr/wtwrib.htm.

Institute for Women's Policy Research. 1996. "Measuring the costs of domestic violence against women." *Research-in-Brief.* Washington, DC: IWPR.

Institute for Women's Policy Research. 2004. *No Time to Be Sick: Why Everyone Suffers When Workers Don't Have Paid Sick Leave.* Washington, DC: IWPR.

Interfaith Worker Justice. 2005. *Why the U.S. Needs a Raise in the Federal Minimum Wage.* Chicago: Interfaith Worker Justice.

Jansson, Bruce S. 1988. *The Reluctant Welfare State: A History of American Social Welfare Policies.* Belmont, CA: Wadsworth.

Jarrett, Robin L. 1994. "Living poor: Family life among single parent, African-American women." *Social Problems.* 41: 30–49.

Jarrett, Robin L. 1996. "Welfare stigma among low-income African American single mothers." *Family Relations.* 45: 368–374.

Johnson, Hans P., & Sonya M. Tafoya. 1999. *The Basic Skills of Welfare Recipients: Implications for Welfare Reform.* San Francisco. Public Policy Institute of California.

Johnson, Rucker C., & Mary E. Cochrane. April 2003. "The Road to Economic Self-Sufficiency: Job Quality and Job Transfer Patterns After Welfare Reform." Cited in Shawn Fremstad, *Recent Welfare Reform Research Findings: Implications for TANF Reauthorization and State TANF Policies.* Washington, DC: Center on Budget and Policy Priorities, January 30, 2004.

Joint Center for Housing Studies at Harvard University. 2003. *State of the Nation's Housing, 2003.* [Online] Available: www.jchs.harvard.edu.

Jones, Edward Ellsworth, & Richard E. Nisbett. 1972. "The actor and the observer: Divergent perceptions of the causes of behavior." In *Attribution: Perceiving the Causes of Behavior.* Edward E. Jones, David Kanouse, Harold Kelley, Stuart Valins, and Bernard Weiner (Eds.). New York: General Learning Press.

Kahn, Alfred J., & Shelia B. Kamerman. 1975. *Not For The Poor Alone: European Social Services.* New York: Harper and Row.

Kaiser Commission on Medicaid and the Uninsured. 2003, January. *The Uninsured and Their Access to Health Care.* [Online] Available: www.kff.org/about/kcmu.cfm. Accessed July 20, 2003.

Kamerman, Sheila, & Shirley Gatenio. 2002. *Tax Day: How do American's Child Benefits Compare?* New York: The Clearinghouse on International Development in Child Youth and Family Policies. Retrieved July 15, 2002 from www.childpolicyintl.org/issuebrief4.htm.

Kaplan, April. 1997a. *Domestic Violence and Welfare Reform.* Welfare Information Network, HN 5449, Vol 1, No. 8, September [Online] Available: www.igc.apc.org/handsnet2/welfare.reform/Articles/art/874022785.htm.

Kaplan, April 1997b. *Domestic Violence and Welfare Reform.* The Welfare Information Network.

Kaplan, April. 1998. *Transportation and Welfare Reform.* [Online] Available: www.welfareinfo.org/transita.htm.

Karger, Howard J. 1992. "Income maintenance programs and the Reagan domestic agenda." *Journal of Sociology and Social Work.* 19: 45–61.

Katz, Michael. 1986. *In the Shadow of the Poorhouse: A Social History of Welfare in America*. New York: Basic Books.

Kelley, Harold H. 1973. "The process of causal attribution." *American Psychologist. 28*: 107–128.

Kessler-Harris, Alice. 1982. *Out to Work: A History of Wage Earning Women in the United States*. New York: Oxford University Press.

Kluegel, James R., & Eliot R. Smith. 1982. "Whites beliefs about blacks' opportunity." *American Sociological Review. 47*: 518–532.

Kobal, Heather, & Desiree Principe. 2002. "Do nonresident fathers who pay child support visit their children more?" *Urban Institute Brief*, No. B-44. Washington, DC: Urban Institute.

Kozol, Jonathan. 1991. *Savage Inequalities*. New York: Crown Publishers.

Lamont, Michele, 2003. "Who counts as 'them': Racism and virtue in the United States and France." Contexts. www.contextsmagazine.org/advertise_listtopics.php.

Lampard, R., & K. Peggs. 1999. "Repartnering: The relevance of parenthood and gender to cohabitation and remarriage among the formerly married." *British Journal of Sociology. 50*: 443–456.

Leadbeater, Bonnie J., & Sandra J. Bishop. 1994. "Predictors of behavior problems in preschool children of inner-city Afro-American and Puerto Rican adolescent mothers." *Child Development. 65*: 638–648.

Leahy, Peter, Terry Buss & James Quane. 1995. "Time on welfare: Why Do people enter and leave the system?" *The American Journal of Economics and Sociology. 54*: 33–48.

Lerman, Robert. 1995. "Increasing the employment and earnings of welfare recipients." In *Welfare Reform: An Analysis of the Issues*. Isabel V. Sawhill (Ed.) Washington, DC: The Urban Institute. [Online] Available: www.urban/org/welfare/overview.htm.

Lewin, Tamar. 1991, April 28. "The ailing health care system: A question of access." *The New York Times*. pp 1, 28.

Lewis, Oscar. 1966. "The culture of poverty." *Scientific American. 215*: 19–25.

Lipset, Seymour Martin. 1990. *The Continental Divide: The Values and Institutions of the United States and Canada*. London: Routledge.

Lloyd, Susan. 1997. *The Effects of Violence on Women's Employment*. Chicago: Joint Center for Poverty Research, MacArthur Foundation. [Online] Available: www.uchicago.edu/Poverty Center/violence.html.

London, Andrew S., John M. Martinez, & Denise F. Polit. 2001. *The Health of Poor Urban Women: Findings from the Project on Devolution and Urban Change*. New York: Manpower Demonstration Research Corporations (MDRC).

London, Rebecca. 2004. *The role of Postsecondary Education in Welfare Recipients' Paths to Self Sufficiency*. The Center for Justice, Tolerance, and Community. [Online] Available: repositories.cdlib.org/cjtc/pis/cjtc_RL-2004_02.

Loprest, Pamela. 2003. "Fewer welfare leavers employed in weak economy." *Snapshots of America's Families. 3*, No. 5. Washington, DC: Urban Institute. [Online] Available: www.urban.org/url.cfm?ID=310837.

Loprest, Pamela, & Gregory Acs. 1996. *Profile of Disability Among Families on AFDC*. Washington, DC: Urban Institute Report to the Henry J. Kaiser Family Foundation.

Loprest, Pamela, & Gregory Acs. August 2003. "Disconnected welfare leavers face serious risk." *Snapshots of America's Families. 3*, No. 7. Washington, DC: The Urban Institute. [Online] Available: www.urban.org/url.cfm?ID=310839.

Lott, Bernice. 1994. *Women's Lives: Themes and Variations in Gender Learning*, 2nd ed. Pacific Grove, CA: Brooks/Cole.

Lutz, Steven, Janet R. Blaylock & David M. Smallwood. 1993. "Household characteristics affect food choices." *Food Review. 16*(2): 12.

Mackie, Gerry. 1996. "Ending footbinding and infibulation: A conventional account." *American Sociological Review. 61*: 999–1017.

Magnuson, Katherin A., & Sharon M. McGroder. 2002. *The Effect of Increasing Welfare Mothers' Education on Their Young Children's Academic Problems and School Readiness*. Working Paper 2002-280. Chicago: Joint Center for Poverty Research.

Manpower 2005. *Profile*. Retrieved October 3, 2005 from www.us.manpower.com/uscom/contentSingle.jsp?articleid=297.

Manpower Demonstration Research Corporation. 2001. *The Health of Poor Urban Women: Findings from the Project on Devolution and Urban Change.* New York: MDRC. [Online] Available: www.mdrc.org/Report2001/UC-HealthReport/UC-HealthRpt.2001.pdf.

Mathur, Anitia, Judy Reichle, Julie Stawn & Chuck Wiseley. (2004). *From Jobs to Careers: How California Community College Credentials Pat Off for Welfare Participants.* Washington, DC: Center for Law and Social Policy. Retrieved May 13, 2004 from www.clasp.org/publications/Jobs_Careers.pdf.

Matthews Hannah, & Danielle Ewen. February 7, 2005. *Presidents' Budget Projects 300,000 Low-Income Children to Lose Child Care by 2010.* Washington, DC: Center for Law and Social Policy.

Marx, Karl, & Friedrich Engels. 1959. "Manifesto of the communist part." In *Marx and Engels: Basic Writings on Politics and Philosophy.* L. S. Feuer (Ed.). Garden City, NY: Doubleday.

Marx, Karl, & Friedrich Engels. 1968. *Selected Works.* New York: International Publishers.

Massey, Carrie D. 1995. *Child Support Enforcement: Measures Available in the State of Florida for AFDC Recipients.* Tallahassee: Florida Commission on the Status of Women.

Mayer, Susan E., & Christopher Jencks. 1989. "Poverty and the distribution of material hardship." *Journal of Human Resources* 24: 88–113.

McGuire, Merideth B. 1992. *Religion: The Social Context* (2nd ed.). Belmont, CA: Wadsworth.

McLanahan, Sara, & Gary Sanfer. 1994. *Growing up with a Single Parent: What Hurts, What Helps.* Cambridge, MA: Harvard University Press.

Mead, Lawrence M. 1986. *Beyond Entitlement: The Social Obligations of Citizenship.* New York: The Free Press.

Mead, Lawrence M. 1992. *The New Politics of Poverty: The Non Working Poor in America.* New York: Basic Books.

Meyer, Carol. 1994. "The latent issues of welfare reform." *Affilia.* 9: 229–231.

Meyers, Judith, & John E. Kyle. 1996. *Critical Needs, Critical Choices: A Survey on Children and Families In America's Cities.* Washington, DC: National League of Cities.

Meyers, Marcia K., Anna Lukemeyer & Timothy M. Smeeding. 1996. *Work, Welfare, and The Burden of Disability: Caring for Special Needs Children in Poor Families.* Syracuse, NY: Center for Policy Research, Maxwell School of Citizenship and Public Affairs, Syracuse University, Income Security Policy Series, Paper No. 12.

Michalopoulos, Charles, Kathryn Edin, Barbara Fink, Mirella Landriscina, Denise Polit, Judy Polyne, Lashawn Richburg-Hayes, Savid Seith & Nandita Verma. 2003. *Welfare Reform in Philadelphia: Implementation, Effects, and Experiences of Poor Families and Neighborhoods.* New York: MDRC, October, 2003.

Miller, Dorothy C. 1992. *Women and Social Welfare: A Feminist Analysis.* New York: Praeger.

Mills, C. Wright. 1956. *The Power Elite.* New York: Oxford University Press.

Mills, Frederick B. 1996. "The ideology of welfare reform: Deconstructing stigma." *Social Work.* 41: 391–396.

Mink, Gwendolyn. 1995. *The Wages of Motherhood: Inequality in the Welfare State 1917–1942.* Ithaca, NY: Cornell University Press.

Mink, Gwendolyn and Rickie Solinger, eds. 2003. *Welfare: A Documentary History of U.S. Policy and Politics.* New York: New York University Press.

Minkler, Meredith, & Robyn Stone. 1985. "The feminization of poverty and older women." *The Gerontologist.* 25: 351–357.

Moffitt, Robert. 1990, March. *Incentive Effects of the U.S. Welfare System: A Review.* (Special Report, Series No. 48). Madison: University of Wisconsin, Institute for Research on Poverty.

Monitoring the Future. 2005. *Monitoring the Future: A Continuing Study of American Youth.* [Online] Available: www.monitoringthefuture.org.

Moody, Anne. 1968. *Coming of Age in Mississippi.* New York: Laurel.

Moore, Kristen A., Martha J. Zaslow, Mary Jo Coiro, Suzanne M. Miller & Ellen B. Magenheim. 1995. *The JOBS Evaluation: How Well are they Fairing? AFDC Families with Preschool-Aged Children in Atlanta at the Outset of the JOBS Evaluation.* Washington, DC: U.S. Department of Health and Human Services.

Office of the Assistant Secretary for Planning and Evaluation.

Morrow, Lance. 1993. "The temping of America." *Time*. March 29, pp. 40–41.

Morse, Janice M., & Peggy Anne Field. 1995. *Qualitative Research Methods for Health Professionals* (2nd ed.) Thousand Oaks, CA: Sage.

Moynihan, Daniel P. 1965. *The Negro Family*. Washington, DC: U.S. Department of Labor.

Murray, Charles. 1984. *Losing Ground: American Social Policy 1950–1980*. New York: Basic Books.

Murray, Charles. 1988. *In Pursuit of Happiness and Good Government*. New York: Simon and Schuster.

National Center for Health Statistics. 2004. *Health, United States, 2004*. [Online] Available: www.cdc.gov/nchs/products/pubs/pubd/hus/poverty.htm.

National Council on Domestic Violence and Abuse. 2003. Homepage. [Online] Available: www.ncdva.org/ Accessed March 05, 2004.

National Governors' Association Center for Best Practices. 1997. *Current Trends and Emerging Issues in Welfare-to-Work*. [Online] Available: www.nga.org/Pubs/IssueBriefs/1997/971204WelfareWork.asp.

National Institute of Justice and Centers for Disease Control and Prevention. 1998. *Prevalence, Incidence, and Consequences of Violence Against Women: Findings from the National Violence Against Women Survey*. Research in Brief. [Online] Available: www.ojp.us-doj.gov/hii/bubs-sum/172837.htm.

National Low Income Housing Coalition. September, 2002. *Out of Reach: Rental Housing for America's Poor Families in 2002*. Washington, DC: NLIHC. [Online] Available: www.nlihc.org.

National Opinion Research Center. 2005. *Codebook Variables BLKSIMP and AFFRMACT*. [Online] Available www.webapp.icpsr.umich.edu/GSS.

Needleman, Herbert L., Alan Schell, David Bellinger, Alan Leviton & Elizabeth N. Allred. 1990. "The long-term effects of exposure to low doses of lead in childhood." *New England Journal of Medicine*. *322*: 83–88.

Newsweek. 1970. "Why the welfare bill is stuck" December 7, 1970, Pp. 22–23.

Nightingale, Demetra S., Regina Yudd, Stacey Anderson, & Burt Barnow. 1991. *The Learning Disabled in Employment and Training Programs*. Washington, DC: U.S. Department of Labor.

Nitz, Katherine, Robert D. Ketterlinus & Linda J. Brandt. 1995. "The role of stress, social support, and family environment in adolescent mothers' parenting." *Journal of Adolescent Research 10*: 358–382.

Oliker, Stacey J. 1995. "The proximate contexts of workfare and work: A framework for studying poor women's economic choices." *The Sociological Quarterly*. 36: 251–272.

Olson, Krista, & LaDonna Pavetti. 1998. *Personal and Family Challenges to the Successful Transition from Welfare to Work*. [Online] Available: www.urban.org/welfare/report1.htm. The Urban Institute.

Page, Marianne E., & Ann Huff Sevens. 2002. *Will You Miss Me When I am Gone? The Economic Consequences of Absent Parents*. NBER Working Paper No. 8786. Washington, DC: National Bureau of Economic Research.

Panzarine, Susan, Elisa Slater & Phyllis Sharps. 1995. "Coping, social support, and depressive symptoms in adolescent mothers." *Journal of Adolescent Health*. 17: 113–119.

Pavetti L., and Duke, A. 1995. *Decreasing Participation in Work and Work Related Activities: Lessons from Five State Welfare Reform Demonstration Projects*. Washington, DC: Urban Institute.

Pear, Robert. 1995. "House backs bill undoing decades of welfare policy." *New York Times*. March 25, 1995. Section I, p. 1.

Peterkin, Betty. 1964. "Family food plans, revised, 1964" *Family Economics Review*. October 3: 12.

Peterkin, Betty, & Richard L. Kerr. 1982. "Food stamp allotment and diets of U.S. households." *Family Economics Review*. *1*(Winter): 23–26.

Petersen, Carol D. 1995. "Female-headed families on AFDC: Who leaves welfare quickly and who doesn't." *Journal of Economic Issues*. 29: 619–628.

Peterson, Paul E., & Mark C. Rom. 1990. *Welfare Magnets*. Washington, DC: Brookings Institution.

Peterson, Richard R. 1996. "A re-evaluation of the economic consequences of divorce." *American Sociological Review*. *61*: 528–536.

Popenoe, David, & Barbara D. Whitehead. 2004. *The State of Our Union: The Social Health of Marriage in America 2004*. The National Marriage Project. [Online] Available: http://marriage.rutgers.edu/Publications/SOOU/TEXTSOOU2004.htm.

Posner, Jill, & Deborah Lowe Vandell. 1994. "Low-income children's after-school care: Are there beneficial effects of after-school programs?" *Child Development*. *65*: 440–456.

Powers, Elizabeth T. 2003. "Children's health and material work activity: Static and dynamic estimates under alternative disability definitions." *Journal of Human Resources*. *38*: 3.

Presser, Harriet B. 1995. "Job, family, and gender: determinants of nonstandard work schedules among employed americans in 1991." *Demography 32*: 577.

Presser, Harriet B. 2003. *Working in a 24/7 Economy: Challenges for American Families*. New York: Russell Sage Foundation.

Presser, Harriet B., & Amy G. Cox. 1997. "The work schedules of low-educated American women and welfare reform." *Monthly Labor Review* April, 1997: 25–33.

Pyke, Karen D. 2000a. " 'The normal American family' as an interpretive structure of family life among grown children of Korean and Vietnamese immigrants." *Journal of Marriage and the Family*. *62*: 240–255.

Pyke, Karen D. 2000b. "Ideology of 'family' shapes perceptions of immigrant children." *Family Focus*. F13–F14.

Quadagno, Jill. 1988. *The Transformation of Old Age Security: Class and Politics in the American Welfare State*. Chicago: University of Chicago Press.

Quadagno, Jill. 1994. *The Color of Welfare. How Racism Undermines the War on Poverty*. New York: Oxford.

Quint, J., H. Bos, & H. Polit. 1997. *New Chance: Final Report on a Comprehensive Program for Young Mothers in Poverty and their Children*. New York: Manpower Demonstration Research Corporation.

Rainwater, Lee, and Timothy M. Smeeding. 2005. *Poor Kids in a Rich Country: America's Children in a Comparative Perspective*. New York: Russell Sage Foundation Publications.

Rank, Mark Robert. 1989. "Fertility among women on welfare: Incidence and determinants." *American Sociological Review*. *54*: 269–304.

Rank, Mark Robert. 1994. *Living on the Edge: The Realities of Welfare in America*. New York: Columbia University Press.

Rank, Mark Robert. 2004. *One Nation, Underprivileged: Why American Poverty Affects Us All*. New York: Oxford University Press.

Rankin, Nancy. 2002. "The parent vote." In *Talking Parenting Public* Sylvia Ann Hewlett, Nancy Rankin and Cornel West (Eds.) (pp. 251–264). Lanham, MD: Rowman & Littlefield.

Raphael, Jody, & Richard M. Tolman. 1997. *Trapped by Poverty, Trapped by Abuse—New Evidence Documenting the Relationship Between Domestic Violence and Welfare*. Ann Arbor, MI: Taylor Institute and University of Michigan School of Social Work: April.

Rasinski, Kenneth. 1998. *Effects of Media on Support of California's Civil Rights Initiative*. National Opinion Research Center. [Online] Available: www.norc.uchicago.edu/library/californ.htm.

Rausch, Paula. 1997. "Welfare job needs worry officials." *The Gainesville Sun*. February 19, 1997. Pp. 1A, 7A.

Reagan, Ronald, Home Page. 1997. *Social Welfare Expenditures Under Public Programs*. [Online] Available: www.dnaco.net/~bkottman/social_spending.htm.

Rector, Robert E. 2004. "Welfare reform: Progress, pitfalls, and potential." *Research Welfare WebMemo #421*. Heritage Foundation. [Online] Available: www.heritage.org/Research/Welfare/wm421.cfm.

Reichman, Nancy E., Julien O. Teitler, Irwin Garfinkel & Sandra Garcia. 2003. *Variation in Maternal and Child Wellbeing Among Financially Eligible Mothers by TANF Participation Status*. Princeton, NJ: Princeton University Press. Center for Research on Child Wellbeing, Working Paper #03-13-FF.

Resnick, M. D., L. J. Harris & R. W. Blum. 1993. "The impact of caring and connectedness on adolescent health and well-being." *Journal of Pediatric Child Health*. 29 (Supplement 1): S3–S9.

Rhoades, J. 2004. *The Long-Term Uninsured in America, 1999 to 2000: Estimates for the U.S. Population under Age 65* (No. Statistical Brief #52). Rockville, MD: Agency for Healthcare Research and Quality.

Roberts, Paula. 1997. *Pursuing Child Support: More Violence?* The Center for Law and Social Policy [Online] Available: epn.org/clasp/970916.htm [1997, May].

Roberts, Paul, & Mark Greenberg. 2005. *Marriage and the TANF Rules: A Discussion Paper.* Washington, DC: Center for Law and Social Policy.

Rogers-Dillon, Robin. 1995. "The dynamics of welfare stigma." *Qualitative Sociology*. 18: 439–456.

Rosier, Katherine Brown, & William A. Corsaro. 1993. "Competent parents, Complex lives: Managing parenthood in poverty." *Journal of Contemporary Ethnography*. 22: 171–204.

Ross, Lee D. 1977. "Problems of interpretation of "self serving" asymmetrics in causal attribution." *Sociometry*. 40: 112–114.

Rowe, Gretchen, & Victoria Russell. 2004. *The Welfare Rules Databook: State Policies as of July 2002.* Washington, DC: the Urban Institute.

Rubin, Lillian B. 1994. *Families on the Fault Line*. New York: Harper Collins.

Ruggles, Patricia. 1990. *Drawing the Line: Alternative Poverty Measures and Their Implications*. Washington, DC: Urban Institute Press.

Saluter, Arlene F. 1989. *Singleness in America*. U.S. Bureau of the Census, Current Population Reports, Special Studies, Series P-23, no. 162. Washington, DC: U.S. Government Printing Office.

San Francisco Chronicle. February 22, 1993. "A different kind of Chicago housing project: Urban Blacks find new hope and pain in suburbs." P. A1.

Sard, Barbara, & Will Fischer. July 15, 2004. *Further Action by HUD Needed to Halt Cuts in Housing Assistance for Low-Income Families*. Center on Budget and Policy Priorities. [Online] Available: www.cbpp.org/4-26-04hous.htm.

Schlein, Michael. 1997. "Fraternity life today." *Gainesville Sun*. September 28. Pp. D1, D5.

Schulman, Karen. 2000. *The High Cost of Child Care Puts Quality Care Out of Reach for Many Families*. Washington, DC: Children's Defense Fund. Retrieved April 9, 2005 from http://www.childrensdefense.org/earlychildhood/childcare/highcost.pdf.

Scott, Marvin B., & Stanford M. Lyman. 1968. "Accounts." *American Sociological Review*. 33: 46–61.

Seccombe, Karen. 1993. "Employer sponsored medical benefits: The influence of occupational characteristics and gender." *The Sociological Quarterly*. 34: 557–580.

Seccombe, Karen. 1995. "Health insurance coverage and use of services among low-income elders: Does residence influence the relationship?" *The Journal of Rural Health*. 11: 86–97.

Seccombe, Karen, Delores James & Kimberly Battle-Walters. 1998. "They think you ain't much of nothing": The social construction of "the welfare mother." *Journal of Marriage and the Family*. 60: 849–865.

Seccombe, Karen, & Cheryl Amey. 1995. "Playing by the rules and losing: Health insurance and the working poor." *Journal of Health and Social Behavior*. 36: 168–181.

Seccombe, Karen, Heather Hartley, Jason Newsom, Clyde Pope & Kim Hoffman. 2005. *Final Report: Access to Healthcare and Welfare Reform*. Center for Public Health Studies. Portland, OR: Portland State University.

Segura, Denise. 1994. "Working at motherhood: Chicana and Mexican immigrant mothers and employment." In E. Nakano Glenn, G. Chang, & L. R. Forcey (Eds.) New York: Routledge.

Segura, Denise. 1994b. "Inside the work worlds of Chicana and Mexican immigrant workers." In *Women of Color in U.S. Society*. M. Baca Zinn and B. Thornton Dill (Eds.). (pp. 95–111). Philadelphia: Temple University Press.

Sexton, Joe. 1997. "In Brooklyn neighborhood, welfare fraud is nothing new." March 19. *New York Times*. [Online]. Available at www.nytimes.com. Accessed December 5, 1997.

Shipler, David K. 2004. *The Working Poor: Invisible in America*. New York: Vintage.

Shulman, Beth. 2003. The Betrayal of Work: How Low-Wage Jobs Fail 20 Million Americans and their Families. New York: New Press.

Singh, R., & C. Peacock. 2003. *News Release: 49 States Have Planned or Implemented Medicaid Cuts in FY2003; 32 of Them Have Taken Action Twice*. Kaiser Commission on Medicaid and the Uninsured. [Online] Available: www.kff.org/about/kcmu.cfm. Accessed February 5, 2004.

Singh, Gopal K., T. J. Mathews, Ally C. Clarke, Trina Yannicos, and Betty L. Smith 1995. "Annual Summary of Births, Marriages, Divorces, and Deaths: United States, 1994." *Monthly Vital Statistics Reports 43, no. 13*, Hyattsville, MD: National Center for Health Statistics.

Skocpol, Theda. 1992. *Protecting Soldiers and Mothers*. Cambridge: Harvard University Press.

Smeeding, Timothy M. 1992. "Why the U.S. antipoverty system doesn't work very well." *Challenge. 35* (January/February): 30–35.

Smeeding, Timothy M., Lee Rainwater and Gary Burtless. 2000. *Luxembourg Income Study: Working Paper No. 244: United States Poverty in a Cross-National Context*. Syracuse, NY: Maxwell School of Citizenship and Public Affairs.

Smith, Dorothy E. 1993. "The standard North American family: SNAF as an ideological code." *Journal of Family Issues. 14*: 50–65.

Smith, Kevin B., & Lorene H. Stone. 1989. "Rags, riches, and bootstraps: Beliefs about the causes of wealth and poverty." *The Sociological Quarterly. 30*: 93–107.

Smock, Pamela J., and Wendy D. Manning. 1997. "Nonresident parents' characteristics and child support." *Journal of Marriage and the Family. 59*: 798–808.

Sonenstein, Freya L., Joseph H. Pleck, & Leighton C. Ku. 1989. "Sexual activity, condom use, and AIDS awareness among adolescent males." *Family Planning Perspectives. 21*: 152–158.

Sorensen, Elaine. 1997. "A national profile of non-resident fathers and their ability to pay child support." *Journal of Marriage and the Family. 59*: 785–797.

Spalter-Roth, Roberta, Heidi Hartmann, & Beverly Burr. 1994. *Income Insecurity: The Failure of Unemployment Insurance to Reach Working AFDC Mothers*. Washington, DC: Institute for Women's Policy Research.

Stack, Carol B. 1974. *All Our Kin: Strategies for Survival in a Black Community*. New York: Harper and Row.

Sterner, Richard. 1943. *The Negro's Share: A Study of Income, Consumption, Housing, and Public Assistance*. New York: Harpers and Brothers Publishers.

Straus, Murray A. 1991. "Physical violence in American families: Incidence, rates, causes, and trends." In *Abused and Battered: Social and Legal Responses to Family Violence* Dean D. Knudsen and JoAnn L. Miller (Eds.) (pp. 17–34). New York: Aldine de Gruyter.

Straus, Murray A., and Richard Gelles. 1986. "Societal change and change in family violence from 1975 to 1985 as revealed by two national surveys." *Journal of Marriage and the Family. 48*: 465–479.

Straus, Murray A., and Richard Gelles. 1988. "How violent Are American families? Estimates from the national family violence resurvey and other studies." *Family Abuse and Its Consequences: New Directions in Research*, Gerald T. Hotaling, David Finkelhor, John T. Kirkpatrick, and Murray A. Straus. (Eds.). (pp. 14–36). Newbury Park, CA: Sage.

Strauss, Anselm, & Juliet Corbin. 1990. *Basics of Qualitative Research*. Newbury Park, CA: Sage.

Strawn, Julie. February, 2004. *Why Congress Should Expand, Not Cut, Access to Long-Term Training in TANF*. Washington, DC: Center for Law and Social Policy.

Sun, Yongmin, and Yuanzhang Li. (2002). "Children's well-being during parent's marital disruption process: A pooled time-series analysis." *Journal of Marriage and the Family, 64*, 472–488.

Super, David A., Sharon Parrott, Susan Steinmetz, & Cindy Mann. 1996. *The New Welfare Law—Summary*. The Center on Budget and Policy Priorities. [Online] Available: www.cbpp.org/WCNSUM.HTM August 13, 1996.

Sutton, Paul D., & T. J. Mathews. 2004. *Trends in Characteristics of Births by State: United States, 1990, 1995, and 2000–2002*. National Vital Statistics Reports. Vol. 52, No. 19, Hyattsville, MD: National Center for Health Statistics.

Sutton, Paul D., & M. L. Munson. 2005. *Births, Marriages, Divorces, and Deaths: Provisional Data for July 2004*. National Vital Statistics Reports. Vol. 53, No. 13. Hyattsville, MD: National Center for Health Statistics.

Swanson, Mark, Mahendra K. Agarwal & Charles E. Reed. 1985. "An immunochemical approach to indoor aero-allergen quantitation: Studies with mite, roach, cat, mouse allergens." *Journal of Allergy and Clinical Immunology*. 76: 724–728.

Swarns, Rachel L. 1997. "Welfare mothers prep for jobs, and wait." *New York Times, p. A1.* August 31.

Szanton, Peter L. 1991. "The remarkable 'quango': Knowledge, politics, and welfare reform." *Journal of Policy Analysis and Management 10*: 590–602.

Tanner, Michael, Stephen Moore, & David Hartman. 1995. "The high value of welfare benefits keeps the poor on welfare." In C. P. Cozic and P. A. Winters (Eds.) (pp. 75–82). *Welfare: Opposing Viewpoints*, San Diego CA: Greenhaven Press, Inc.

Taylor, Patricia A., Patricia A. Gwartney-Gibbs, & Reynolds Farley. 1986. "Changes in the structure of earnings inequality by race, sex, and industrial sector, 1960–1980." In Robert V. Robinson (Ed.) (pp. 105–138). *Research in Social Stratification and Mobility*, Vol. 5. Greenwich, CT: JAI.

Teti, Douglas M., Michael E. Lamb, & Arthur B. Elster. 1987. "Long-range socioeconomic and marital consequences of adolescent marriage in three cohorts of adult males." *Journal of Marriage and the Family*. 49: 499–506.

Thomas, Susan. 1995. "Exchanging welfare checks for wedding rings: Welfare reform in New Jersey and Wisconsin." *Affilia. 10*: 120–137.

Thompson, Linda. 1992. "Feminist methodology for family studies." *Journal of Marriage and The Family. 54*: 3–18.

Thurer, Shari L. 1994. *The Myths of Motherhood: How Culture Reinvents the Good Mother*. Boston: Houghton Mifflin.

de Tocqueville, Alexis. (2004). *Democracy in America* (Arthur Goldhammer translation). New York: Penguin Putnam (original work published 1835).

Trattner, Walter I. 1989. *From Poor Law to Welfare State*, 4th ed. New York: The Free Press.

Trent, Katherine, and Kyle Crowder. 1997. "Adolescent birth intentions, Social disadvantage, and behavioral outcomes." *Journal of Marriage and the Family. 59*: 523–535.

Uchino, Bert N. 2004. *Social Support and Physical Health: Understanding the Health Consequences of Relationships*. New Haven: Yale University Press.

United Auto Workers. 2002. "The benefits of unions." *Research Bulletin* [Online] Available: www.uaw.org/publications/jobs_pay/02no3/jpe05.html.

U.S. Bureau of the Census. 1997a. *Poverty in the United States: 1996*. Current Population Report Series P-60. No. 198 Washington, DC: U.S. Government Printing Office.

U.S. Bureau of the Census. 1997b. *Statistical Abstract of the United States*, 117th ed. Washington, DC: U.S. Government Printing Office.

U.S. Bureau of Labor Statistics. No date. *The Value of the Federal Minimum Wage, 1954–1996*. [Online]. Available: www.dol.gov./dol/esa/public/minwage/chart2.htm.

U.S. Bureau of Labor Statistics. 1992: *Employment and Earnings* 39 (1 January). Washington, DC: U.S. Government Printing Office.

U.S. Census Bureau. 2001. *Statistical Abstract of the United States*. Washington, DC: Author.

U.S. Census Bureau. March 13, 2005. "QT-H10. Units in structure, householder 65 and over, and householder below poverty level: 2000." *American Factfinder*. [Online] Available: www.factfinder.census.gov/.

U.S. Census Bureau. 2005. *Statistical Abstract of the United States: 2004–2005*. Retrieved April 5, 2005 from www.census.gov/statab/www/.

U.S. Congress, Office of Technology Assessment. 1992. *Does Health Insurance Make a Difference?—Background Paper.* (OTA-BP-H-99) Washington, DC: U.S. Government Printing Office.

U.S. Department of Agriculture. December, 2004. *Food Stamp Program: Frequently Asked Questions* [Online] Available: www.fns.usda.gov/fsp/faqs.htm.

U.S. Department of Education. 1994. *The Condition of Education: 1993.* Washington, DC: National Center for Education Statistics.

U.S. Department of Health and Human Services. July 1997. *Health United States, 1996–97.* Washington, DC: U.S. Government Printing Office.

U.S. Department of Health and Human Services, Administration for Children and Families. January 1998. *Changes in Welfare Caseloads.* [Online] Available: www.acf.dhhs.gov/news/case-fam.htm.

U.S. Department of Health and Human Services, Administration for Children and Families. July 2002. *Child Support Enforcement Program Fact Sheet.* [Online] Available: www. acf.dhhs.gov/news/facts/csnew.html.

U.S. Department of Health and Human Services, Administration for Children and Families. 2003. *Indicators of Welfare Dependence, Annual Report to Congress.* U.S. Government Printing Office, Washington, DC.

U.S. Department of Health and Human Services, Administration for Children and Families. November, 2004. *Temporary Assistance for Needy Families (TANF) Sixth Annual Report to Congress.* Office of Family Assistance [Online] Available: www.acf.hhs.gov/programs/ofa/annualreport6.htm.

U.S. Department of Health and Human Services, Administration for Children and Families. 2005. *Welfare Rolls Continue to Fall. Press Release* [Online]: Available www.acf.hhs.gov/news/press/2005/TANFdeclineJune04.htm.

U.S. Department of Health and Human Services. February 9, 2005. *Welfare Roles Continue to Fall.* [Online]. Available: www.acf.gov.news/press/2005/TANFdeclineJune04.htm.

U.S. Department of Health and Human Services. March 23, 2005. *The 2005 HHS Poverty Guidelines: One Version of the [U.S.] Federal Poverty Measure.* Washington, DC: Author.

U.S. Department of Justice. 1994. "Violence Between Intimates." *Bureau of Justice Statistics Selected Findings: Domestic Violence.* Nov. No. NCJ-149259. Washington, DC: Author.

U.S. Department of Justice. 2004. *Criminal Victimization, 2003.* Washington, DC: Author.

U.S. Department of Labor. 1994. *Employment and Earnings.* 30 (4). Washington, DC: Author.

U.S. Department of Labor. 2002. *Characteristics of Minimum Wage Workers.* [Online]: Available: http://bls.gov/cps/minwage2002tables.htm#6.

U.S. Department of Labor. September 2004. *Highlights of Women's Earnings in 2003.* [Online] Available: www.bls.gov/cps/cpswom2003.pdf.

U.S. Department of Labor. December 2004. *Minimum Wage Laws in States-January 1, 2005.* [Online] Available: www.dol.gov/esa/minimum/america.htm.

U.S. Department of Labor. April 5, 2005. *Characteristics of Minimum Wage Workers: 2004.* [Online] Available: www.bls.gov/cps/minwage2004.htm Accessed October 24, 2005.

U.S. Department of Labor. 2005. *Employment Status of the Civilian Population by Race, Sex, and Age.* [Online]: Available: http://bls.gov/news.release/empsit.t02.htm.

U.S. Department of Labor. May 6, 2005. *Employment Situation Summary.* [Online] Available: www.bls.gov/news.release/empsit.nr0.htm.

U.S. Department of Labor. 2005. *Women in the Labor Force: A Databook.* Retrieved August 15, 2005 from www.bls.gov/cps/wlf-databook2005.htm.

U.S. Department of Labor, U.S. Bureau of Labor Statistics. (2005). *Consumer Expenditures in 2003: Report 986.* Retrieved October 3, 2005 from http://www.bls.gov/cex/csxann03.pdf.

U.S. Federal Bureau of Investigation. 1995. *Crime in the United States 1994.* Washington, DC: U.S. Government Printing Office.

U.S. House of Representatives, Committee on Ways and Means. 1996. *1996 Green Book.* Washington, DC: U.S. Government Printing Office.

U.S. News Online. August 18, 1997. "Fast food and welfare reform." [Online]. Available: www.usnews.com/usnews/issue/970818/18burg.htm.

U.S. News Online. April 26, 1996. "Raise the minimum wage?" [Online]. Available: www.usnews.com/usnews/ISSUE/WAGE.htm.

U.S. Social Security Board. 1940. *Social Security Yearbook 1939: Annual Supplement to the Social Security Bulletin.* Washington, DC: U.S. Government Printing Office.

U.S.A. Today. July 2, 1996. "Welfare Mistrust." P. 1A.

U.S.A. Today. September 16, 1997. "Call of the Road." P. 3A.

Valentine, Charles A. 1968. *Culture and poverty: Critique and Counter-Proposals.* Chicago: University of Chicago Press.

Van Manen, Max. 1990. *Research in Lived Experience.* London, Ontario: Althouse Press.

Walzer, Susan. 1998. *Thinking about the Baby: Gender and Transitions into Parenthood.* Philadelphia: Temple University Press.

Warner, Judith. 2004. *Perfect Madness: Motherhood in the Age of Anxiety.* East Rutherford, NJ: Riverhead.

Weitzman, Lenore. 1985. *The Divorce Revolution: The Unexpected Social and Economic Consequences for Women and Children in America.* New York: The Free Press.

Welfare Information Network. 2005. *Domestic Violence.* [Online] Available: www .financeprojectinfo.org/WIN/domestic.asp.

White House Working Group on the Family. November 13, 1986. *The Family: Preserving America's Future.* Washington, DC: U.S. Government Printing Office.

Williams, Dave. December 17, 1997. "State's Rich-Poor Gap Among the Widest." *The Gainesville Sun.* Page 3B.

Wilson, Mark. 1996. *The Folly of Increasing the Minimum Wage.* Backgrounder Update, No. 275. April 22. The Heritage Foundation. [Online] Available: www.nationalsecurity. org/heritage/library/categories/theory/ bgup275.html.

Wilson, William J. 1987. *The Truly Disadvantaged: The Inner City, the Underclass, and Public Policy.* Chicago: University of Chicago Press.

Wilson, William J. 1993. *The New Urban Poverty and the Problem of Race.* The Tanner Lecture, Ann Arbor: University of Michigan.

Wilson, William J. 1996. *When Work Disappears: The World of the New Urban Poor.* New York: Alfred A. Knopf.

Wise, P. H., W. Chavkin, & D. Romero. 1999. "Assessing the effect of welfare reform policies on reproduction and infant health." *American Journal of Public Health.* 89: 1514–1521.

Woolsey, Lynn. 1994. "Reinvent Welfare, Humanely." *New York Times,* 22, January. p. 21.

World Values Survey. 1994. *World Values Survey, 1990–1993.* Ann Arbor, MI: Inter-university Consortium for Political and Social Research.

Yaniv, Gideon. 1997. "Welfare fraud and welfare stigma." *Journal of Economic Psychology 18*: 435–451.

Yount, Kathryn M. 2004. "Symbolic gender politics, religious group identity, once the decline of female genital cutting in Minya, Egypt." *Social Forces.* 82 (3), 1063–1090.

Zedlewski, Sheila R. 2003. "Work and barriers to work among welfare recipients in 2002." *Snapshots of America's Families.* No. 3. Washington, DC: The Urban Institute.

Zedlewski, Sheila, R. 2003. *Work and Barriers to Work among Welfare Recipients in 2002. Urban Institute.* Retrieved March 15, 2005 from www.urban.org/url.cfm?ID=310836.

Zedlewski, Sheila R. May 19, 2004. "Have New Policies Made a Difference?" *Recent Trends In Food Stamp Participation.* Washington, DC: The Urban Institute.

Zimmerman, Shirley L. 2001. *Family Policy: Constructed Solutions to Family Problems.* Thousand Oaks, CA: Sage Publications.

Zucchino, David. 1999. *Myth of the Welfare Queen.* New York: Scribner.

INDEX